ISBN 978-90-819840-4-1

9 789081 984041 >

ISBN 987-90-819840-4-1

Contact info: info@masteringarchimate.com

Mastering ArchiMate

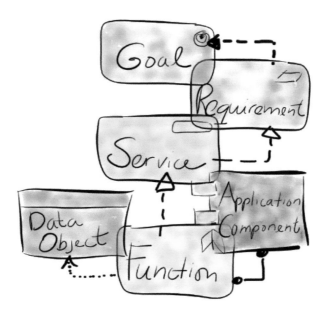

Edition II

Table of Contents

Table of Contents

Introduction

Introduction

1. Why This Book?

This book grew out of the desire to share the things I learned over the course of several years with respect to seriously employing the ArchiMate® Enterprise Architecture Modeling language. As Lead Enterprise Architect, working for the Asset Management unit of the largest Fiduciary Manager in the world (B€ 343 Assets under Management as of October 2013), I introduced the use of ArchiMate because it seemed to me — for a variety of reasons — the only reasonable choice for our modeling in the line of our Enterprise Architecture work. The choice was based on an estimate of the practicality of the language, and I am satisfied with how it works in our daily practice. This practice includes — next to models for projects and target architectures — the maintenance of a single very large (tens of thousands of objects and relations) 'current state' model of our enterprise, built along strict guidelines and used for analysis, reporting and as source for other systems (e.g. the CMDB of Infrastructure Management), as well as use for future state and project architectures. The scope and detail of our modeling has taught us very valuable lessons about ArchiMate modeling, which I am sharing in this book.

When we started using ArchiMate, I decided to stick almost religiously to the official definitions and not think or talk about diverging until we had a reasonable body of experience. After all, only when you have enough experience are you capable of really estimating the effect of the choices you have when changing the language. We still stay very close to what ArchiMate prescribes to this day, even if the depth of our experience has led me to some criticism and improvement proposals (see Chapter "Discussing ArchiMate" on page 179).

This book also grew out of the desire to provide a better introduction than what was available. In my experience, what is available is often pretty limited in scope and in my opinion sometimes even damaging in its explanations as you will not learn the things to become a *good* modeler in ArchiMate but you will learn some random patterns without learning the pitfalls of those patterns. No introduction I have seen actually explains the language well enough and I have not seen introductions that actually prepare you for sizable modeling work.

The best document until now (if you ask me) is the original paper from (then) the Telematica Instituut (Telin, now called Novay) of the Technical University Twente in The Netherlands, describing the pre-1.0 original ArchiMate standard. This comes close to the official specification — which itself is of course by definition right — but not automatically the best way to get educated. This book is an attempt at something better.

I intend to do three things:

- Give a decent initial introduction in the concepts and relations that make up the language;

- Present a number of patterns and uses that may be useful when modeling in the language;

- Give enough content so you can develop a feel for the subject.

The latter means that you will find some pretty deep and arcane discussions and examples in this book, here and there. These are not meant as practical examples to follow, but they are there because thinking about at the 'edges of practicality' improves your choice and understanding of practical solutions.

1.1 Uncle Ludwig

Here and there, you will find references to 'Uncle Ludwig'. Uncle Ludwig stands for the twentieth century philosopher Ludwig Wittgenstein, who some characterize as the most important analytic philosopher (as opposed to, say, moral philosopher) to date. Wittgenstein in his entire philosophical life concentrated on 'meaning'. His result came in two parts. The first part in his youth, where he tried to build meaning on top of logic. The results were limited (but sadly had the most influence in the computer science discipline of all of his work). Later in life he tried to answer what meaning then was for all the rest of what we say, where logic does not give you the definitive answer. He came up with the solution 'meaning lies hidden in correct use'. Given that ArchiMate is in part a service- (and thus use-) oriented language, this maxim is useful here and there. Actually, I find the maxim extremely useful for work even beyond modeling, e.g. wondering about the actual use of documents sheds light about their meaning.

If you want to know more about Wittgenstein, I suggest "Wittgenstein's Place in 20th Century Analytical Philosophy" by P.M.S. Hacker. Wittgenstein has been misinterpreted by many (e.g. when people misinterpret him as having stated that "meaning is *equivalent* to use"). Hacker not only understands Wittgenstein (he has written extensive and insightful analyses) but he also can explain it rather well. Wittgenstein often sounds daunting to people, but in my experience it can be pretty practical.

2. Enterprise Architecture

So you're working in an organization. The organization consists of many people, organized in organizational structure, in groups, departments and sections, and — if large enough— business units or even separate companies. If you look at what these people do, you look at business functions — say, 'after-sales' — or business processes — say 'handling a warranty claim from a customer'. These business functions and processes are a way to look at the behavior of your organization.

Now, these days, you have computers to support your work. You might not look at them anymore as computers (e.g. the iPhone or iPad you are reading a book on), but they are. And if your work is not shoe repair, plumbing, building, etc., your work will involve handling information. And even if it *is* shoe repair, the informational aspects of your work (planning, billing, accounting, etc.) are supported by IT. You *use* IT in the line of your work. The IT that supports people also has structure and behavior, just like the business itself. You use *applications*, and these 'running' applications have *functions* (i.e. behavior) and deliver *services* (support) to the business process. The applications themselves need an IT infrastructure to 'run', maybe large servers, maybe just your laptop or iPhone (where the applications are called 'Apps'), and there have to be all kinds of networks so all these systems can communicate with each other.

For about half a century now, the information revolution has moved most data from paper and other non-electronic media to IT systems, even the data that eventually is printed on paper. Not a multimedia, but a *unimedia* revolution has taken place: from all kinds of different storage and transport media, the information has been digitized and been moved to being small electrically charged or magnetized spots, each of these spots representing a single yes/no choice: a bit. We hardly think about that level, but we all know what a *file* is these days, and generally we do not think of the paper original that the term originally stood for.

In large organizations, all these applications and files that support the business have become an almost impossible to control, complex landscape, where many things can and do go wrong and where change is fraught with peril. Because changing something here will crash something somewhere else over there, in a landscape that is one big web of dependencies of business and IT. And even if that was not the case, translating business strategy and requirements to the right IT-support, or using IT-innovations to improve your business are difficult. Because, contrary to popular belief and partly as a result of that inertia-building web of dependencies, IT does *not* change fast. Mostly because its rigid logic lacks the flexibility of human compensating behavior. Building a new office is generally a process that takes less time than implementing (let alone building and/or implementing) a new core IT system.

This web of objects (products, bank accounts, bills, roles and actors, applications, data, servers, files, networks, etc.) and relations between them is what Enterprise Architecture is about. It is about the design of your business and the IT that supports it. It is about having the right business organization, having the right IT for your business and letting the business innovate on the basis of the possibilities of IT, now and in the future. Especially, it is meant to lead to better IT choices, because, as stated above, IT is often more difficult to change than the business.

The appearance of Enterprise Architects in this field is relatively recent. Not too long ago, if you would try to find that role you would end up looking at an organizations management. 'The' Architect of an organization is its manager. He or she finally decides on how the business is organized, how it is run and what IT is implemented. But the field has become complex enough that a special function has appeared: the (Enterprise) Architect. The management has in fact outsourced the (rough) design of its solutions to a specialized function, whose task it is to handle all that complexity. Here at least is already one important point: Enterprise Architecture should be the responsibility of (organizational *management* of) the business, not of the IT provider. It is meant to help management to make fundamental decisions, not leave them to someone else with some requirements and then say "make it so".

Now, the Enterprise Architecture function has proliferated and also fragmented. There are now business architects, security architects, application architects, data architects, information architects, integration architects, enterprise architects, infrastructure architects, domain architects, IT architects, solution architects, integration architects, the list seems endless. And to make matters worse: the same job name may mean quite something different depending on who and where you ask for the definition. What one company calls a business architect, the other company calls an enterprise architect or a lead architect and what one company calls an enterprise architect another may call information architect, etc..

So, I am going to lay out my own definition and fragmentation of Enterprise Architecture. First, in line with the Enterprise Architecture modeling language ArchiMate, I divide Enterprise Architecture into the following layers:

- Business & Information Layer
- Application & Data Layer
- (Technical) Infrastructure Layer

Enterprise Architecture for me has nothing to do with the organizational unit (department, business unit, project) that the architect has as his *domain*, but everything with the fact that he or she is architect on all *layers*: business & information, application & data and infrastructure. *Enterprise Architecture is about the coherent design and modeling of all layers*. For me, a Project Architecture is also an Enterprise Architecture, because a project is also a domain and an 'enterprise' in itself.

I do recognize specialization of architects at a layer: a Business Architect is concerned with the business & information layer and an Infrastructure Architect with the infrastructure layer. Some call these layers 'domains' as well, but I find that confusing. I reserve domains for recognizable divisions of the organization, such as departments, business functions or projects. So, for me, an Domain Architect is an Enterprise Architect within a certain domain.

If enterprise in 'Enterprise Architect' does not denote organizational level, how do we then call the chief enterprise architect of the organization? My favorite job name for such a function is 'Lead Enterprise Architect' (and he or she should fulfill (amongst other things) a role comparable to that of the 'Lead Legal Counsel').

You can forget all of this, except for one thing: in the context of ArchiMate, 'Enterprise Architecture' says nothing about being in the top of the organization, but about the fact that an 'enterprise' is a coherent landscape that can be divided in business, application and infrastructure layers (or very roughly: people, software and hardware) and Enterprise Architecture is about *all* of them.

A second division, is often made in our field: a division between 'architects' and 'designers'. For me, there is no fundamental difference between the two, both are forms of design and the only difference is the level of detail they are concerned with. Leaving out details is not to be taken lightly, though. It is one of the most difficult aspects of Enterprise Architecture. In my view, an Enterprise Architect is concerned with all details, but sparingly goes into those details. Architecture is (in part) "the art of leaving out *irrelevant* details". Leaving out details, sadly, often derails into religiously ignoring details. The key word, however, is 'irrelevant': as the Chinese proverb says: people stumble over molehills, not over mountains. An architect consciously leaves out details that he or she has decided are irrelevant to the decisions to be made.

In the early 90's, I had to follow a basic course on safety when working as a contractor for Shell. Here I learned a very valuable lesson: working safely is not about *avoiding* risks, it is about *consciously taking acceptable* risks. There is

no such thing as *not* taking risks. For me, the same applies for abstraction in design. *Abstraction* is not about *ignoring* detail, it is about *consciously leaving out* detail. And luckily, as we will see later, ArchiMate is equipped for that, as it has a mechanism that supports having coherent detailed and non-detailed views of the same model.

There is a third division one can make in Enterprise Architecture. Basically, an organization can use architecture in the following three settings:

The Current-State (or As-Is or IST) architecture. This is a descriptive model of how the current landscape of business and IT is. It can be used for reporting (e.g. to regulators) and analysis;

The Future-State (or To-Be or SOLL) architecture. This is a (rough) prescription on how the future landscape should be. It generally consists of both high level models and guidelines for the more detailed work done in the line of moving towards the intended state;

Change architectures. These are the descriptions of what Change initiatives like projects will produce. A common form is a Project (Start) Architecture. Like the Future-State, this is a combination of models and guidelines, but the detail should generally be comparable to the Current-State as the Change initiative actually results in a very specific change of that Current-State.

Enterprise Architecture is in the end about:

- Making good *choices* in the light of the strategic goals and positions of your enterprise;
- Making coherent *choices* across your enterprise
- Making good *choices* in themselves (e.g. in sense of total cost of ownership, etc.)

In all of these, modeling your existing state and your choices in ArchiMate can be really helpful.

2.1 Where are the principles and guidelines?

You might wonder, with all this talk about modeling: where are my architecture principles and guidelines that architecture is all about and that guide development for instance? I can say this about it here:

There are many definitions of what Enterprise Architecture is. The widely quoted ISO/IEC/IEEE 42010 standard, for instance, defines (system) architecture as

> *fundamental concepts or properties of a system in its environment embodied in its elements, relationships, and in the principles of its design and evolution*

There are two aspects: the *design itself* (elements, relationships) and the *principles of design*. This book is about the first aspect. I know many Enterprise Architects who are of the opinion that it is all about the second aspect. I could not agree less, and hence my approach to Enterprise Architecture is above all about the *actual* Business-IT landscape decisions that have to be made. Whether the use of principles and guidelines is a good way to come to such decisions is a question that is outside the scope of this book. It is the subject of another book I might try to finish in the foreseeable future...

2.2 Disclaimer

I have to warn you: in case you did not know: you almost can't learn anything from a book (the exception being do-books like Bobby Fisher's *Chess Lessons*). The only way to learn something is by *doing* it (which is why Bobby Fisher's book is an exception). Knowledge is about 'know how' not about 'know what'. It's funny that — while being convinced of this — I have written a *book* to teach ArchiMate. But anyway, *you won't really learn ArchiMate from this book*, you need to seriously *use* the language to really learn it. But if you do that, this book is meant to help you out and speed you up. Writing the book, by the way, is almost as much (but not quite) as much fun as teaching a class (and educational in itself).

3. Gratitude

I am very grateful for the assistance of the following people:

- First and foremost: Jos Knoops, colleague at APG, who has been an invaluable sparring partner from the start when discussing how we would be using ArchiMate, e.g. patterns;

- APG colleagues Joost Melsen, Floris Hack, and Paul Hamers for more real world pattern discussions;

- Leon Joosten, former colleague at APG and my then-time boss, who supported me at APG when I wanted to introduce ArchiMate to the organization in 2009.

Without that opportunity I would not have been able to gather the experience to be able to fill this book;

- Peter Spiers of Adobe Forums, who helped me get started with Adobe InDesign and helped me solve serious issues in my first attempts at the document and without that help, I would not have a tool to produce this properly;

- And of course, last but certainly not least: my family, who — while I was writing — have carried the burden of the fact that I was writing and thus had less time to do my chores and be a sunny, active part of family life.

4. License

This book comes in four different versions:

- A hardcover version distributed via normal channels for printed books (ISBN 978-90-819840-4-1);

- A paperback version distributed via normal channels for printed books (ISBN 978-90-819840-2-7);

- A full electronic version (PDF) that is restricted (printing not allowed) and stamped (ISBN 978-90-819840-3-4);

- An excerpt electronic version (PDF) containing only the basic introduction to the language.

You can contact me at the following e-mail address:

info@masteringarchimate.com

Heerlen, The Netherlands,

Gerben Wierda

5. Release Notes for Edition II

March 2014:

- There is also something more to add, e.g. I would have liked to add a really complete picture of a scheduled automated workflow, but one has to stop at some point.

This page intentionally not left blank

ArchiMate
Basics

ArchiMate Basics

1. Elements and Relations: 3x3x3

When modeling Enterprise Architecture, we need a language that knows about the concepts of Enterprise Architecture, and ArchiMate does a good job. To start with, you need to know that ArchiMate is built from three types of *elements*:

- elements that act (active elements)

- elements that represent the behavior of those 'elements that act' (behavioral elements)

- elements that cannot act and which are acted upon by that behavior (passive elements)

The three element types, connected by *relations*, can form sentences of sorts. A pickpocket (the application) steals (the application function) a wallet (the data). This is what makes ArchiMate a grammar, although people generally call it a language. The structure of the ArchiMate grammar is partly based on the subject-verb-object pattern from natural language.

Your model is therefore a story of sorts. It tells the reader the basic structure of the story: who acts on what.

We will start somewhere in the middle, at the application & data level of Enterprise Architecture.

1.1 Application and Business

An application is modeled in ArchiMate as seen in View 1.

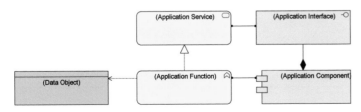

View 1. *The Basic Application Pattern*

This is possibly the first snippet of ArchiMate you have ever encountered, and it already has five element types and four relation types, so we are going to take our time to describe it.

Roughly, the two yellow and two blue elements in the image together make up the 'application' and the green element is the data the application operates on; i.e. think of it as the blue and yellow elements representing the word processing application and the green element representing the document being edited. The lower three elements represent the *internals* of the application and the data. The two upper elements represent how the application can be used by and is visible for a user.

One of the most essential aspects of ArchiMate is that modeling the behavior is separated from modeling the structure. The blue elements in the figure represent the active structure ('who') and the yellow elements represent the behavioral aspects of the 'who' elements — they are two sides of the same coin: in a certain sense one can't exist without the other.

It seems rather excessive that you need four elements to model one application. We will later see that you can simplify this, even to a single one of these elements, but for the moment it is very important to understand what the underlying structure looks like. Actually, the lack of addressing this in documents and courses I have seen, has been a major reason for writing this book. An understanding of the foundation is required to model *well* in ArchiMate.

Having said that, here is a short explanation of the 5 element types in View 1:

 This is the Application Component. It stands for the 'actor' that an application in your Enterprise Architecture landscape actually is. It is one side of the coin of which Application Function (its behavior) is the other.

 This is the Application Function. It stands for the behavior of the Application Component, how the application can act. It is one side of the coin of which Application Component is the other.

Application Component and Application Function are, in fact, inseparable. You cannot have an actor that does not act unless the actor is dead, and in that case it should not appear in your architecture. Without magic, you cannot have an act without an actor. Again, later we will see how to leave things out of our views and models, but for now we stick to the details.

(Data Object) This is the Data Object. It is what the Application Function acts upon. The Application Function might create, read, write, update or delete the Data Object. Conceivably, the Data Object might not be needed; you can imagine behavior that does not access a passive element. You can also imagine that you do not model Data Objects that only exist *inside* your application. Not every variable in the application code is modeled. But as soon as the Data Object is visible to other parts of your landscape, or when it is persistent, it should be there. Generally, that means we generally only model (semi-)persistent Data Objects. Note: this is not the file or the database itself — those are represented on a lower level: the infrastructure level. We are still one abstraction level up. To illustrate the difference: an RTF file can be both an MS Word Data Object or an Apple TextEdit.app Data Object, depending on which application is used to access it.

Two elements in the image have not been explained yet. They have to do with how the application is used/seen (by the business or by other applications):

(Application Interface) This is the Application Interface. It stands for the route via which the application offers itself to the business or to other applications. Note: both separate concepts (used by people and used by other applications) are supported by this one element. One example would be a Graphical User Interface (GUI), but it can as well be an Application Programming Interface (API), a Web Service or one of the many other ways an application offers itself to other 'actors' in your landscape. Given that difference in use (and thus, as Uncle Ludwig would say, meaning), it is unlikely that the same interface will be used by both a human or another application. But it can be; e.g., in the case of a Command Line Interface (CLI) used by a scheduler system. Application Interface is a 'handle' of the 'actor' that is the Application Component. It is one side of a coin of which Application Service is the other.

(Application Service) This is the Application Service. It stands for the 'visible' behavior of the Application, how the Application Interface can act *for a user*. It is one side of the coin of which Application Interface is the other side. Here again, the service may be 'technical' in that it is offered by one application to other applications or it may be part of your Business-IT integration: services offered to business processes (behavior of humans). The same type of element is used for both.

Now, apart from the elements, there are relations between the elements. There are four in the initial image:

⟵┄┄┄┄┄ This is the Access relation. The access relation always depicts a behavioral element accessing a passive element. Here it depicts the behavior of the applica-

tion (the Application Function) accessing a passive data element (the Data Object — something that in the end generally resides in a file or a database). The arrowhead is optional and it may depict read access or write access (e.g. two for read/write).

◆——— This is the Composition relation. It means that the element at the end with the diamond is the *parent* of the element on the other end and that the child *cannot exist independently* from the parent. The relation depicts the composition of larger wholes out of smaller parts, but it does not mean the set of children modeled must be necessarily complete in your model: there may be parts that are not modeled. This relation could also for instance be used to show that an Application Component has various subcomponents.

┄┄┄┄▷ This is the Realization relation. This has two types of use in ArchiMate. Here it means that the element at the end without the arrowhead is the element that 'creates' the element at the end with an arrowhead: the application's internal functionality realizes a service, which is the externally usable functionality of the application.

●———● This is the Assignment relation. This also has more than one meaning in ArchiMate. Here, it means that one side (the active element) *performs* the behavior that is the behavioral element on the other side.

Important and possibly initially confusing aspects of ArchiMate are thus that — while we have multiple elements (structural and behavioral) representing what is in the mind of many a single thing (an application or an application interface) — we also have single elements (and as we will later see, relations) that can be used with multiple meanings. When you get the hang of it, everything becomes pretty natural just like it is with natural language, but if you are looking for a strictly disjunct (made of independent concepts) approach to a modeling language (e.g., like a programming language or like UML), it might be confusing in the beginning.

Having modeled an application, we can turn to modeling the way this application is used by the business. And before that, we need to look at the way the business & information layer of Enterprise Architecture is modeled in ArchiMate. Luckily, it looks a lot like what we saw in the application layer so it is easy to understand now and it can be seen in View 2.

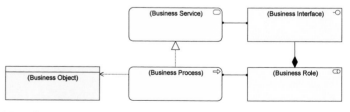

View 2. *Basic Business Process Pattern*

I have left out the actual human actor — the one that fulfills the Business Role — for now to stress the equality between this pattern and the one about the application in View 1 on page 15. It looks quite the same and that is not a coincidence. The relations are the same as with the application image above. The new element types are:

This is the Business Role. The Business Role is an 'actor' in ArchiMate, but it is slightly more complicated than that, because it is an abstract sort of actor based on 'being responsible for certain behavior'. The real actors are people and departments and such. ArchiMate has an element type for those as well, but we leave that for later. Business Roles can perform Business Processes.

This is the Business Process. It stands for a set of causally-related activities that together realize services or create elements. Roles can be assigned to a Business Process, they perform the process, just as the Application Component performs the Application Function. Just as in the application layer, a Business Process cannot exist without a Business Role (which does not mean you must model both, I am talking about the reality you are modeling), they are two sides of the same coin. We also have Business Function, but we leave that for later.

This is the Business Object: the (generally) abstract element that is created or used by a Business Process. Think of objects like 'a payment' or 'a bank account' or 'a bill'. Though it is named Business *Object*, it is more like a *Concept*. It may represent non-informational objects as well, e.g. if your company produces steel beams, you may have a 'Steel Beam' Business Object representing the beam itself and not information about the beam. This usage is not very commonplace, though.

Again, just as with the application, these elements can make sentences of sorts. The proverbial 'second hand car sales' role performs the 'sell second hand car' process, which creates a 'bill'. Criminal, crime and — in this case, possibly — proof of crime.

This is the Business Interface: the way the role interacts with others. You can think of it as a 'channel'; e.g., phone, mail, meeting, etc.. The interface is the visible manifestation of a role.

And this is the Business Service: more or less what it is always about in an organization. This is the reason for the existence of the process. This is the service it offers to (and thus can be used by) others (either inside or outside the company). A company might offer many services; e.g., a bank offers at the most abstract level a 'savings' service or a 'loan' service.

Having set up a couple of basic elements and relations, we can now fill in the missing links. Because on one hand we have the business that offers services to others, on the other hand we have IT that offers supporting services to the business. Together they look like View 3.

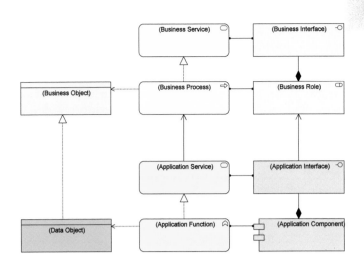

View 3. *Basic Application is used by Basic Business Pattern*

The application level is connected to the business level by three relations. On the left we see the already familiar Realization relation (┈┈┈▷). Here it means that the Data Object realizes the Business Object. In a concrete example: the 'bank account' Business Object may be data (a Data Object) of an accounting application; it is the same item's representation in a different architectural layer.

In the middle and on the right we see a new relation:

←———— This is the Used-By relation. It means that the element at the end without the arrowhead is used by the element at the end with the arrow head. The Application Service, for instance, is Used-By the Business Process. The Application Interface (e.g. the Graphical User Interface) is Used-By the Business Role. Note especially that the definition is passive: it is not 'uses' but 'is used by'. The reason for that is that the direction of relations is important in ArchiMate, something that will be explained later on.

The fact that an Application Interface can be used by a Business Role is the 'other side of the coin' of the same Used-By relation between Application Service and Business Process. They are twins. Both illustrate the 'service oriented' way that ArchiMate relates one layer to the next as far as actors and their behavior goes.

With what has been explained so far, you can already do much of the modeling you need in terms of 'Current State' or 'Change/Project' Enterprise Architecture. There are two more things that need to be explained before the basic setup is complete: applications using other applications, and business processes/roles using other business processes/roles. Here again, what happens at business level and application level is identical, so we are going to illustrate only one.

1.2 The double use of Used-By

So far, our example has only shown Used-By as a relation *between* levels in your architecture. But the same relation type can also be used *within* a level. The business may use an application, but an application can also be used by another application.

In View 4 you see the same Used-By relation (◄——) twice. Once between the 'A' Application Service and the Business Process that uses the 'A' application, and once between the 'B' Application Service and the 'A' Application Function. This means that the 'A' application makes use of the 'B' application. Though the relation is Used-By in both cases, it has quite a different role to play. Often, the definition of an Application Service that is used by the Business is pretty business-like in its description, something you discuss with a senior user or a process owner. But the relation between applications is more of a technical nature and you discuss it with application architects. The difference generally shows itself clearly in the types of names and descriptions of the service. It is hard to truly imagine an Application Service that is both used by another application and a Business Process. After all, both uses will be pretty different, unless we are talking about a fully automated business process, which we will handle later.

1.3 Business Function

So far, we have modeled business behavior always as a Business Process. But ArchiMate actually has two main work horses for business behavior: Business Process and Business Function. The differences are subtle and in most situations you can use either. In section 10 "Business Function and Business Process" on page 75 we will look into the difference in more depth and see that there is a nice way of combining them both when modeling your business layer. Business Function looks like this:

For now, as we are doing the superficial introduction, it is best to use the following guidelines:

- You use a Business Process if you are thinking of a causally-related set of behaviors ('activities') that in the end *produce* something, normally a service or an object. Business Process is an outside-in view of business behavior, based on what the behavior *produces*. You normally assign a single Business Role to a Business Process or Business Function, but that leaves you free to have sub-roles assigned to sub-processes or sub-functions. If disjunct roles do something together, you should (officially) use a Business Interaction in ArchiMate (see Section 2.1 "Collaboration and Interaction" on page 23) but you often have quite some freedom to

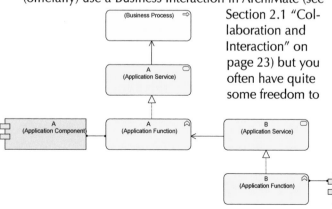

View 4. *An Application Using Another Application*

choose a different 'not-proper' pattern (we'll get into this later).

- You use a Business Function if you are thinking of a grouping of related behavior based on — for instance — same tools, same skills or same role that performs it. In fact, Business Function is best seen as an inside-out view of the business behavior.

1.4 Business Actor

Earlier we encountered the Business Role. The Business Role

View 5. *Business Actor in Context*

is an abstract sort of actor. But in a business architecture there are of course *real* actors: people, departments, or even business units or companies or maybe regulators. ArchiMate has an element for that: the Business Actor, as seen in context in View 5.

On the left we see the already familiar Business Process to which a Business Role is Assigned. The Business Role *performs* the Business Process. On the right we see the new element type Business Actor, which is Assigned-To the Business Role. This must be read as the Business Actor *fulfills* the Business Role. ArchiMate was designed to be economical with relation types, so it re-uses the relation for a slightly different meaning.

1.5 Adding Technical Infrastructure to the Mix

Just as the Business Process needs the Application Service to be able to be performed, the Application Function needs infrastructure to run. If we add the infrastructure to the application layer, we get View 7 on page 19.

There are no new types of relations here, but there are new element types:

 This is the Node. This is a slightly complicated concept in ArchiMate and more details follow later, but for now, think of it as the hardware and its system software, where files are stored or applications can run. We'll see the details later.

This is the Infrastructure Function. Just as with the Application Function and the Application Component, the Infrastructure Function stands for the behavior of the Node. They are two sides of the same coin. Note: the Infrastructure Function is new since ArchiMate 2.0. If you use older tooling or you encounter older views, it might not be there. Instead, in ArchiMate 1.0, the Node directly Realizes the Infrastructure Service. The ArchiMate 2.0 designers did the right thing and made sure all layers have this same basic structure-of-four (service-function-interface-'performer').

(Infrastructure Service) This is the Infrastructure Service, the visible behavior of the Node. In many ways, this is what the infrastructure is all about, what it can do for the applications, its reason of existence. This is what the applications need to function. Typical examples of Infrastructure Services are for instance a 'file share' or 'application execution' or a 'database service'. The latter may cause confusion, because you might wonder why that is an *Infrastructure* Service and not for instance something at the *application* level. We'll get back to that in Section 5.6 "Why two types of software?" on page 37, but for now, it is enough to say that the Node comprises both the hardware and the system software. A database system is generally modeled as system software and the database as an Artifact (see below).

(Infrastructure Interface) This is the Infrastructure Interface. This is not that easy to explain. For Application Interface, one can easy dream up an easy example: the (graphical) user interface. But for the Infrastructure interface, ArchiMate is not very clear; it says it might be best thought of as a kind of contract that the 'user' (the application) has to fulfill. An example would be a protocol, like the SMB or NFS protocol for file sharing and the TCP/IP or UDP/IP ports where the service is offered. Unless you are a dedicated infrastructure architect, you can generally do without this one. I am just mentioning it here to be complete and leaving it out here would introduce the concept of 'pattern' before it is wise to do so.

(Artifact) The last new element (for now) is the Artifact. This one is pretty simple. The best example is a file. Another often-used example is the actual database where your application's data resides. Another example is the actual 'executable' (file) also known as 'the binary': what your application is when you look at the 'byte' level. Your application. The 'data bytes' Artifact in the model above is the one that realizes the Data Object that is ac-

cessed by the Application Function. The 'executable bytes' Artifact forms the bytes (a file, or a set of files often called a 'software distribution') that the system can read and interpret as a program. On the infrastructure level, 'a byte is a byte' in the sense that both passive (Data) elements and active (Application) elements are in the end nothing but a collection of bytes. Deep down, we get to the basic level of zeros and ones as we should.

The relations are mostly pretty straight-forward. The Assignment relations (•——•) between Node and Artifacts stand for the fact that the Artifacts *resides* on the Node. In other words, it depicts where in your infrastructure you can find a file. Also pretty simple are the Used-By (←——) relations between Infrastructure Service and Application Function and between Infrastructure Interface and Application Component. If an Application Function needs access to a file that resides on a file system, the file system is an Infrastructure Service that is Used-By the Application Function. And its mirror is the Used-By relation from Infrastructure Interface to Application Component. This mirroring is depicted by the Assignment relation (•——•) between Infrastructure Interface and Infrastructure Service, exactly as happens in the levels above between the 'interface' and the 'service'.

And lastly, there are the Realization relations (·······▷) between an Artifact and both Data Object and between Artifact and Application Component. This one is also pretty simple and easiest to explain by example. Suppose your application is Microsoft Word, then the file you are editing could be called "foo.doc". And if the application is MS Word, the Artifact realizing the Application Component could be "word.exe".

I have a detailed example model for you in View 6 to see everything in a single context. The model shows someone writing a letter to a customer that contains an answer, supposedly to a question the customer has asked. Two infrastructural services are needed for this to work. The

View 7. *Basic Application uses Basic Infrastructure*

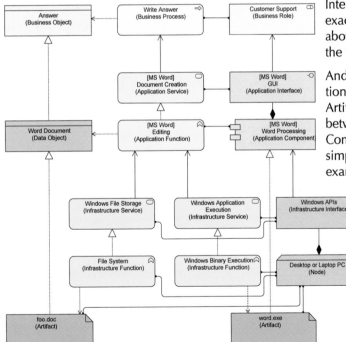

View 6. *Write Answer Process, supported by MS Word and a Standalone PC*

application should run and the document must be stored. In this example, everything happens on a standalone PC.

If you are an 'enterprise' architect you may think that all this detail is irrelevant and that the language looks like a language for detailed design only. Don't worry: using ArchiMate does not mean you absolutely must model all these details, the language can handle both: a roughly sketched Business Operating Model down to the nitty-gritty details you have to confront when you are in a project. I am simply using an example everybody knows, to illustrate how it works in ArchiMate. And even in View 6, I have left some things out, and I have combined the Infrastructure Interfaces into one element. I could also have combined the Infrastructure Services into one element, this is a question I will address later when I am discussing 'modeling patterns'.

One more comment, before we go on with the rest of the language. As you might have noticed, the initial example with infrastructure in View 7 had no Access relation between the Infrastructure Function and the 'executable' Artifact. But the 'write answer' example of View 6 does have that kind of a relation (shown in red). Here an explicit Infrastructure Function for application execution was modeled and that function needs access to the 'executable' artifact. So which one is correct? The answer is: whatever your brief is and what you want to show. ArchiMate is a grammar, so it is *your* choice what you want to put in that grammar and how you put it. You have considerable freedom and you will certainly develop your own style. You can certainly model incorrectly in ArchiMate, just as you can write false statements or make grammatical errors in any language. So there are wrong models. The syntax of the ArchiMate language does not by definition lead to correct statements, just as with other languages. Later, we will address choosing your style and patterns, the latter being like 'common phrases in the language'.

1.6 System Software and Device

Our first use of infrastructure elements was pretty limited. We added the Infrastructure Function, the Infrastructure Service, the Node, the Infrastructure Interface and the Artifact. ArchiMate adds two useful active structure concepts to model the actual infrastructure layer of your architecture:

Device and System Software. The best way to explain them is by giving an example of how they can be used.

In View 8 we see a model of a database server in our landscape. The name of the server is 'srv001' and that could be the name it carries in a CMDB for instance.

The new element types are:

 This is the Device, the actual hardware, the 'iron' of our infrastructure. In this example, two elements of the type System Software have been installed on it (Assigned-To it). The little logo of the element is an image of a keyboard/screen.

 This is the System Software element. It stands for software that we consider to be part of our infrastructure layer and not our application layer. Most common uses are operating systems or database systems. In our example both are available: the Red Hat Linux operating system and the PostgreSQL database system. Modeled too is that the PostgreSQL software uses the Red Hat software. (If we have our existing landscape modeled in such detail, we could by analysis find all PostgreSQL databases that run on Red Hat, handy if we are planning an update and there is something about PostgreSQL running on Red Hat that merits extra attention).

Both are a type of Node. A Node like in View 7 on page 19 can be either System Software or Device, or a collection of both (see below).

Note that not just technical low-level software is System Software. In fact, even some end-user applications may also be System Software. What really sets software apart from Application Component as System Software is that System Software is always a sort of *platform*. It is an environment where other software can run. So, for instance, Java on your computer is System Software. It can read and execute JAR files which contain Java instructions. See also section 5.6 "Why two types of software?" on page 37.

1.7 Composition and Aggregation

We already met the Composition relation (◆——) earlier. The composition represents a whole-part relation. It is best to look at the ArchiMate version of this common relation as the relation between a tree (a real one from your garden, not the computational concept) and its branches. A branch is branch of a single tree and cannot be a branch of multiple trees. If the tree is destroyed, all of its branches are destroyed as well.

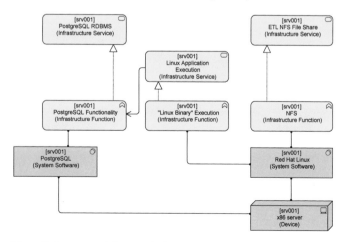

View 8. *Device and System Software*

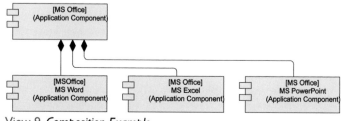

View 9. *Composition Example*

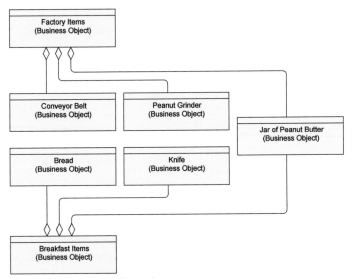

View 10. *Aggregation Example*

Generally, you may always create a Composition relation between two elements of the same type (or 'super-type', explained later). View 9 contains an example.

The Aggregation relation (◇—) is a variation on the theme. It looks like View 10.

It is best to look at the Aggregation relation as a kind of grouping (note: in Section 2.8 "The Grouping Relation" on page 27 we will see an official 'grouping' relation). The 'parent' (on the end with the diamond) represents a 'collection' of the children. But other than with Composition, the children may be a member of multiple Aggregations as you can also see in View 10: The 'Jar of Peanut Butter' is both part of the 'Factory Items' of the peanut butter factory and the 'Breakfast Items' of a consumer's home. It's a like the number 4 being both part of the collection of squares of integers and the collection of even numbers. Composition versus Aggregation is sometimes described as 'has-a' versus 'part-of', the difference being not directly clear form the terms. Also, composition is sometimes referred to 'strong ownership', whereas aggregation is sometimes referred to as 'weak ownership', again somewhat problematic as the aggregation does not 'own' the child at all.

1.8 Nesting

There are three relation types that may be drawn by nesting an element inside another element: Composition, Aggregation and Assignment. Note: tooling often allows more than the language does, especially if you use tooling that is

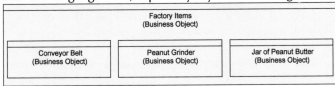

View 11. *Nested Aggregation*

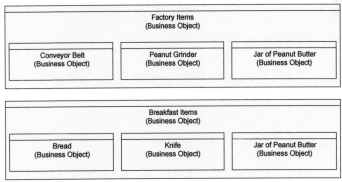

View 12. *Two Nested Aggregations with Shared Object*

nothing more than a good model-drawing application such as Visio for Windows or OmniGraffle for Mac OS. Anyway, let's take the 'Factory Items' from View 10 as an example. Nested, it looks like View 11.

That looks a lot cleaner and that is why many modelers like it. But we can already see a disadvantage: you no longer see anymore what the relation is between parts and whole: Composition? Aggregation?

It gets worse, when you want to model both Aggregations from View 10 in Nested form in one view as in View 12.

Not only are you unable to see the actual relations, it has now become necessary to include the 'Jar of Peanut Butter' element twice. And though the name is the same, there is nothing that will tell you if 'under water' it is the same element. You can have two different elements with the same name in ArchiMate, after all, the label has no meaning inside the language (as the language' is in fact a *grammar*) even if it has a meaning in the world of an architect. Besides, even if your modeling guidelines force different names for different elements, think of a very large view with the same element twice. Are you going to spot that the same element occurs twice? Probably not. So are you going to see the dependencies in full? Again: probably not.

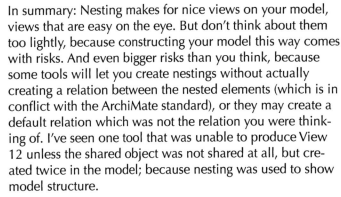

View 13. *Assignment Nesting, Two Levels Deep*

View 13 contains an Assignment example of Nesting, two levels deep.

In summary: Nesting makes for nice views on your model, views that are easy on the eye. But don't think about them too lightly, because constructing your model this way comes with risks. And even bigger risks than you think, because some tools will let you create nestings without actually creating a relation between the nested elements (which is in conflict with the ArchiMate standard), or they may create a default relation which was not the relation you were thinking of. I've seen one tool that was unable to produce View 12 unless the shared object was not shared at all, but created twice in the model; because nesting was used to show model structure.

1.9 Using a Node to encapsulate infra-structure

Now that we have seen Composition and Nesting, we can look at View 8 on page 20 that introduced System Software and Device and show in View 14 how it might be modeled.

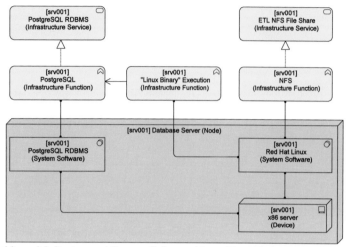

View 14. *Device and System Software Nested in a Node*

In this example, the System Software and Device elements are children (Composition) of an abstract Node element (the Composition relations are not explicitly shown here, but instead modeled as Nesting). This is kind of a nice grouping of an infrastructure element as the composition's children have no independent existence or use. We can also go further: in View 17, the Infrastructure Functions too have been Nested in the Node. This is possible, because we can also Assign the functions to the overall Node and we may Nest an Assignment relation.

In this example, the Node realizes two Infrastructure Services: the PostgreSQL software realizes an RDBMS service that is available to Application Functions, and the operating system also realizes a network file system shared directory. Basically, all structure below the Infrastructure Services is modeled inside the Node. Later, we will go one step further with this example when we discuss patterns.

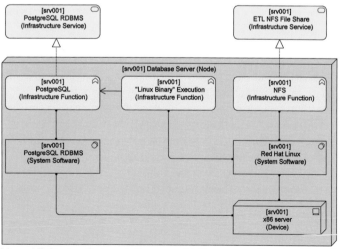

View 17. *Device, System Software and Infrastructure Function Nested in a Node*

In Section 7.2 "A Basic TI Pattern: A Database" on page 47, we will see that it might be handy to restrict ourselves here, to make analysis of the model easier. You have the choice of course if you want to model these details (and you can go as far and deep as you like). It all depends on the use you want to make of your model (in other words: Uncle Ludwig was right). Here, it is only shown to explain what the element types are and how they relate to each other.

1.10 Event, Trigger and Flow

So far, we have handled the 'structure' of your architecture and all relations so far were so-called 'structural relations'. ArchiMate is not big on the dynamics of an architecture, but it does have two 'dynamic relations': Trigger and Flow, and one operator to combine these into a dynamic structure (see Section 2.9 "The Junction Relation" on page 29).

View 15. *Trigger and Flow*

In View 15 we find Trigger (──▶) and Flow (----▶) relations in a business layer example. We see three Business Functions here from the asset management world: 'Portfolio Management' is taking investment decisions, which result in orders for the 'Trading' function. So, 'Trading' starts trading when it receives an order from 'Portfolio Management'. Triggering means there is a causal relation between the two functions. The flow between 'Portfolio Management' and 'Trading' says information flows from one to the other. In this case it is the 'Order'.

But the Trading function also regularly receives a list of allowed counterparts, countries and currencies from the 'Risk Controlling' function. This information Flows from one to the other, but it does not Trigger a trade. A Flow relation between two Business Functions can also be modeled as Business Objects written (Accessed) by one function and read (Accessed) by another. If we add those, it looks like View 16.

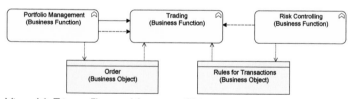

View 16. *Trigger, Flow and Access to Objects*

So, how useful is the Flow relation if you can also use the Business Objects and the Access relation? Well, it has a few advantages:

- You can make simpler view by leaving the Business Objects out and for instance label the Flow relations. The problem, though, is that such a label generally cannot be used to analyze what goes on your landscape, I'll say it already here: watch out for relying too much on labels and properties of elements, they often live outside the 'analyzable' structure of your model.

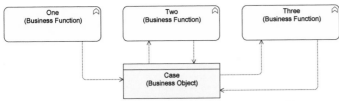

- But, most importantly, your dependencies can become clearer with a Flow. Take, for instance, the example of a 'Case' flowing though your business from Business Function to Business Function. Having read/write relations from these Business Functions to that single Business Object tells you nothing about how information flows. Take the example in View 18.

This does not tell you how the 'Case' Flows through your organization. What do you think? Look at View 19 and it becomes clear what the flow of information is.

Without the Flow relations, would you have known? Could you have drawn the wrong conclusion? Certainly. Is that a bad thing? After all they all depend on that Business Object. Well, take this example: without the Flow relation, you might think that the roles behind function One, Two and Three may have to agree concurrently on all the contents of the Case Business Object. But, in reality, you might only need to set up talks between One and Two on the one hand and Three and Two on the other and depending on the issues at hand, that might be simpler.

Trigger and Flow relations may generally be drawn between behavioral elements within a layer; e.g., from Application

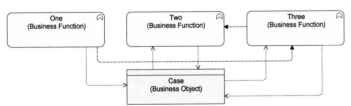

View 19. *Business Functions sharing Access to a Business Object, with Flows*

Function to Application Function or from Business Process to Business Process.

ArchiMate also has a special element that depicts a Business Event. A Business Event is 'something that happens'. Events can trigger a Business Process or a Business Function and they can be raised by a Business Process or Business Function, which is also depicted with a Trigger relation. Business Events are normally used for standalone 'things that happen'. An example can be seen in View 20.

ArchiMate does not fully support detailed process modeling, it only has a limited support for the dynamics of behavior. In section 25 "Linking BPMN and ArchiMate" on page 156 I will present a method to use ArchiMate for EA while using BPMN for process modeling.

View 20. *Business Event Triggers Business Process*

1.11 The (almost) complete Picture

We have described 14 of ArchiMate's 31 element types, so in that sense we are only half way. But, with the elements and relations of this section, you can probably do 95% of an architect's work, if that work is focused on normal business-IT integration and modeling things like Project Architectures.

The title of this section is "Elements and Relations: 3x3x3". It has this title because ArchiMate:

- divides Enterprise Architecture into a Business & Information layer, an Application & Data layer and a Technical Infrastructure layer. These are the rows in ArchiMate's meta-model and this division is fairly standard in the Enterprise Architecture world.

- divides architecture in any layer 'strictly' into Active Structure, Behavior and Passive Structure. Put in a sentence: "Who/what does what to what?". The clear separation of actors and their behavior is not common in Enterprise Architecture and it is a main foundational aspect of ArchiMate.

- has three kinds of relations: Structural Relations, Dynamic Relations and 'Other' Relations (next section). The reason for this division becomes clear in the section on Derived Relations.

2. Other Elements and Relations

With the elements and relations of the previous section you can probably do most of an enterprise architect's work, if that work is focused on 'Current State' and 'Change/Project' Architectures. Here is the rest:

2.1 Collaboration and Interaction

Suppose you have two Business Roles in your organization that need to work together to get some specific work done. For instance, the 'sales' and the 'legal' Business Roles need to work together to create the offer for the prospective client.

Within ArchiMate there are generally two ways of modeling this.

Using the elements and relations we already described, you can put one of them in the lead and let the second provide a service. In our example: 'sales' produces the offer, but it uses the (internal) services realized by (the processes of) 'legal' in its processes (see View 21 on page 24).

In this set-up, it is clear who is in charge. 'Sales' decides to send the offer out, not legal. 'Legal' must provide something (and for instance withholding approval means 'sales' cannot

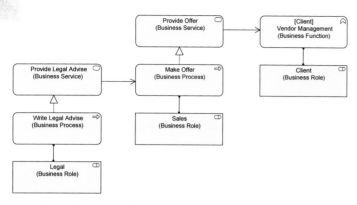

View 21. *Collaboration: Sales Uses Legal on Order Creation*

proceed), but the service to the client is realized by the process of 'Sales'.

ArchiMate offers a second way to model such collaborations. You can create a Business Collaboration that is made up of the Business Roles that are part of that collaboration. Then, you can assign a Business Interaction to that collaboration, the interaction being the behavior of that collaboration. It looks like View 22.

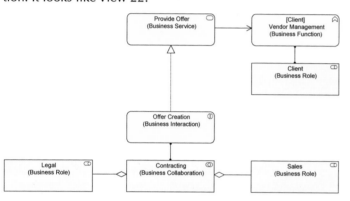

View 22. *Collaboration: Sales and Legal Collaborate on Order Creation*

The whole 'offer creation' 'process' is now modeled as not one of the parties 'owning' it, but both. There are a few new elements:

> This is the Business Collaboration. It is a special kind of Business Role that Aggregates multiple other Business Roles (or Business Collaborations, of course, as these are also types of roles, see Section 2.3 "The Specialization Relation" on page 25). It is the concept that defines multiple roles forming a (specific) single 'collective' role to do something together.

> This is the Business Interaction. It is the behavior of that Business Collaboration, the activities they do together. Note that, while the Business Collaboration Aggregates two or more Business Roles, the Business Interaction does *not* Aggregate Business Functions or Business Processes. What is not

clear in ArchiMate is if we want to see a Business Interaction as functional or process-oriented. Given that it generally produces a result, it is probably best to see this as process-oriented.

One consequence of using a Collaboration is that it is not clear who is in charge. This might be more acceptable to the organization in terms of sensitivities, but sometimes it is just true: nobody is really in charge. In Section 10.2 "Business Function or Business Process?" on page 76, I will present a 'modeling pattern' of the business that uses Collaboration to show the loosely coupled nature of some of the organization's 'end-to-end' processes.

Both methods (using a service and interaction) are correct, it is a matter of style what you want to use and both approaches have some consequences. If you think about it, you could even model the sales-client interaction as a collaboration, after all the transaction requires decisions of both sides. For this introduction, it suffices that you have seen this.

Actually, there is a quick and dirty way to do this too. Archi-

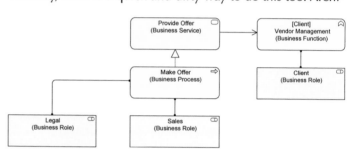

View 23. *Informal Collaboration.*

Mate says that a Business Process is assigned to a single role, but it does not enforce this in the formal definition. Nothing stops you from assigning multiple roles to a single process. So, we can model it quick-and-dirty as shown in View 23.

This way, we also show that the 'Make Offer' process is assigned to two roles, in fact forming a de facto collaboration. This will, however, be frowned upon by ArchiMate purists. Besides, why is this a collaboration? Maybe *either* of the two performs it. The meaning of multiple alike relations (like multiple Realizations to one element) is not defined by ArchiMate, leading to some vagueness in models if it is modeled. For Business Role to Business Process or Business Function, ArchiMate suggests limiting yourselves to a single role performing the behavior. After all, for multiple collective performers, collaborations exist. But for other such situations like multiple Data Objects Realizing a single Business Object, the vagueness is there.

At the application layer, something likewise exists, as is shown in View 24 on page 24.

The Application Collaboration stands for the collaboration of two Application Components. The behavior of that collaboration is the Application Interaction and such a behavior may realize

View 24. *Application Collaboration*

an Application Service. Here too, it is not clear who is in charge, but an architect may like it because it is 'fairer' to the importance of both. Also, it gives the architect a clear central place to document how applications interact. In the Used-By model, the description gets divided over multiple elements This is a matter of style, and we'll get back to that in Section 8.1 "Application Collaboration is an Anthropomorphism" on page 66.

2.2 The Association Relation

The weakest relation, the 'catch-all' relation of ArchiMate, is the Association relation which is depicted as a simple line (———). It has a couple of formal roles in ArchiMate, but it also has the role of 'relation of last resort'. If you want to model the relation between two elements, if you know they are related somehow but you cannot model how, you can use Association. It is, therefore, often a sign of lack of knowledge or effort, so it is a matter of style if you want to use it (we'll talk about style later). For now, know that it exists and below we will see some official uses.

2.3 The Specialization Relation

All relations we have seen so far are relations between actual elements in your landscape. The Specialization relation (◁———) is different. From a software engineering perspective, I can explain it easily: all other ArchiMate relations are element-level relations, this one is a class-level relation. The Specialization relation says that an element is a kind of another element. For instance, a 'car insurance' and a 'travel insurance' are both a kind of 'insurance'. Or a 'stock' and a 'bond' are both a kind of 'liquid investment'. An example is shown in View 25.

Here, we say that 'Cash' is a kind of 'Liquid Investment' (a liquid investment is an investment that you can easily trade) and another kind is 'Security' which again can be specialized into 'Stock' (a deed to a partial ownership of a company) and 'Bond' (a loan to an organization or country). If an element is a specialization of another element, whatever relations are true for the 'parent' (the element at the arrowhead) must be true for the child. If a Business Process handles 'Liquid Investment' (e.g., a reporting process), it must be able to handle both 'Cash' and 'Security'. On the other hand, if a business process handles 'Security', it must be able to handle both 'Stock' and 'Bond' but it does not need to be able to handle 'Cash'.

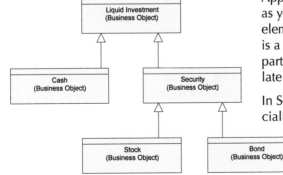

View 25. *Specialization Example: Investment Types*

In Object-Oriented (OO) design, the specialization is sometimes called the 'Is-A' relation. Its counterparts are the 'Has-A' relation, which in ArchiMate is Composition (◆———) and the the 'Refers-To' relation, which in ArchiMate is Aggregation (◇———). Generally, what you can do with an 'Is-A' Sub-classing (which is what you do with the Specialization relation), can have complex consequences. Take for instance 'Cash' from the current example. Suppose our company says we may only use cash as collateral for securities we lend and not (other) securities. We would have a new Business Object in our landscape called 'Collateral' and 'Cash' could be a kind of 'Collateral'. It looks like the example in View 26.

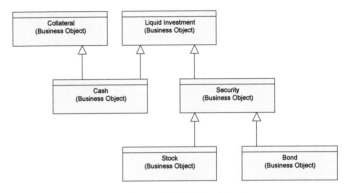

View 26. *Specialization Example: Multiple Inheritance*

What we have here is called in OO-terms 'multiple inheritance': Cash is both a kind of collateral and a kind of security. Most OO languages do not support true multiple inheritance (C++ does, more modern Objective-C, Java and C# do not) and for a reason: it tends to become messy because the 'parents' may have conflicting rules of behavior for the 'child' to inherit (a bit like parenting in real life, true, but maybe not the best paradigm for software engineering or business architecture modeling).

What is interesting to know is that Specialization also plays a role inside the ArchiMate meta-model. For instance, Device and System Software are both Specializations of Node, a Business Collaboration is a Specialization of Business Role and an Application Collaboration is a Specialization of Application Component. What this means above all is that as you can have Compositions and Aggregations between elements of the same type, and, for instance, since Device is a subtype of Node, you can have a Device as Composite part of a Node (as in Section 1.9 "Using a Node to encapsulate infrastructure" on page 22.

In Section 7.21 on page 63, I'll show an example of Specialization use in a current state or change model, but largely I would advise you to be careful when using this relation type in models that are meant to describe a concrete (project (end) state or current state) reality. In other words, you can forget most of what has been written in this section and still properly create good ArchiMate models.

2.4 Product, Contract and Value

If you want to model the offerings of your organization to the outside world (anyone who uses what you produce, be it clients or regulators), a handy element is Product. A Product is a simple enough concept. It is an Aggregation of one or more services and (optionally) a Contract. It is Associated with a Value. It looks like View 27.

As you can see, the Product element type is a bit weird: it is part of ArchiMate's Passive Structure (elements acted upon), but it also Aggregates Behavioral elements (the actions themselves). And it is a business-layer element, but it may aggregate an application-layer or infrastructure-layer element. If I was a purist, I would say this element type is a 'kludge'. Still, it can be useful. The new element types are:

This is the Contract. It represents the formal or informal agreement that covers the delivery of the service provided. This might be a specific Service Level Agreement or General Terms & Conditions.

This is the Value of the Product. A Value is a pretty abstract kind of element in ArchiMate. It has wide-ranging use. It can be the value to the consumer, but also to the producer. It could be described in monetary terms, but it may just as well be described in emotional terms (e.g., an insurance service may be associated with the value of 'economic security' or 'be able to sleep easy at night'. 'Be able to' since 'sleep at night' is the actual Business Process). In the standard view of the ArchiMate model, it is generally Associated with the Product (and this is also the case in the underlying meta-model as shown in the standard), but the actual ArchiMate definition of Value Associates it with the service and mentions the Association with Product only as 'indirect'.

View 27. *Product, Contract, Value and a Product's Constituents*

This is the Product. It is what you offer to the outside world. For a department of your organization, the Product may be something offered 'internally'. It can be handy to make

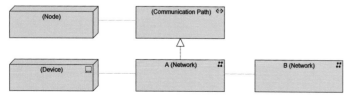

View 29. *Network and Communication Path*

the link between your Enterprise Architecture and how management looks at the organization.

2.5 Representation and Meaning

Earlier we encountered the Business Object, the work horse of passive structure in your business layer architecture. And we saw how this business-level element could be Realized by an application layer Data Object. Take for instance the 'Answer' Business Object that was Realized by the 'Word Document' Data Object in View 6 on page 19. ArchiMate also has another way to Realize a Business Object, it can be realized by a Representation. A good example would be a

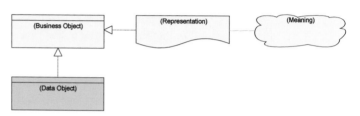

View 28. *Representation and Data Object Realizing a Business Object*

print of the answer letter you are sending to your customer. The relation between a Business Object and its direct surroundings looks like View 28.

The new element types are:

This is the Representation. While the Data Object is the element in our application layer that represents the Business Object, the Representation is another way of representing the Business Object and it stands for a representation that can be shared with others, e.g. a print, a PDF file you send as attachment in a mail message, or a web-page. Or the actual real Steel Beam we mentioned in 1.1 "Application and Business" on page 15.

This is the Meaning of the Representation. ArchiMate says it is the "information-related counterpart of a Value" and it "represents the 'intention' of a Business Object or a Representation".

For corporate strategy-level Enterprise Architects, they can be useful, e.g. in the future state architecture, but in most practical circumstances (current state architecture, project architecture) they do not add a lot of value. Specifically, Meaning runs against Uncle Ludwig's idea about what a meaning is, but that is a philosophical issue, not an architectural one, so we will not be discussing it here. Representation is sometimes a useful link to the physical world, but the description ArchiMate gives with links to 'RTF' or 'HTML' overlaps with the IT-levels of your architecture. We'll return to this issue later.

2.6 Network and Communication Path

ArchiMate offers two elements to model communication at the infrastructure level: Network and Communication Path. A simple overview of use is shown in View 29.

The new element types are:

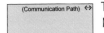

This is the Network. It stands for the physical communication medium just as the Device stands for the physical computer hardware. A typical example could be '1Gbps Ethernet'.

This is the Communication Path. What the Network is at physical level is the Communication Path at the logical level. It is a way for nodes to exchange data. The example ArchiMate 2.0 gives is 'message queuing'.

A Network Realizes a Communication Path. The other relations are all Associations. To be honest, I have never seen these used in practice. Maybe I haven't seen enough practice or maybe they were thought of in a time that such aspects were still important in Enterprise Architecture work while they are now more or less a given like the air we breathe.

Network and Communication Path can be drawn both as 'boxes' with the association relation and also as connec-

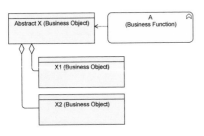

View 31. *Aggregation can be used as grouping*

tions, even though they technically are elements. Basically that would mean that you have to draw a Realization relation between two connections and my tool of choice cannot do that, so you're not seeing it here.

2.7 Automated Processes

So far, our landscape was based on a business process performed by people (actors fulfilling a role). But what if a process is fully automated? ArchiMate has the following solution: If a process is run by people, a Business Role is Assigned-To the Business Process and a Business Interface is Assigned-To a Business Service. The Business Role *performs* the Business Process. If a Business Process is *performed* by an application, we draw an Assigned-To between the Application Component and the Business Process. And consequently, we also draw an Assigned-To between the Application Interface and the Business Service. View 30 shows them (in red).

This way, we can model an application that by itself performs a process that realizes a service. In Section 28.2 "Automated Processes" on page 188, we discuss this approach in more detail as part of a Chapter on proposed improvements for ArchiMate..

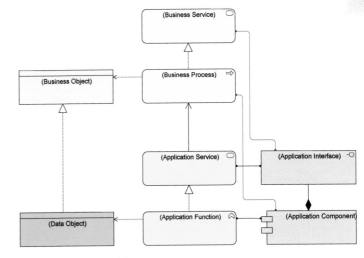

View 30. *Automated Process*

2.8 The Grouping Relation

In ArchiMate you can group elements visually in two ways: Nesting (see Section 1.8 "Nesting" on page 21) and Grouping. Nesting is in fact a way to draw *three* types of relations: Composition, Aggregation and Assignment. According to the standard, you may *only* use Nesting for one of these relations (tools often allow more nestings than ArchiMate allows). But what if you want to visually group other elements? Suppose you want to group the different Business Objects accessed by a Business Function? You can, for instance, use Aggregation and create an abstract Business Object in your landscape as you can see in View 31. On the left of that view you see the actual relations, and on the right the Aggregations are drawn using Nesting. It works if you can Aggregate and if you do not mind adding an abstract (non-existing) element in your model.

But what if you cannot aggregate? For this, ArchiMate has the Grouping relation. This is a relation, but it looks like an element with other elements nested like the gray boxes with labels in View 32.

The Grouping relation is a catch-all kind of relation. It says that all elements in the box have 'something' in common, in the example: legal status. So, in the left box, we find a Business Process 'BP1' and an Application Service 'AS1' that are regulated by law, and in the right box we find a Business Process 'BP2' and an Application Service 'AS2' that are non-regulated. Given the catch-all nature, you can think of grouping as a visual way to show Associations, but ArchiMate does not define it that way. Though Grouping is formally a relation in ArchiMate, it tends to be used in a purely graphical way to make certain views of your model clearer for the reader.

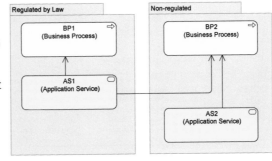

View 32. *Grouping Relation*

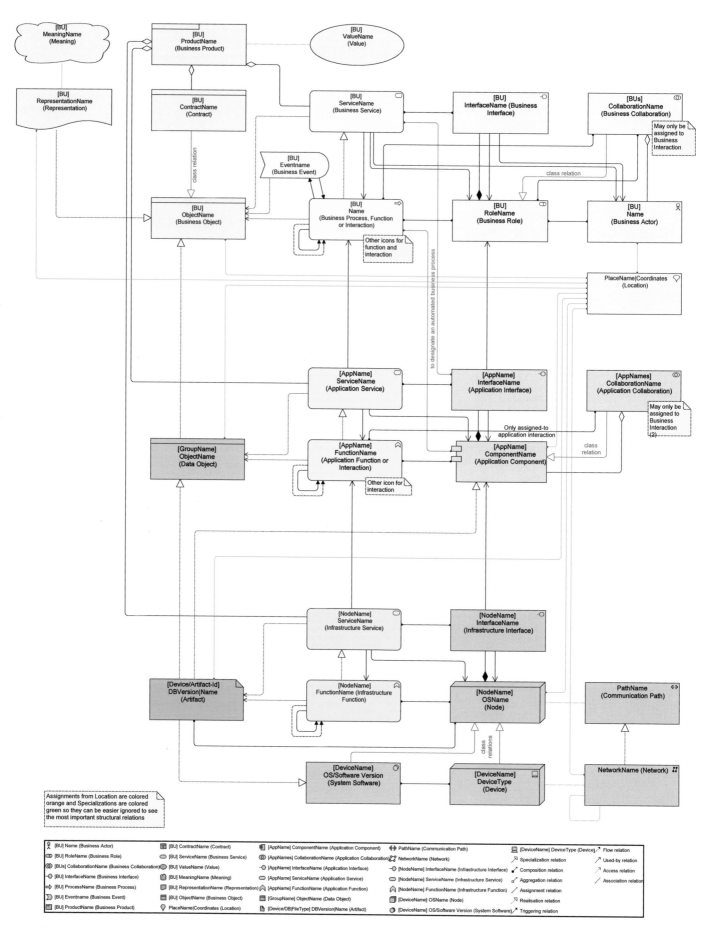

View 33. *ArchiMate 2 Metamodel*

2.9 The Junction Relation

Finally there is the Junction relation. This is very special because it is a *relation* that can relate other (dynamic: Flow and Trigger) relations to each other. An example is shown in View 34.

The big dot in the middle is the Junction. You can label the incoming

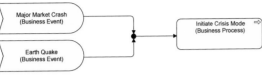

View 34. *Junction relation (join)*

or outgoing dynamic relations, e.g. in a case of a choice as shown in View 35.

View 35. *Junction relation (split)*

The Junction is very generic. The ArchiMate 2.0 Standard suggests that it might be handy to extend it (Section 9.2 of the ArchiMate 2.0 Standard) to And-Split, Or-Split, And-Join and Or-Join. But that is not part of ArchiMate itself. The tool I use comes by default with an And-Junction and an Or-Junction (not separated in splits and joins).

2.10 Location

The final ArchiMate element to explain is Location. This is new in ArchiMate 2.0 and an example is given in View 36.

This is the Location element. This element stands for a geographical location where something resides. You can use the Assignment relation to link it to several other element types to model where they are located.

2.11 The Complete Picture

ArchiMate is reasonably rich. There are 31 element types and 10 relation types in Version 2.0, excluding the Motivation and Implementation extensions.

In View 33 on page 28 you'll find the overall picture of ArchiMate's element types and their relations. This is often referred to as the ArchiMate Meta-Model. Note:

- Business Process, Business Function and Business Interaction take the same place and are represented by the Business Process icon in this view of the meta-model;

- You may Access passive elements from *any* behavioral element (so far I modeled only Access from *internal* elements to keep thing simple). More about this in section 19.4 "Where to relate your information to" on page 29.

- The labels used for the elements in View 33 (and in this book) are not required like that; they represent the

standard labeling pattern I normally use and I explain why in Section 6.6 "About labels" on page 45. Labels are not regulated in the ArchiMate standard, but as with natural language, play an important role along with grammar in producing meaning.

View 33 is repeated on page 219. During the rest of the book, you might want to look back at the meta-model to check for things. If you keep your finger between that page and the one before it, the meta-model is always readily available.

2.12 Closing Remark on the core ArchiMate meta-model

We have seen relations that look like elements (Grouping) and elements that may look like relations (Communication Path). If you get the feeling that ArchiMate is not 100% clean, I cannot fault you. But even with these issues (which we will visit later) I must stress that in my experience, ArchiMate is *extremely* usable. Creating Project Start Architectures based on detailed ArchiMate models has, in my experience, substantially reduced delays and unforeseen issues — having a detailed 'Current-State' model has seriously improved our control over and our reporting on our landscape to regulators.

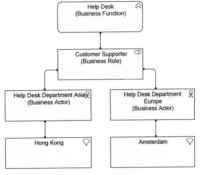

View 36. *Example use of Location object*

When we started to use ArchiMate, we initially had many doubts about how the ArchiMate designers had set up the language. But, we did follow the rule that we would strictly stick to the meta-model and not change or adapt it in any way (even though our tool supported that). We did this for two reasons:

- Any future tool update might break our models or require a lot of work;

- Understanding something comes only after a lot of experience. Though we did sometimes dislike what we saw, we decided to distrust our (beginner) skills more than the skills of the language designers. This was wise: when our experience grew, we learned to appreciate most of the choices the designers had made.

If you focus on finding faults (something that comes naturally for architects as they are always for the lookout of something that may break) you will. But in my experience, that does not affect the usability much. ArchiMate is very, very usable.

3. Derived Relations

3.1 Derived Structural Relations

So far we have included every concept, every element type and all connecting relations. ArchiMate, however, offers a mechanism to create 'shortcuts'. The researchers, business users and students that created ArchiMate even offered a mathematical proof that their definition of the shortcuts are 'correct'. Adding these shortcuts to the model was originally seen as extending 'ArchiMate proper' to a sort of 'Archi-Mate+', but these shortcuts are so handy and useful that most practitioners (or teachers) do not really distinguish between the fundamental and shortcut relations anymore (which is a bad thing, as we will see). Add to that, tools generally do not support the actual difference and it is easy to understand that the shortcuts are probably one of the most (implicitly) used but least (explicitly) understood aspects of ArchiMate.

Officially, ArchiMate calls these shortcuts 'derived structural relations' and I generally explain them by saying that the derived relations are a summary of a 'dependency route' that lies between two elements in a model. All tools I know allow you to model a summary without modeling the underlying 'true' route of elements and relations, but in the end each summary relation implicitly assumes that such a route with real elements and relations is there, even if you have not (or need not have) created them in your model.

The best way to illustrate them is by using an already familiar example, the earlier used 'write answer' example, It is shown again in View 37 for easy reference (ignore the redness of one relation this time).

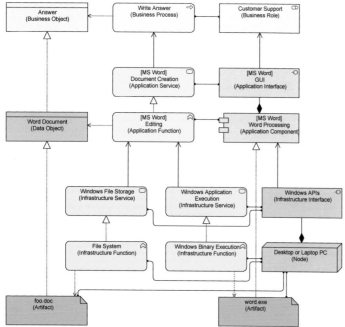

View 37. *Write Answer Process, supported by MS Word and a Stand-alone PC*

Given this example, the questions we may want to ask are:

a. What is the relation between the 'Desktop or Laptop PC' Node and the 'Write Answer' Business Process?

b. What is the relation between the 'word.exe' Artifact and the 'Document Creation' Application Service?

c. What is the relation between the 'Desktop or Laptop PC' Node and the 'Answer' Business Object?

For this, ArchiMate comes with the following procedure:

*   Find a route from one element in the model to another following the *structural* relations between them. There is a additional requirement: a route is only valid if all relations followed are followed in the *same direction*. All relations have a direction, except Association which is bidirectional (Assignment was also bidirectional in ArchiMate 1.0).

*   Every structural relation has a *strength*. If you have a valid route, the derived relation between both ends of the route is the *weakest* relation found on the route, much like the weakest link in a chain. The strengths are (from weak to strong):

    1. Association (bidirectional))

    2. Access (direction: always from behavioral element to passive structural element, independent from arrow which depicts read or write; that the direction may be opposite to the arrow is a pitfall when starting with ArchiMate.)

    3. Used-By

    4. Realization

    5. Assignment (in each layer from actor to behavior and in the infrastructure layer from Node to Artifact, bidirectional in ArchiMate 1.0)

    6. Aggregation (direction: from parent to child)

    7. Composition (direction: from parent to child)

Using this procedure, we can answer the questions above:

a. From the 'Desktop or Laptop PC' Node, via Assignment (strength: 5) to 'Windows Binary Execution' Infrastructure Function, via Realization (strength: 4) to 'Windows Application Execution' Infrastructure Service then via Used-By (strength: 3) to the 'Editing' Application Function then via Realization (strength: 4) to the 'Document Creation' Application Service then via Used-By (strength: 3) to the 'Write Answer' Business Process. The weakest relation encountered is Used-By, which is the (derived) relation between the PC and the Business Process: *the PC is Used-By the Business Process*, which makes good sense.

b. The 'word.exe' Artifact Realizes (4) the 'Word Processing' Application Component, which is Assigned-To (5) the 'Editing' Application Function which Realizes (4) the

'Document Creation' Application Service. The weakest is Realization, so *the 'word.exe' Artifact Realizes the 'Document Creation' Application Service*. Which also makes sense.

c. If we take the route from (a) we need just one extra step: from the 'Write Answer' via Access (strength: 2) to the 'Answer' Business Object. The weakest of that route is now Access, so *the PC Accesses the 'Answer' Business Object*.

The Open Group's ArchiMate Forum's decision to make Assignment unidirectional in ArchiMate 2.0 solved the problem that quite a few nonsense derivations were possible. In ArchiMate 1.0 it would for instance enable the route from the 'foo.doc' Artifact via the PC Node to the 'Windows File Storage' Infrastructure Service with Realization as the resulting relation, or in other words: 'foo.doc' Realizes Windows File Storage. Hmm, I think not.

But still, sometimes, multiple shortcuts do exist. For instance, there is an alternative answer to question (c): From the PC Node via Assignment (strength: 5) to the 'foo.doc' Artifact, then via Realization (strength: 4) to the 'Word Document' Data Object and via another Realization to the 'Answer' Business Object. The result is: the PC Realizes the 'Answer' Business Object.

In other words: the PC *Accesses* the 'Answer' Business Object and it also *Realizes* that same 'Answer' Business Object. Here it is clear that we are looking at two aspects of this PC, it both executes the application and it stores the data. If the data were to reside on another server, we would not have both routes. So, the two routes are in fact a true aspect of the situation: the PC does both and so both relations dutifully appear. No problem.

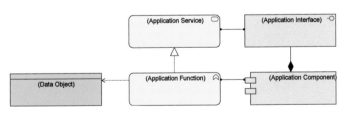

View 38. *The Basic Application Pattern*

So, all is well? It gets a little more complicated. Have a look at the Basic Application pattern again in View 38.

If you go from Application Component to Application Service, you can follow two routes. The first route (via the Application Interface) leads to Assigned-To as the (weakest) derived 'summary' relation. But the one via the Application Function leads to Realization as the (weakest) derived 'summary' relation. ArchiMate does not tell you which one to take if two possible routes exist. That is OK, as we saw in the previous example, when two routes stand for two different aspects. But in this case, either derived relation says something about how you view the concept of Application Component. If you choose Assigned-To, you keep to the strict separation of active component and its behavior. If you

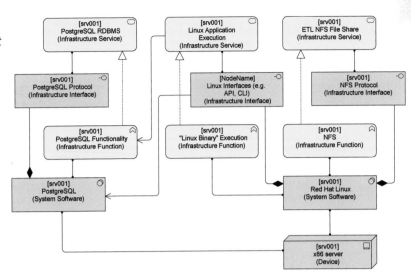

View 39. *System Software and Device with Interfaces*

choose Realization, you look at the Application Component from a more behavioral point of view. We get back to this confusing issue when we discuss the language and look at possible improvements in Chapter "Discussing ArchiMate" on page 179.

What all of this so far implies is that derived relations are useful to make summary views or abstract representations of a complex landscape, but there are risks involved in using them without (or mixed with) the underlying reality. The risks we have seen so far are still benign. But there are some pitfalls we will see later.

Finally, returning to View 8 on page 20 in System Software and Devices, if we add a couple of Infrastructure Interfaces to that view we get View 39.

You might understand why I did not show this in View 8: very complicated for something as simple as a server that provides a file share and a database. But using derived relations, you can conclude that View 40 is a correct representation of the same.

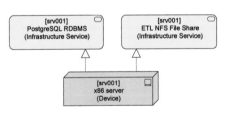

View 40. *Simplified/derived version of View 39*

So, if you want to keep it simple: you can just model these. Keeping it simple and using abstractions make your models and views easier for the reader, but there are some caveats. We'll get back to more of this later.

3.2 Derived Dynamic Relations

Quite a bit simpler, but since ArchiMate 2.0 there is also the possibility to create derived relations from *dynamic* relations. Take a look at the example in View 41.

Suppose we start with the Flow relation B, between 'Business Process 1' and 'Business Process 2'. ArchiMate says:

- You may move a begin *or* end point of a dynamic relation to an element that is Assigned-To the current element.

- You may move a begin *or* end point of a dynamic relation to an element that is Realized by the current element.

Moving *both* begin and end points *simultaneously*, we can turn Flow B into Flow A and turn Flow B into Flow C. Note that we cannot turn Flow C into Flow B or A or turn Flow A into Flow C, according to the text of the standard.

You can of course move *only one* of the begin or end points. E.g. from Flow relation B, you can derive a Flow relation D between 'Business Role 1' and 'Business Service 2'.

The same is true for the Trigger relation and the same derivations can be made on the application layer and — since ArchiMate 2.0 — on the infrastructure layer.

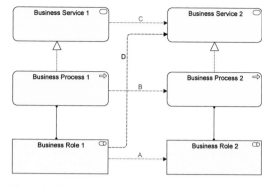

View 41. *Derived Dynamic Relations*

Incidentally, the ArchiMate 2.1 standard contains a table with allowed relations, including all allowed derived relations and it does not allow Flow D (and others like it) while it does allow a large number of (seemingly) derived dynamic relations which are in conflict with its own definitions of those derived relations (see 27.1 "Hidden Structure and Specialization Confusion" on page 180).

It is not allowed to combine structural and dynamic relations in a derivation.

4. Beginner's Pitfalls

4.1 Pitfalls of Derived Relations

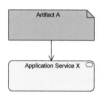

View 43. *Artifact Used-By Application Service?*

I once encountered the snippet in View 43.

The modeler intended to model a file that was accessed by an application. He used an Artifact for the file (which makes sense), but his tool did not allow him to draw an Access relation from Application Service X to the Artifact. His tool suggested, though, that the Used-By was possible.

Having an Access relation from Application Service to Artifact is not in the core meta-model. Having an Access relation from Application Service to Artifact as a derived relation is also not possible in ArchiMate as it requires traveling a route with relations in opposite directions (Realization from Artifact to Data Object and Access from Application Service to Data Object). But his tool did allow him to model a Used-By from Artifact to Application Service. The Architect just used what was allowed, and from a human language point of view, it made sense: "the file is 'used by' the application service'. If you say this to a fellow human being, he or she will know what you mean. So, he assumed that all was well and driven by an understandable desire to be productive carried on.

But in ArchiMate, this is not what it means because ArchiMate's Used-By is not equivalent to natural language's 'used by'. Since this Used-By is not a core relation, it is some sort

of a derived relation. So, the question is, what route lies behind this derivate? What hidden assumptions are there

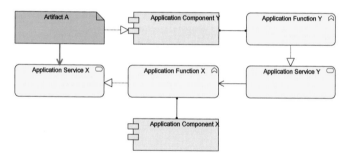

View 42. *Artifact Used-By a Business Service: the hidden objects*

that make this relation possible? View 42 shows a possible expansion of what his derived Used-By relation means (his original relation in red).

As you can see, the Used-By from Artifact A to Application Service X was possible, because an application can use *another* application (and not so much data), and that *other* application is then Realized by our Artifact A. He thought he modeled the use of data but he did model the use of another (hidden) application.

If the language allows the relation, it is not certain that the relation actually means what you think. That shortcut leaves intermediary structure out, and sometimes (as shown here) that structure in ArchiMate must be something that is not what you intended to show. This is one reason why I generally say that it is best to keep as close as possible to the core relations in the meta-model and not use derived relations too much when modeling. You can of course use them for reporting, but using them in modeling is risky.

Pitfall 1. Derived relations may not mean what you think.

4.2 Don't trust the language or the tool blindly: know what you are doing

A tool sometimes offers you to draw a 'default relation' between two elements. If you draw a relation between an Application Component and a Business Process, it may prefer the core relation Assigned-To above the derived relation 'Used-By'. I have seen quite a few beginner models that had Assigned-To relations between Application Components and Business Processes while it was *not* an automated business process. They meant to write that an Application Component was Used-by a Business Process (a derived relation and also what they meant to model) but ended up drawing an Assignment and thus effectively writing that the application automatically performed the Business Process.

View 44. *This was possible in ArchiMate 1.0*

Another beginner modeled View 44 (in the ArchiMate 1.0 days).

For this one I could not find a derived route at all. Here, it turned out, the ArchiMate 1.0 specification did allow it (it was in the table that has all the possible relations and derived relations). This was a leftover of earlier versions before ArchiMate was officially standardized. It was never removed from the table and dutifully implemented by the tool builder. Sadly, though, it was an error in ArchiMate 1.0. The error, by the way, has been fixed in ArchiMate 2.0, so decent tools in recent versions will not allow you to draw

View 45. *Not quite what ArchiMate intended,*

this relation anymore.

Pitfall 2. Not checking if your relation makes sense in the meta-model.

And finally, I once modeled an Interaction and a Collaboration. To my surprise, the tool allowed an Aggregation from Interaction to Function, but not the other way around as I wanted. It can be seen in View 45. Now, this is not exactly how ArchiMate defines the Interaction elements (Interaction elements are not defined as an Aggregate of functions/processes, they are just the behavior of a Collaboration, which

is an Aggregation (of roles or application components, recall Section 2.1 "Collaboration and Interaction" on page 23).

Whatever I did, I could not get the Aggregation relations on the left the way they are on the right, the way they make sense when you want to model this detail. It turned out, the tool makers had forgotten to implement the meta-model relation between Interaction and its constituent Functions and when you tried to create it, the tool found an other relation that was possible because of Specialization: because Interaction and Function were both implemented as Specializations of an underlying behavioral element in the meta-model, and because any type of element can Aggregate its own kind, it was possible to Aggregate an Interaction under a Function.

Pitfall 3. Trusting your tool blindly.

Lastly, ArchiMate (and several tools) support 'viewpoints'. Viewpoints are in fact subsets of the ArchiMate meta-model (the subset may include derived relations). A viewpoint may restrict which types of elements you may model and what relations are allowed between them. They are a sort of patterns, but not quite, as they do not so much prescribe *how* to model but only offer constraints in *what* you can do.

I use 'view templates' for modeling (see Section 21 "Construction & Use Views" on page 135). A tool will constrain your use of elements and relations in an ArchiMate Viewpoint and not being able to create a relation may not be because it is not allowed, but because it is not allowed in the active Viewpoint.

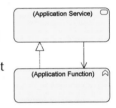

Pitfall 4. Using a viewpoint without knowing that you are.

View 47. *How Function and Service are displayed in the Meta-model*

4.3 Misunderstanding the standard meta-model diagram

I have seen beginners often just copy the relations they see between element types in the basic meta-model (View 33 on page 28). This is generally fine, but there are some snags.

A common snag is the way the standard meta-model shows the relation(s) between a function/process and a service. This looks like View 47.

What the view illustrates is that 'a' function can realize 'a' service and that 'a' service can be used by 'a' function. But in real modeling, we model generally not 'a' service or function. We model specific services and functions.

So, when a beginner models something like View 47 as the relations between a specific function

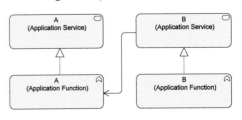

View 46. *How the function/service relations in the meta-model are intended.*

and the service that it provides, he actually says the function also uses the service it provides: it uses itself. Now, as a way of modeling recursion, this could be OK, but that is generally not what is meant (we generally do not model this kind of technical details in Enterprise Architecture). In short: the pattern of View 47 should generally *not* appear in our models.

What the above snippet illustrates is that *an* element of the *type* Application Function can Realize *an* element of the *type* Application Service, and that *an(other)* element of the

type Application Function can use *an element* of the *type* Application Service as illustrated in View 46 on page 33.

The Realize and Used-By relations are between the same *types* of element, but not between the same *elements*. And of course, the same is true at the business and infrastructure levels.

Pitfall 5. Copying relations in the meta-model to your model blindly.

5. Some Noteworthy Aspects of ArchiMate

5.1 Introduction

ArchiMate started out as a University Institute project, supported by a couple of large organizations. Its initial version was finalized in 2004. In 2009 it was adopted as an open standard by The Open Group. ArchiMate is — as far as I know — the first *Open* Standard for Enterprise Architecture modeling (if you do not count UML as an EA modeling language). Enterprise Architecture is not new and quite a bit of modeling has been done, most of it not in ArchiMate.

People create models for projects, often just as a set of images in an 'architecture' document. Sometimes, some modeling for projects is done in UML, but most of the time, you will look at some non- or semi-standardized use of boxes, arrows, dotted lines, nesting, etc., generally some sort of free-format graphical tooling will be used like Microsoft Visio for Windows or OmniGraffle for Mac or worse: Microsoft PowerPoint. One of the 'nice' aspects of such modeling is that it is often ambiguous enough for all stakeholders to see their own preferred reality in it. A more vague and ambiguous approach enables this often 'politically' expedient modeling. Everybody is happy, that is, until it turns out there is a problem somewhere during a later phase of a project. In my experience, people do not understand detailed Visio images either, but they seldom have to understand them anyway, so everybody is happy. When ArchiMate arrives, suddenly people are confronted with views that they have to agree on as a definition of sorts, and suddenly they have to understand what the image says. And the result is that some of them will fight adoption of the language. They want to stick to the old simpler way.

It gets even worse with the modeling of your current state. Once every few years, the lack of insight in the existing landscape will cause an effort to create an overview. People work for months at unearthing the situation, and generally in the end you will have a few large posters with boxes and lines (and a legend to explain what every box type, arrow type and color signifies. The model is never maintained and after a year, it becomes so outdated that it becomes pretty useless for anything but a general introduction. Now, also in ArchiMate, this can happen, if you just draw your visuals in ArchiMate without the support of tooling that can keep thousands of elements and relation in a single coherent model.

The fact that a single coherent model is useful is of course clear to many. So, sometimes modeling is done in Enterprise Architecture tooling. These tools often have their own internal proprietary model, a model that also comes with a certain philosophy on what Enterprise Architecture is. These days, some of these tools will have ArchiMate as an option, often (more or less successfully) implemented on top of their own proprietary language. I'll say a bit more about tooling in Chapter "Tooling" on page 201.

Modeling in ArchiMate brings the advantage of a fixed syntax of your models with reasonably clearly defined element and relation types. Modeling with a tool brings you the possibility to have those different views on what you are modeling to be actually related 'under water' and it brings more possibilities to actually maintain your models. Modeling in ArchiMate also brings modeling that is independent of your modeling tool: if you ever decide to move it is possible to another tool that supports ArchiMate. In the worst case the migration cannot be automated and migration is a lot of hand work, but it is possible.

In Chapter "Discussing ArchiMate" on page 179 I will discuss some of the areas where I think ArchiMate could be improved. In this chapter I'll say a few things about its strengths and some weaknesses I have no suggestions about. But, though I have my criticisms, *my overall conclusion is that the language is very practical in actual use*. I would not have written a book about it if I were not convinced that ArchiMate can be extremely useful for Enterprise Architecture work.

In the final document of the original university project, the authors write:

> *During the initial design of the ArchiMate language no explicit attention was paid to any desired formal properties of the metamodel itself. Emphasis was put on the applicability of the language.*

And this is also what has resulted: a very *usable* language, which is not perfectly logical. This sometimes offends architects who desire a formal, certain language which can be used without interpretation (or so some architects think). ArchiMate offers a 'rational' way of looking at Enterprise Architecture, but it does not offer a 'perfectly logical' way. Later versions of ArchiMate have improved the language and some original choices leading to severe problems (like the original bi-directionality of the Assignment operator) have been fixed. But it still remains noticeable here and there that the language never was based on a formal model.

5.2 Separation of Actor and Behavior

At the business level, separating process (behavior) from role (actor) is common practice. There is some confusion with respect to a business function (as will be discussed in Section 10.2 "Business Function or Business Process?" on page 76).

Some approaches see a function as behavior embedded in some sort of actor-like element, you can recognize it in the language used: a function *is* behavior (as in ArchiMate) versus a function *does* something (function *performs* behavior, it seems to be an actor of sorts). ArchiMate is a language where the separation is fundamental and the separation has been replicated in all layers. This clarity in the meta-model really helps to make good models, but it is important to stress that at every layer, the actor and its behavior are fundamentally inseparable. You can choose not to *model* one and use derived relations to pass them by, but they are assumed to be there.

The split often is confusing for those coming from ways of thinking that do not have that split, e.g. Process Modelers who do often not use the function concept at all (for more depth, see: 10.4 "The 'End-to-end' Business Process" on page 79) or Software Architects where (like in mathematics) a function is both structure and behavior in one.

There is another misinterpretation I've come across. If you say 'passive element' to people, they sometimes interpret that as 'not taking initiative', as 'reacting only'. This I encountered for instance when a colleague first was told about the interface concepts in ArchiMate. He found it illogical to say that an interface is an active element. Because an interface does nothing by itself, it needs to be used before it does something. In his use of the words active and passive, that meant an interface is passive. But ArchiMate does not mean 'reactive' by the word 'passive' and it does not mean 'taking initiative' by the word 'active'. In ArchiMate terms:

- Active means *capable* of performing behavior (either acting or reacting);
- Passive means *incapable* of *performing* behavior.

Behavior is what links active to passive elements: Active elements are Assigned-To behavior and behavioral elements Access passive elements. The passive ArchiMate elements are philosophically speaking 'objects' and the active ArchiMate objects are philosophically speaking 'subjects'. It is not wrong what the colleague said, it is just not how ArchiMate intends the terms 'active' and 'passive'. For completeness, here are ArchiMate's official underlying core definitions of active, behavior and passive:

An active structure element is defined as an entity that is capable of performing behavior.

A behavior element is defined as a unit of activity performed by one or more active structure elements.

A passive structure element is defined as an object on which behavior is performed.

And service and interface are defined as:

A service is defined as a unit of functionality that a system exposes to its environment, while hiding internal operations [...].

An interface is defined as a point of access where one or more services are made available to the environment.

5.3 One View Type

One of the beautiful aspects of ArchiMate is that it is a true Enterprise Architecture language. ArchiMate has been designed to model the interrelations across *all* layers in your Enterprise Architecture: from Business via Applications down to Infrastructure and vice versa. Though tooling often offers you all kinds of different view types, ArchiMate itself only has one single view type: the entire Enterprise Architecture. ArchiMate *Viewpoints* (which I do not strictly use) restrict what is in an ArchiMate view, but it is not a fundamentally different view.

At the software level, UML with all its different kind of views on the same objects and classes might be more precise, to model the whole shebang, ArchiMate does a very good job.

5.4 On the direction of structural relations under the assumption of 'worst case'

In ArchiMate 2.0 the structural relations all have a single direction except Association, which is bidirectional. This direction plays an important role in calculating the derived relations between elements that are indirectly related in a model.

The idea behind it seems logical. Take the example in View 48.

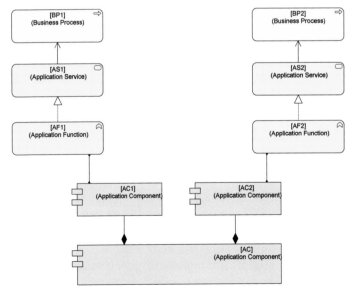

View 48. *Example used for discussing 'worst case' versus 'happy flow' assumptions about dependencies*

If you look at it, having a derivation mechanism that makes Business Process BP1 independent from Application (sub) Component AC2is logical. After all, Business Process BP1 uses only Application Function AF1 and not Application Function AF2. But the question is, what do we mean exactly by dependence? Business Process BP1 is clearly not *meant* to depend on Application Function AF2, but does that mean it is independent? Suppose Application Function AF2 has a fault and it breaks the Application Function of Application Component AC and *as a consequence* Application Function AF1? In that case, there *is* a relation between Application Service AS1 and Application Function AF2, even if the relation is not *meant to* play a role and even if the relation from Application Component AC2 to Application Component AC has the opposite direction as the one from Application Component AC1 to Application Function AF1.

Or that interesting example of an Infrastructure Service that does not depend on what Application Function or Infrastructure Function uses it, except of course when the Application Function or Infrastructure Function overwhelms the resources of the Infrastructure Function which for instance happens when a Denial-of-Service attack hits your web servers, but it can also happen in normal cases. Suddenly, in that 'worst case' there *is* a dependency from 'user' to 'used'.

We can see that how you interpret 'dependence' has to do with the scenarios you take into account. Look at 'happy flow' only, and it makes sense that for instance Composition and Aggregation have a direction. But look at 'worst case' (a natural way of looking from an architectural point of view) and the Composition and Aggregation relations will link elements the other way too.

So, if you look at 'worst case' instead of 'happy flow', all structural relations become bidirectional. Going back to the example above: there seems no way Business Process BP1, Application Service AS1, Application Function AF1 and Application Component AC1 can depend on Business Process BP2, because whatever breaks in Business Process BP2 cannot influence Application Service AS2. But if BP2 overwhelms AS2, AS1, AC1 and thus AC, BP1 will be affected. BP1 then depends on BP2.

Maybe in a well-designed model you could give properties to the relations about their influence strength in both directions and then calculate the strength of dependence across a model (but now I am dreaming).

5.5 On the limitations of derived relations

So, relations in ArchiMate have a direction and this direction plays a role when creating valid derived relations.

The directionality of relations was required during the development of ArchiMate because of the way derived relations were set up mathematically. In that set up, bidirectional relations (Assignment and Association) were for the sake of analysis replaced by two unidirectional relations.

In ArchiMate 2.0, the bi-directionality of the Assignment relation was replaced by a unidirectionality. This is a good thing and it removed quite a few nonsense derived relations.

The ones that made sense (like a Business Service being Used-By an Actor) were added explicitly to the meta-model (which is why my version in View 33 on page 28 has these explicitly added, often these are forgotten in views of the metamodel as they were not necessary in ArchiMate 1.0).

If I look at the relations and their direction and I want to have some sort of criterium to be able to decide on making summaries and which combinations should and should not be allowed, I end up choosing the concept of 'dependence'. If element A depends via relation R on element B, but B does not via the same relation depend on A, then the relation from B to A is unidirectional. The clearest example is the Used-By relation: if an Infrastructure Service X is Used-By an Application Function Y, Y depends on X, but not the other way around. For the Infrastructure Service X it is totally irrelevant if it is actually used or not, it does not depend on being used (but as we saw above: this is not quite true, as real-world Denial-of-Service attacks prove). But — in a simplified design-sense — for Application Function Y, life stops when Infrastructure Service X is not available and not the other way around.

Take also, for instance, the Access relation. It has a direction that runs from the behavioral element to the passive element. Now, I can understand that in part: a Data Object that is created or deleted by an Application Function depends for its existence on the work done by the Application Function. It also fits with subject-verb-object like structure of ArchiMate. But a Data Object that is read by an Application Function does not depend on it at all, it is the other way around: if the Data Object is not there or broken, the Application Function may fail. The object may influence the subject, as in "The broken tile caused him to fall". In natural language, objects without behavior may be used as causes (become active). In ArchiMate, passive elements are not like that.

Or think of a Business Process that requires access to a certain document. The document is a Data Object that is Realized by a file Artifact and that itself Realizes a Business Object (e.g. a letter). The file Artifact resides on a server (Node). When you look at that situation, there is nothing weird or 'wrong' with thinking that the Business Process Accesses the Artifact and your business people will in reality really think that way. They often think in files, not in abstract Business Objects. But the derived relation is *not* allowed because of the direction of Realization. You can create derived relations from Infrastructure to Process (a few are illustrated in View 49), but *not* the other way around.

One of the things that initially attracted me to ArchiMate was not only the reasonable meta-model that is its foundation. It was the promise of derived relations. To have a model where you can have all the necessary details for a decent analysis as well as views where you have summarized the complex views in simpler ones. And both views are correct and come from the same underlying structure.

I must admit, the official ArchiMate derived relations have lost a bit of their attraction for me. There are too many problems where you as an architect know that the language does not allow you a (derived) relation, but where you know

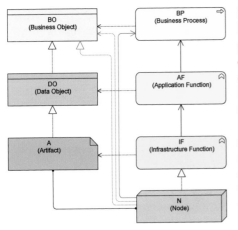

View 49. *From Node to Business Layer*

it makes sense to have one. In my practice, it turns out the official derived relations have a very limited use. They are too limiting in many situations. It turns out that depending on the patterns you model with, you develop the need for quite different 'derived' relations.

I also have not seen a tool yet with decent support for derived relations. The original ArchiMate project created them as an extended set of relations on top of what is in the (powerful) basic meta-model. And they provided a mathematical proof that if they were defined as they were defined, the new set of 'basic + derived' relations was again a closed set. The current standard actually says they are as proper relations as the core relations. It also is being presented in courses and educational material. I haven't seen much material that goes into the limitations of this approach.

The use of derived relations in a model creates a lot of new analysis routes in models. And if you use tooling, the number of possible routes quickly overwhelms your effort to keep your analysis viewpoints (often some sort of viewpoint logic) working. This is why I advise to stick as much as possible to the basic meta-model and *only* use derived relations in the creation of your *patterns* (which we will see in Section 7 "Patterns"). That way you create a stable subset of all the possibilities that makes analysis of your models achievable. I advise against using too many derived relations other than those of your patterns.

Finally, it is easy to draw false conclusions from derived relations. Have a look at View 50.

View 50. *Drawing false conclusions from derived dynamic relations*

The lower blue Flow relation is the source. According to the rules of derived dynamic relations, you may derive all four upper Flow relations from the lower one. But if you read the diagram, it is obvious that the red Flow relations are wrong. Another Uncle Ludwig moment: linguistic meaning does not follow from grammatical rules.

5.6 Why two types of software?

ArchiMate has two types of elements for software:

- At the Infrastructure Level, there is System Software, which is Assigned-To an Infrastructure Function which Realizes an Infrastructure Service;

- At the Application Level, there is the Application Component, which is Assigned-To an Application Function which Realizes an Application Service.

Now, if you know a bit about computers, you know that this distinction is technically nonsense. After all, — with the exception of the operating system — software is software, whatever its use. That Relational Database System that you model at the infrastructure layer (e.g. Oracle, SQL*Server, DB2, PostgreSQL) is technically just another application that runs on the operating system. So, an IT-engineer will probably initially balk at ArchiMate's separation of software in two types, where it is also can be a matter of taste (or confusion) how you model something. Take for instance the spreadsheet :it will be shown in Section 7.3 "Modeling Spreadsheet Applications" on page 48 that it can be modeled in two ways: either at the application layer or at the infrastructure layer. That seems stupid, why should there be such confusion possible in the language?

But if you look at the reality of Enterprise Architecture, the discussion is *not technical*. It is about modeling for the enterprise how business, applications and infrastructure together (should) work. And when you take the *business perspective* and not the technical perspective, it is quite clear that such a mission-critical application which has all that specific business process oriented logic embedded in its code is quite something different from that generic database that is needed to support it. If you look at the separation as 'business-specific' (i.e. containing business logic) versus 'generic', then the separation becomes understandable. Hence, the database is System Software, but the business-specific logic that is written inside it should be modeled as an Application Component, which is realized by that same database which, in fact, acts as an application *platform* in itself. As will be shown in the Application Deployment Patterns in Section 7 "Patterns" on page 46, it can become quite complex to create patterns for modeling modern architectures like three- (or even four-) tier application architectures and modern inventions like SaaS. On the other hand: you have to invent the patterns only once (or take them from his book ;-), but you can use them many times.

For sake of argument, we could try to imagine if we were to try to have only one software type in ArchiMate. The System Software at the Infrastructure would become (the equivalent of) an Application Component. Then, either the Application Function should be able to realize an Infrastructure Service (which kind of makes the Infrastructure Service a clone of Application Service) or the Infrastructure Service realized by Software should become an Application Service (which means you have in fact software service versus hardware service). This leads to all kinds of problems with the business perspective on Enterprise Architecture. We either have application-layer elements in the infrastructure layer, which is confusing, or we have to limit infrastructure to hardware only. But the latter is also problematic because you can have many infrastructural components that can be Realized by both hardware and software. A couple of examples:

- A virtual hard disk in memory (RAM Disk);

- Software RAID;

- A network filter built from a general purpose computer with two network interfaces and dedicated software.

I think especially this latter problem is what makes a single type of software type in ArchiMate maybe technically superior, but in terms of a business perspective (and a usable view on Enterprise Architecture) inferior. From a technical perspective the meaning comes from how it is *implemented* (is it a Device or an Application Component?), but from a business perspective the meaning comes from its *use* (is it business-specific or generic functionality?). I think for the usability of ArchiMate for Enterprise Architecture modeling it is a good thing ArchiMate has the (technically flawed) concept of two types of software. Uncle Ludwig wins every time...

5.7 There is more than one-to-one

An Artifact can Realize an Application Component. It can also Realize a Data Object. One data object can even Realize both. As will be described in more detail in Section 12 "Secondary and Tertiary Architecture" on page 89, realizing both will lead us to more complete thinking about our Enterprise's Architecture. Or the same Artifact can Realize both active and passive elements, as will be shown for instance in 7.3 "Modeling Spreadsheet Applications" on page 48. ArchiMate is very powerful, because of that, but it might take some getting used to.

Sometimes, concepts from the real world you are modeling will end up in quite different ways in your model. This has not specifically to do with ArchiMate, but ArchiMate does have support for it. A good example is a customer. That customer is both an Actor in your Enterprise Architecture, but it might *also* be a Business Object. ArchiMate can let you do both and so catch the two quite different aspects of your customer (what he does and how he is represented inside your business) very well.

5.8 Abstraction versus Precision

We architects love abstraction. Abstraction makes the nitty-gritty and complex details disappear. Abstraction makes the unmanageable manageable.

Our business colleagues also love it when we produce abstractions. It makes our end products easier to digest.

In the ArchiMate language, you can do both, which means that – apart from the precision-like modeling that you do, for instance, when building 'Current State' or 'Project/Change' detailed models – you can use the ArchiMate language in a more 'loose' set-up; e.g., when designing a landscape top-down, even in a rough way with broad strokes.

For instance, when designing, if you have a Business Process that requires the services of an application, you generally start with defining that application service in terms of 'what the business needs', and then you design how this service will be realized by one or more applications.

The ArchiMate language has enough freedom to be used to make models with a lot of abstraction, and as such it also supports an approach to Enterprise Architecture design that sees services as abstractions defined top-down (from the needs of those that use the service). In fact, such thinking was an important aspect of the design process of the ArchiMate language in the first place.

But the ArchiMate language also supports a more specific and precise use that is useful for creating precise 'Current State' or 'Project/Change' models that can be used for documenting or designing your enterprise.

There is much more that can be said about this, but you can rest assured that the power of expression of the ArchiMate language is good for both, even if the concepts have been explained so far in the 'precision approach'. Besides, the ArchiMate language has another important way of simplification: the use of derived relations (with their limitations, as we saw in section 5.5 "On the limitations of derived relations" on page 36).

Together, both ways ('more abstract use of the concepts' and 'derived relations') create a powerful set that enables very high-level/abstract modeling in the ArchiMate language. More of this in Section 17 "Using Abstractions" on page 114 and in other places in this book.

5.9 ArchiMate Extensions

There are two official (that is, form the Open Group) extensions to ArchiMate: The Motivation Extension and the Implementation and Migration Extension.

The Motivation Extension is meant to model not so much the elements of the Enterprise but some elements of Enterprise Architecture (such as drivers, goals, requirements, constraints, principles, etc.. It is described in section 13.3 "The Motivation Extension" on page 97.

The Implementation and Migration Extension is meant to model some elements of a change process: work packages, deliverables, plateaus. It is described in Section 20 "The Implementation and Migration Extension" on page 130.

Both are not intended for modeling the enterprise itself but for modeling architectural and project management aspects.

This page intentionally not left blank

Style &
Patterns

Style & Patterns

6. Aesthetics (Style)

6.1 Why aesthetics matters

If your views are simple, with only a few elements and relations, it will not be difficult for people to read them. But soon you'll find the need to create larger, more encompassing, views. And when you start having several tens of elements and many relations in a view, you'll find that it is hard for people to read them. It will even become hard for yourself if you get back to that view a few months later. It gets worse, when the view is a mess, visually.

Modeling with ArchiMate in that sense is not so different from writing ordinary text. Though in the end it is the conceptual that matters, layout can have a devastating effect on the readability of text. The use of a lot of different fonts, sizes, styles, colors, etc., creates a chaos that overwhelms the senses and makes it difficult to get at the concepts. And that is exactly what style does: when style is good it becomes invisible, at its best it even helps making things clearer. The main task for visual style — when used to improve readability, that is — is to become as little a distraction as possible.

When the Apple Mac ushered in the area of graphical computers in the 80's and formatting of text became for the first time something everybody could attempt, the first consequence was that the world was confronted with a lot of very ugly documents with disastrous visual styles and layouts. People tended to use every effect that was available in a single document. You see the same often when children start to create their first documents on computers. The same thing happened when the web went graphical in th 90's , you might remember the web sites with a lot of blinking, distracting, banners, for one.

In terms of Enterprise Architecture modeling we're — as I'm writing this — at the same 'childish' stage: most views look very ugly, are chaotic in their layout and style and in the end, are much less usable than they could be.

So, in this section, I'm going to give some simple suggestions to improve the readability of your views. Note: architects, especially the ones that tend to create the more complex models, belong to the somewhat smarter demographics and as such also on average somewhat to the more 'lazy' demographics. Laying out your views cleanly takes some energy. Keeping the views well laid out when you change them even more: add one element and you might well up having to rearrange tens more. So be prepared to put some time in this. In my experience: it repays itself many, many times over.

The basic idea behind a good visual style is that the view should be `easy on the eyes'. That means it should be 'quiet'. And next to that, you need some ways to fight ambiguity and you need some redundancy. To give an example, have a look at View 51 on page 42, it contains the ArchiMate meta-model in an unreadable layout. The readable layout was View 33 on page 28.

6.2 Arranging relations

The first thing to do is:

> Style Guide 1. Make your relations in general go in vertical and horizontal directions only.

Keeping your relations like that immediately makes the view easier to look at. A lot of lines under a variety of angles overwhelms the HVS (Human Visual System). Very rarely, I do use a line segment under an angle. Only when I think it makes the view easier on the eye, I will do it. The same goes for you: develop and follow your 'designer' instincts (which I think you should have if you're an architect). Generally, horizontal/vertical lines work best.

You must watch out for overdoing it, though. Many people will make their view even easier on the eye by using overlapping lines. But overlapping lines have a danger of being ambiguous. Have a look at View 52 on page 42.

Can you see which Business Objects are accessed by which Business Processes? You can't, so it might be easier on the eye, but it hides essential information. Therefore, it is generally better to model non-overlapping lines as in View 51.

So the next guideline is:

Style Guide 2. Don't let relations overlap.

As you can see in View 51, I have also rearranged the order of the Business Objects to prevent lines from crossing each other. Thus:

Style Guide 3. Minimize the number of line crossings.

And finally, in View 51, I have arranged both Access relations starting from Business Process X to lie close to each other, while having a larger distance to the Access relation starting from Business Process Y. I have created some sort of grouping on the first two

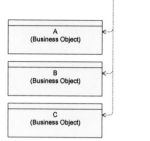

View 52. *Style: Overlapping Lines*

relations, supporting the fact that they both are attached to Business Process X. Thus:

Style Guide 4. As much as possible: Group relations according to either source or destination.

What also helps is to align relations. Say, you have three elements in a row and two relations (between left and middle, and middle and right), it is easier on the eye the have the relations aligned vertically. Have a look at the example in View 54 on page 43.

Now compare with the one in View 53.

You can see that even in this small view the second one is slightly 'quieter'. The effect is larger the more complex your model becomes. Hence:

Style Guide 5. Align relations, even unrelated ones.

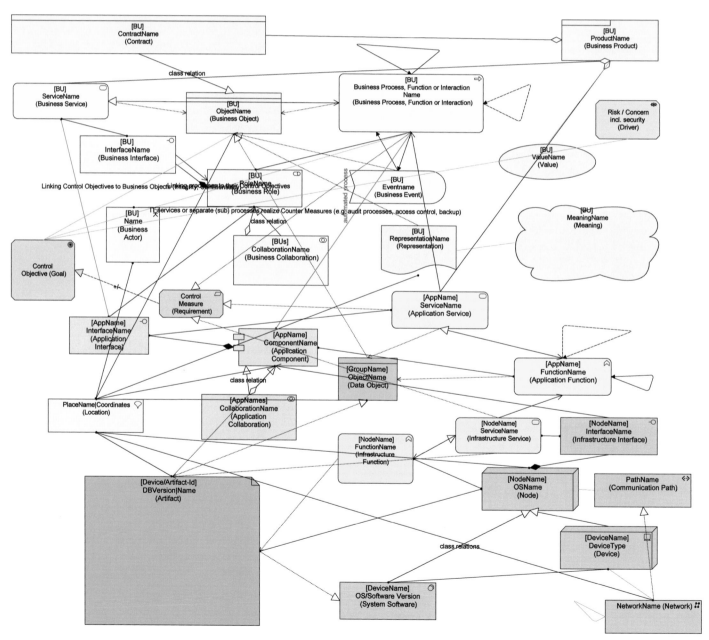

View 51. *ArchiMate Metamodel in Bad Layout*

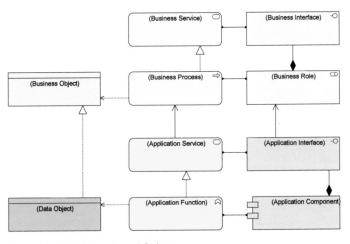

View 54. *Style: Non-aligned Relations*

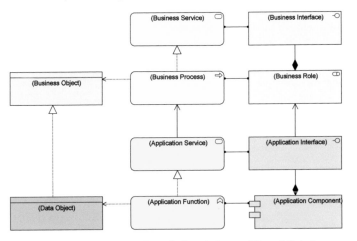

View 53. *Style: Aligned and Equally Sized objects, Aligned Relations*

6.3 Sizing and Arranging elements

There are a few simple rules on sizing and arranging your elements that makes the view easier on the eye. So far, the last views above had all the elements created at the same size and laid out in a grid. Have a look at the variation on View 54 in View 55.

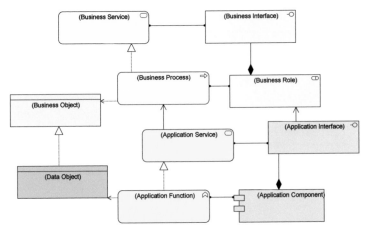

View 55. *Style: Equally-sized, non-aligned objects*

As you can see, removing alignment of the elements makes the view again more cluttered. So, the fifth guideline is:

Style Guide 6. Align elements, even unrelated ones.

Then, of course, we can make View 55 more noisy even, by varying element sizes as in View 56.

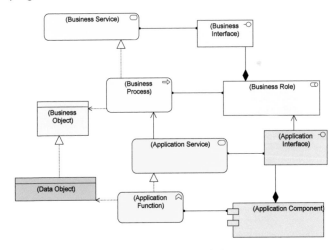

View 56. *Style: Variable-sized, non-aligned objects*

This is again more cluttered, so the next guideline is:

Style Guide 7. Use as few as possible different element sizes (this is like not using too many font sizes in a text document).

Preferably, most of your elements have the same size. Note: you could have different sizes for different types of elements (say, all application services have one size and all application functions have another), but though the extra distinction might make it easier to spot different element types quickly, having multiple sizes quickly makes more chaos and that chaos overwhelms the advantage of the extra clue to separate element types. Besides, there is a better way to help separate element types (see below). So, in general, use as few sizes as possible in your view.

We can matters even worse still as can be seen in View 57.

Just by rearranging the elements, I have created a view with 5 unnecessary line crossings. Note: there are no unnecessary crossings here (under the constraint that I not go around the outside). Try to imagine what would happen if I would change the order of attachments of relations on the Appli-

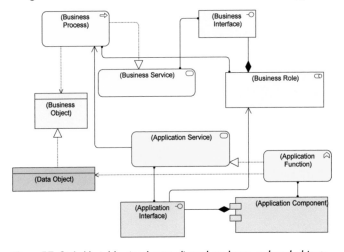

View 57. *Style: Variable-sized, non-aligned and non-ordered objects*

cation Interface in this example. Hence, the next guidelines are:

> Style Guide 8. Align elements and attach relations such that relations are as simple as possible and with the least number of line crossings, preferably straight lines from one element to another.

And:

> Style Guide 9. If you have a nested element or groupings, align the elements that are on the inside as well.

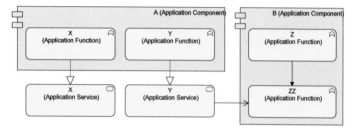

View 58. *Style: Align nested objects*

Note that in the example in View 58 Application Function Z is aligned with Application Functions X and Y and that Application Components A and B are also aligned.

Thus:

> Style Guide 10. Distribute elements evenly within their `group`.

With a group, I mean that you might have a couple of related elements, I do not mean just actual ArchiMate groupings or nestings, though there it holds too. Such a group in my views will have elements of all the same size, be aligned and evenly distributed. A non-even distributed variation on the previous example can be seen in View 59.

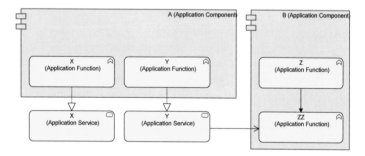

View 59. *Style: Objects not distributed evenly in their 'group'*

Again, these rules are basic rules. Always, your main goal must be:

> Style Guide 11. *Make a view as easy on the eye, as 'quiet' as possible without losing essential information.*

Sometimes, you must break a rule to get the quietness you desire, and so be it, unless you will lose information in the process. Aesthetics is never a matter of just following rules anyway.

One important final remark on sizing and arranging: the above guidelines lead to views that are rather 'boring'. For technical views for your fellow architects, that should not be

a problem. But when you communicate to non-architects, you will need to take far more freedom to get the message across (technical views do not have a 'message' per se).

Therefore, when I want to communicate with non-architects (e.g. management or users), I will relax the approach above, or, I will use something else than ArchiMate for that specific message. A message is often only valid at a certain moment in time anyway, so doing a one-off is not really a problem.

6.4 Using color

Color is a powerful tool for communication. And it's easy to start using different colors for different (type of) elements in your view, say, you could color all elements of one business unit blue and of another business unit green. I think most of those uses for color can be done with labels and grouping (see below). I use color to mark certain *types* of elements consistently to improve readability of the *structure* I have created.

The official ArchiMate specification is colorless. The original ArchiMate project of Telin (Telematica Instituut), before the first Open Group standardization, used colors in a consistent way, though they were never a part of the original specification, they were a more something of a custom.

Those original `ArchiMate Colors` were blue, green and yellow. Blue was used for the active elements, like Actor and Role at the business level, Application Component on the application level and Device on the infrastructure level. Yellow was used for behavioral elements, like Business Process and Business Service on the business level, Application Function and Application Service on the application level and Infrastructure Service on the infrastructure level. Green, finally, was used for passive elements, like Business Object at the business level, Data Object at the application level and Artifact on the infrastructure level.

But another way of separation, using the same colors was later introduced as well. This was mainly because there is one 'problem' with the original color scheme, and that is that the `interface`, `service` and `data/business object` elements all have the same form/icon and would become indistinguishable, and the same is true for 'function' elements. Hence, if such an element was to be found in a view, it would neither from the form, nor from the color be immediately clear if we were looking at a Business Service, an Application Service or an Infrastructure Service. So, some people started to use the yellow/blue/green separation for business layer, application layer and infrastructure layer instead. This way of using colors also became the standard way for some tools.

ArchiMate is color-agnostic, but I have a strong preference for the original coloring which is also still used in the foundational images of the specification. The reason is that one of the strong points of ArchiMate is the way it focuses on behavior as the link between 'actors' and `acted-upons`. In my modeling work, behavior is actually leading. For instance, when somebody started a discussion on adding the 'owner' of a system to our model, I realized that owner is a *role* and hence the ArchiMate-driven question arises: what is the *behavior* (process/function) of this role? And what does this behavior actually change, what is the `acted-upon' here? This led to what has been described in Section 12 "Secondary and Tertiary Architecture" on page 89.

Using the original color scheme strengthens that basic strong point of ArchiMate because it keeps a focus on the different roles the different elements in the ArchiMate grammar play and I find it especially useful because it supports my preference for modeling with behavior as the central axis around which everything revolves.

Still, it is still handy to be able to discern in a view which layers elements belong to. So, I came up with the color scheme I am using in this book too and which can be seen in View 33 "ArchiMate 2 Metamodel" on page 28 (never mind the color used to signal aspects of certain relations in this image, this is just about the colors of the elements).

As you can see there, I kept the blue-for-actors, yellow-for-behavior, green-for-acted-upon separation of the original ArchiMate coloring, but with a twist. I strengthened the colors for the infrastructure level, and softened those of the business level as the higher you go in the meta-model, the 'softer' reality becomes. Colleague Joost Melsen tells me:

> Our usual demarcation is such, that a business process allows for a larger degree of freedom in behavior than an application function, which in turn is 'richer' in behavior than an infrastructure function. We will probably never take away too much freedom on the human processing level in favor of IT, because it allows each of us humans to act and decide according to our own values of correctness, and thus be meaningful.

Now, if we create overview views with all levels represented (e.g. for a Project Start Architecture), it is with this color scheme immediately clear what is business, what is application and what is infrastructure. It is also immediately clear what are actors, what is their behavior and what does this behavior change. It is easy to explain this to business and developers alike.

6.5 Grouping

ArchiMate has an official 'grouping' relation (see Section 2.8 "The Grouping Relation" on page 27) and for three relations (Composition, Aggregation and Assignment), you are also allowed to depict it by Nesting (see Section 1.8 "Nesting" on page 21). Here, I want to say something about 'visual grouping' as a means to keep views easy on the eye. For this, you can of course use the ArchiMate Grouping relation, but you can also do it purely visual. For instance, you can put all the elements from the Business Layer close together, so that you can focus on one part of the view to see the business aspects. Or you can group on the basis of subprocesses in a view. The goal here is to make the layout of your view such that they eyes have to travel a minimum distance, based on what you want to convey. We'll see a few uses later in a few examples in the book.

6.6 About labels

ArchiMate has been labeled an `architecture language'. It certainly has aspects of a language. The combination of actors, behaviors and acted-upon elements resembles subject-verb-object of a normal language. And that is intentional: the designers of the language had this in mind. But what makes a language?

There are two issues I'd like to discuss here (and yes, they have a practical application in Enterprise Architecture work):

- Redundancy in a language;
- Syntax versus semantics (grammar versus meaning).

To start with the latter: take the following natural language sentence: "The customer drinks a bicycle". Assuming that there is no cocktail called 'the bicycle', this is not a meaningful sentence in the English language. You can't *drink* a bicycle. Grammatically (syntactically), the sentence is correct, but semantically, it is nonsense.

We can do the same in ArchiMate. It is easy to use relations to connect elements in a grammatically correct but meaningless way. E.g. using a word processing application to steer the magnets of the Large Hadron Collider in Geneva. Easy to model in ArchiMate, but meaningless in practice.

So, not only the *form* your sentences take is important, but also the *words* themselves. So, take a good look at ArchiMate: its elements are word-*types*, *not* actual words. Without a label in each element, views become meaningless (incidentally, we use an anonymizing script in our tool before we send models to the tool company's help desk to help prevent the leaking of confidential business information). ArchiMate, therefore, looks more like an architecture-*grammar*, than an architecture-*language*. This means that thinking about the labels becomes important. If you are language speaker with perfect control of grammar, you still need to find the right words.

The single most effective choice I made with regard to communicating our views was to keep the *type name* of an element *in the label* of an element. This is of course redundant, as (with the right color coding) every element type is already visually different from another. But it is very effective. For people who do not read models every day, the addition '(Business Process)' at the end of the label hugely speeds up understanding the model. 'Business Process' immediately triggers the right concept in their mind, the icon itself does not. This is even true for experienced architects that use ArchiMate every day. In fact, adding this simple redundancy has in my opinion immensely enhanced the usability of ArchiMate views in our organization. For instance, already early on, infrastructure specialists expressed an interest to replace their own visualizations (spreadsheets, drawings) with our ArchiMate views. That is something you generally are told is not to be expected. "Don't expect to be able to use large and complex ArchiMate views outside of your core architect group", you are told when you go to your first ArchiMate course. In practice: a little redundancy goes a long way towards readability.

I also use other guidelines for labeling of elements. These have to do with easy use and especially reconciliation and integration with other models that exist in other tools in the organization, e.g. the CMDB, the process- or risk modeling tool, the software design tool and others.

So, is this practical? In my experience yes: forget the nice grammar for a moment: the power of language in the end lies in semantics. And there, redundancy improves communicability. There is nothing new there: nature has done it first: natural language is full of communication-enhancing redundancy (to the great pleasure of code breakers through the ages, by the way).

Architects are normally inclined to simplify, have a single definition, etc., in other words do everything that reduces complexity, to rationalize — to make logical. But Enterprise Architecture relates strongly to the real world, where logic, certainly pure logic, has its limitations and much of it actually may make matters worse.

The pattern I use generally puts three things in a label:

- First line: some grouping information between square brackets. In the infrastructure layer, generally the device name, e.g. '[winsv001]', in the application layer, generally the application name and in the business layer the business unit name.

- Last line: type name between brackets, e.g. '(Application Service)' for the Application Service.

- In between: whatever short labeling you want there, but generally the 'name' of the element as ArchiMate calls it.

6.7 Don't Use the 'Children's Forms'

After having gone into things you can do to improve readability, here is in my view one thing you generally should *not* do: use ArchiMate's 'playful' element forms like the big puppet for Actor or the big PowerPoint-like arrow for Business Process, etc.. In my opinion, these forms are for children, not for grown ups and they are not visually 'quiet'. Maybe for the absolutely simplest views with only a few elements that are shown to people who never have to look at ArchiMate views again, but in that case I would probably not use ArchiMate at all but create a funny drawing with Greek columns, jumping dogs, images of police constables, etc.. ArchiMate is intended for serious messages and using the 'funny forms' is akin to writing your serious design document in limerick form. Your views are serious business, they should look the part.

7. Patterns

Note: From now on, it might be practical to keep a finger on page 219 so you can easily move there and back.

7.1 The Use of Patterns

Asking "How do you model X?" is probably the most asked question by those starting to use ArchiMate. This chapter intends to offer solutions for many such questions, like "How do you model a spreadsheet?" or "How do you model a Business Rule Engine?". These patterns are certainly not the only way to do it and I will even offer some alternatives here and there. In the end, if you become experienced, you will tend to create your own patterns. Modeling style is after all like writing style. And good modeling is like good writing: a mixture of good content and good style.

But there is more to patterns than just a nice way to model something. If you end up using ArchiMate to model your Current State Architecture, the model that contains your existing Enterprise Architecture, that model becomes much more usable (and thus following Uncle Ludwig, much more meaningful) because using the same pattern in comparable situations for instance enables you to create (depending on your tool of choice) automated exports and analyses.

Imagine you have that large Current State model and it enables you to do an analysis that can tell you that if a certain Business Process needs a Return To Operations (RTO) of 4 hours, you can easily find all the servers that need to support that requirement. Or if you have a Information Manager, you can easily find which applications he or she is respon-

sible for. Or you have a server nearing the point where its capabilities are overwhelmed and you can easily identify the business processes responsible. ArchiMate is an Enterprise Architecture language, which entails *all* the layers and it is well suited to provide the foundation for such information.

In the coming sections I will present several patterns. I will start with a basic Infrastructural pattern. The reason for that is that this pattern will return in a few guises and also as

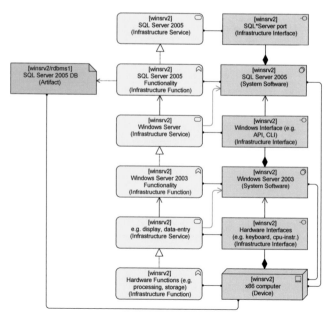

View 60. *Full details of deploying a database*

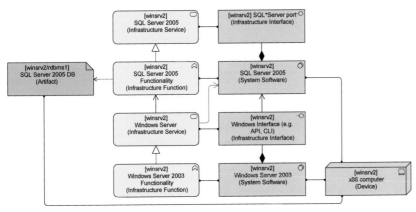

View 61. *Deploying a database, without the hardware details*

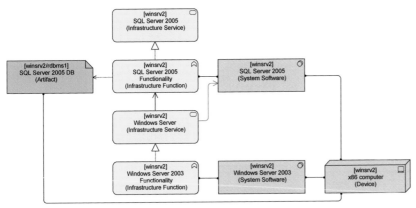

View 62. *Deploying a database, without hardware details and interfaces*

underlying pattern for some application patterns. So, without further ado, here is:

7.2 A Basic TI Pattern: A Database

ArchiMate has its three layers and some of what happens in your architecture will be classified as Infrastructure. In ArchiMate, that is more than just hardware. It is also artifacts like files and it is software with its behavior: operating systems, surely, but also other systems like relational databases and so forth. ArchiMate has software on two levels, and though that is useful, it can also be confusing. Because if you have software, how do you model it? As System Software or as Application Component? If you look at it from an IT perspective, the difference is illogical: after all software is software. But from a business perspective it makes kind of sense. For the business, its business-critical applications are what count as 'application', the software beneath it like databases are 'infrastructure'.

If you want a fully detailed model for a database at the infrastructure level, you get something like View 60.

Unless you are an Infrastructure Architect interested in modeling these details, you will probably never model it like this. But it is the basis from which we are going to simplify to get to the practical pattern we will use.

This is what is modeled in View 60: Bottom-right, there is a Device, the actual computer hardware, in this case an

x86 server. This is hardware, thus an *active* element, and thus it has *behavior*: it has functions it performs and services it provides. Installed on the Device (the Device is Assigned-To the System Software) is an Operating System. This active element again has behavior: the functionality of the Operating System and the services it can provide. Its functionality requires the use of the hardware services that the *Device's* functionality provides. Also installed on the Device (Assigned-To it) is the SQL*Server 2005 Relational Database Management System (RDBMS). The SQL*Server 2005 System Software performs (Assigned-To) its behavior (the SQL*Server 2005 Functionality Infrastructure Function) which in turn Realizes a SQL Server 2005 Infrastructure Service which can be used by Application Functions elsewhere in your model. The SQL*Server 2005 Functionality requires the Operating System's Infrastructure Services to function. On the left, there is the actual database Artifact, the Device is Assigned-To this Artifact, signaling the Artifact resides on the host. The SQL*Server's functionality accesses that database artifact.

Since the Assigned-To relation in ArchiMate 2.0 is unidirectional (mainly: from active element to behavior), ArchiMate 2.0 has a few explicit extra relations to show that all active elements can use services. Normally, with such a detailed view, we would not add these. I have added these in red in View 60, though, because we use them below to simplify.

Now, for the pattern I want to use, I must decide what I *need* as elements for future use, e.g. for analysis or reporting. The first thing I really do not need is all the details of the hardware. Removing those gives me View 61.

A second thing I generally do not model are interfaces. I look at Enterprise Architecture from the perspective of *behavior*. I am interested how behavior of the applications are used by the business for instance. I am interested in the services the infrastructure must provide for the applications to function. How this is technically done (Infrastructure Services for instance represent infrastructure protocols like HTTP, SMTP or database server protocols) is not something that interests me as an Enterprise Architect, though it might of course interest the TI-Architect.

Without the interfaces, View 61 turns into View 62.

Actually, for reasons of Enterprise Architecture, I am also not interested in the internal behavior of my infrastructure. What I want to know what System Software has been installed on it and what Infrastructure Services and Artifacts they provide for the outside world. So my View 62 can be simplified to View 63 on page 48.

Now, when I removed the internal behavior elements, links between active infrastructure elements and the Infrastructure Service and Artifact, that are exposed to the outside world, were lost. These have been replaced by derived relations (in

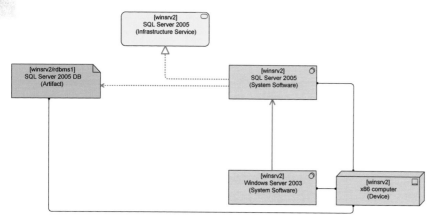

View 63. *Deploying a database, without hardware details, interfaces and internal behavior*

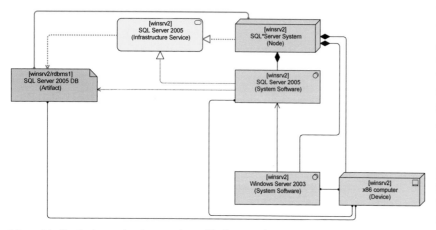

View 64. *Deploying a database: using a Node to make an abstract device*

red). For instance: from the Windows Server System Software via Assigned-to the Windows Server Functionality via Realization to the Windows Server Infrastructure Service via Used-by to the SQL*Server 2005 System Software (here we need that extra Used-by from View 62 on page 47).

For infrastructure, I can adopt the use of an intermediate (abstract) Node to encapsulate everything below what is exposed to the outside world as already suggested in Section 1.9 "Using a Node to encapsulate infrastructure" on page 22. This is shown in View 64. This Node has the internal System Software and Device elements as Composite parts. From the Node, we can create new derived relations from that Node to the Artifact and Infrastructure Service that is

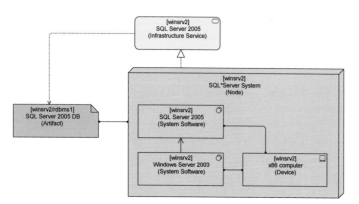

View 65. *Deploying a database: Nesting details in a Node*

exposed to the outside world. These are shown in red in View 64.

When we then use Nesting to get all the Composite parts inside the Node, we get View 65.

This is actually the pattern I prefer for modeling basic infrastructure items. I do not model all the omitted intermediary elements and internal structures that I used to come to this summary pattern. I used derived relations to get this result. There is no need for the other details in my Project Architectures or Current State Architecture. But even if I model the above, I can still when it suits me present an even simpler view on that pattern as can bee seen in View 66.

Now, this is a pretty simple TI-structure pattern. We have a Node that embeds a single Device to which two System Software elements are Assigned. We Realize the Infrastructure Service directly from the Node, making the Node (and the Infrastructure Service and the Artifact) a sort of cut-off between Infrastructure use and Infrastructure structure. The Node is used in fact as a sort of object in an object-oriented approach, hiding its internals, exposing its interfaces. Later, we will see a few more complex examples when we look at 'clustered' infrastructure setups. An important aside: a server can of course Realize multiple Infrastructure Services, say a RDBMS service *and* a File Share.

View 66. *Deploying a database: Collapsing the Node*

7.3 Modeling Spreadsheet Applications

Excel Spreadsheets are IT's (and an Enterprise Architect's) nightmare. First, there is no way of tracking them, so you may have all kind of mission critical stuff in spreadsheets that have no access control, no logging or auditability, and which are written poorly, etc.. But except being a nightmare, they are also a fact of life in any modern organization. And it is worse: Excel is often augmented by all kinds of plug-ins from all kinds of vendors. SaaS-vendors, Data vendors, functionality vendors etc. distribute plug-ins (statistical plug-ins, access to tooling plug-ins, etc.) that become part of the Excel application environment.

So, all that mission critical application behavior that is in Excel is something that gives headaches to Enterprise Architects (and Support Organizations) because it generally is not tractable. In architecture descriptions, people end up with models that have elements like 'Excel' in them that stand for 'anything that is done in Excel' and that generally means 'we have no idea at all what is happening there'.

Personally, I think most of what is in Excel is not a real problem (except for that access control, auditing and logging and such, if these are required) for Enterprise Architects if looked at properly. First, those little spreadsheets that employees create for their daily job are mostly not that mission critical at all. They tend to improve the efficiency of what they otherwise would have to do by hand (and can do by hand if need be). (Some, however, are not that innocent at all, like the spreadsheet I once saw that had all the information of another application copied into it for easy reference and that was two years out of date). Also, in some organizations you will find literally hundreds of thousands of spreadsheets, that on closer inspection tend to be some sort of smart form. One person enters data, another reads the data. And afterwards the form is never used again. It sits on your servers as an archive copy of something that happened once. It's not an active element, it is an old passive element, which probably never will bother you again.

But, if you look into your organization, you will probably find there are indeed some mission critical applications that are in fact spreadsheets and for which there is no business case to turn them into properly built and maintained applications. Think of the analysis models Asset Management Portfolio Managers use and play around with. Turning these in formal applications with change procedures and lead times of weeks (if not months) defeats their object. You still want these in your models, though, and you don't want them in there as a generic 'Excel' element. So, there is need to decide on how to model a spreadsheet application.

Initially, you might want to start with adding Excel as an Application Component to your landscape as shown in View 67.

Excel's functionality Accesses 'spreadsheet' Data Objects that are Realized by .xls Artifacts. There are two spreadsheets in this example, one of which depends on a vendor plug-in that connects to an outside data service. Think for instance a stock market plug-in that delivers live price data for stocks and bonds.

In the example, spreadsheet B is a normal spreadsheet based on Excel's functionality only. Its data is contained in the spreadsheet and so is its logic (macros, programming). The Excel Application Component is Assigned-To the generic Excel Application Function (all of Excel's functionality). This functionality reads the spreadsheet data object, and with the logic contained in the Data Object and based on its internal engine to process that logic, it Realizes the Application Service that is used in a Business Process.

Spreadsheet A requires the use of a vendor plug-in. This is modeled as follows here: the plug-in is generally installed as a part of the Excel installation. On the infrastructure level we are generally talking of some sort of Windows dynamic loadable library (DLL) which is loaded by Excel and the plug-in becomes a component that becomes part of Excel. This

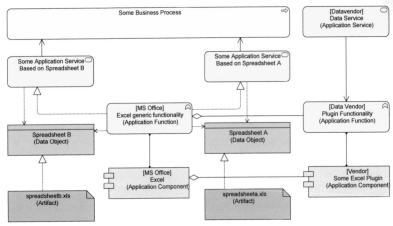

View 67. *Excel as an Application Component*

has been modeled with an Aggregation. On the functional side, both Application Components have their Application Function, covering everything what the Components can do. The main Excel Application Function is in the lead and it Accesses spreadsheet A, and realizes Application Service A. It is the plugin's functionality that accesses the outside vendor's Application or Infrastructure Service.

So far so good, but there are a few disadvantages to modeling it this way:

- Because the generic Excel functionality is in charge of Realizing all Application Services, everything is related via that Application Function. Application Service B depends on the plug-in, while it does not need the plug-in. It is in fact not possible to discriminate between Application Service A and B if you want to know who depends on the vendor's data service and plug-in.

- The .xls artifact contains both data and logic, but the logic does not end up in a recognizable Application Function. Application Functions are nice to have when discussing creation and maintenance of IT.

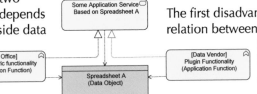

View 68. *Excel as an Application: linking a plugin to the Application Service*

The first disadvantage can be solved by having a relation between the plugin's function and Application Service A (and not B) as seen in View 68.

Though not wrong in the sense of the language, the Realization (in red) is not true in a real sense of course, because it is Excel that creates the Application Service *using* the plug-in, and not the plug-in directly in some way.

If you want to do this properly in ArchiMate, you should in fact use Application Collaboration and an Application Interaction as in View 24 on page 24.

Both alternatives are not really attractive to me, so on the application level I would stay with the first solution. And the dependence of spreadsheet B on the plug-in is not really a problem: after all, the functionality of the plug-in could actually still break spreadsheet B, so in that sense the dependency is still real as we noticed in 5.4 "On the direction of structural relations under the assumption of 'worst case'" on page 35.

The other disadvantage (no visibility of the functionality, the behavior, that comes from the logic (macros and such) inside the spreadsheet) remains. A spreadsheet itself can be a kind of application, people 'program' spreadsheets, but this application nowhere shows up as such in this approach. That is why I prefer another solution. I consider the .xls as an Artifact that Realizes *both* a (passive) Data Object and an (active) Application Component. The spreadsheet itself is an application also, not just data. Excel then becomes the (generic) *platform* on which the application runs, a bit like a Java Virtual Machine being the platform within which the Java application (that is Realized by a '.jar' Artifact) runs. This can be seen in View 70.

Here, the spreadsheeta.xls Artifact Realizes not only a Data Object from the data in the spreadsheet, but it also Re-alizes an Application Component from the logic in the spread-sheet. That Application Component is assigned to the Applica-tion Function that stands

View 69. *Excel and the plugin as an Application Collaboration*

for the *behavior* of the spreadsheet. This behavior has access to the data (in fact, the Excel formulas and Macros have access to the (passive) data that is *also* in the spreadsheet, this happens internally). The behavior then Realizes the Application Service for B that is used by the Business Pro-cess. This can be extended to a spreadsheet like A that uses the plug-in to access a vendor's data service. This can be modeled in various ways, here it is modeled as the plug-in being an aggregate child of the Excel Infrastructure Service so that we still have the link between the plug-in and Excel (if the plug-in breaks, Excel can be affected). But for the rest, the plug-in service is used by the Application Function that represents the behavior of spreadsheet A. Also modeled is a direct Used-By at both the application layer and the infra-structure layer to show the use of the vendor's data service. Technically, the Used-By from the data vendor's Infrastruc-ture Service to the plugin's Infrastructure Service is not fully modeled. The data vendor's Infrastructure Service should ArchiMate-technically be modeled as being Used-By an Infrastructure Function, which in its turn Realizes the plugin's Infrastructure Service. As it is, the Used-By is a derived relation.

The biggest advantage of modeling Excel as an Infra-structure Service is not that stuff with the plugins. It is that it so clearly shows that a spreadsheet can be an *application*. Spreadsheets are used as passive elements and as active elements. We tend to think of passive elements as 'harmless' but the fact that all those spreadsheets are the nightmare for IT and Enterprise Architects is because they often are not harmless passive elements at all, they often are applications and should be treated that way. And that Excel

wizard Asset Manager is a programmer even if he or she does not think so.

Next in line: another 'application' that is not an application.

7.4 Modeling an Internet Browser

It is illustrative to think about the reality of what happens when you use a web site. You start up your browser and you type in an URL, e.g.:

```
https://archimatemusings.wordpress.com/wp-admin/
post.php?post=99&action=edit&message=10
```

The browser connects to the web server and loads a web page that the web server sends. What the web server sends is based on the URL, which is composed of three parts: a protocol identifier (e.g. `https://`), a domain name (e.g. `ar-chimatemusings.wordpress.com`) and the request part (the rest of the URL, e.g. `/wp-admin/post.php?post=99&ac-tion=edit&message=10`). (ArchiMate buffs will recognize an interface, a service and a passive structural object, the request, in that one URL.)

Now, based on that request part, the web server returns bytes to the browser using the 'https' protocol as requested. That data could theoretically be any-thing, but in this case, the data conforms to a standard language, HTML, which the browser understands. HTML originally was just a simple description of (passive) markup/layout, but browsers these days are far more powerful. They have functionality that allows them to present *active* components to the user, say buttons, pop-ups and so forth and ways to run almost arbitrary code. This code is normally JavaScript code, which is an application platform built into almost every browser. JavaScript, by the way, has nothing to do with the programming environment 'Java'. JavaScript was originally called "Mocha", then "Live-Script" until somebody at Netscape thought it a good idea to

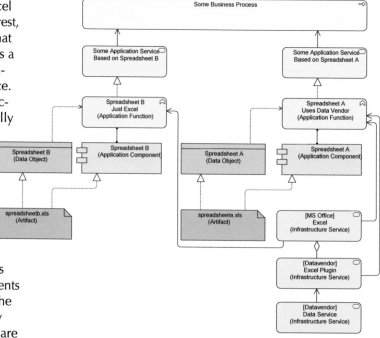

View 70. *Excel as Infrastructure Service (Application Platform)*

change the name so it could profit from the hype surrounding Java at that time. But I digress.

Anyway, what is being sent from web server to web browser is just a file, a stream of bytes. In ArchiMate terms, that is an *Artifact*. Now, this Artifact Realizes both passive (the text you read) and active (behavioral) elements like those buttons, clickable maps and so forth. What actually happens is that your browser interprets the file (HTML/JavaScript) and realizes *both* a passive Data Object and an active Application Component. This is just like Excel did in the previous pattern: Excel interprets the spreadsheet and Realizes both passive (Data Object) and active (Application Component) elements.

But there is a difference. With a web browser getting the file from a web server, the file may be just 'in memory' and the whole setup is created 'on the fly'. There is no Artifact on a disk needed, it may just exist fleetingly in memory of the desktop running the browser. Close the browser and it is gone. The pattern is shown in View 71.

This pattern is useful to make clear where the application is.

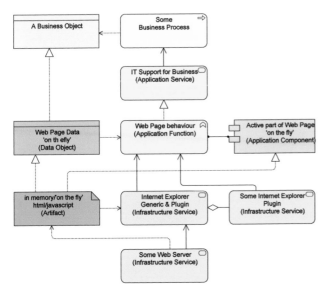

View 71. *The Internet Browser as Infrastructure Service (Application Platform)*

Sometimes you see models where the web site is modeled as an application. But that muddles the picture because it suggests that the application does not run on your infrastructure. In reality, with browser-based applications, the application runs *in the browser platform* which in turn is part of your own infrastructure. It *looks* like everything runs elsewhere, but that is not true. It only *seems* that way because it is downloaded 'on-the-fly' and destroyed as soon as you quit the browser. You have a temporary, downloaded application that generally connects back to the same server (or another one) to interact with. The only reason that your security people do not get scared about you downloading and executing applications is because the JavaScript 'runtime' in the browser is a 'sand box' that is properly separated from your local infrastructure. But change the JavaScript run time to some browser plug-in that is used as platform, e.g. Flash or

Java, and your security people will become restless. Because Java and (especially) Flash are plugins that have been known for security breaches.

What we have seen with the spreadsheet and web browser so far is that they are not so much applications per se, they represent a *platform*. This idea of looking at platforms is very useful when modeling.

Note: this is not the entire story. After all, what is sent to us is often just the 'presentation layer' and not the entire functionality. We'll get back to this in 7.13 "Deployment Pattern: Three-Tier Application" on page 56.

7.5 More 'application platforms'

So what are good example of application platforms of which we now have seen two (spreadsheet and browser)? Here are a few:

- JavaScript (Browser built-in, loads parts of the HTML page, namely the part inside a <script type="text/javascript"> tag. Another script language that can be delivered inside an HTML Artifact is for instance VBScript (only Microsoft browsers support this);

- Tcl is another scripting language that can be delivered inside an HTML document with a <script> tag. It requires a plug-in;

- Adobe Flash (Browser plug-in). Loads .swf ("shockwave-flash") Artifacts and Realizes Flash applications);

- Microsoft Silverlight (like Flash).

The above are browser-based platforms. But there are others:

- Java (Java Virtual Machine that loads .jar Artifacts which Realize Java applications). Sometimes the Artifact is also delivered via a browser, but the downloaded Artifact runs in its own Java sandbox, not in the browser. Citrix provides VPN-functionality for working from home that way, for instance;

- Perl, Python, Ruby, etc. are languages where a script is read by an application that acts like a platform. This is like the earlier Excel pattern. Perl is not the application, but the Perl script is an Artifact that Realizes an Application Component;

- Unix shell scripts or Windows .bat or .cmd batch files are examples of Artifacts that are read by platforms and turned into Application Components. The platform here is the operating system;

- Enterprise Service Buses;

- Relational Databases. These may have programming languages embedded. E.g. In Oracle you can program in PL*SQL: you can see how this would look, expanding on the earlier basic infrastructure pattern which was also explained using a database. As you can see in View 74 on page 52, the PL*SQL code is an Artifact that is a composite part of the database it resides in. This PL*SQL code Artifact Realizes an Application Component, which uses the Oracle db001 Infrastructure Service,

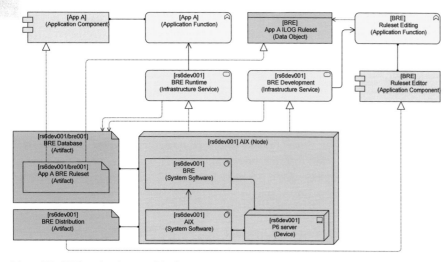

View 72. **BRE as Application Platform**

both to be able to run the logic as well as access the data in the database;

- Business Rule Engines. This one is illustrated in View 72. This example is a bit more complete as a platform than the previous ones. Here you see that the rule set is modeled as an Artifact that Realizes an Application Component, which uses the BRE runtime environment to function. Next to the runtime, you see that the BRE distribution also contains a development environment to create and edit the rule sets. In this example the development environment runs on the server. In reality, this probably will be some sort of browser based or Java-based environment that has a thin client somewhere and Artifacts will be promoted from development to a runtime, but for simplicity of this example it has been assumed here that development happens on the runtime server. An noteworthy aspect of this example is that the rule-set Artifact Realizes *both* an Application Component and a Data Object. For the developer, the rule-set is *data*. But for the business, the rule-set is an *application* that is used in its business process. That business process is primary to the business, the development of the rule-sets is secondary. That is why I call the direct use of IT by the business Primary Architecture and processes like application management or application development Secondary Architecture. There is also Tertiary Architecture (e.g. The processes of Enterprise

Architecture, leading to for instance requirements for Primary and Secondary Architecture. We'll get back to that in a section 12 "Secondary and Tertiary Architecture" on page 89.

If you add all these platforms to your landscape, you will begin to appreciate the amount of programming still going on in your environment. This is what I would call 'hidden programming'. And because it is hidden we tend not to see the hidden complexity we have created in our environments. Not only the end users tend to do their 'end user computing' (EUC). These days, looking at EUC is on many organization's radar. But your infrastructure people who write Perl and shell scripts, batch jobs and so forth are not on many radar screens yet. They happily go on creating their landscape of many little applications without much notice, until someone want to change something, that is. And that simple off the shelf database might hide application programming as well. When we are done looking at EUC, we

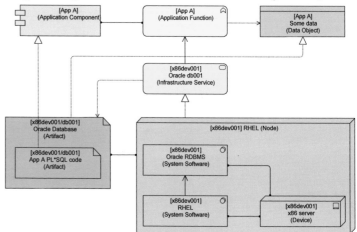

View 74. **Database as an Application Platform**

might pick up IMC (Infrastructure Management Computing). And after that, we might realize that Business Rule Engines do not remove programming, they just move it from the programmer to that poor business analyst who, just like the sales manager programming his Excel spreadsheet, is a programmer even if he of she does not realize it.

Summarizing: if an environment can be programmed and it provides a kind of run-time environment, you probably are looking at something that can be modeled using the 'platform' approach. Modeling the applications hidden in these platforms is necessary if you want a complete view of your Enterprise Architecture, because they contain essential business logic.

A suite like MS Office contains both end-user applications (like MS Outlook) and applications that are a mix of platform and application (such as Excel & Access). More on this in section 18.2 "Complex Software Stacks" on page 119).

View 73. **TI Building Blocks**

7.6 Infrastructure 'Building Blocks'

In View 65 on page 48 we encountered a basic TI Pattern. The TI Pattern is that you model the TI as a single Node that hides the internal complexity, then you let that Node Realize Infrastructure Services and the Node is Assigned-To any related Artifact. This makes the Infrastructure Service and the Artifact the linking pins between the infrastructure layer and the application layer.

But in most enterprises, infrastructure is shared between various applications. A file share may be used by many applications, and even databases may be shared by different applications, say, one application that uses the database to store transactions and another separate application that creates management reports on those transactions from the same database. Both use the same database and thus both use the same database Infrastructure Service. The way I prefer to do it is to have the Infrastructure Services clearly named for the Nodes that realize them, whereas an abstract 'aggregate' Infrastructure Service aggregates these into the specific set that is needed for each application to function (and hence is Used-By the Application Function). This abstract Infrastructure Service is then named the 'Exploitation' Infrastructure Service for that particular application, and it is the ideal service for the infrastructure people to provide a Service Level Agreement for running the application. It looks like View 73.

In this example, App A (the 'transaction application') runs on a Windows desktop and uses both a file share and a database. App Y (the 'reporting application') runs on a RS6000 server and accesses the same database as App A.

There is a big advantage to this pattern: the application layer of your architecture generally does not change if the deployment changes.

The pattern has a slight disadvantage: given the direction of the Aggregation relation, you cannot create a derived Used-by relation from either of the Nodes to either of the applications, whereas you know that this relation certainly exist. The abstract 'aggregate' Exploitation Infrastructure Services break the possibility to derive the relation in ArchiMate terms. In reality, this is not really a problem because tooling will generally allow analyses that go beyond derived relations and tooling will allow you to traverse the aggregation relation in the opposite direction.

We do not add Infrastructure Services that we do not Realize ourselves to the exploitation aggregation. See 7.12 "Deployment Pattern: Two-Tier Client-Server with a Remote Server (ASP)" on page 56 for an example.

7.7 Application Deployment Patterns

We already saw a couple of basic deployment patterns (e.g. the PL*SQL and BRE 'platforms') earlier in this section, Now, we are going to look at a series of examples that are pretty common.

7.8 Deployment Pattern: Standalone PC Application

We are going to start with the simplest: an application running on a standalone PC which can be seen in View 75.

Here, a couple of common choices in my example deployment patterns can be seen again:

- I encapsulate TI in a Node like in View 65 on page 48. It is the Node, and not one of its constituents, (which are all composite parts) that Realizes the Infrastructure Service. In reality, it is the Windows System

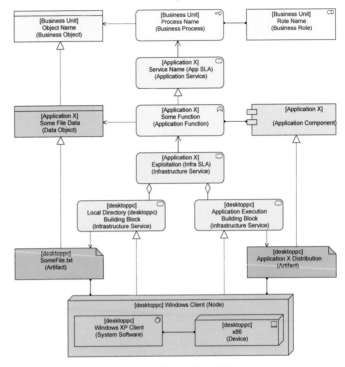

View 75. *Deployment Pattern: Standalone PC*

Software on the desktop PC that Realizes the Application Execution Service but we 'hide' those details;

- Any Infrastructure Service and its related Artifacts are coupled with Access relations;

- The Node is named after the Device that is embedded. In fact, this is often the Domain Name from the DNS system that gives access to the Infrastructure Service;

- The Infrastructure Services are named such that it is clear which Node realizes them;

- As described in 7.6 "Infrastructure 'Building Blocks'", all Infrastructure Services needed to actually run an Application, including its data, are Aggregated into one abstract 'Exploitation' Infrastructure Service which has the name of the application in its label. The actual Infrastructure Services are 'building blocks' and the result is a service which a IT delivery organization could have an Service Level Agreement on;

- The Infrastructure Service Realized by the Node has been split in two: one for the actual running of the application and one for access to the data. In this example, that separation does not make much sense yet, but in more complex situation it becomes useful. So, the simple situation has been modeled slightly more complex than necessary here so it stays in line with the coming patterns.

7.9 Deployment Pattern: Standalone PC Application with File Server based Data

Next is a slight variation on the basic standalone pattern and in fact one which still should be pretty common in most organizations: a standalone desktop application, but with the data stored on a file server. Most organizations do not allow data to be stored on the local disk of a desktop, basically because that make backing up that data practically impossible. It can be seen in View 76.

Not much changes here with respect to the previous pattern. Note:

- It is the Windows Server System Software that actually Realizes the File Share Infrastructure Service, but as in the previous example (and all coming examples) our pattern uses the Node as an encapsulation that hides

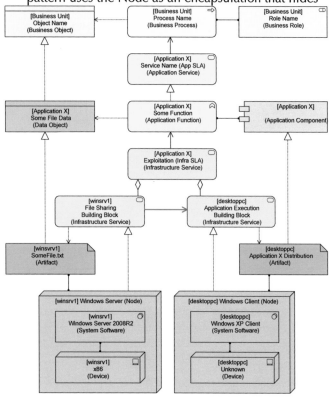

View 76. *Deployment Pattern Standalone PC using a File Share*

internal structure and behavior;

- It is the Infrastructure Function Assigned-To the System Software on the desktop PC that actually uses the File Share Infrastructure Service, or in other words in this case: the Windows client mounts (in Windows lingo: 'maps') a remote file share under some drive letter. So, if I want to be exact, I need to draw a Used-By between the File Share and the Windows software on the PC.

But as I want the Node to completely hide the internal structure, I have two choices:

- * Let the File Share Infrastructure Service be Used-By the desktop PC Node;

- * Let the File Share Infrastructure Service be Used-By the Application Execution Infrastructure Service (which is a derived relation of the former one and the fact that the desktop PC Node Realizes the Application Execution Infrastructure Service. My choice is this one for two reasons:

  - ° If in a future pattern the Node Realizes multiple Infrastructure Services, not all of these may actually use what in this example is the File Share Infrastructure Service. Going via the Node may in the future create derived relations that are not there at all;

  - ° I keep the relations between the Infrastructure Services visible even if I do not show the Nodes in a view. Say, for instance, I model the "Internet" Infrastructure Service that my IT Department provides (as some of my systems may depend on it and I want to be able to take that into account), but I do not model the Nodes such as routers, switches and so forth that are needed to provide that services. The IT Department itself may model them of course. And in my own model, using a division of models in certain fixed 'construction views' makes this choice better, but we get into that in Section 21 "Construction & Use Views" on page 135.

So you see, my patterns do not always follow the exact and complete way the world is in core ArchiMate. For my role as Enterprise Architect, it is enough to have the relations as chosen now. You can of course choose differently.

7.10 Deployment Pattern: Classic Two-Tier Client-Server Application

The Classic Two-Tier Client-Server application consists of a client application that talks to a database (the server). It can be seen in View 77.

I have modeled a variation in red line/outline. This specific database system consists of independently running 'instances' (in operating system terms: it 'forks' multiple copies of itself). Suppose your large model is input for the CMDB and the infrastructure people need to know quickly what instance of the RDBMS system is at fault when there is a problem with an application. You can then choose to augment your database pattern with this information. In that case, you would have to model the instance inside the Node, while the Artifact is outside the Node. So, this augmentation breaks the basic idea of a Node encapsulating all information. I'll repeat it again: you can create any pattern you want. The most important is that you stick to certain patterns if you want the model to be at its most usable.

The next pattern is a variation on the Classic Client-Server.

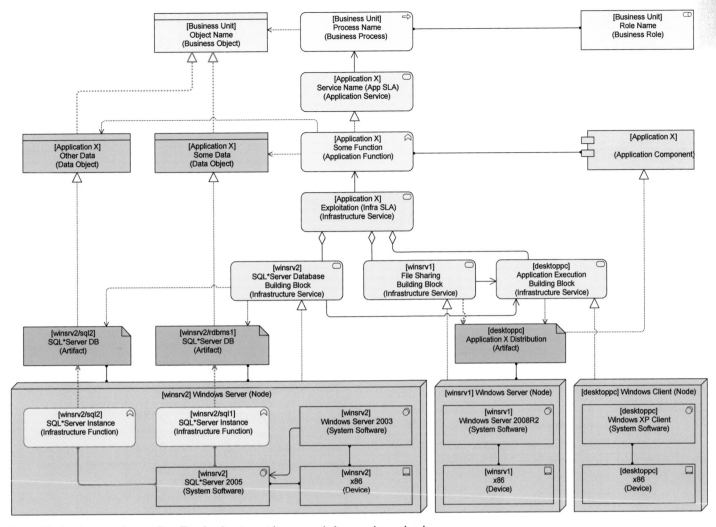

View 78. *Deployment Pattern: Two-Tier Application with mounted client and two databases*

7.11 Deployment Pattern: Two-Tier Client-Server Application with mounted Client Application and two databases

If the client application in client-server is deployed on a different (file) server, the pattern becomes slightly more complicated, as can be seen in View 78. In this example, I have created two 'instances' of the database software on the server and two databases. That was the variation that I talked about in the previous example.

If you take a look at how the situation is in reality, you know that the *operating system* of the desktop PC mounts/maps the file share on which the application is deployed. Formally, I would have to model a Used-By between the File Share Infrastructure Service and the Windows XP Client operating system's Infrastructure Function on the desktop. But I try to prevent as much as possible any relation to the inside structure of the Nodes. So, I create a derived relation in this pattern between the File Share Infrastructure Service and the Application Execution Infrastructure Service. The big advantage of this choice is that I do not have to show the Nodes (or worse: their internal structure) in a view to get the interdependencies.

Both derived relations I use to shield the inside structure of the Node can be seen in View 79.

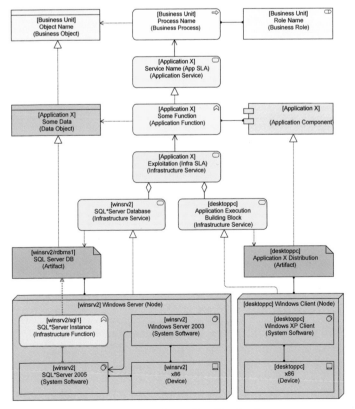

View 77. *Deployment Pattern: Classic Two-Tier Application*

That the desktoppc Node realizes its Application Execution Infrastructure Service (red) is the result from the fact that the Windows XP System Software is a Composite part of the desktoppc Node and the Windows XP System Software Realizes the Application Execution Infrastructure Service (via the omitted Infrastructure Function). That the File Share

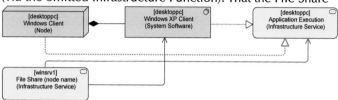

View 79. Deriving the relations from Infrastructure Service to Infrastructure Service (Used-By) and from Node to Infrastructure Service (Realization)

Infrastructure Service is used by the Application Execution Infrastructure Service (blue) is the result of the fact that the File Share Infrastructure Service is Used-By the Windows XP System Software and the Windows XP System Software Realizes the Application Execution Infrastructure Service.

Note: the 'Application X Distribution' is Accessed by both the file share and the processing Infrastructure Services. This is correct, but you could leave out the blue one as you already have the dependency via the Used-By from the file share to processing Infrastructure Service.

7.12 Deployment Pattern: Two-Tier Client-Server with a Remote Server (ASP)

The pattern in View 80 is another variation on the Classic Two-Tier Client-Server.

Here, the server is not your own, but it is provided by an external party. This is sometimes called an Application Service Provider, though the terminology for all these patterns is not very fixed.

This pattern might sound strange, but it actually happens. An example from Asset Management would be Bloomberg's AIM portfolio management and trading application. The Classic two-tier pattern was a client talking a database protocol to some database system. These days, the clients often talk to the server using the world wide web protocols (http or https) and exchange XML-formatted objects. But fundamentally, it is still the same. Another example would be Apple's iTunes application.

Note that the external service has not been made part of our Exploitation Infrastructure Service Aggregation.

7.13 Deployment Pattern: Three-Tier Application

A Three-Tier application is an application where a thin client (often not more than a presentation layer without its own data) connects to an 'application server' where an instance of the 'second tier' application is launched specifically for that thin client. The second-tier application contains the actual business logic. This second-tier

application itself then connects to the third-tier: the database layer. A first attempt can be seen in View 81 on page 57. The fact that it has three tiers is nicely reflected in the interrelations of the Infrastructure Services (Used-By relations between Infrastructure Services). Modeled here is a very basic three-tier, where Tier 1 is an application in itself that is actually deployed on the desktop. These days, the first tier is often browser based, you can combine both patterns.

Now, in the normal Three-Tier case, the first-tier 'thin client' is generally nothing more than a presentation layer and having the actual Application Functions Assigned-To it is stretching it: it is just not true that the presentation layer performs the functionality. The actual business logic is after all in the second tier: the application server. When we looked at the language's 'two types of software' we introduced the notion that if it has business logic, it should be software in the application layer and when it is generic software it should be software in the infrastructure layer. We used that distinction already to set up patterns like the spreadsheet pattern and other 'platform' patterns.

Personally, I like to see all the business logic in software at the application layer. In that case, I would propose another variation on the pattern, which can be seen in View 82. That business logic that is deployed on the application server is now visible as an Application Component (the business logic). The thin client is also an Application Component (the presentation layer). Together they make up the system. It is quite a large net we are casting here, because we end up creating a composition of Application Components that in the deep down technical IT reality can hardly be seen as

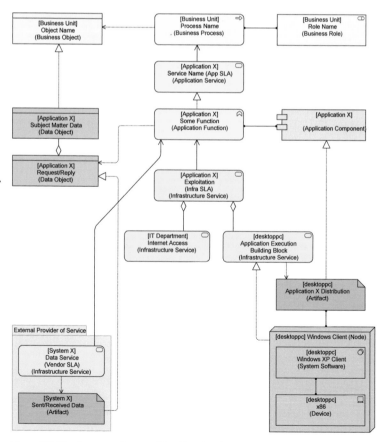

View 80. Deployment Pattern: Two-Tier Application with remote server

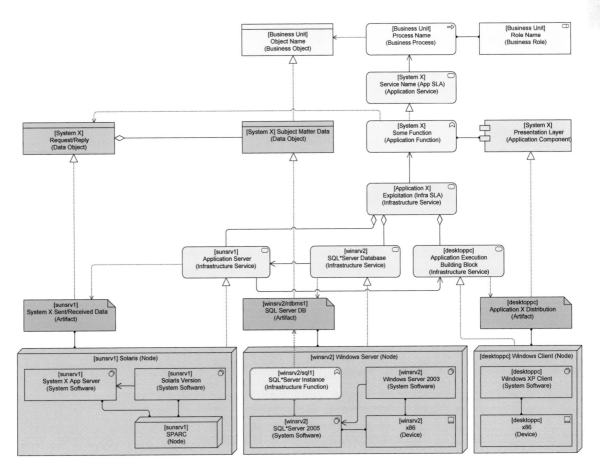

View 81. *Deployment Pattern:Three-tier Application (with missing business logic)*

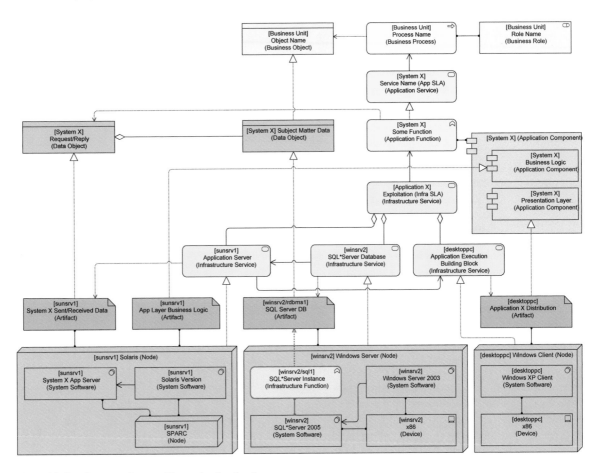

View 82. *Deployment Pattern:Three-tier Application*

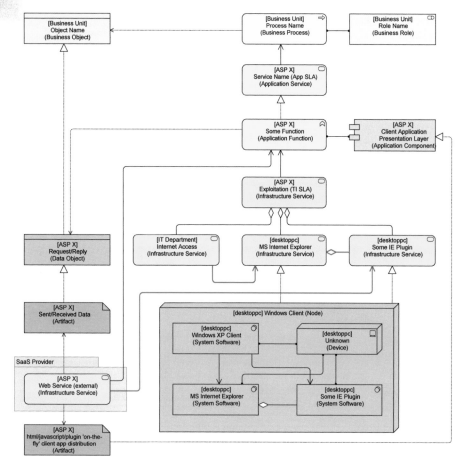

View 83. *Deployment Pattern: Software as a Service (SaaS) - variation I*

mands from us the installation of a certain plugin for the browser (e.g. Silverlight, Flash or some other proprietary plugin). I have used an Aggregation relation (next to the Used-By) for the interdependencies of Infrastructure Services, to point out that the relation between the browser and the plugin it *loads* is much stronger than the relation between the browser and the other services (Internet access, remote web server) it *uses*.

This pattern shares with the initial three-tier pattern, however, that the application that runs locally in the browser platform is nothing more than a presentation layer. The business logic runs not locally, but remotely. This has the rather unpleasant consequence that we have to Assign the Application Component representing the *presentation* layer to the Application Function representing the *business logic*.

Therefore, we can better turn our original perspective (our IT provides services to our business) on its head. It is not *our* IT that provides the Application Service to our business, it is *their* IT, it is SaaS after all. *We* just offer *them* Infrastructure Services (a platform for the thin client and an internet connection) so that *they* can offer *us*

one 'program' at all. But on the other hand: the entire system's functionality that provides the service for the business is indeed a combination of presentation layer and application layer. I do not think using an Application Collaboration is proper here, as Collaborations are meant for loose collections performing temporary behavior.

Question 1. What Style Guide are we breaking in View 81 and View 82?

Answer 1. Switching position of Application Tier and Database Tier leads to less line crossings.

7.14 Deployment Pattern: Software as a Service (SaaS)

Another variation is a pattern that is often called 'SaaS' for 'Software as a Service'. It is both a variation on the two-tier pattern and the three-tier pattern. The difference between this pattern and 'Two-Tier Client with a Remote Server' (ASP) is normally that an internet browser is used as a platform for a very thin client to access the software. As we saw earlier, when we were discussing the browser-based application, the Application Component here is created on the fly from the HTML/JavaScript/etc. Artifact sent by the web server. So, in SaaS, the outside provider provides not only the server, he also provides the (JavaScript) 'presentation' application on-the-fly and we just provide the platform that the application needs to run. In the example in View 83, I made matters a bit more interesting by modeling a SaaS provider which de-

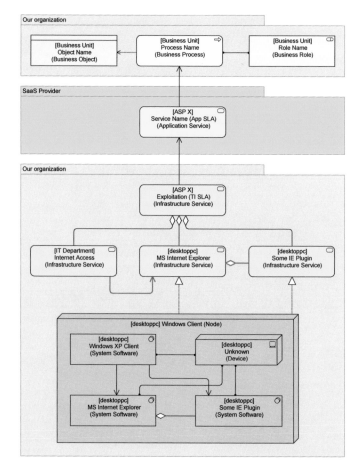

View 84. *Deployment Pattern: SaaS Provider uses our Infrastructure*

the Application Service as can be seen in View 84 on page 58.

This pattern makes it very clear that the external party is providing an Application Service to our business. Our Business Objects that are Accessed in our Business Process do not even have a representation at the application layer as they only exist *outside* our architecture in the 'IT cloud'. Of course, when that same SaaS-provider offers a way for us to get a copy of the data, we can model that too in addition to what is shown above.

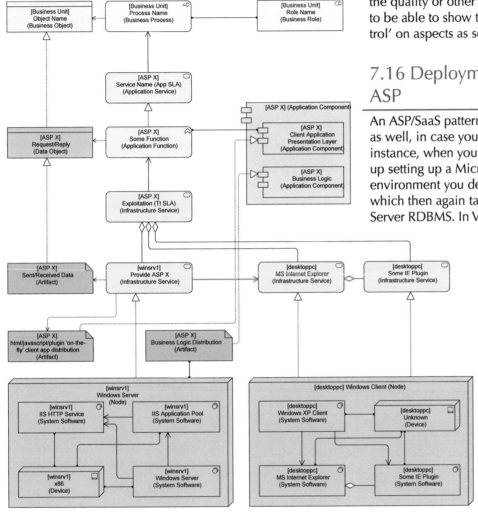

View 85. *Providing your own ASP*

7.15 We only model what we can see/'change'

You might wonder why I did not include the Application Functions and Application Components in the SaaS-variant in View 84. The reason is a sort of golden rule: "we only model what we can *change*". Modeling the internal structure of how your SaaS provider functions internally (something sometimes found in its documentation) is not only unnecessary, it distracts you from how *you* as an organization are functioning, which is what your Enterprise Architecture is all about. If your organization has outsourced its IT in a SaaS-manner, modeling data objects and infrastructure

of the SaaS-provider gives a false picture of your Enterprise Architecture. It is outside your scope.

So, I suggest to draw the line for modeling at what you actually directly can see from the perspective of your own organization. Everything you model, should be part of what is under the control of your organization (both make and buy). You yourself should be able to check your model against reality to see if it is correct.

Now, there are reasons why you sometimes need to know more. For instance, regulators may force you to be aware of the quality or other aspects of your provider. You might have to be able to show to your regulators that you are in 'control' on aspects as security and such.

7.16 Deployment Pattern: Providing a local ASP

An ASP/SaaS pattern can be used inside your company as well, in case you use application servers internally. For instance, when you deploy Microsoft Dynamics, you end up setting up a Microsoft IIS Web Server, within which environment you deploy second-tier applications you build, which then again talk to an underlying Microsoft SQL*-Server RDBMS. In View 85 on page 59, you can actually see what is going on under the hood of the ASP/SaaS pattern, because you are providing it to yourself. If you look closely, you'll see that the pattern looks a lot like the three-tier pattern in View 82 on page 57, but without the third tier. This is no coincidence, because the ASP pattern is just like the three-tier pattern, with the only difference that the presentation layer (the first tier) runs in the browser *platform*.

Of course, the reality of your Local ASP is far more complex. Say, a reporting server is used to create reports every day. And your Local ASP based solution has to send out mail as well to alert people in certain circumstances. And of course, there is a Third Tier: that data must be stored in a database. Or, if the second tier calls upon the reporting server for some functionality we actually have sometimes *four* tiers: thin client → application server → reporting server → database server. The extended example can be seen in View 86 on page 60.

Question 2. Which relation is missing in View 86?

Answer 2. The Assignment from the Business Logic Artifact to Node winsrv1.

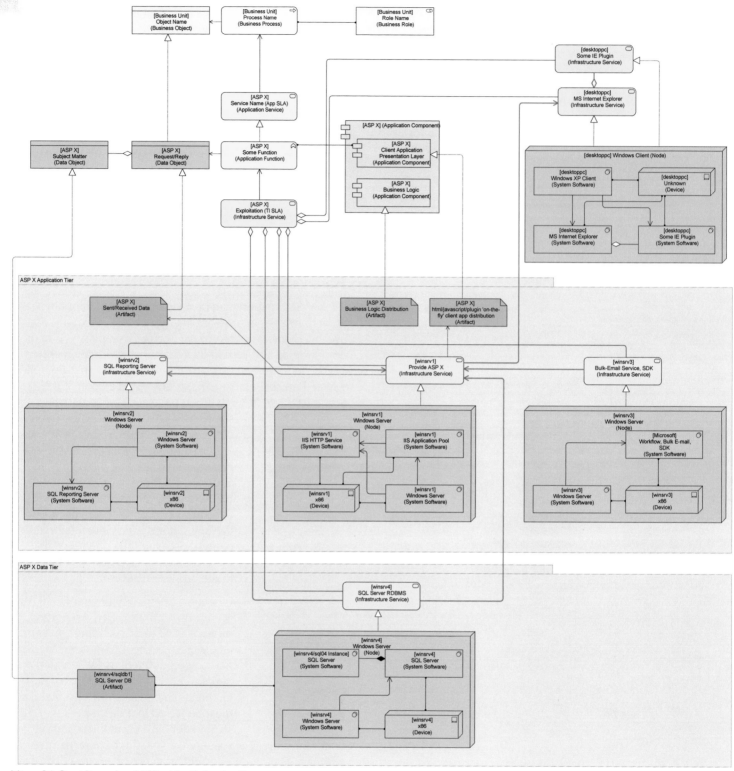

View 86. *Providing a local ASP with all the details*

7.17 The Use of Patterns (reprise)

We will now move to a couple of TI-specific patterns that have to do with types of infrastructure clustering. Infrastructure clustering is generally used to improve performance or reliability.

So far we have seen pretty simple TI-structures, starting with View 65 on page 48. We had Nodes that embedded a single Device and the System Software that was Assigned-To

that Device. Then, we Realized the Infrastructure Service directly from the Node, making the Node (and the Infrastructure Service and the Artifact) a sort of cut-off between Infrastructure use and Infrastructure structure. The Node is used in fact as a sort of object in an object-oriented approach, encapsulating its internals.

This approach in combination with the Building Blocks approach (View 73 on page 52) creates fixed routes between TI and applications. For instance, if you want to know which

Application Function depends on a certain Device, you follow the following route: Device is Composite part of Node, which Realizes Infrastructure Service which is part of an Aggregate 'Exploitation' Infrastructure Service which is Used-by an Application Function. This is not a valid route for a formal ArchiMate 'derived relation', but when you use the patterns consistently, this route will always give you the Application Functions that depend on the device. Such consistent pattern use in your modeling will give you (depending on your modeling tool) all kinds of useful (and more importantly: reliable) automated analyses. The less discipline while modeling, the more variation in your patterns, the more difficult it becomes to define 'standard' dependency routes and use your model effectively. Archi-

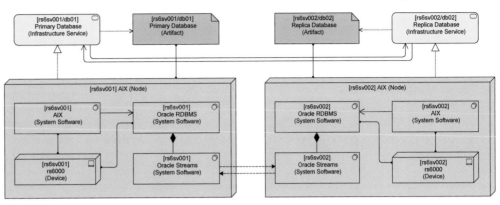

View 87. *Infrastructure Pattern: Database Replication*

Mate is not just a language or a grammar, it is a *modeling* grammar, and if you combine a wild selection of modeling styles and patterns, the result becomes less usable. If you do not use patterns at all, you're at the mercy of painstakingly letting a human (probably yourself) analyze the model, something that may overwhelm you if the model becomes large (which it most likely will, if you model your Current State).

However, we will now get into a bit of IT complexity where we might (for sake of aesthetics for instance) decide to introduce alternative patterns. E.g. another level of Node embedding or another level of Infrastructure Service Aggregation. When we do this, it is important to remember the price one pays: for every alternative pattern, you need a second route if you want you standardized (and thus including automated) analyses to be complete.

7.18 Infrastructure Pattern: Database Replication

The first example of a very lightweight sort of 'cluster' is database replication and it can be seen in View 87. Actually, this is not really a cluster if one defines a cluster as a combination of items that present themselves as a *single* item to the outside world. In database replication, the main database replicates all its actions to a second read-only database. This is above all useful for performance. Suppose you want to run complex management summary reports on your core system's database, such queries may degrade the performance so much that the actual work being done on them suffers. Maybe you have even queries that take hours of heavy 'data crunching' to complete. You do not want to let those queries bring down the performance for your users. The simplest solution is a database replication. Now, a replication is not a purely one-way process, even if it sounds like one. As we need to be certain that *both* databases have *exactly* the same data, the primary database needs to be told that the change at the replica succeeded, and if not, it should turn back its own change. Databases generally have

some sort of 'persistence' mechanism (in SQL terms a COMMIT) that turns whatever data it has written to cells, rows or tables to permanent storage. Now, what replication needs to ascertain is that if one of the commits fails for whatever reason, the other is rolled back too. Hence, performance wise (though only on COMMIT and ROLLBACK) the primary database will suffer. And since you generally cannot ROLLBACK after a COMMIT has been executed, the 'commit' operation needs another level of 'roll back'. For the rest, both databases can be (except for the replica being read-only) used independently. They turn up as two 'independent' databases in your infrastructure (which is why this is not really a 'cluster'). These tricks have of course been extended to writing in both databases, but for that better solutions have been created.

In View 87 you see a couple of standard database patterns side by side. Each has its own database, each Realizes its own Infrastructure Service. But the 'clustering' has been modeled in two ways:

- As a flow between the replication components of the databases. Note: we break our pattern here that we do not model to the internals of the Node. If you dislike it you can of course model the flow between the Nodes. I break it however because for complex Nodes it is rather limiting not to know which sub-components actually talk to each other;

- As two Used-By relations between the Realized Infrastructure Services. The reason is that, as earlier, we want to be able to see the dependency when we only view the Infrastructure Services 'Building Blocks' (and Artifacts) and not the Nodes. If you offer an 'Exploitation' Infrastructure Service to an application that contains the 'primary' database, you want to be able to see that one of its Building Blocks depends on another Infrastructure Service still. As the replica database is not really used by the application, the Used-By is a nice alternative that shows the indirect dependency.

7.19 Infrastructure Pattern: High-Available Database Cluster

If we create a true cluster from multiple databases, they will behave as a 'single entity' to the outside world. That is, they present a single Infrastructure Service to the outside world and the outside world does not know which actual database is being used. An example is modeled in View 88 on page 62. In that example I have modeled a database cluster that provides two databases. I have also put in a little detail about the technical situation. Server rs6sv001 has two databases: rdbms11 and rdbms21 (Assignments in red). Rdbms11 is the rdbms1 database on the first server. Rdbms21 is the rdbms2 database on the first server. In fact only the rdbmsxy databases exist physically, The rest are just aliases in the database system. Rdbms1, for instance, is the alias for either rdbms11 on rs6sv001 or rdbms12 on rs6sv002. The setup in the example uses the second server for the first database as first server for the second database and the first server for the first database as second server for the second database (you might need to read this sentence multiple times, in short: they are each other's fall back but also provide their own primary database). So, it is a pretty efficient setup. The fall back server is used and not just idling expensively in the background. Of course, this requires that — in the case of a failure of either of the Nodes — the applications can do with roughly half the database performance. As extras I have modeled the upper Artifacts. They are aliases in the database's naming scheme. They may be used by some applications and we therefore need them in our model. The nodes also contain a batch-job agent. Both devices need such an agent, e.g. to start jobs on them during the night (e.g. a backup job for rdbms2 on rs6sv002 and a backup job for rdbms1 on rs6sv001).

Now, applications that access this cluster always go to 'rs6sv001'. For the outside world, that is the name of this cluster. In this specific example, the Oracle RDBMS has its own databasename-to-system mechanism that handles this (as far as I know, I'm not an expert) This is modeled as an extra Aggregation layer of Infrastructure Services.

Variations are of course possible. We could for instance have chosen to model only one abstract Node. But that would have meant we lose the information on which Device the actual physical databases are, unless we would have Assigned them to the Device instead of the Node. Or we could have modeled an extra layer of Node-embedding and just have the top Infrastructure Services being Realized by that outer Node.

7.20 Infrastructure Pattern: High-Available Server

The third example of clustering is a high-available operating system or server. Here, two devices run an operating system and on top of that they run software that makes them act as a single system. So, we can approach the cluster as a single system where we can for instance install

View 88. *Infrastructure Pattern: Database Cluster. Set up pioneered by colleague/hired gun Roy Zautsen* software on. In the example in View 89, we see a Node that contains two RS6000 Devices running IBM's AIX. On top of AIX, HACMP software (HACMP stands for "High Available Cluster Multi-Processing") has been installed which delivers a HACMP Service. The flows between the HACMP system software elements are used to model the clustering dynamics. The result is in fact a virtual single operating system, which has been modeled explicitly.

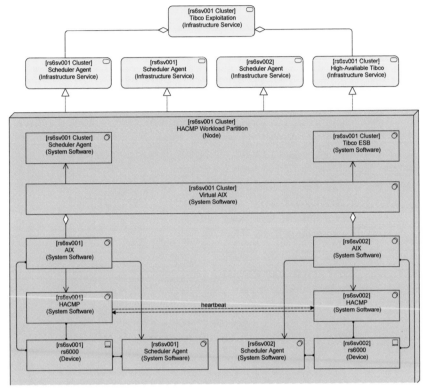

View 89. *Infrastructure Pattern: High Available Server. This set up pioneered by colleague/hired gun Roy Zautsen. (services approach from Edition I was dropped)*

In this example, Tibco has been installed on that virtual operating system. Tibco itself is unaware that there are *two* Devices and *two* operating systems it runs on: it sees only a single operating system and a single file system thanks to HACMP. (And yes, I know it is called Power-HA these days, but I have limited time, so the diagrams and story remain as they are).

I have also modeled three installed scheduler agents here. One on the operating system of each device and one on the cluster. If, for instance, a batch job for Tibco needs to be started (e.g. a scheduled restart), the scheduler must use the "[rs6sv001 Cluster] Scheduler Agent (Infrastructure Service)", but if for instance some housekeeping job on one of the underlying devices is necessary, it should use "[rs6sv001] Scheduler Agent {Infrastructure Service}". Not visible in the view: the Tibco and 'cluster' Scheduler Agent System Softwares have been Assigned to the Node.

This is one of many ways this can be modeled and it is actually not the one we use. There are often constraints to the way you want to model things, based on the way your model is used. More about this in Section 22.3 where the actual pattern I ended up using is discussed.

7.21 Using Collections and Abstraction in a model

When you make large models to describe your current state architecture, it tend to become useful to have certain groupings in your model. I am not talking about grouping in a view, but grouping elements 'together', e.g. via Composites, Aggregations or Specializations. For instance, if you have multiple versions of MS Excel in your landscape, you might want to group all instances of Excel 2003 and Excel 2007 in your model so it is easy to find them when for instance you have to do an analysis that has to do with upgrading one or the other (e.g. which business processes are affected when I will upgrade all MS Excel instances to MS Excel 2010?). You might think of doing it like in View 90.

Here abstract elements have been created to stand for the different types of Excel we have in our landscape. After all, the 'real' MS Excel 2007 on a PC somewhere, is an instance of a generic type 'MS Excel 2007', which in turn is a subtype of 'MS Excel'. (Incidentally, most organizations would love to be able to know all spreadsheets that are used in their business, but few do). A different approach is using an Aggregation as in View 91 on page 64, which looks almost the same.

The first has the advantage that it is using a true abstraction relation for the abstractions: in other words: these generalizations do not exist in reality, they are *types*. Hence, using a specialization is 'proper'. The second looks not so much at a Type/Class, but sees all those Excels out there as a large *collection* of real instances. This is not a real 'abstraction', but it is 'proper' too.

The second has the advantage, though, that derived relations from the abstract elements to the real elements are possible: 'Spreadsheet C' uses 'Excel'.

You can probably get pretty heated discussions amongst architects over one or the other. But if your tool does not restrict your analyses to only derived relations, they both

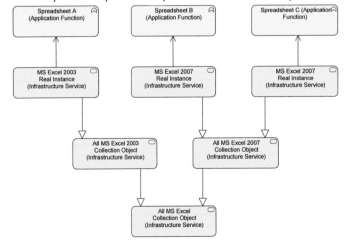

View 90. *Adding collections to your model by Specializations*

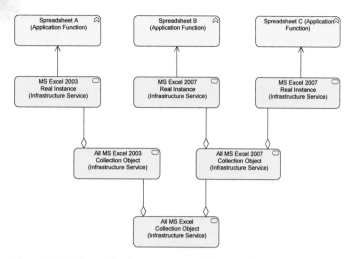

View 91. *Adding collections to your model using Aggregations*

work out equally in practice. In practice I have settled on using the second because of the following unlikely scenario: If my tool ever in a new release restricts me to doing analyses through proper ArchiMate derived relations, that pattern will still work.

More on this subject in section 17 "Using Abstractions" on page 114.

7.22 External Data Services

Suppose you have an application that uses an external data provider. For instance, you have a pricing process that uses a system that gets its data from a price feed from a data vendor. There are generally two ways to model this. The first is to model the external provider as an Application Service as shown in View 94. The second is to model the Data Vendor as an Infrastructure Service as shown in View 95.

Following the same argumentation as in section 7.15 "We only model what we can see/'change'" on page 59, my preference is the second one for data services. The first has the advantage that you can directly model the dependency of the business process on the data provider, but the second

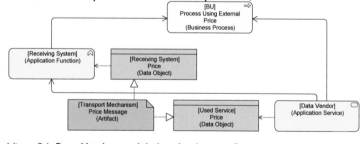

View 94. *Data Vendor modeled as Application Service*

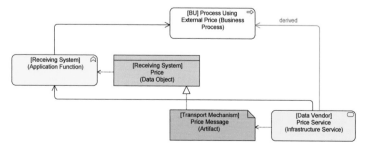

View 95. *Data Vendor modeled as Infrastructure Service*

one only contains items we can 'change', elements that we can actually see and verify at our end. 'Change' in this case means of course that we can either use the service or not. These Infrastructure Services are kept outside an 'exploitation' Aggregate (see View 80 on page 56 for an example).

If all is well, the relation between the data vendor's service and the process still exists as a derived relation.

Note that if the service used in the process has direct human interaction, like a SaaS-solution, there is of course an externally provided application in play, which should be modeled as Application Service.

7.23 Concurrent Realization?

In ArchiMate, a function (or in the business layer, a process) can Realize a service. Nothing in ArchiMate stops you from having multiple functions all Realizing the same service. But what does it signify? Generally, it is meant by those that use the pattern that both functions together Realize the service. This construct, however, is somewhat problematic. Let's start with the example in View 92.

This is what you often see in a model and it is intended to mean that both functions

View 92. *Two Business Functions Concurrently Realize One Business Service*

together realize the service and not 'either of them can realize the service', though I can imagine situations where for instance three locations of a function all are modeled separately (as they are performed by different roles that are fulfilled by different actors) and all three perform *exactly* the same service to the outside world. The pattern is ambiguous (which is almost never a good sign).

But back to the commonly intended meaning, of two different processes that *together* realize a service. Now, if these two functions provide the service together, we have two options:

- Both functions work together to provide a single unified service;

- Both provide a sub-service of the overall service.

The first, however, should be modeled using Business Interaction (and if active components are added: Business Collaboration). See View 93.

Note that we do not strictly follow ArchiMate here as ArchiMate says an Interaction is the behavior of a Collaboration and not so much an Aggregation of functions or processes like a collaboration is an Aggregation of Roles or Application Components. But this is in the spirit of ArchiMate. And the

View 93. *Two Functions Interact to Realize a Service*

second looks like View 99.

If you expand the Nesting of View 99, it looks like View 96 (ignore the red associations for now).

Now, the question is: what is the relation between Function A (or B) and the 'Service provided by Functions A and B'? In the image, these relations are depicted by the red lines. Well, since the Realization between the

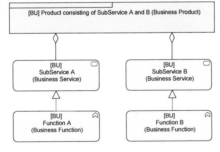

View 99. *Two Business Functions each Realize a Sub-Service of an Overall Business Service*

Function and the corresponding Sub-Service has a direction opposite to the relation between the Sub-Service and the overall Service, there is no official derived ArchiMate relation. And if you look at dependency in a certain way, it is also logical: Sub-Service A does not depend on Function B. So, if we have two independent sub-services, we should not model a Realization between each function and the overall service because *they do not exist*.

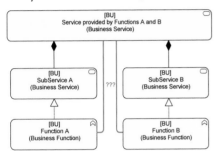

View 96. *Two Business Functions each Realize a Sub-Service of an Overall Business Service, expanded*

In the case of a collection of independent sub-services that are offered to the outside in a 'package', you can probably better use the Business Product element as in View 97.

So, summarizing:

- If an overall Business Service is truly realized by two or more functions (or processes) in collaboration/interaction, you can better model the true collaboration/interaction;

- If it is not so much function A *and* function B Realize a Service together, but function A *or* function B Realize the *same* Service *independently*, we could use the pattern in View 92 on page 64;

- And if functions A and B Realize Sub-Services for an overall Service or Product, we can best use View 99 or View 97.

View 97. *Two independent (Sub-)Services make up a single Product*

All in all, I suggest to stick to a 1:n relation between:

- In the business layer: Business Process (or Business Function) and the Realized Business Service;

- In the application layer: Application Function and Application Service;

- In the infrastructure layer: Infrastructure Function and Infrastructure Service.

More on this in section 17 "Using Abstractions" on page 114.

Realizing a service by two functions is also possible in the application layer of ArchiMate, as can be seen in View 98.

Here too, you need to wonder what is being meant. If two independent functions can provide the same service, this is a possible pattern. You might think of two applications that both provide the same and you can use either of the two to do what you need, as in "there are two allowed ways to calculate travel distances for your travel expense calculations".

But as a pattern showing two functions Realizing a service

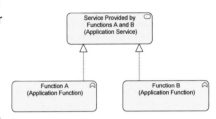

View 98. *Application Service Realized by Two Application Functions*

together (which is how you will see most modelers using it), you run into the same sort of questions as above. Of course, ArchiMate also offers the Application Collaboration and Application Interaction as an element to model the way two Application Functions may offer a single service. I personally think this should be avoided in your models, as I'll explain in Section 8.1 "Application Collaboration is an Anthropomorphism". As such, this would be an example of an 'anti-pattern'.

7.24 Summary of Basic Patterns

A summary of the most important points of the patterns above, and a bit more:

- As mentioned in Section 7.2 "A Basic TI Pattern: A Database" on page 47, I do not model interfaces. As I keep a 1:1 relation between interfaces and services, and a 1:n relation between internal and external behavior (hence, no (ambiguous) 'concurrent Realizations' for instance), interfaces do not add anything to the model, they are that 'other side of the coin' and nothing else;

- I use a Node to encapsulate infrastructure. Infrastructure Services are Realized directly by the Node, Artifacts are Assigned-To the Node. With a few exceptions (throughout the book) there are no relations between elements outside the Node and elements inside the Node;

- I Aggregate Infrastructure Services as 'building blocks' into an Infrastructure Service explicitly meant to model the support for a certain application. Relations between the child-Infrastructure Services (e.g. Used-Bys) are optional;

- I only model what I can change/see. I do not model assumptions about matters I cannot check (e.g. internals of counter-parties).

8. Anti-patterns

8.1 Application Collaboration is an Anthropomorphism

The designers of ArchiMate added two collaboration concepts to the language: a Business Collaboration and an Application Collaboration. In Section 10.2 "Business Function or Business Process?" on page 76, we will see that Business Collaboration has an equivalent in the real (business) world. But this is hardly true for Application Collaboration (though with an exception, see below).

In ArchiMate there are two basic `cooperation' patterns. One is Used-By. A behavioral element (process, function) can use another behavioral element (service). We repeat View 21 on page 24 here in View 100.

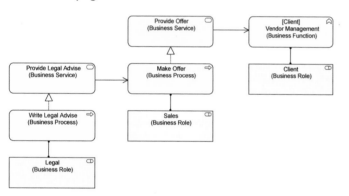

View 100. *Collaboration: Sales Uses Legal on Order Creation*

The other is a Collaboration. We repeat View 22 on page 24 in View 101.

In the business layer this is both an understandable way to look at it. But when do you choose one, and when the other? If you look at the concept of 'collaboration' from a human perspective — which is OK at the business level — it is about decision making. I would go for Collaboration when both processes must actively negotiate to make decisions *together*. An example is the 'exception collaboration' mentioned in Section 10.2 "Business Func-

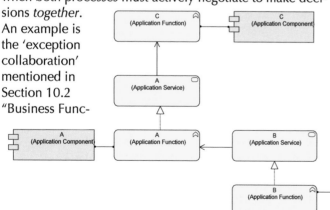

View 102. *Application C uses Application A which uses Application B*

tion or Business Process?" on page 76. I would use Used-By when the process or function used has no real say in the matter, the decision power lies all with the 'user' and not with the 'used'.

If you try to imagine how a real Application Collaboration would work, you have to differentiate between the two uses of Used-By (see section 1.2 on page 17). One is an application used by a business process or business function, the other is an application used by another application. In the latter case, the question is: which application provides the service that the 'user' application connects to? Basically, there are two options:

- The 'user' application C uses another application A which itself uses yet another application B as can be seen in View 102;

- The 'user' application C uses both application A and application B as can be seen in View 103 on page 67.

The difference between these two is where the application logic is that *combines* the functionality of A and B. If A has logic to combine itself with B and then deliver the result to C, the pattern of View 102 is the case. If C has the logic to combine the results of A and B, then the pattern of View 103 is the case.

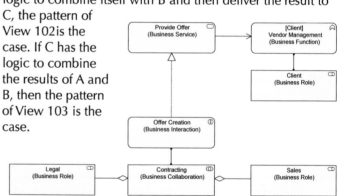

View 101. *Collaboration: Sales and Legal Collaborate on Order Creation*

Now suppose we would draw this using an Application Collaboration as can be seen in View 104 on page 67. It neither fits the first nor the second option. It introduces elements that are abstract and that do not exist in reality. It certainly does not fit the second option: the actual interaction does not take place outside of C, it takes place *inside* C. And in the case of the first option, it suggests an equality between A and B that is not there.

So, in the case of applications using a service provided by two other applications, we shrink the amount of elements from 8 to 7, but at the price of introducing 3 elements that do not exist in reality and that muddy the picture of what is really going on in a substantial way.

And that is not all: try to add the Application Interface to the mix and you get View 105. Given that an application can only use *one* interface for a service, we now also have introduced an interface that *cannot* exist in reality. In terms of creating a good model of what is going on, matters have gone from problematic to bad. To make matters even worse, if you use an

View 103. *Application C uses Application A and Application B*

Interaction to describe behavior (and properly document the Application Interaction element), you will still need to fully document the separate behaviors that make up the Interaction if they are used elsewhere in solitary form or in another Application Interaction. The same documentation will be in different places and it will be difficult to keep it in sync (a typical thing for IT-people to forget: documentation).

Is it possible to think of a pattern where Application Collaboration makes sense when the 'user' is another application? Yes, but it is pretty convoluted. Here is an example:

Suppose there are multiple applications that provide the same service, say a search service. A request for such a service is given concurrently to all that can provide the service. All possible search providers calculate a quality of the answer they can provide: how much 'trust' they have in the answer they can give. All write this 'trust' value in a common data object. After a fixed time, all look in

View 104. *Application C uses a Collaboration of Applications A and B*

the common data object if they had the highest trust value and only the one who has the highest trust value delivers the service. Basically, what is described here is a sort of AI with autonomous software agents: on the basis of internal rules (which they all share but have implemented separately, which in this case is possible in a practical sense because the rule is very simple) the applications amongst each other decide who is going to provide the service. Given that all applications participate in making that decision, you can argue that there is a single application function that is in effect distributed across multiple application components: hence a collaboration of all applications is assigned to that single function. The interface for that solution will be a nice piece of engineering too. In practice, software engineers will most likely design a 'master application' and the architectural relation reverts to Used-By of View 103.

So, using Application Collaboration for a pattern where applications are using multiple other applications is not a very good idea, I think. Basically, what the Application Collaboration element in most cases breaks is the guideline "the best model of the world is the world itself". This is an old adagium from AI where they learned over a couple of

decennia that creating abstractions actually decreased usability. The same is true for Enterprise Architecture modeling, especially when you are busy modeling your Current State or the end state of a Project. I do not think using such abstractions is always wrong, they are perfectly reasonable. Enterprise Architects, being creatures that love the simplification that comes with abstraction, especially love it. My problem with too much abstraction in your Enterprise Architecture models is that it is pretty unmanageable, just like in AI. Stay close to what is really there and less confusion and more usability is your reward.

Anyway, what about using Application Collaboration for an Application Service that is used by the business and that is thus described more in business (human) terms? Well, an Application Service for the Business is of course defined in business terms and as such, a collection of services thrown together is possible from a human point of view. But think again of the interface which messed things up before. Each of these applications has its own GUI. Using an Application Interaction again forces you to create a non-existing (abstract) Application Interface that under water consists of the two separate GUIs collected in one.

All in all, you're generally better off by not using multiple realizers for one service at both the business layer and the application layer. It looks simple, but it also introduces many untrue aspects in your model, so in many cases there will be a too high price to pay.

But there is an exception.

Recall the multiple-tier application deployment patterns like for instance View 82 on page 57. There the presentation layer of the multi-tier application and the business logic layer each are an Application Component Realized by an Artifact. In that View, the complete system was modeled as an Application Component with each of the Artifacts Realizing a sub-component. And while technically it is the presentation layer that *Uses* the business logic layer, it is quite nice to model this as a true Application Collaboration as my colleague Jos Knoops proposed. This is shown in View 106 on page 68.

I must admit I rather like this use of Application Collaboration.

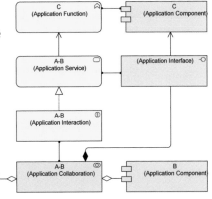

View 105. *Application C uses a Collaboration of Applications A and B, with Application Interface*

We also decided not to use it, though it is more aesthetically pleasing. The reasons is that it meant we had to change our analysis viewpoints such that everywhere the script is looking for an Application Function, we would also have to model the alternative routef. But we might still do it, because it is also nice to have a way to differentiate between single- and two-tier applications where the business logic resides with the presentation in one component, and three-and-more tier applications where the business logic is spread out over multiple components working together.

Question 3. If you want to add an Application Interface to '[System X] Service Name (App SLA) (Application Service)', of which Application Component is it a Composite child?

Answer 3. '[System X] Presentation Layer (Application Component)' and derived from the '[System X] {Application Component)'.

8.2 Using the Association Relation

The Association relation has a couple of official uses in ArchiMate. As the Association relation is allowed between all concepts, it is a kind of catch-all. It is always allowed and it is always possible.

As far as I'm concerned, most of the time, the Association relation is for wimps. It is a sign that you haven't thought out what the real relation is. It is often a sign of sloppy modeling. So, here are my rules regarding the use of the Association relation:

• Don't use the Association relation where another more specific relation can be used;

• If you cannot use a more specific relation, consider if elements are missing that would make modeling without the Association relation an option. Only fall back to the Association relation if a complete model would be too complex or detailed for the use you are going to make. In that case, develop a fixed pattern for the situation using the Association relation and reuse that exact pattern in comparable situations. In such cases, you should have at least once have modeled (analyzed) the complete situation in full without the Association relation as underlying foundation for the choices in your pattern. An example will be given later in the book when we will be talking about modeling ownership of applications and such;

• For the rest: only use the Association relation in its formal roles in the meta-model.

Summarizing: use the Association relation only where it appears in the meta-model and in situations where doing a real model of what happens becomes too unwieldy. A pattern where we use Associations that way can be found in Section 12.9 "Making it Practical: shortcuts" on page 93.

8.3 Using properties too much

There is also an anti-pattern that has not so much to do with ArchiMate itself, but with tooling. Most tools let you add all kinds of information to an element or relation that is modeled. This is a good thing, for instance if the tool (almost all do) let you add the documentation for that element to that element.

Some tools also have the option to add explicit properties to an element type. This can even be in the form of free fields where you can add information. For instance, you could add the cost of an Infrastructure Service to the element and use that information to provide analysis of running costs of your Architecture.

Properties of elements and relations can be very useful, but they also have a danger: they are invisible most of the time. ArchiMate is a graphical grammar and those properties do not always show up when you want and they are not always available for the easy analyses you can make on the basis of a model. So, for instance, you might add the application's owner as a property to an Application Component, but that makes it impossible to connect that property to that same Actor that lives as a real Actor element in your model.

So, the bottom line is: only use properties for things you cannot model and even then be careful as they live outside of ArchiMate's grammatical structure.

The same limitations hold for labels. Labels do have a positive role to play in readability of course (see Section 6.6 "About labels" on page 45), but do not rely on them for analysis and structure.

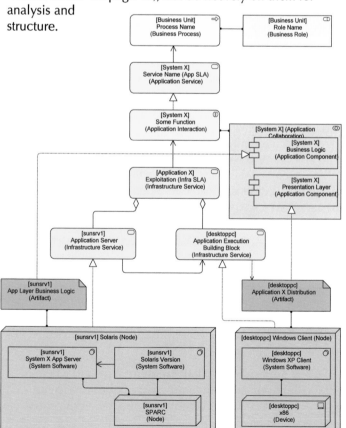

View 106. *Using Application Collaboration to model a multi-tiered software system*

9. An Example from the Real World

Ending this chapter I want to present you with a real-world example. This is about receiving files from an external data provider and using them. These files have to be received, moved to the right location in your landscape and then loaded in some application.

For this, the company employs a Managed File Transfer system, a Scheduler System and a human. The MFT System is programmed to receive certain files and depending on what it receives from whom, to move those files to a directory on a server in the landscape. There, the Scheduler watches for the file to arrive, and if it does, it starts a script that copies the file over to yet another location, using simple copy commands and shared file systems. After having done that, the Scheduler is done. The human (supposedly at some time of day) looks for the received file and loads it in the application by hand.

Now this situation is unnecessarily complex. After all, you could let the MFT system drop the file on the server where the receiving system can read it. Assume that there are reasons not to do it that way.

In View 109 on page 70, this setup has been modeled. The MFT system works like this. In the Demilitarized Zone (DMZ) of our network, a 'Relay Server' (srv001) receives communication from the outside, e.g. an SFTP file transfer initiation. It checks if this party is allowed to and if so, patches the incoming communication through to a 'Gateway Server' (srv002) on the inside of our network. Here the actual receiving of the file happens and the file (Artifact filexxx. yyy) is stored locally. Here the MFT system runs a work flow that decides where the file has to go. In this case, it goes to srv003, a dedicated MFT transport end node: it receives all files together with signal files for the Scheduler. From here the Scheduler is taking over.

But before we go further I want to draw your attention to the other two Artifacts on srv002.

- One is the distribution of the MFT Gateway System. This Artifact Realizes the '[Transporter] Workflow Maintenance (Application Component)'. This application is used by IT Management to control the MFT System, create work flows for it etc.;

- The other is '[srv002] Transporter Workflow Configuration' (Artifact). This Artifact Realizes two different elements. One is the '[Transporter] Workflow (Data Object)', which is the *passive* element that is maintained by

the 'Workflow Maintenance' application. The second is the '[Transporter] Workflow (Application Component)'. This element represents the workflow as an *actor* in our landscape which is responsible for automatically performing the 'Receive Incoming Files (Business Process)'.

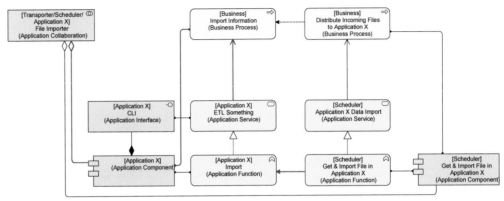

View 107. *Scheduling example: Scheduler triggers ETL*

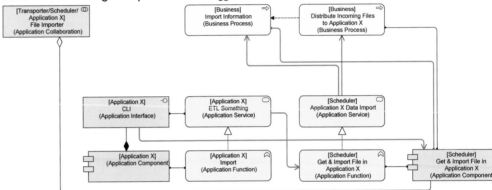

View 108. *Scheduling example: Scheduler uses ETL*

What you see here is both the architecture of *using* the workflow as well as *creating or maintaining* the workflow. In Section 12.3 "Secondary Architecture: Development" on page 89, this will be explained in detail.

The same primary (used by the business) and secondary (created/maintained by the developers) split is modeled again for the Scheduler.

I also want to draw your attention to the way the file ends up on srv003 from srv002. On srv003 an MFT software agent is running that can receive files. This System Software Realizes the 'Dedicated Transporter End Node Service' that is used by the software on srv002. Following our deployment patterns, we do not model this in deep detail but we model this as a dependency between both Infrastructure Services.

The deep details of the Scheduler starting local scripts (jobs) on servers which then use mounted file systems to copy files are not modeled, there is no need. A shortcut is modeled, the File Share of srv004 is used by the Scheduler. Agent on srv003.

Have a look at the '[Scheduler] Specific Job/Flow Exploitation (Infrastructure Service)'. This is the 'exploitation' service we saw before (see View 73 "TI Building Blocks" on page

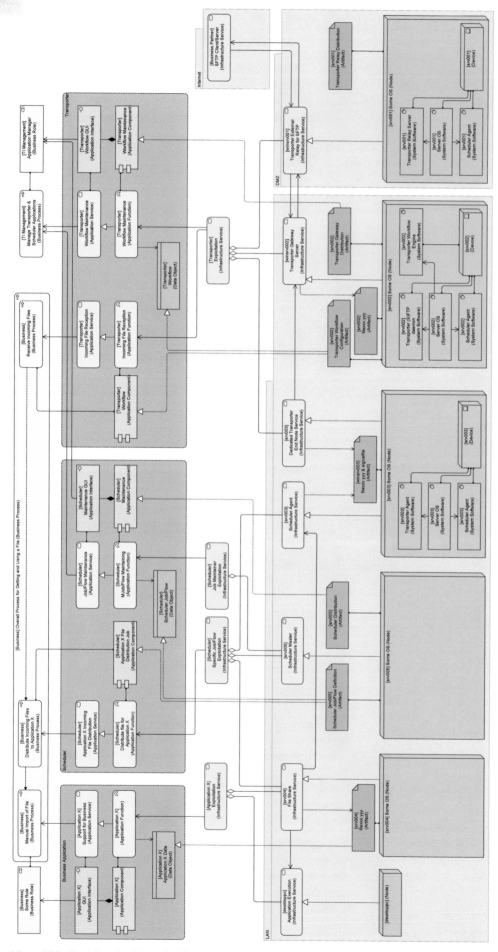

52). It is made up of the File Share where the file has to go, the Scheduler Master which is in control of the whole operation and the Scheduler Agent which is needed to do the actual copying. The Scheduler Agent therefore needs the File Share, and that is modeled by the Used-By between them.

Finally, at the top of the view, you see the entire business process. Two subprocesses/steps are automatically executed by applications (the Transporter and the Scheduler systems) and one is performed by a human.

But that doesn't need to be the case. In many organizations such business processes may run fully automatic. This has been modeled in View 110 on page 71. This view is identical to the previous one, except in the upper-left corner. If the final step is not done by hand (by a human Business Role) but by a system, there are two ways to look at this (and probably more), shown in red and blue in View 110 on page 71.

- Following the blue relations and shown separately in View 107, we model that the loading is done by Application X, behavior that is *Triggered* by the Scheduler;

- Following the red relations and shown separately in View 108, we model that the loading is done by the Scheduler which *Uses* Application X.

Both are correct. But the one with the *Trigger* does not depend solely on structural relations, while the one with *Used-By* does. I find that somewhat cleaner.

There is another advantage for using the one with only structural relations. I generally do not model Interfaces, something that is more or less superfluous when you model the behavior well. (If someone disagrees with me, he or she can write his or her own book ;-). So, without those (and without the collaboration that I generally also do not use because in ArchiMate I cannot model a Collaboration of automated and non-automated actors, you get the result shown in View

View 109. *Modeling the Use of a Managed File Transfer and a Scheduler use for your business, a human user loads the retrieved data*

111 on page 72. And for the entire
setup, only one relation is left.

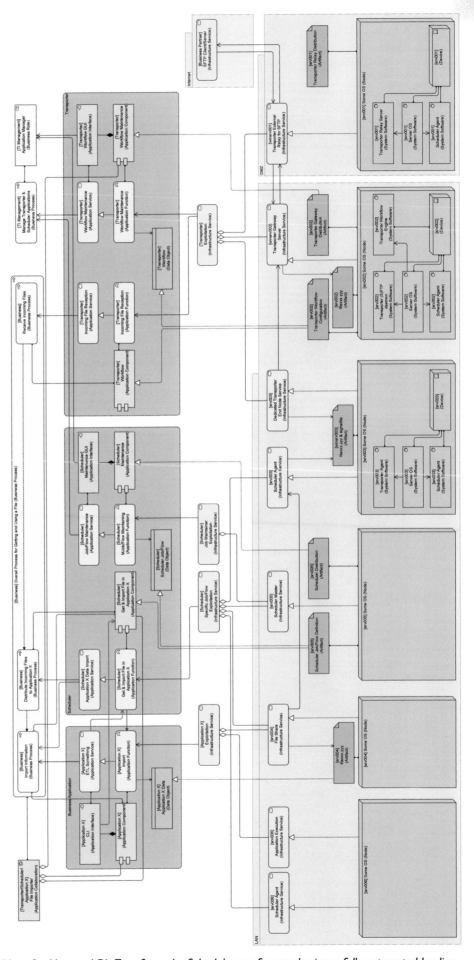

View 110. *Modeling the Use of a Managed File Transfer and a Scheduler use for your business, fully automated loading*

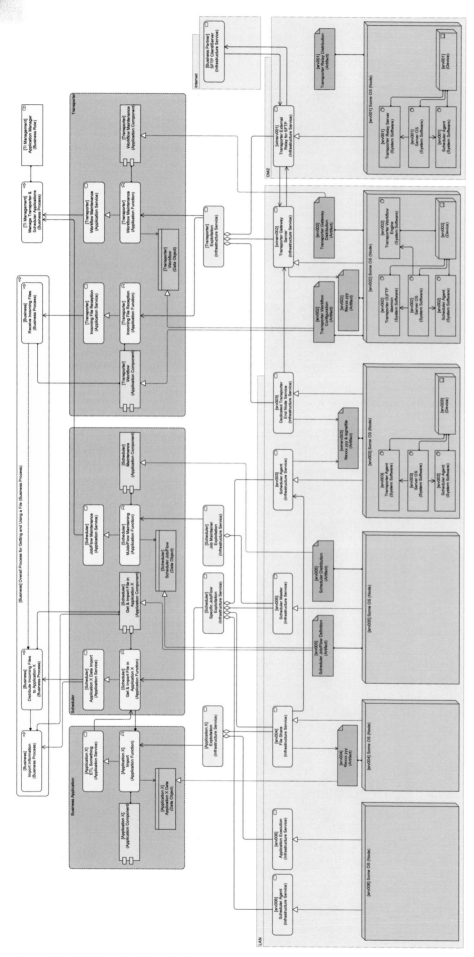

View III. *Modeling the Use of a Managed File Transfer and a Scheduler use for your business, fully automated loading (cleaned up)*

This page intentionally not left blank

Advanced Subjects

Advanced Subjects

10. Business Function and Business Process

10.1 On ArchiMate's divide between behavior and structure

ArchiMate is divided into structure and behavior. Active structure elements (like Business Roles and Application Components) perform behavior (like Business Processes/ Functions and Application Functions) and these behaviors act on passive structure (like Business Objects and Data Objects. This division is a fundamental property of the language, but it is slightly different than other ways to look at architecture (e.g. traditional view of software architecture or business architecture) and that does sometimes lead to discussion.

What I have noticed is that especially ArchiMate's Business Function element is problematic in this sense. It has been customary in some circles to see a Business Function as a somewhat visible 'part of the *organization*' that *performs* a certain function in that organization. And that description shows already where the problem lies. In non-ArchiMate ('old school') business architecture speech, a business function often *performs* something and both there and in ArchiMate terms, something that *performs* behavior is an *active* structure, while ArchiMate's Business Function is not an active structure element at all, but a *behavioral* element that *is* performed.

Application Function also suffers from this problem. In the field of Software Engineering, a function is both a piece of code (which is structural) as well as the behavior of that piece of code. Historically, there have not been two terms in software engineering to separate that structure and its behavior (nor in the related subject of mathematics, where formula and behavior of a function are one and the same). Also, coming from software engineering, in UML the division between structure and behavior is different from that in ArchiMate. In UML, we have a set of elements, some of which may play both a structural and a behavioral role, depending on the type of diagram they are in. Take for instance an Object Diagram in UML, which is structural, and a Sequence Diagram, which is behavioral, and both may use the same objects in either a structural or a behavioral role. In other words: UML allows objects that can be both structural and behavioral, depending on the views they appear in (structure type of view or behavior type of view). This follows the paradigm of Object-Orientation in software engineering, where objects are structural but encapsulate behavior (and some data even). In ArchiMate, there is but one type of view (even if you are free to restrict yourself to certain element and relation types in different viewpoints) which combines structure and behavior, but the elements *themselves* are separated in behavioral and structural (active and passive). Coming from one world, the other doesn't fully match. (UML is big, complex and mostly directed at the world of object oriented software engineering, it is not really a good placeholder in this section for software engineering in general and much more can be said about it, but I thought the juxtaposition was nice).

So, both in business descriptions and in software engineering, many people see structure as something that 'encapsulates behavior'. In ArchiMate, it is possible to suggest a structure that encapsulates behavior as can be seen in View 112.

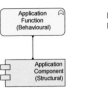 

View 112. *Nesting a behavioral object inside an active object to suggest encapsulation*

On the left you see the un-nested model, with an Assignment relation between the Application Component and the behavior of that component: the Application Function. On the right, a visualization suggesting encapsulation using ArchiMate's Nesting relation, here used for Assigned-To (nesting is one of those parts where ArchiMate is pretty unclear as it can mean (a mix of) three different relation types. I personally almost exclusively use Nesting for Composition between elements and, with a bit of reluctance, Aggregation). Note: though this nesting suggests encapsulation, it does not *mean* encapsulation. "Encapsulation of behavior equals structure" does not exist in ArchiMate.

Back to the business layer. ArchiMate's definition for a Business Process is:

A business process is defined as a behavior element that groups behavior based on an ordering of activities. It is intended to produce a defined set of products or business services.

ArchiMate's definition of a Business Function is:

A business function is defined as a behavior element that groups behavior based on a chosen set of criteria (typically required business resources and/or competences).

In summary, both are behavioral and both group the *same* activities (but from a different perspective). ArchiMate 2.1 makes also clear in its explanation that both process and function are the behavior of a single role and that if you want to model behavior of multiple roles, you should use a Business Interaction, which is the behavior of a Business Collaboration.

So, a Business Process groups behavior based on what it *produces*. It is a grouping based on an 'outside' parameter: the *result* of the activities. A Business Process is therefore an 'outside-in' grouping of behavior. A Business Function groups activities based on an 'inside'-parameter: what resources and capabilities it needs. A Business Function is therefore an 'inside-out' grouping of (potentially the same) behavior.

Both Business Process and Business Function both are *behavior* in ArchiMate. For Business Process, that is not surprising for most of us. But for Business Function, that differs from other approaches where a function is considered 'structural'. In ArchiMate, Business Function is *purely* behavioral, it is itself behavior that may be a grouping of (sub)behavior. So, where is the structure that performs it? Well, according to the definition, a (single) Business Role (in practice often a role fulfilled by a department). So, where a business function in other approaches may be a structure that encapsulates behavior and thus be structure and behavior in one, in ArchiMate, a Business Function is pure behavior and it is performed by a different, structural element: a Business Role. (ArchiMate 2.0 repaired the somewhat confusing definition of a Business Role in ArchiMate 1.0 as (named) *behavior*).

And what about grouping/encapsulating of Application Component and Application Function? Same here and even nicer. Because at the application level, ArchiMate kind of sees the same sort of 'encapsulation' on both sides. Application Function may be an encapsulation (by means of a composition) of other Application (sub)Functions and Application Component may be an encapsulation (by means

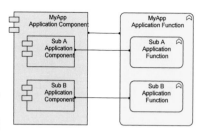

View 113. *Encapsulation of Application Sub-Components and Application Sub-Functions*

of a composition) of other Application (sub) Components. Between the Application (sub) Functions and Application (sub)Components is a one-on-one Performed-By relation. As can be seen in nested form in View 113.

Seeing the composition of Application Functions on the right easily makes one use the word 'structure'. And indeed, in a sense, there is a 'structure' in the Application Function, as it is a composition of Application (sub)Functions. But though there is a 'structure', that does not mean the element itself is 'structural' *in ArchiMate's sense*. Paraphrasing Uncle Ludwig: watch out for 'bewitchment by language'. The fact that you are using (almost) the same word ('structure') does not automatically make it the same meaning.

10.2 Business Function or Business Process?

So, a rather tricky part of ArchiMate is the difference between Business Process and Business Function. Both stand for behavior at the Business Level. Both generally encapsulate in the end the same activities. Choosing between a Business Function and a Business Process is sometimes difficult. It is like the eternal question about the chicken and the egg. Note: there is a large part of the architectural community that thinks it is not difficult at all. For them, a process is a chain of functions. But the story is more complex.

Question 4. Now that I'm mentioning it: Which *was* first, the chicken or the egg?

Answer 4. The egg. The first chicken egg was a mutation laid by a pre-chicken from a mutated seed or egg cell. A chicken is the means by which an egg makes another egg.

ArchiMate in its prenatal form used to have a concept called Business Activity. This would stand for a lowest level, indivisible, piece of business behavior It was not to have any constituent parts. Business Function and Business Process would then be an Aggregation of- business behavior elements, either Business Function, Business Process or Business Activity. In an 'unfolded' picture that lacks the abstract 'Business Behavior' concept, it looks like View 114.

View 114. *Pre-ArchiMate 1.0 relations between Business Process, Business Function and Business Activity*

TOG dropped activity in the 1.0 spec. I do not know why exactly, but I can imagine a couple of reasons:

- It is difficult to decide when something becomes indivisible;

- It is difficult to come up with a clear distinct definition of Business Activity that is neither inside-out or outside-in.

My initial approach to combining the different roles of Business Function and Business Process in our ArchiMate models was close to this original, but with a small twist. In our company it was still customary to think of Business Processes as being a sort of 'chain' of Business Functions (as is often the way architects look at the division) and in ArchiMate this can become a Business Process that has aggregated Business Function children. I proceeded to make that view symmetric in that one could also say that a Business Function aggregates the Business Processes it contributes to. This can be seen in View 115.

(I had removed activity as it is not part of ArchiMate 1.0) In this way, I took the classic approach and made it nicely symmetric. Both are then just overlapping (not necessarily orthogonal) views of the *same* business behavior. Say, a wave/particle

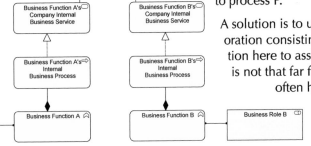

View 115. *A Business Process Aggregates Business Functions and a Business Function Aggregates Business Processes*

view of something that is essentially the same thing, one 'measured' from the aspect of what it produces (process, outside-in) and one of what it requires (function, inside-out). I can personally live with that Quantum-Mechanical-like ambiguity, but it is not to everybody's liking. Therefore, I dropped that way for another, because we actually can be more precise in our thinking using ArchiMate's core relations from the metamodel as guidance.

Suppose we do indeed see process as a kind of 'chaining' of functions, what are we actually saying, ArchiMate-wise? Chaining is not an ArchiMate relation, after all. Luckily, ArchiMate has a good relation for this: Used-By. So, what we can say is that a Business Process *uses* the Business Functions in some way (instead of both being aggregates of each other). But, in ArchiMate, how does a process use a function? Well, a Business Process can use a Business Service, which in its turn is provided by the Business Function.

But if you want to model the behavior that *Realizes* something (like a Business Service), the preferred option is a Business Process and not a Business Function. After all a Business Process is 'intended to produce a service'. So we must ask ourselves: if a Business Function Realizes a Business Service what *process* actually realizes that service? Well, that must then be an *internal* process of the Business Function. The result is something like View 116. Here we see a Business Process that uses ('chains')

two different Business Functions to realize a Business Service. The roles are assigned to the functions, that according to ArchiMate should be performed by a single role. The internal processes of the functions have here been modeled as composites of the function, not aggregates. That is logical, because the *internal* process of a business function ceases to exist if you delete the business function.

This pattern can of course be repeated infinitely, i.e. the internal process uses multiple internal sub-functions and their internal sub-processes. I think you should be careful with that, as it fragments your model. It depends on the future questions you want to answer with the help of the model if those details are really useful.

You may prefer nesting to strengthen the visual message here. Under water, the composition relation is still there, but showing it embedded is kind of nice in this case, as can be seen in View 117.

Now, the question must be asked: which role(s) actually perform(s) "Business Process P" in View 117? This depends on the organization of the company. Maybe there is an explicit steering role for that process (which has some difficulties if you go into it). In absence of such a steering role we could think that both Role A and Role B are assigned to Process P. But the (ArchiMate) derived relations between said roles and process from the model above are not Assigned-To but *Used-By* (performs+composite+realizes+used-by = used-by), so it would be confusing to have both Assigned-To and Used-By from roles B and A to process P. Therefore, we need another separate role to assign to process P.

A solution is to use a Business Collaboration consisting of the roles in question here to assign to the process. This is not that far from what in reality often happens. In many companies we will see some sort of very loose and thin 'collaboration'. Payments just pays what Claim Handling has approved and they only communicate when it is about the process itself or when something is amiss (which in turn is often all that they collaborate about). There is no separate role making sure that everything happens. Yes, there are (as oversight) process

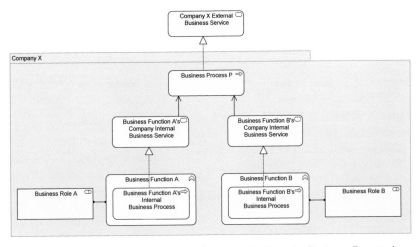

View 116. *A Business Function's internal process Realizes a Business Service*

View 117. *A Business Function's internal process Realizes the Business Function's service, nested view*

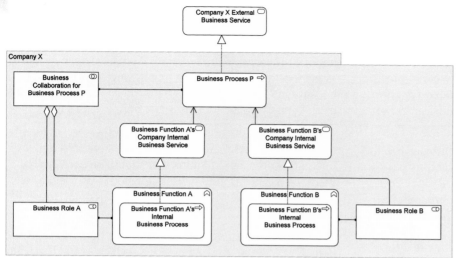

View 118. *A Business Process using Business Functions is performed by a (loose) Business Collaboration*

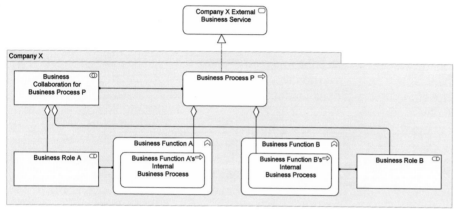

View 119. *End-to-end process made up from parts of functions instead of using independent functions*

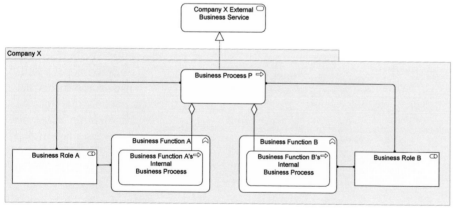

View 120. *End-to-end process made up from parts of functions instead of using independent functions, with informal collaboration*

owner roles for the internal processes of function A and B so their internal process is such that collaboration *can* actually happen. But these, as we will see in Section 12 "Secondary and Tertiary Architecture" on page 89, are quite different roles than those that are assigned to performing the function. Anyway, an example of loose/thin collaboration would be something like View 118 (note: this is sloppy ArchiMate as the collaboration is assigned to a process and not to an interaction as is proper).

Depending on how the operating model of your organization actually is, a different picture may emerge of course.

If instead of using an 'end-to-end' process that *uses* functions, but we model the End-to-end process as a Business Interaction and notice that it can Realize a Business Service, you can wonder about the internal setup of that interaction. ArchiMate just says the interaction is performed by the collaboration and leaves it at that. But if you look deeper, what happens when different roles collaborate?

The first thing is that if different roles collaborate, it is their separate behaviors in the collaboration that *together* create the interaction. These separate behaviors will somehow be recognizable as such also, or you will not be able to define the interaction in your business manuals. If two Business Functions together somehow create the Business Interaction, it is either an 'interaction of processes' or 'an interaction of functions'. Since an interaction is directed at *realizing* something (a service for instance) it is best to use processes. We'll show an example below when we look at the relation between ArchiMate Enterprise Architecture modeling and Business Process Modeling.

The *Business Process P* in View 118 is modeled as some independent entity: a separate process that uses the services provided by the internal Business Processes of the separate Business Functions. But a problem exists: that separate process using the services of other does not really exist. In reality, that process is made up of the processes of the different functions. So, we can simplify. The first step in simplification can be seen in View 119. Here the Business Services have been removed and the internal Business Processes of the Business Functions have been Aggregated into the End-to-end Business Process P.

Actually, we can simplify one more time. Using the 'informal collaboration' technique (see section 2.1 "Collaboration and Interaction" on page 23) we can make a very simple diagram indeed. This is not 'perfect ArchiMate' but it clearly can be interpreted as the same. Using 'informal collaborations' has the added advantage that you do not have to name that collaboration, which is especially advantageous if you have many of these that nobody but your Enterprise Architecture modeling language requires. View 120 just communicates a lot easier than View 118.

In section 25 "Linking BPMN and ArchiMate" on page 156 we will see an even more drastic simplification when the whole process structure of the enterprise has been siphoned off to BPMN models which are linked to ArchiMate models.

If we take the approach in View 118 and map it to the application layer, we would get the situation that we might say that an Application Function has its own internal Application Process, a concept that does not exist in ArchiMate. Should it? The 'Application Process' realizes Application Service and Application Function is grouped based on Data Objects and Infrastructure Services required? Should Application Process stand for the algorithm that produces the result? It might give a nice starting point when you think about business rule engines. Still, as we are not discussing changing the language here, but describing how to use it as it is, we will not go into that here. Besides, at the Application Layer, it is pretty difficult to split the idea of a function and a process. However you model it, one can be turned perfectly into the other.

10.3 Good Old Fashioned Business Function

In Section 10.1 on page 75, I discussed the structural/behavioral divide in ArchiMate and how it differs from the 'old school' Business Function (something I call the GOFBF or Good-Old Fashioned Business Function in honor of Hubert Dreyfus, the philosopher who wrote *What Computer's (Still) Can't Do*, but I digress), the 'structural' function that encapsulates 'behavior'. Here, I'll show a way to model this in ArchiMate.

The full world of a Business Function delivering services to the organization can be modeled like View 121. The gray box contains the 'old school' business function. The structure (role with sub roles) and the behavior (function and internal processes). That doesn't look like 'encapsulation' yet, but using ArchiMate's Nesting visualization, we can make a view that suggests the encapsulation as in View 122. It is a bit nasty, this one, because the relation between 'A Business Role' and 'ArchiMate Type Business Function X' is Assigned-To, something not always expected of an ArchiMate Nesting.

We can simplify this picture further as can be seen in View 123 (note, all these views come from the same model, they are just presented in different ways to convey a different message). The Realization relations from 'ArchiMate Type Business Function X' to 'Service A of Function X' and 'Service B of Function X' are derived from Composition (from function to process) and Realization (from process to service).

We can remove ArchiMate's Business Function from the view and summarize one level further to get one single element in the gray grouping of View 124. And there you have it: a GOFBF viewed as a structure encapsulating behavior. Conclusion: If you want to model a GOFBF, you should use Business Role in ArchiMate. Incidentally, ArchiMate says that a Business Function or a Business Process must be seen as the *internal* behavior of a Business Role. So, there you have it, the solution was there already from the start...

10.4 The 'End-to-end' Business Process

In Business Process Modeling many model without functions at all. They model so-called 'end-to-end' processes that consist of steps and subprocesses that are performed by different roles. This is different from ArchiMate and that has to do with ArchiMate's split of active and behavioral elements.

To explain that, I am starting with a view that depicts the thinking of a process modeler (View 125 on page 80). The process modeler looks at the end-to-end process as a series of subprocesses or process steps that are performed by different roles or actors in the organization. Note: View 125 suggests something not exactly ArchiMate. For instance, though the subprocesses are nested in the roles (thus modeling swim lanes) the subprocesses are *also* embedded in the end-to-end process. In my model, the subprocesses are aggregate children of the end-to-end process, but in the view, the end-to-end process is positioned *graphically* behind the role 'swim lanes'. (I can also nest the roles inside the end-to-end process in my tool, even if they stick out.)

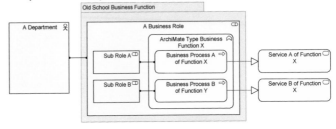

View 122. *An ArchiMate Business Function, with two internal processes (nested), roles and services realized*

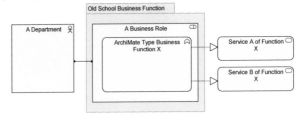

View 123. *An ArchiMate Business Function realizing two services with internal processes omitted from View 122*

View 124. *A Good-Old-Fashioned-Business-Function becomes a Business Role in ArchiMate, further simplified from View 123*

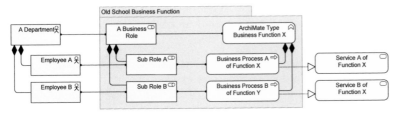

View 121. *An ArchiMate Business Function, with two internal processes, roles and services realized*

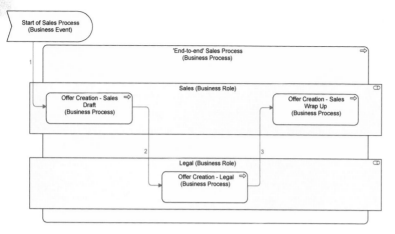

View 125. *How the process modeler looks at the 'end-to-end' process in a 'swim lanes' kind of view*

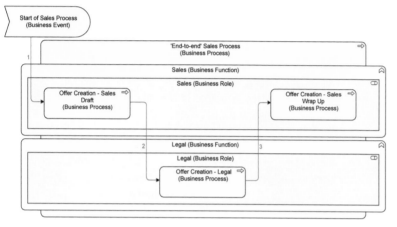

View 126. *Business Functions added to the process modeler's View 125, the GOFBF way*

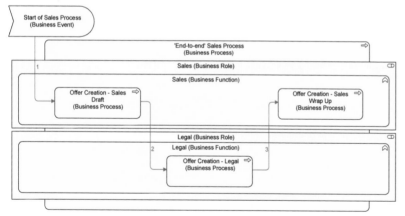

View 127. *The process modeler's View 125, with functions added the (kind of) ArchiMate way*

The first thing you may wonder about is the question where the Business Functions are. And indeed, most of the time I have talked with business process modelers they tend to ignore the functional division of the organization, other than the roles. In fact, this is one of the ways the GOFBF-thinking manifests itself. The process modelers do not make the separation of role and function too clearly. Process modelers tend to see a business function as an 'actor' of sorts in the GOFBF way. The Process Modeler's 'business function' X *performs* Y, whereas in ArchiMate the business function is just another categorization of behavior *of* actors (X is *performed by* a role).

We can add the Business Functions for which the subprocesses are internal processes. This can be seen in View 126 and View 127.

If you think in the GOFBF-way, where 'functions' are structural with roles inside them, you get View 126 (remember, this all is not really proper ArchiMate) In ArchiMate, the nesting of roles and functions toggles: a function may be nested *within* a role (thus depicting the Assigned-To relation to the roles' behavior). This can be seen in View 127.

Note, this is borderline clean modeling in ArchiMate. The Nestings of processes inside functions depict Compositions, the Nestings of functions inside roles depict Assignment and the Aggregation relation between the end-to-end process and the subprocesses is not really shown.

We can model the end-to-end process in ArchiMate also according to the patterns used in Section 10.2 "Business Function or Business Process?" on page 76. View 128 on page 81 is in fact equivalent (with the exception of the added client) to View 127, though some relations are now shown explicitly but instead in the form of Nesting.

We have another option. We can use a Business Interaction to model the 'end-to-end' process. After all, the 'end-to-end' process is performed by a collaboration of the roles that perform the processes that 'make up' the interaction. This can be seen in View 129 on page 81.

If we follow strictly what ArchiMate says about interactions being just the behavior of a collaboration (ArchiMate, remember, says nothing about the interaction being an Aggregate collection of processes like it says the collaboration is an Aggregate of roles) we get View 130. The problem here is that you lose the direct relation between the 'end-to-end' process and its constituent parts. Since ArchiMate does not forbid the approach of View 128 or View 129, these can be used. The advantage of using the Business Interaction as in View 129 is that you can see for every 'end-to-end' process exactly which roles are required where and this remains the case when you start to get more complex models with sub-roles, etc.

10.5 Business Process Modeling versus Business Layer Architecture

There is one aspect with modeling where I have encountered a fundamental different outlook between some Business Process Modelers and ArchiMate. That difference is their attitude towards automation.

When these process modelers look at the position of automation in the business processes, some tend to focus solely of what they can describe of the human part of the process. The automation part has to be described elsewhere (in the documentation of the systems). This means that if a process is automated, in the eyes of these business process modelers

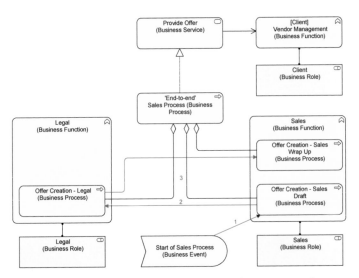

View 128. *The end-to-end process as a chain of processes, without using collaboration and interaction*

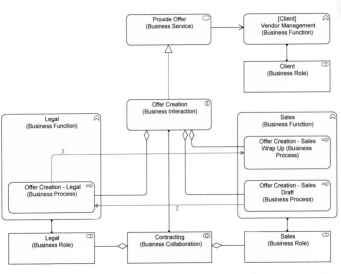

View 129. *End-to-end process modeled as Business Interaction (with added Aggregate relations to the subprocesses)*

it disappears from their radar. It has become automation, not process. ArchiMate, however, looks at it differently. Even if a business process is automated, there still is a business process.

Personally, I think ArchiMate is superior. The way to look at automation as something that is 'used-by' human processes is only part of the story. More and more, automation runs processes entirely by itself. For most companies, fully automating certain processes and making the business architecture 'STP' (Straight-Through Processing) and 'Exception Based' is the norm. But process modelers are not often well aware of Enterprise Architecture's integral view of the landscape and look at it 'the old way'. The best way to confront the issue is to ask what would happen in their models if a process was fully automated. Where, in that case, do we find the process?

Note that the process modeler's view is easier on the business user who generally does not think in abstractions like a 'Report Definitions (Business Object)' but thinks of the 'reportdefinition.xls' file.

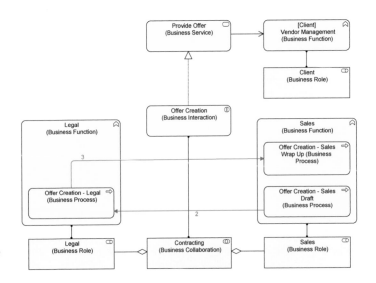

View 130. *The end-to-end process modeled as a Business Interaction, strictly following the description of Business Interaction in the Archi-Mate 2.0 specification*

11. How ArchiMate Can Help To Choose Your Business Functions

11.1 Dividing your enterprise's behavior into Business Functions

Having discussed how to combine Business Functions and Business Processes, let's look at an actual discussion I once had with other architects. For this, I first need to make a short and simplified description of what was under discussion.

In Asset Management, portfolio managers (or fund managers, etc.) manage assets. They have a portfolio of holdings,

stocks, bonds, or maybe ownership of shopping malls etc. They manage these holdings generally along three aspects:

- Performance: what does this investment actually deliver in profits?

- Risk: what is the risk associated with this investment? How uncertain are the profits or the value of this investment?

- Compliance: are we following the restrictions set upon us? An example may be that the client has told you not to invest in weapons. Or the organization has generic risk-minimizing rules like that you are not allowed to invest in certain countries, or trade with certain counter-parties, or invest in certain types of instruments (like junk bonds).

Asset Managers try to maximize financial performance while minimizing financial risk. In the meantime they all work under the assumption that there is generally an inverse relation between the two, so if there are more risks, they will want to see more performance. E.g.: riskier bonds have to pay out more interest, safer bonds deliver less. They try to mix assets with different risk profiles as these combine generally into a lower risk of the portfolio. They also try to minimize their own cost and they have to comply to the compliancy rules.

Now, the process (simplified) is as follows. Each day, the portfolio manager inspects his portfolio and the news in the world. When inspecting his portfolio, he tries to assess future performance, he assesses risk (often based on all sorts of statistical calculations) and then he may decide to buy or sell something. When he has decided (say, buy $100 million worth of Zimbabwean diamond mining stock), there will be a phase of so called 'ex ante' (Latin for 'before') compliance checking. There are many kinds of checks, based on rules set by a different department, the `investment control' department. Generally, this department monitors performance, risk and compliance and sets the rules for compliance. One of those rules may be that there is a limited list of countries the portfolio manager is allowed to invest in, and Zimbabwe is not on that list. The check bears this out and such the order is not passed on to the trading desk.

Some asset managers let the portfolio managers or traders do their own compliance checking on the basis of the instructions, like the `allowed country list'. Some separate these duties away from the portfolio manager to make it less likely a portfolio manager enters into a deal that has to be rolled back. Of course, the risk difference between the two are limited as any compliance break will turn up when the 'ex post' (Latin for 'after') checking at the end of the day is performed by investment control.

Now, here is the discussion: When architects discuss the business architecture of this asset manager and they want to divide the activities up into business functions, the question arises: is 'ex ante' (what happens before the deal) compliance checking part of the 'portfolio management' business function or part of the 'compliance control' business function, which also has 'ex post' (after the deal) checking? Two things get easily mixed up here: functions and processes on the one hand and roles and actors on the other. But let's start with an initial view of the processes and objects involved as seen in View 131. `Investing' processes are:

- Check the portfolio against performance and risk parameters;
- Make an investment decision;
- Check the decision against compliance rules;
- Make the deal (trade).

The compliance processes (we have limited ourselves to compliance here, you have also processes that measure risk and performance) are:

- Create the compliance rules and objects;
- Monitor the trades and positions against compliance rules;
- Check the decision against compliance rules.

The latter can be seen as part of both 'investing' and 'controlling', it seems, and in fact organizations disagree on this point. Some see it as 'investing', just as checking performance and risk are part of the normal activities of a portfolio manager (View 132). Others see it as part of all of the 'compliance' activities that are performed by a different group than the portfolio managers, say the investment control department (View 133). This difference is in fact based on difference in actors more than in other differences. In ArchiMate that is actually a pretty decent reason for separating activities into different Business Functions as functions are groupings based on shared resources, skills, etc., which are performed by a single role.

So far, so good. Let's add those roles and actors to the main Business Functions in both solutions. The Portfolio Manager role performs the Portfolio Management Business Function and the Compliance Officer role performs the Compliance Control Business Function. When the 'Ex-Ante Compliance' is seen as part of 'controlling', performed by a compliance officer, it looks like View 135 on page 84. When 'Ex Ante Compliance' is seen as part of 'investing', it looks like View 134. Both are pretty clean views.

But 'being performed by a compliance officer' is just *one* possible reason to separate activities into a Business Function. There are many more, other resources, for instance. And suppose we would have the following situation: the

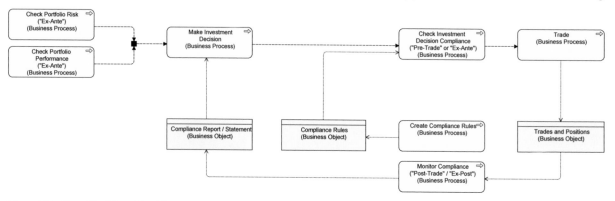

View 131. *Simplified Portfolio Management without Business Functions*

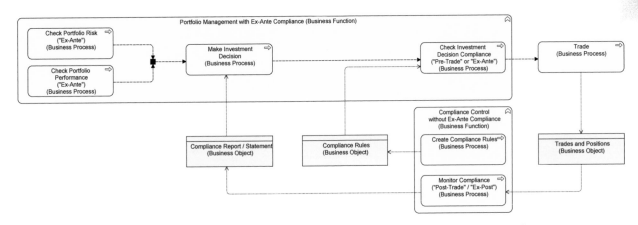

View 132. *Simplified Portfolio Management with Ex-Ante Compliance as part of Portfolio Management function*

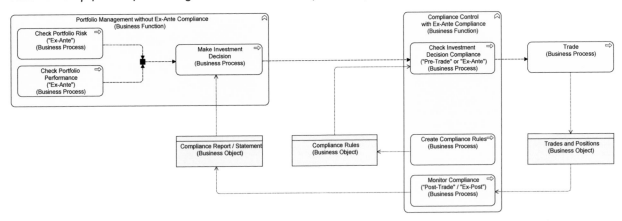

View 133. *Simplified Portfolio Management with Ex-Ante Compliance as part of Compliance Control function*

portfolio manager does the 'Ex Ante Compliance' check, but 'Ex Ante' compliance checking is still seen as part of the 'compliance' *function*, e.g. because it is supported by the same IT services as the other processes that are part of the compliance function. Well, that is possible as well. It looks like View 136 on page 85. The 'compliance' function now has two processes that are performed by the compliance officer and one that is performed by the portfolio manager.

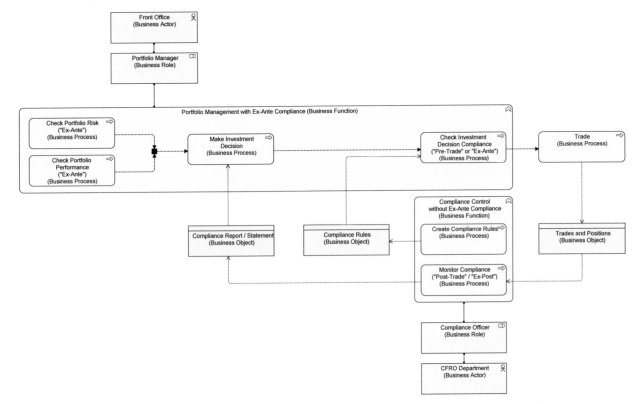

View 134. *Simplified Portfolio Management with Ex-Ante Compliance as part of the Portfolio Management function*

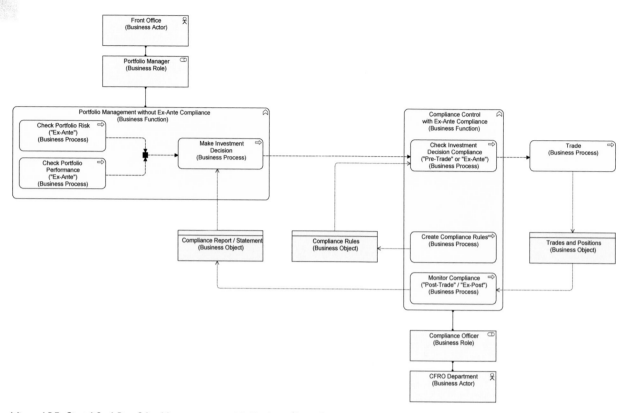

View 135. *Simplified Portfolio Management with Ex-Ante Compliance as part of the Compliance Control Function*

View 137 contains the reverse split: the compliance officer role performs a step in the portfolio management function. ArchiMate has no formal problem with writing it this way (though it may be frowned upon), we look at Business Functions and Business Roles independently and we can have a Business Function where the internal processes are performed by multiple roles. The question that arises of course is: what Business Role needs to be assigned to the overall 'compliance' Business Function in View 136 on page 85? We have a function, but who performs it? It must be a single role, according to ArchiMate. The solution is to use a Collaboration, as in View 138 on page 86.

Summarizing: if you want all 'compliance' activities in one Business Function, but not all processes of that function are performed by the same role, you end up with a Collaboration that is needed in your model to perform the function. To make the set of examples complete, have a look at View 140 on page 87. Here the Portfolio Management function is performed by a Collaboration.

Question 5. Can you spot the incorrect ArchiMate in View 138 and View 140?

Answer 5. Collaborations may only be Assigned-To Interactions.

Though ArchiMate suggests that a function should be performed by a single role, this role can well be a Collaboration (which itself is a type of role), though the function then becomes an interaction. Function and *actual* Role being disjunct could therefore very well be the case if you have other characteristics that drive your grouping into Business Functions. I personally would advise against it, though. Because if your Business Function landscape differs widely

from your Business Role landscape, it will be very difficult for everybody to keep track. In other words: being performed by a single recognizable role is an important potential dividing characteristic for dividing your landscape up in Business Function, just as ArchiMate suggests.

Now, if you step back from all the possibilities of modeling for a while, and you look at it from an Asset Management perspective, some of these models will be considered as plain silly by investment professionals. But that is in fact more about how they are used to look at things, than that the models are 'wrong'.

Personally, I would indeed use the 'single Business Role' as an important characteristic for separation into Business Functions. So, at an Asset Manager where the portfolio manager does 'Ex Ante' compliance checking, I would go for separating into Business Functions according to View 134 on page 83 (and not like View 135). But if the compliance officer does the 'Ex Ante' compliance checking, I would probably *still* go for View 140 on page 87 and not View 136, the reason being that the whole chain of portfolio management to trading has quite a different beat to it (continuous, straight through processing) than the batch-like daily measurement of *the rest of* compliance, let alone the once in a while change (creation) of compliance rules. In other words: Business Role is an important characteristic for separation into Business Functions, but it is not by definition the *only* characteristic. Time patterns may be an important characteristic as well. And there are more. In fact, 'Ex Ante' compliance checking is so weakly connected to the skills of either portfolio manager or compliance officer, if you choose View 134 on page 83 or View 140 on page 87, your main division into Business Functions stays the same, even if

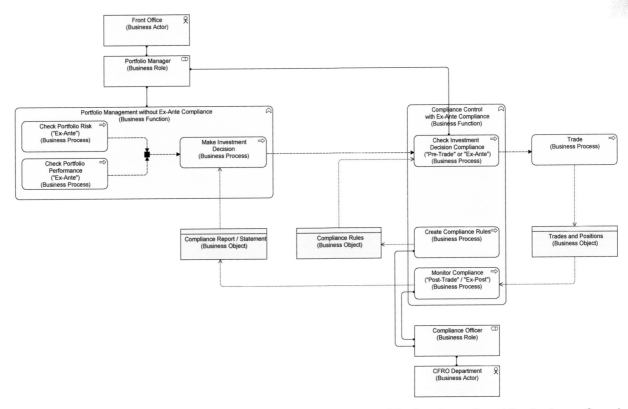

View 136. *Simplified Portfolio Management with Ex-Ante Compliance part of the Compliance Control function but performed by the Portfolio Manager role*

the company decides to change the assignment of 'ex ante' compliance checking from a portfolio manager to a compliance officer (or the other way around).

So, here you see it again: there is no simple answer on how you should model, just as having a grammar does not mean

you know which sentences evoke the best effect in your reader.

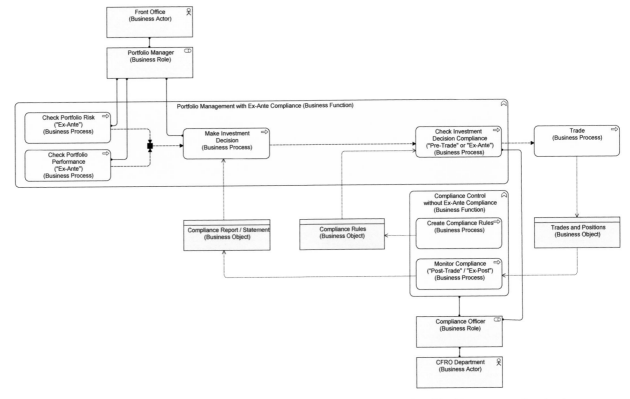

View 137. *Simplified Portfolio Management with Ex-Ante Compliance part of the Portfolio Management function but performed by the Compliance Officer role*

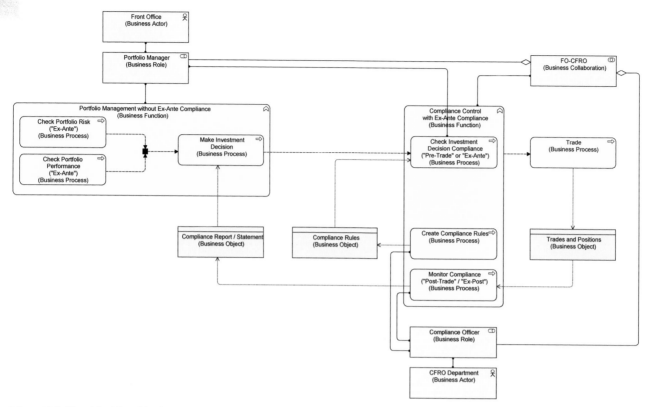

View 138. *Simplified Portfolio Management with the Compliance Control function performed by a Collaboration of Portfolio Manager and Compliance Officer*

11.2 Concurrent Functional Landscapes

So, among the most difficult Enterprise Architecture discussions are discussions on separating your business layer into Business Functions. The previous example already gave an example on how something can easily (and properly) be seen as a part of two different functions. But even after you have created your ideal functional decomposition, keeping it for all uses may not be the best thing to do.

Take the following example: in Asset Management, we can have — amongst all our functions — the following two functional decompositions: 'fund accounting' on the one hand and 'payments & cash' on the other hand. Both generally have to do with business objects that are being held in the outside world: banks have the bank accounts where the cash is, custodians have the custodian accounts that hold the non-cash assets, e.g. stocks and bonds. If we buy stock from another party via the stock exchange, we enter into a deal, which is then confirmed by both sides and then follows 'settlement'. Settlement means: we instruct our bank to

send cash from our bank account to the other party's bank account and they instruct their custodian to send stocks from their custodian account to ours. It often takes some time for this to be completed, say 3 business days. At the end of each day, our bank sends us a bank statement with all our transactions of that day and the end cash position on that account. The custodian does the same on our holdings. When we strike the deal, we put in our accounting system that we will receive the stocks in three days, and we also put there that we will have pay out cash which they will receive in 3 days. But in both cases, we also check afterwards if what has actually happened is the same as what we said would happen. Such checking is called `reconciliation'.

Functionally, we might have a 'Cash & Payments' Business Function and a 'Fund Accounting' Business Function. This is because handling custody and handling cash are quite different in processes, outside contacts, skills, etc.. So, our 'Cash & Payments' Business Function cotains a daily 'Reconcile Cash Accounting with Bank Statements' Business Process, while the 'Fund Accounting' Business Function contains a 'Reconcile Holdings against Custodian Records' Business Process.

So far, so good, but reconciliation is a pretty basic set of activities: you have the records of someone else, you have your own records, you compare records and you handle the exceptions (called 'breaks' in reconciliation lingo). In terms of IT support, the activities are almost the same, even if they differ substantially at the business level. Hence there are systems that in a generic fashion support 'reconciliation': comparing two sets of data and support the work flow of those checks and the handling of any finding.

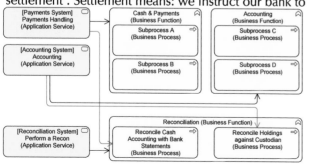

View 139. *A separate Reconciliation Business Function still uses the accounting and payments systems for exception handling*

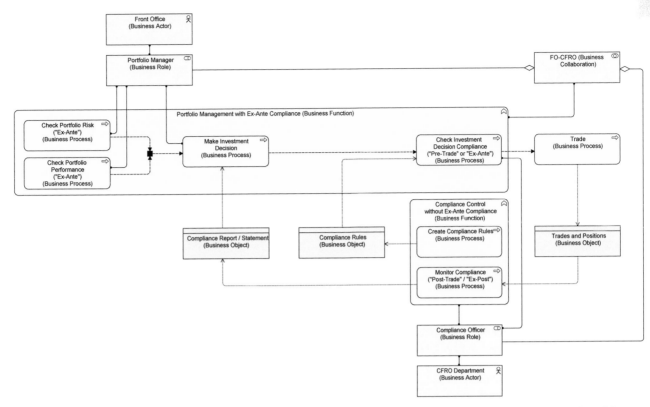

View 140. *Simplified Portfolio Management with the Portfolio Management function performed by a Collaboration of Portfolio Manager and Compliance Officer*

So, when you let Enterprise Architects — instead of the Business — discuss the functional decomposition of your business, they — knowing how much each reconciliation technically and operationally looks like another — tend to want to group all reconciliation in a 'Reconciliation' Business Function. They look not just at the business layer, they are focused on the effects on the IT landscape and when you take those underlying operations into account, a single grouping of all reconciliation seems logical, especially if in the back of your head, you are already thinking forward to the process of selecting the right platform for 'Reconciliation'. Feeling strongly, both sides, business and architecture, fight fanatically for what they see as the 'correct' separation in disjunct Business Functions.

The simplified view without a separate Reconciliation Business Function looks like View 141.

The Cash & Payments Business Function is supported by the Payments System, the Accounting Business Function is supported by the Accounting system. Both have reconciliation processes, which are supported by the Reconciliation system. Note: I am not saying Asset management is to be modeled like this, say, that the Cash & Payments Business Process does not need the Accounting system, I am just

making a theoretical example as simple as possible. The real world is more complex.

When we model a separate Reconciliation Business Function, it might look like View 142.

I have, however, not been entirely complete. Because even if technically and operationally the actual data reconciliation only requires the Reconciliation system, handling 'breaks' (exceptions) will still require the Accounting System for holdings reconciliation and the Payments system for the cash reconciliation. If these are added, it looks like View 139 on page 86.

The added red Used-By relations show that the reconciliation (as seen from a *business* and not *IT* perspective) still requires access to the accounting or payments system. In fact, in a derived way, these relations were already there in View 141, so one could argue from this example that you need not create a separate Reconciliation Business Function in your model, but that is not the point of this story.

View 141. *Cash & Payments function and Accounting Function both have a reconciliation process*

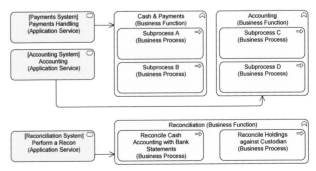

View 142. *A separate Reconciliation Business Function*

The point is that if you look at it from a technical point of view, there is something like the bare technical and operational capability to handle reconciliations generically. In the views, it is what the 'Perform a Recon' Application Service supports. And if you start looking for ways how your IT is going to support your business, it is not a smart idea to handle both reconciliations separately. You might end up with an IT solution for the first one that is incompatible with the second one, forcing you to two systems or a migration. It is a smart idea to look at supporting the technical and operation aspects of doing a reconciliation in one go. The fact that business-wise the reconciliation process need access to their respective source systems to handle the exceptions does not mean that reconciliation itself is supported by either an Accounting or a Payments Application Service.

The two ways of looking at it are based on two different approaches to separation into Business Functions which we described above. One approach sees a Business Function akin to a capability to *do* something. The Business Processes make use of that capability or are made up of 'strings' of those capabilities. In that way of looking, the 'Reconcile Holdings against Custodians' makes use of both the Reconciliation capability and the Accounting capability. Both capabilities offer services to that Business Process. In this approach, the Business Processes are not the internal structure of a Business Function, the Processes are 'on top' of the Business Functions. Both ways of looking (as described here) are valid, in my opinion.

If you want to choose between making Reconciliation (or whatever your choice) a separate Business Function or not, ArchiMate helps in the sense that it says that a Business Function should be performed by a single Business Role. So, in case you have a clearly defined single Business Role that performs all 'reconciliations' (e.g. in an operational or technical sense that hands the results to other functions like Accounting or Payments to handle the exceptions), there is a decent reason to have a separate Business Function. But in a case like this, it is probably more important to combine monitoring and exception handling of 'holdings reconciliation' into one process that is performed by a single role: someone with knowledge of accounting and custodians and their processes. And the same is true for cash reconciliation. So, though we have reconciliation capabilities in our business, it will be performed in many places by many different roles in different contexts. Creating a single function of it at the business level which is performed by a single *real* role is not a good idea.

Now suppose we do indeed conclude that reconciliation is not a separate Business Function in our business because it is more like a capability that is part of different separate processes. How do we make sure we can take account of all those separate processes when we are looking at supporting the business with IT? Because in that case, it *is* useful to have a 'reconciliation function' that is to be supported by reconciliation Application Services.

The answer is that you nothing stops you to have a different separations into separate Business Functions for that specific goal. Let's go back to ArchiMate's description of what a Business Function is:

A business function is defined as a behavior element that groups behavior based on a chosen set of criteria (typically required business resources and/or competences).

And the specification continues with this explanation:

Just like a business process, a business function also describes internal behavior performed by a business role. However, while a business process group's behavior is based on a sequence or "flow" of activities that is needed to realize a product or service, a business function typically groups behavior based on required business resources, skills, competences, knowledge, etc. that 'make up' the behavior.

There is a potential many-to-many relation between business processes and business functions. Complex processes in general involve activities that offer various functions. In this sense a business process forms a string of business functions. In general, a business function is behavior that delivers added value from a business point of view. Organizational units or applications may coincide with business functions due to their specific grouping of business activities.

As described in Section 10.2 "Business Function or Business Process?" on page 76, if a Business Function is to deliver added value, it has to provide a Business Service. But as a Business Service is to be produced by a Business Process, a Business Function must have *internal* Business Processes that actually Realize those Business Services. Other, higher level, Business Processes may be based on that 'string of Business Functions', but that means the *internal* Business Processes of a Business Function are Used-By the (to the Business Function) *external* Business Processes.

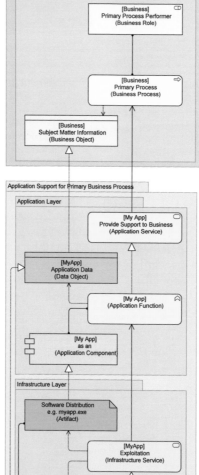

View 143. *The Primary Architecture: Business uses an Application that uses Infrastructure*

But when we use a different set of criteria, we get a different grouping of behavior. If we want to group our business behavior on the basis of the criterium of IT-use, we get a different landscape. In that case, we might prefer the model where Reconciliation is a separate Business Function. In our example, if we follow the criterium 'competences' we get one landscape and if we follow 'IT-resources' we get another.

In summary:

- You divide business behavior up into Business Functions based on criteria;

- Different criteria produce a different landscape;
- Forcing everybody always in one specific landscape, produces irreducible conflicts. Hence, you might end up using multiple 'landscapes';
- Any landscape is based on a grouping of the internal Business Processes of the Business Functions, these must be the same for all landscapes to make sure all landscapes are not contradictory to each other.

I have named the separate IT-resource enterprise landscape the BITMAP: Business-IT Mapping.

12. Secondary and Tertiary Architecture

12.1 Introduction

A while back, when we were building our Current State model somebody posed the question: How are we going to add the 'application owners' to our model? The question arose, because we had decided to use our Current State ArchiMate model as source for our CMDB on which the help-desk software is based. In that database, the help-desk people need to be able to find the owner of the application if something is wrong with it. In fact, our ArchiMate model partly became our CMDB.

Now the easiest way is to create a Business Role that you connect to the Application Component with an Association. That is the quickest way. But working with ArchiMate a lot influences your thinking. So, when somebody came up with the word 'owner', my thought was: "Wait a minute, that sounds like a role...". So, if owner is a Business Role, what Business Process is actually assigned to that Business Role? What, in other words, is 'the owner's process'? What does an 'owner' do actually? And that made me think about other roles surrounding the use of IT: application manager, developer, exploitation manager, architect maybe even. The thinking resulted in an approach that I have christened 'Primary, Secondary and Tertiary Architecture'.

12.2 Primary Architecture

Primary Architecture is what it is all about and what is generally on everybody's mind and what we have been using as example most of the time. An example summary is in View 143 on page 88.

This is what generally is the sole focus of Enterprise Architects: how the business processes are supported by IT. More or less, you see here a small summary of the essentials of the ArchiMate meta-model.

12.3 Secondary Architecture: Development

But as we all know, there is a lot that is needed for this 'Application Support for the Business' to work. Assuming we build our own application (comparable things happen when the application is not built but bought), we need to model the *development* of the application. Application development is a Business Process in itself, which as a result produces the application to be deployed and

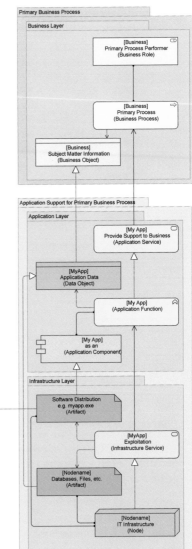

View 144. *The Primary Architecture with the Secondary Development Architecture*

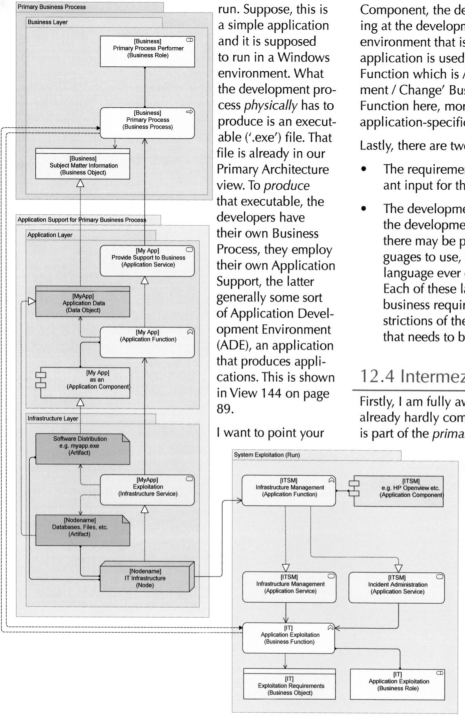

run. Suppose, this is a simple application and it is supposed to run in a Windows environment. What the development process *physically* has to produce is an executable ('.exe') file. That file is already in our Primary Architecture view. To *produce* that executable, the developers have their own Business Process, they employ their own Application Support, the latter generally some sort of Application Development Environment (ADE), an application that produces applications. This is shown in View 144 on page 89.

I want to point your

Component, the developer Accesses a Data Object. Looking at the development process, we see the development environment that is used to create the application. That application is used by the 'Application Change' Business Function which is Assigned-To the 'Application Development / Change' Business Role. Note: I have used a Business Function here, more or less because this behavior is not application-specific. I could have used a process as well.

Lastly, there are two Business Objects:

- The requirements for the application. This is an important input for the development process;

- The development requirements. There are some things the development function cannot handle. For instance, there may be policies regarding the development languages to use, because supporting every development language ever created is just too expensive and risky. Each of these languages comes with restrictions. If a business requirement would be in conflict with the restrictions of the development function, there is a conflict that needs to be resolved. We get back to these later.

12.4 Intermezzo

Firstly, I am fully aware that in most organizations it is already hardly common practice to model everything that is part of the *primary* architecture. So, modeling the development process is something that is generally thought of as 'nice to have'. I agree and that is why I call this 'secondary'. However, the development role must see this as its own *primary* process and would do well to actually get it under control. Having said that, I am not expecting you to model every nook and cranny of your organization. I am using ArchiMate modeling here to make an analysis of the situation, in the end, I will present a short and usable summary that only slightly extends primary architecture.

Secondly: the labeling of the business layer elements has between the []-brackets the proposed part of the organization responsible, generally 'business' or 'IT'.

View 145. *The Primary Architecture with the Secondary Exploitation Architecture*

attention to the fact that the executable Artifact now realizes *two* elements in the Application Layer:

- For the primary business process, the Artifact Realizes an Application Component: an active element that supports the primary process with automation;

- For the (secondary) development process, however, that same Artifact Realizes a Data Object, that is created/updated by the development environment which supports the development process.

In other words, what for the business user is an application, is data for the developer. The user Uses the Application

12.5 Secondary Architecture: System Exploitation

When the developers have delivered the application, it needs infrastructure to function. The application may be deployed on the hardware (the Node), but the 'run' people keep track of the infrastructure smoothly running, etc.. The 'run' people also have a help desk, where users can go to with problems. An example is modeled in View 145. The 'run' people also have Business Processes that are supported by their own Application Services Realized by IT Service

Management (ITSM) software. Two are modeled in the example:

- Infrastructure Management, which means keeping an eye on the infrastructure to check if it is still running properly;
- Incident Management to keep track of incidents, requests etc.

In the example, the Infrastructure Service that the Node Re-

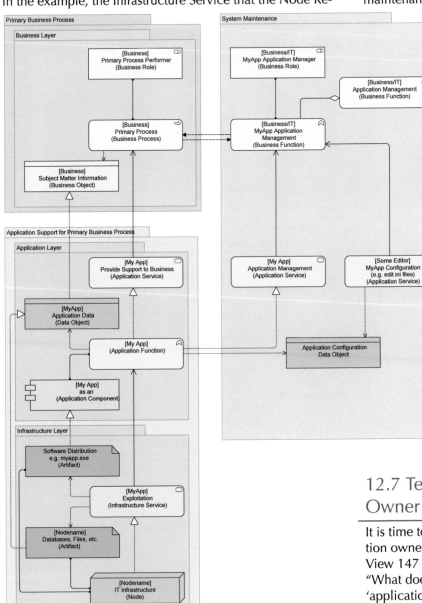

View 146. *The Primary Architecture with the Secondary Application Management Architecture*

alizes for the Infrastructure Management software to use has been left out, what you see is the derived relation between Node and Infrastructure Management software. Additionally, the incident and request information and answers that flow from the primary process to the exploitation process (and back) have been modeled as Flow relations.

In reality, all of this is far more detailed and complex, but the idea of this example is to show how the various aspects of using IT in your organization are related.

12.6 Secondary Architecture: Application Maintenance

The last aspect of Secondary Architecture is application maintenance. Application maintenance consists of things like managing settings of an application, such as user profiles, authorizations, or other maintenance jobs like management reports and such. Generally, in an organization, the larger applications have dedicated application managers who are responsible for these activities.

View 146 on page 91 contains an example. In that example, two patterns have been modeled:

- the application MyApp itself offers application management itself (e.g. screens to modify user's rights and so forth);
- some other (not shown) editor is used by the application manager to edit configuration files which are Accessed by the application.

Furthermore, the business users will communicate with the application managers, this has been modeled by a Flow relation between both Business Processes. And finally, the application management for MyApp has been modeled as being part of an overall Application Management Business Function.

12.7 Tertiary Architecture: Application Owner

It is time to add the role that started this analysis: application owner. The expanded example model can be seen in View 147 on page 92. We return to the original question: "What does an application owner do?", or — since the 'application owner' is clearly a Business Role — "What is the application owner's process?". Here you need to separate the 'application owner' role from all the other roles that actual person may be assigned to, e.g. information manager, department head or whatever. If you think about it that way, than the 'application owner' is above all about one thing: deciding about the 'requirements'. The 'application owner' may tell the developers what to build (remember: a comparable situation arises when systems are bought instead of built) and probably foots the bill. The 'application owner' is a spider in the web: he or she communicates with the users, the developers, the application managers, the infrastructure managers, all of which have a role to play with regards to the requirements. The users want a change? That is a change

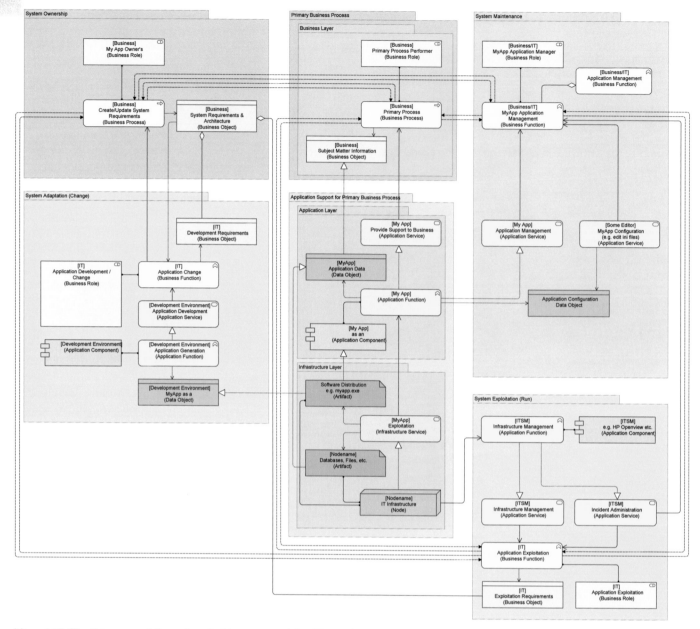

View 147. *The Primary and Secondary Architectures and the (Tertiary) Application Owner Architecture*

of the requirements that has to be decided upon by the 'application owner' role, all the while communicating with other stakeholders like developers and infrastructure managers. Infrastructure managers have their own requirements and so have the developers, their requirements have to be aggregated into the system requirements as well.

You can see there are more spiders in this web: the application managers communicate with all stakeholders and so do the infrastructure managers. After all: who are they going to call when there is a problem with the application which needs a change of that application?

12.8 Tertiary Architecture: other roles

We're almost done with this description. In View 148 on page 93 the final expansion of the example is shown. It adds a few other tertiary roles in summary form. These are: Process Owner, Data Owner and Enterprise Architecture. Remember, these are *roles* (the actual actors may overlap

with other roles). They are shown here primarily because they also have requirements that have to be taken into account by the application owner.

The 'process owner' is responsible for the process description and decides how a business process should run. Often, the 'process owner' is the same as the 'process executive' (which is not shown in this example), the one who is responsible for the execution of the process. Think of a department head who is responsible for the execution of the business process while a business control department may in the end be responsible for way the process must be executed (the process description). The user generally is a subsidiary of the process executive, and often either the process executive or some 'information manager' of his unit fulfills the role of application owner. Anyway, the process description is part of the requirements for an application, as the application is there to support that process after all.

The Data Owner may set policies for data, like retention, security, etc. This role also adds requirements.

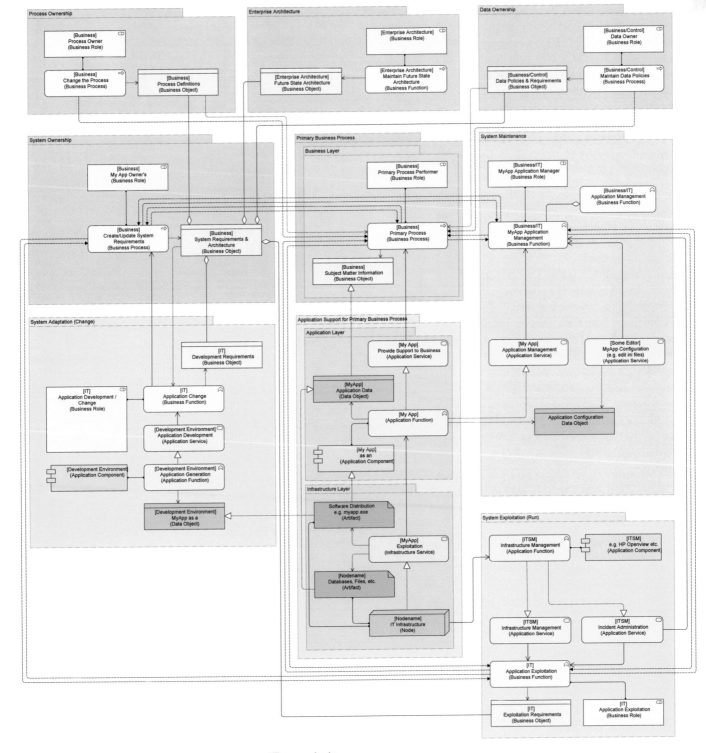

View 148. *The Full Picture: Primary, Secondary and Tertiary Architecture*

Enterprise Architecture may set policies and goals for the way applications are set up and how they interrelate, another addition to the requirements an 'application owner' has to manage.

Finally: the purple groupings are clearly 'business', the orange ones are clearly 'IT' and the gray one can be either.

12.9 Making it Practical: shortcuts

Now if you're in an average organization, you are probably far from realizing the complete model coverage of primary, let alone secondary or tertiary architecture. Maybe, when our discipline matures in a few decennia, it will be normal to do so. But for now, if you have to model all the secondary and tertiary aspects, it is probably a bridge too far. However, it might be good to model the most important roles regarding IT without fully modeling their processes and relate them to the primary architecture. A following set of 9 roles (as seen in View 149) may be sufficient in most cases:

- Run Manager. This is the role that is responsible for the smooth maintenance and running of the infrastructure. This role may be accountable for any SLA that has been agreed on Infrastructure Services, hence we model this as an Association Relation from the Run Manager Role to the Infrastructure Service. The role is generally fulfilled by the IT department.

- Application Manager. This is the classic application manager, the role that changes application settings (e.g. adding/deleting users or authorizations, changing application settings). It is the application functionality that is changed by this role, so we Associate it to the Application Function. This role is in practice fulfilled by many different actors in organizations. Some application managers are part of a business function, some are part of the change/development function, some are part of an IT delivery organization. In View 149, the role is Assigned to the IT Delivery organization.

- Change Manager. This role is responsible for the delivery of the application. If the application is built, these are the people responsible for development. If it is bought, these are the people doing the implementation and configuration. This role is generally fulfilled by IT-oriented (but business-aware) people.

- Application Owner. In the full Secondary-Tertiary approach, this role is responsible for the requirements of the system. What these requirements above all describe, is how the system is going to support the business. This is, so to say, the primary requirement, whereas the requirements from others (run, change, application management, architecture, etc.) are in the end always secondary. That primary part of the requirements is realized by the service the application delivers (to the business), so we Associate the Application Owner role to the Application Service. This role is often fulfilled by a Business Executive or in larger organizations this is delegated to an 'Information Manager'. A nice consequence is that we mirror the difference between 'owner' and 'user' of ITIL, a widely used framework for aligning services with business needs.

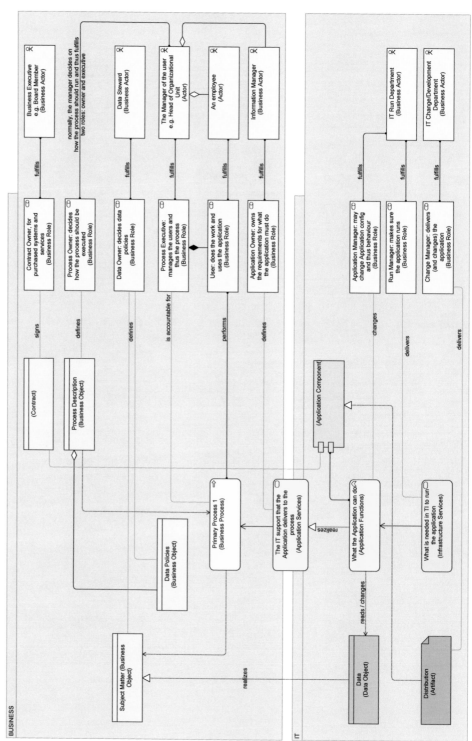

View 149. *Simplified way to model roles from the Primary/Secondary/Tertiary Architecture Analysis*

- User. This is simple, this is the person using the system. We do not need an Association relation, because the User role is part of the primary architecture and the role is already Assigned-To the process that uses the Application Service.

- Process Executive. This is the role that is accountable for the execution of the process. It is generally fulfilled by the management of the user's department. The Process Executive is often not recognized in these descriptions and is often confused with the Application Owner. But in my setup, there is a difference. For instance, in a scenario with a major disturbance to the process because of IT failure, you inform the one responsible for the *process* (the User in this setup) and the one accountable for the *process* (the Process Executive, generally the management). The Information Manager as such does generally not have accountability for the process's execution, he has no operational role. Note: if these roles are fulfilled by the same person, you end up talking to the same person, but that does not mean that person is at that time fulfilling all his or her roles. In the example, I have made the Process Executive the manager of the Information Manager by Aggregating the latter under the former. What I have done here is using the Head of a Department and the Department interchangeably. How you model the manager role of a department is an interesting subject, by the way, which I'm not going further into here, I am just using this shortcut.

- Data Owner. Often, policies, regulations and laws govern data use. A separate owner of the data of a system may be used to design that role.

- Process Owner. This is the role accountable for the way a process is run. In the example, I have Assigned it to the Manager of the User, who also fulfills the Process Executive role. Indeed in practice, these roles are often fulfilled by the same executive. However, in larger organizations, it may be delegated to, for instance, the Information Manager. Note that I have not been perfect with RACI (Responsible-Accountable-Consent-Informed) here, I am just creating a shortcut to model a few stakeholders into your Enterprise Architecture without modeling in full the Enterprise Architecture of those stakeholders.

- Contract Owner. Often, a system is (in part) purchased. There will be a contract that is important when looking at requirements etc. I have modeled this role separately and Assigned it to a top executive, who is generally supported by a Vendor Management function & department.

The most important ones to start with in my experience are the ones from the IT exploitation perspective: Application Owner (Associated with the Application Service), Application Manager (Associated with the Application Function) and Change Manager (Associated with the Distribution). But a usability problem appears when you have applications that Realize multiple independent Application Services or have multiple recognizable Application Functions that need to be modeled.

Note: The summary relationship between Change Manager and the IT system has changed with respect to Edition I of Mastering ArchiMate. The association used to be between Change Manager and Application Component. Why this is and more on complex application is described in Section 18 "Complex Applications" on page 117.

13. Modeling Risk & Security

13.1 Security Architecture

As far as Enterprise Architecture goes, one of the most underdeveloped areas is Security Architecture. It has been mentioned in most Enterprise Architecture frameworks and there are some new frameworks under development. Most of those that I have seen have a fundamental problem, which I'll illustrate with an analogy (always dangerous, analogies).

When Apple launched its own calendaring application (iCal) in 2002 they introduced a new architecture for the concept of a calendar. The calendaring application could hold multiple calendars. You could for instance load the calendar of all the sports matches you want to keep track of. Or you could load a view on another person's calendar (served by iCal Server) in your iCal window. Apple did (it now does, at least on Mac OS X) not offer the option to make appointments in your calendar *private*. Apple reasoned: it is not the *appointment* that is private, it is the *calendar* that is private or public. If you want to have appointments in your calendar that other people cannot see the content of, you need to make a second calendar for yourself with the private appointments.

Now, there is a basic flaw in this reasoning. As I am just a single person, I have only a single life. Which means that for people to be able to see if I'm available as a person, they have to see all my appointments. Hence, just giving them access to my public calendar and not to my private one does not work. Apple fixed this (in Mac OS X, not yet as I write this in iOS), probably under the market force of Microsoft Exchange, but it took them years to come around to the correct point of view (such inertia probably comes with the territory of being too often right ;-).

The analogy with Enterprise Architecture is that there is just a *single Enterprise reality* and thus that having a separate Security Architecture is nonsense. To be useful, Security Architecture must be fully integrated with your Enterprise Architecture, it must — ideally — be an *aspect* of it.

What Security Architecture in its core often is about are the following aspects of information:

- Confidentiality: Information is *only* accessible for those that should have access to it;

- Integrity: Information is correct. In practice this means that it cannot be modified undetectably;

- Accessibility or Availability: Information is available for those that need access to it.

These are the original CIA-aspects. Many frameworks add other aspects, like legally driven aspects such as:

- Authenticity: The source of information can be established with certainty;

- Non-repudiation: In practice this means that a party cannot deny certain information, e.g. having received something.

There are many more details with respect to modeling security, depending on the framework used. In fact, there are many discussions on these (maybe even more than on Enterprise Architecture frameworks, who will say). All these aspects have an effect on *risks* that are related to handling information. E.g. a leak in your confidentiality might result in a financial risk, or a damage of your reputation or it might even land you in jail. Which brings us to the fact that these aspects used in Information Security are what in Risk Management are sometimes called *Control Objectives*.

13.2 Risk

If you move over to Risk Management, you find generally a division in three:

- Risk: The damage that can be done. The main aspects of risk are *impact* and *likelihood*;

- Control Objective: What state of affairs you want to achieve with regard to the Risks. In the most simple form, Control Objectives often take the form of the inverse of the Risk. But in more mature approaches, the Control Objectives are separate, as a single Control Objective may be a state of affairs that fights multiple Risks and for a single Risk, multiple Control Objectives may be important;

- Control Measure or sometimes Countermeasure or just Control: What you actually *do* to get to this state of affairs that is the Control Objective.

This division can be found in many frameworks, like ISO27001, ISA 3402. The main issue for us here and now is that if we are able to model the most important aspects of Risk Management in our Enterprise Architecture, we also have the framework to model the most important aspects Security Architecture. I am not saying that everything related to Security or Risk can be brought back to a few simple elements and relations. Risk and Security merit a far more comprehensive approach than that. But modeling Risk, Control Objective and Control Measures in your Enterprise Architecture may offer a good link between your Enterprise Architecture and the Security and Risk Management in your organization.

So, we come to the question if ArchiMate can help us adding Security and Risk Management aspects to our Enterprise Architecture. And — since ArchiMate 2.0 — it can. I am presenting to you here an approach (first collaboratively pioneered at my company by colleagues Jos Knoops and Roy Krout). But first we introduce ArchiMate 2's Motivation Extension.

13.3 The Motivation Extension

ArchiMate 2 comes with an extension called the Motivation Extension. It contains several concepts. It is easiest to illustrate (most of) them in an example as can be seen in View 150.

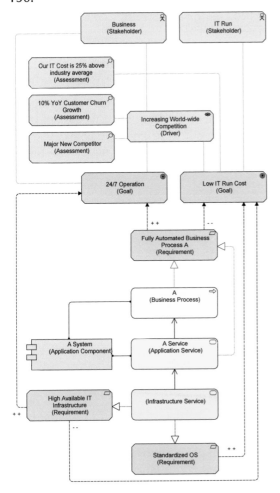

View 150. ArchiMate 2.0 Motivation Extension example

The new elements and relations are:

This is a Goal, which is an end state that a stakeholder wants to achieve. In the example above, the Business wants to achieve 24/7 operations and the IT Run wants to lower IT cost.

This is a Requirement, which is a obligatory aspect of what a system or process Realizes. In the example, there is a Requirement to use standard operating systems only in your infrastructure, to have high-available infrastructure and to have a certain business process fully automated.

This is a Driver, which is something that drives change in the organization. These may be external (e.g. market forces, regulation) but also internal (e.g. the mission or vision of an organization). In the example, there is one driver: 'Increased World-Wide Competition'.

This is an Assessment, which is the outcome of an analysis of a Driver. E.g. if a driver is "customer satisfaction", a poll might result in an assessment. In the example, there are two Assessments: a new competitor has arrived om the scene and we win/lose 10% of our customers each year (because they come to/from the competition)

This is a Stakeholder, which is a Role that is interested in achieving a Goal, or might be associated with a Driver or an Assessment. In our example, there are two Stakeholder roles: Business and IT Run (the responsibility for keeping the systems operational).

This is a Constraint (a Specialization of Requirement), which is a forbidden aspect of what a system or process Realizes. There is no Constraint modeled in the example, but it behaves like a Requirement.

This is a Principle, which is a sort-of Goal that is a generalized Requirement. There is no Principle modeled in the example, but it behaves like a Requirement.

The concepts are not exactly, discretely separated. It is sometimes a matter of taste if something is seen as a Goal or a Driver. Having a certain strategic Goal as an organization may count as a Driver, it seems to me. And the divide between a requirement and a principle is not very clear too. This is not really a problem (we encountered some overlaps earlier, think Business Function versus Business Process), it then comes down to creating your own good patterns to use them.

The relations between the elements are generally Associations. The exceptions are that Realization is used to:

- let a Requirement, Constraint or Principle Realize a Goal;

- let a Requirement or Constraint Realize a Principle;

- let any core ArchiMate concept (except Value and Meaning) Realize a Requirement. In the example, an Infrastructure Service, an Application Service and a Business Process all Realize a Requirement. An interesting question is if you have — as is the case in the example — a Requirement like 'Fully automated Business Process'. Is it the Business Process that Realizes this Requirement (in red) or the Application Service (in blue) or both? There is quite a bit of freedom in choosing your patterns.

and a new relation:

This is the Influence relationship. It is used to model the way Driver, Assessment, Goal, Principle, Requirement and Constraint can influence each other. Normally, a label on the relationship is used to denote the type of influence. In the example, the Requirement to use standardized operating systems in the infrastructure influences positively the 'Low IT Cost' Goal, but the 'High Available IT Infrastructure' influences that same Goal in a negative way. The 'High Available IT Infrastructure' Requirement positively influences the '24/7 Operations' Goal and the 'Fully Automated Business Process A' influences '24/7 Operations' positively but 'Low It Cost' negatively.

The Motivation Extension of ArchiMate 2 shows its origin: the developers wanted to catch the Architecture itself in their modeling language. Hence, the use of the concept of Principle (which is a popular Enterprise Architecture concept) next to Requirement and Goal. What this new part of ArchiMate also shows is how different the world of human intentions and motivations is from the logical world of IT and how difficult it is to map one onto the other ("I have one negative influence and one positive. Now what?"). But what the Motivation Extension does offer us is a basic mechanism to model Risks, Control Objectives (including those from Security) and Control Measures and in that way link ArchiMate models to the world of Risk and Security:

13.4 Modeling Risks and Controls

When modeling Risk, you can use the following mapping:

- A Risk is modeled using ArchiMate's Driver element;

- A Control Objective is modeled using ArchiMate's Goal element;

- A Control Measure (sometimes just 'Control', sometimes referred to as 'Countermeasure') element is modeled using ArchiMate's Requirement element.

We Associate a Process for which there is a Control Objective with that Control Objective. For instance, a payments process may have as Control Objective that it is not possible for a single person to authorize a payment. Such a Control Objective is than modeled as a Goal element that is Associated with the process it is a Control Objective for.

In the overview of View 151 on page 99 the patterns for modeling Risk (including Security Risks), Control Objectives (including Security Aspects of Information) and Control Measures are shown.

In the green grouping, we find a (primary) Business Process 1 that consists of three subprocesses Sub 1.a, Sub 1.b and Sub 1.c, where information flows from Sub 1.a to Sub 1.b and Sub 1.b to Sub 1.c.

Furthermore, 4 Risks have been modeled: Risk X, Y and Z and a Risk called 'Security'. Note that these can in the real world be replaced by a complex tree of Risks, using for instance Aggregation and Composition relations. The Risks X, Y and Z are Associated with Control Objectives 1, 2 and 3 in an n:m way. For instance, Risk Y is Associated with Control Objectives 1 and 2, while Control Objective 2 is Associated with Risk X, Y and Z. The Risk 'Security' is Associated with three Control Objectives: Confidentiality, Integrity and Availability.

The Control Objectives are not only related to the Risks (red Associations) but also to the elements they are Control Objectives of (blue Associations). In the case of Control Objectives 1, 2 and 3 and Control Objectives Availability, the

Control Objectives are Associated with Business Process 1. In case of the Control Objectives Confidentiality and Integrity, they are Associated (blue Associations) with the 'Subject Matter' Business Object they are Control Objectives of. Note that the color of the Associations here is only to make the explanation easier, I am not advocating per sé that blue Associations are used for linking Risks to Control Objectives and blue Associations for linking Control Objectives to the elements they are Control Objectives of. But to be honest, I find the idea attractive, as you can easily focus on the specific type of relation in a view.

Control Measures (or just 'Controls') contribute to the Control Objective. This has been modeled by using the Influence relation from Control Measure to Control Objective. For instance, the '99% uptime' requirement (Control Measure) for the Infrastructure Service contributes positively to the 'Availability' Control Objective.

All Control Measures are either Realized by a Business Process, by an Application Service or by an Infrastructure Service. For the last two holds that the Control Measures are requirements to the service.

Three patterns are shown how Control Measures can be Realized by Business Processes:

- First, there can be a separate process that Realizes the Control Measure. This can for instance be a separate audit process. This is the case for Control Objective 1 in View 151. The audit process requires a flow of information from the audited process and this is true for any external process that realizes a Control Measure for a core process.

- Secondly, the actual Business Process that the Control Objective is about might have to be *changed* because of the Control Objective. For instance, there might be an extra step in the Business Process to perform a check or an authorization. In View 151: This extra step Sub 1.b is really part of core process 1. To denote that this part/subprocess is there *because* of the Control Measure, it has also been made an Aggregate child of the (possibly unrelated) collection of process steps (subprocesses) that together Realize the Control Measure. This aggregation therefore is a collection of all the changed parts of processes that have been changed because they are part of what Realizes the Control Measure.

- Thirdly, a separate process may be responsible for information that the core Business Process. This can be in two different ways:

    * First, a process may produce information that is used in another process. For instance, as a Control Measure to prevent trading with non-allowed parties or in non-allowed countries, the control function may produce a list of allowed parties or countries that is then used in the trading process.

    * Secondly, a process may provide requirements for how a core business process is run. For instance, requiring a four-eye principle on certain activities. Such requirements become part of the process's

documen-
tation and
adhering to
the require-
ments can
become
again part
of an audit
type realiza-
tion.

The first pattern is
the pattern that also
offers the proof that
Control Measures
have been taken
and that therefore
Control Objectives
will be met.

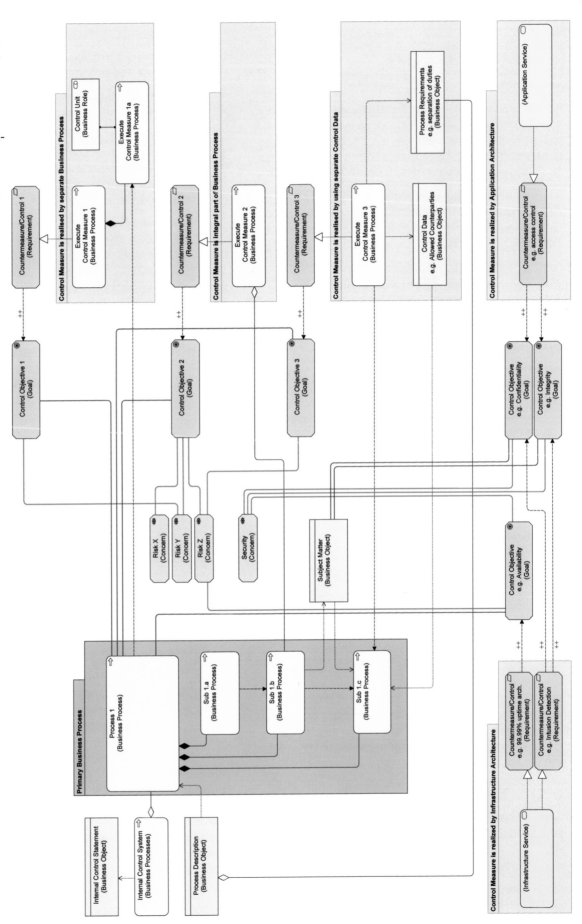

View 151. *Five ways (patterns) the Enterprise Architecture can Realize Control Measures/Controls that contribute to Control Objectives that are associated with Risks*

14. More Platform Thinking

14.1 Low Level Data Entry

Recapitulating our approach with respect to software:

- If it has business logic / functionality used by the business, it is an Application Component. As a result, that spreadsheet your business uses is an Application Component and Excel itself is System Software that Realizes an Infrastructure Service (see Section 7.3 on page 48);

- If it does not have business logic / functionality used by the business, it is either something very generic, e.g. a database system or it is a platform of sorts (see Section 7.5 on page 51) or both.

But consider the following scenario: you have an application (App A) that requires you to load certain data via an Excel spreadsheet document. That is, you need plain vanilla

written for that platform (e.g. a Scheduler or Transporter workflow) *as well* as its own maintenance tooling. So:

- The system's distribution Artifact Realized the System Software that Realized the Infrastructure Service (the *platform*);

- The system's distribution (Artifact) Realized the Application Component that was the *maintenance/development* part (directly used by a 'secondary' business aspect) of that platform.

Actually, this is a pretty common pattern if you reason from the distribution Artifact. Now, go back to the Excel distribution (in fact MS Office, but that is not an important distinction). That distribution Realizes the Infrastructure Service for the spreadsheets that run in the platform. But that distribution *also* Realizes the Excel 'maintenance/development' Application Component just like in the example of Section 9.

Summarizing: Excel is not just an Infrastructure Service, but it is *also* a *development environment* (in case you write business logic in Excel) and a *data entry environment* (in case you have to enter just data).

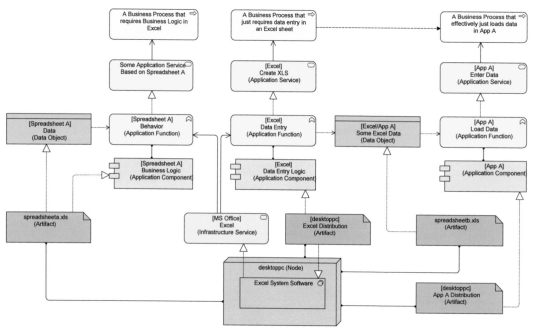

View 152. *Using Excel for Data Entry for a Business Process*

So, in those cases that data entry in an Excel spreadsheet (say a spreadsheet with user names and authorizations that some SaaS service requires to be uploaded to be able to set the users and authorizations) is an essential step in your business process, something you should not leave out because it is very important, you can use for instance a basic '[Excel]

data entry in Excel to create that .xls file. That file is then later loaded into the application. You do not use Excel as an Infrastructure Service *platform* to run business logic in an Excel spreadsheet, you create the spreadsheet using Excel as the *application*.

Since that System Software cannot Realize an Application Service itself in ArchiMate, it cannot be used directly by the Business Process. I suggest you do not read on immediately, but instead think yourself for a while how to solve the puzzle.

Now, that you've thought of a solution, I'd like you to go back to Section 9 "An Example from the Real World" on page 69. What happened there was that a platform was *both* used as Infrastructure Service for some sort of logic

Spreadsheet Maintenance (Application Function)' in your landscape. Worked out in detail the reasoning can be found in View 152. (Incidentally, I would personally leave the Application Component, the distribution Artifact and maybe even the Application Function for Excel's 'maintenance' mode out of my model. Just use the '[Excel] Create XLS (Application Service)' and leave the rest out. In fact the solution to model Excel to create a file becomes pretty simple. It is shown in View 153. The argument for the Realization relation from Node to Application Service is left as an exercise for the reader (I always wanted to write that since having to study Gasiorowicz...).

What this also shows is that Excel is its own development environment. Creating an Excel spreadsheet is data entry when it is just entering data in cells for other applications to read. Or it is just a different way of writing a different kind of document, e.g. a report. But as soon as you start using macros and formulas, you are in fact using the Excel development environment to write an *application*, which is an Excel spreadsheet that runs using the Excel Infrastructure Service as in 7.3 "Modeling Spreadsheet Applications" on page 48. This is not different from the maintenance environments shown in Section 9 on page 69.

View 153. *The 'Create Spreadsheet' Excel Application Function*

14.2 ESB

How do you model an Enterprise Service Bus (ESB)? An ESB is a system that many organizations deploy these days to connect different systems to each other. What an ESB generally offers is a way to 'loosen' the dependencies between the applications that use each other's data. Instead of a large bowl of spaghetti of custom-built point-to-point connections, the ESB offers a more generic solution: a central agent in between that makes sure every application gets his data from other applications. ESBs are particularly good at handling *event-based* data: as soon as something changes in one application, it is sent to the ESB and all the applications that require it immediately get it. This is so-called Straight-Through Processing (STP). However, though ESBs support the STP pattern very well, it is not guaranteed of course that the processing at the receiving end indeed happens immediately. And there are even situations where stability of the data during a period is essential so sometimes STP is even a bad thing in your architecture. The decoupling provided by ESBs also makes the landscape a bit more robust under change. After all, because not all systems need to be technically aware of each other, new connections can be created without anything changing at other endpoints. E.g. you can change your accounting system and the systems providing data to the accounting system need not be aware of this. In the real world, this is often not the case as systems have different demands on the data and some changes need to happen anyway upstream. But it is a big improvement in any case.

Now, what an ESB basically does therefore is:

- Receive data from one application;
- Send that data to any other application that requires it.

There is some more complexity though, because every application may have its own definitions of the data in terms of formats, ranges, etc., so ESBs not only transport data, they also transform it. For this, ESBs generally employ a central Common Data Model (CDM), that is used as a central mapping for everything sent and received. So more precisely, what an ESB does is:

- Receive data in an application-specific format at an end point;
- Transform data to the CDM;
- Route data to other points depending on a routing table (what kind of data goes where);

- At the end point: transform data to the application-specific format for the receiving application;
- Send data to the receiving application (in the application-specific format).

In the basis it's technically not more complicated than that. But the question is, of course, how to put this in your landscape.

Before we look into the details, let's recap a basic approach: an ESB does nothing out of the box. To let it do what it needs to do for your organization, you need to set it up. And though euphemistically you might call that 'setting it up' or 'configuring', what it really is, of course, is a form of programming. It is just not programming with a known 'programming language', it is programming within the confines of the ESB *platform*. And what we program are specific pieces of (business-specific) logic:

- Adaptors to connect the different applications;
- Routing logic to route the data.

So if we follow the platform-pattern, we already know we will have to model a couple of Application Components, namely for the adaptors and for the routing. These Application Components are physically represented by the Artifacts we build (set up, configure) for them.

Now, in our simplified and restructured example we model two applications that are connected via the ESB: *System A* and *System B*. System A produces data that is needed by other systems, one of those is System B. An example would be if System A delivers official prices of what we have in store to all other systems. System B would then for instance be a risk system that requires any price update because it keeps track of those to calculate price variability. Some other system (not in the example) would then keep all our positions. The (pricing) System A needs to know any change in positions because it uses that information to know for which items prices need to be defined. Some other system delivers those position updates, also via the ESB, to System A. Now things like 'prices' and 'positions' are called 'topics' in ESB lingo. And internally there are various 'queues' where these topics are written to or read from.

Virtually, the whole ESB setup realizes an Application Service that provides the delivery to system B of a price produced by System A, and this is one way to look at it. In a real world situation there might be approximately 7 major systems connected to the ESB and on average they might be interested in approximately 4 topics. I such a situation, the whole ESB setup might be reduced to roughly 30 *virtual* Application Services to make sure the right data flows to the right systems. In fact, these 30 or so virtual Application Services are what you would need to build as specific point-to-point data distribution solution if you did not have an ESB. I'd rather have an ESB, though, as it throws in a lot for free, such as guaranteed delivery, exception handling, logging, auditing, etc., stuff which is a lot to build for every connection yourself.

If you choose to model the ESB by modeling the virtual Application Services it provides, you get something resem-

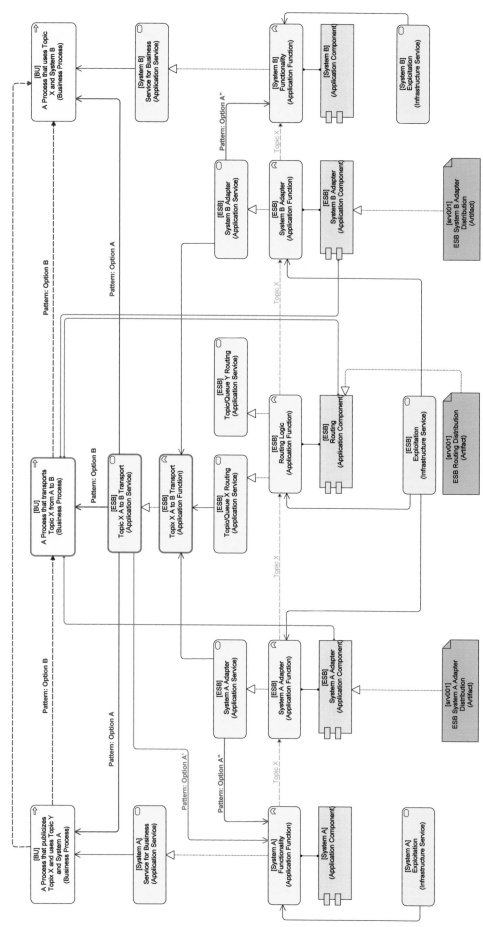

First, have a look at the two red-bordered elements, the *[ESB] Topic X A to B Transport (Application Function)* and the *[ESB] Topic X A to B Transport (Application Service)*. These are the virtual elements that in reality do not exist in the ESB environment but that are implied by it and are modeled in this approach. Technically, you could model it by modeling an Application Collaboration of all Application Components in the ESB and turning the Application Function into an Application Interaction that Aggregates the different ESB Application Functions (adaptors and routing). This can be seen in View 155 on page 103.

We're staying with View 154 for now. In the bottom half of the view you see the typical result of the platform pattern. What we have built in our ESB platform is modeled as Artifacts that Realize Application Components which are Assigned-To Application Functions which Realize specific Application Services. The (red outlined) virtual Application Function and Application Service make use of the real services of the ESB components to provide that specific 'Topic X from A to B' service.

There are a few options shown in View 154. First have a look at the Used-By relations that start from our virtual *[ESB] Topic X A to B Transport (Application Service)*. Option A (blue) shows that this virtual service is Used-By the (business layer) processes that need the functionality of System A, respectively System B. With this approach belongs a dynamic Flow relation directly from one process to the other. Option B (purple) on the other hand says that the behavior of the ESB in fact defines an automated Business Process in itself that is responsible for connecting both processes. This process takes what one process produces and what the other process needs. This automated process is the one using our virtual Application Service. And since it is performed by the ESB, it requires an Application Component that can be Assigned-To it. But because our Application Function is virtual, there is no such component

bling View 154. View 154 contains a few pattern options, though, which I'll explain below.

View 154. *Basic ESB Pattern with Virtual Application Services* available. But I can Assign it from the involved ESB components (pink). Here ArchiMate 2.0 purists will frown as I should use a formal Application Collaboration instead of this informal collaboration (see View 23 on page 24).

Hence the solution in View 155. Here we create another abstraction, but this time satisfying ArchiMate 2.0 purists. We create — specifically for this task — an (abstract) Application Collaboration that Aggregates the necessary ESB components. This Application Collaboration is Assigned-To an (also abstract) Application Interaction. It is possible to add Aggregates from the Application Interaction to the separate Application Functions performed by the ESB components, but those are left out here.

I would like to draw your attention to the olive green Used-By that connects our virtual Application Service to the functionality of System A. As we know that in the application layer System A makes use of the ESB, we need to draw a Used-By. Pattern Option A′ (the olive green one) models it such that System A uses the virtual Application Service that makes transport of Topic X from System A to System B possible. But it is an ugly solution, because connecting something that does not exist (our virtual Application Service) to something that does (our System A's functionality) confuses abstraction with reality. So, we're better off using Pattern Option A″ (green) for the technical connection in the application layer. So, in View 154 on page 102, there are a few usable combinations of patterns we can use:

- Either Pattern Option A or Pattern Option B for the link between application layer and business layer;

- Combined with Pattern Option A″ for the link inside the application layer.

My personal favorite is Pattern Option B for the application-business layer linkage, because it enables you to have a business representation of what the ESB is doing for you in an automated fashion. Having it has the advantage that if you ever change or

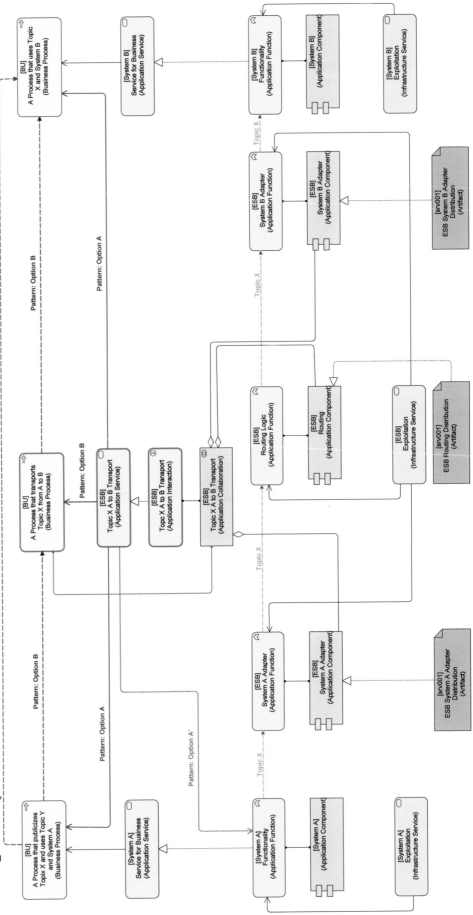

View 155. *Basic ESB Pattern with Virtual Application Service Realized by Application Interaction of ESB Components*

remove the ESB, you will know what you need to re-establish with its successor. I also favor informal collaborations over formal ones, because they keep my models simpler in terms of constructions used. The fewer my types of constructions, the easier analysis becomes. So, leaving formal ArchiMate collaborations and interactions out and using only informal ones simplifies my analysis algorithms.

Pattern Option A'' in View 154 on page 102 is not possible in View 155 because the Application Services inside the ESB environment are missing in that view. Adding them is awkward as they are not used to model the coherence between the various parts: the Application Interaction is already being used for that. And adding them just for the application layer dependencies is also slightly awkward as you are modeling the 'service' of the ESB component twice, once as service and once as the interaction. If you then want to model the application-layer dependency, you are limited to Pattern Option A', which we already noted as being slightly problematic.

As you can see, I have added a few flows to the examples in View 154 on page 102 and View 155 on page 103. In the application layer they are quite straightforward, and that should be so of course: that is where the real actions of the ESB take place. Topic X flows from System A to System B, using two adapters and the routing logic. In the business layer the world is also pretty simple: With Pattern Option A, information flows from one process to another, with Pattern Option B, there is a formally defined automated process linking the two, which is being performed by the ESB components (or the Application Collaboration Aggregated from them as in View 155 on page 103).

In a real language, there are generally multiple ways to convey the same message. And apart from the minor variations above (separate business process for what the ESB does yes or no, collaborations yes or no), there is also a third approach. Instead of modeling details and using Used-By or Application Collaborations, this approach uses Aggregation to group the different Application Services Realized by the ESB components into meaningful groupings. In fact, this is the same approach as used in 7.6 "Infrastructure 'Building Blocks'" on page 53. Our abstract services such as 'flow Topic X from System A to System B' are in fact Aggregations of the 'building blocks' below it. This is shown in View 157 on page 105. Some noteworthy aspects:

- I have left out the option without the

explicitly modeled automated Business Process (Pattern Option A in the previous examples);

- System A does not only publish Topic X, it also is subscribed to Topic Y. The publisher of Topic Y is not shown;

- The data flows in the application layer are shown for Topic X from System A to System B. The orange flows are in native 'System A' or 'System B' format, the black flows are in 'Common Data Model' format. These flows are not modeled to flow from Application Function to Application Function but more precisely from one of the topic- or adapter-specific Application Services Realized by that Application Function;

- Because there is no explicit Application Collaboration modeled, the automated Business Process responsible for transporting Topic X from System A to System B is performed by an informal collaboration of the necessary ESB components;

- View 158 on page 106 contains the same but with added infrastructure layer details. It is possible to extend this to the actual Data Objects needed and have these Realized by actual message Artifacts. A fragment is shown in View 156.

Having shown all this, which solution is best? That is not easy to answer, they all have merits and drawbacks. But for me, I like the 'building block' approach (see section 7.6 "Infrastructure 'Building Blocks'" on page 53) with Pattern Option B, without Data Objects and Used-By between systems and the ESB in the application layer and with Flows and Messages best for a couple of reasons:

- No virtual Application Components (Application Collaborations) or virtual Application Functions (Application Interactions) are created, only Aggregated Application Services are created;

- I can keep my models collaboration- and interaction-free, which simplifies the set of used patterns and thus analysis algorithms;

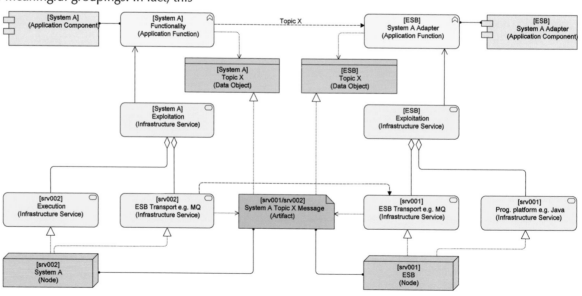

View 156. *Fragment of ESB Example with Messaging Artifacts and Data Objects*

- The 'service building-blocks' approach has been used before at the infrastructure level;
- The underlying structure of how applications connect to the ESB is clear;
- No seemingly hard structural dependencies (Used-By) are created which do not exist in reality. If you remove a publishing system, the subscribed systems will still work, albeit with outdated data. E.g. System B depends on the MQ infrastructure (which will be there) but nothing will arrive (because the ESB will not write to that queue): the flows are broken. This nicely reflects the generally 'loosely coupled' nature of an ESB setup.

A drawback is that you depend on labels to see the relation between Topic X flows and Topic X Artifacts.

As you might guess, these variations and options are only some of all those that are possible. You might come up with even better ones, suiting your circumstances. For one: the patterns described here are for detailed modeling, if you want to produce something for non-modelers (e.g. management), you definitely will have to simplify.

If you start out in a project with a rough design, already identifying which processes need to be executed automatically is supported by View 157 Pattern: Option B. And roughly identifying which Application Services are needed without having to model the underlying building blocks (only the upper row of application layer objects in View 157) is also supported by this approach. In other words, you can create a simplified view of what needs to be implemented, but adding more detail later on does not mean your original view changes. There is more to be said on 'simple views' versus 'detailed views', but as a small example, have a look at View 159 on page 107. Here, we can use just that upper part of View 157 (or View 158) in the rough design phase of a description (or design, or project). The only elements that we have to show at that stage are the automated process and what the applications (including those developed in the ESB platform) have to do for those processes. I have added a placeholder element for yet unknown elements of the ESB that

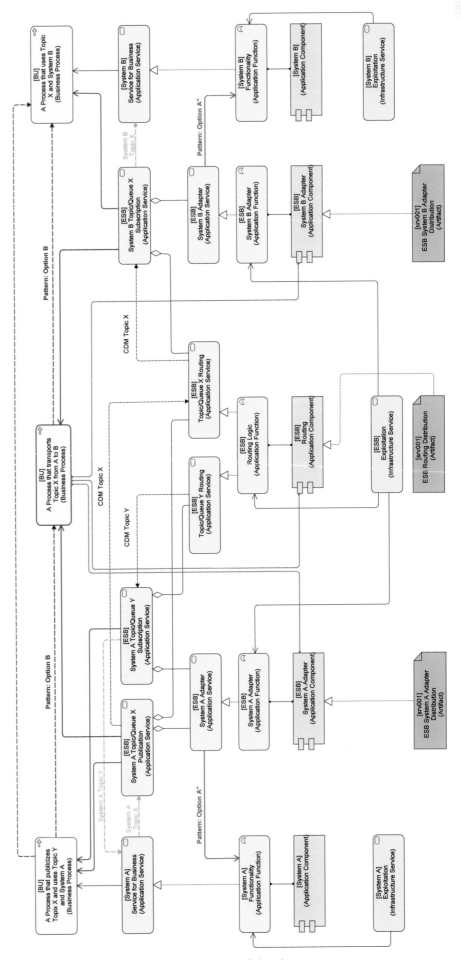

View 157. *Basic ESB Pattern with clear Publish-Subscribe*

have to perform the process and Realize the services. This is to signify during the rough design phase that the process

runs automatically and is performed by ESB components. The placeholder element has a green border and the place-

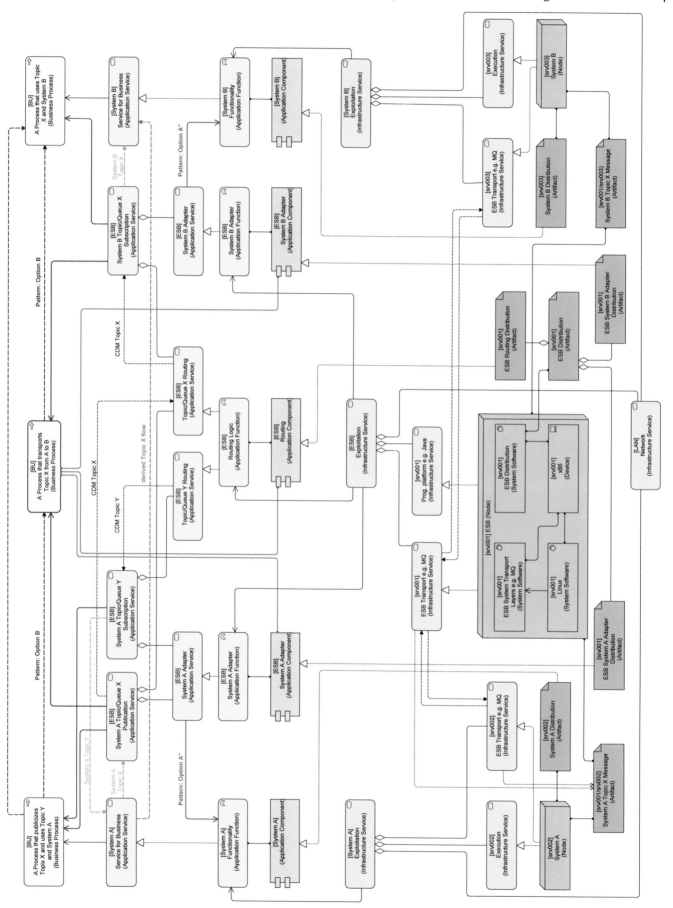

View 158. *ESB - Publish Subscribe with Infrastructure*

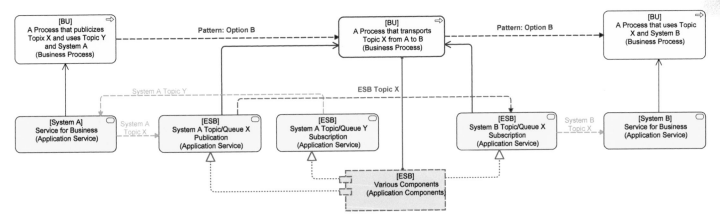

View 159. *ESB Example: rough/simple design of what a project must deliver*

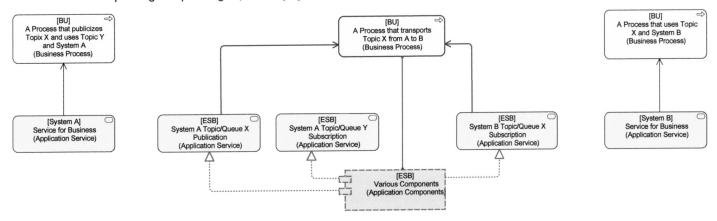

View 160. *View 159 with dynamic relations removed*

holder relations are green in View 159. When in a later stage the model is fleshed out, the placeholder elements and relations are replaced with the real elements and relations. Of course, if at this stage you already know which components have to perform this process, you can add them directly.

You may notice that the ESB Topic X placeholder flow is a derived relation from the CDM flows in View 157 on page 105. But the other placeholder relations cannot be formally derived within ArchiMate 2 proper, not even if you would see the placeholder Application Component as an Aggregate of the required real components (a collaboration of sorts). But as it is so clearly useful and meaningful, it is for me an illustration that while the concept of formally derived relations in ArchiMate is elegant and meaningful, it is too restricted to limit yourself to in the real world (see also 5.5 "On the limitations of derived relations" on page 36).

Finally, in View 160 you can see what happens in this ESB-modeling approach (in this case in the rough model, but the same is true for the detailed model) when you leave out the dynamic relations (which I often do when modeling). Suddenly, it seems System A, System B and the ESB components have no relations with each other. This is of course not true, but the structural relations between the systems and the ESB components are all down in the details in the application layer (e.g. Pattern: Option A'' in green in View 157 on page 105). It is kind of nice that the 'loose coupling' via an ESB does not show up structurally in our rough design. But since we do want to show the 'loose' dependencies, in this case it is best to show the dynamic relations too. This solution, by the way, is not what I prefer. The solution I prefer can be found in 25.8 "Processes communicating via an ESB" on page 174, which is shown after we have looked at ArchiMate–BPMN linkage.

15. Organizational Structure

15.1 Basic Organizational Structure

The actors in the business layer generally form an organization with a discernible structure. This structure can for instance be found in HR systems where the formal hierarchy is often put down in some sort of tree structure. But the HR system generally is only about humans, it is not about Departments or other more abstract structures. The department is there virtually, but only the job profiles normally

have actual data in them. This is illustrated in View 161 on page 108 where – on the left hand side – you see a typical HR structure of the organization. If you want to add more abstract actors like departments or the organization itself, you need the right hand side.

The structure in View 161 is too simple of course. Because in HR we do not only have actual persons, these persons fulfill specific job profiles. In fact, the structure of departments and such from an HR perspective is a structure of job profiles, where the manager profile sits above the various employee profiles. Such a Job Profile is in fact a Business Role, but without the specific Business Processes to perform Assigned from it. The HR department has no use for 'job descriptions of a *department*', that's more something for Enterprise Architecture (Business Role Assigned from that department and Business Function Assigned from that Role). But if we model the Job Descriptions as Business Roles, we can create the structure as seen in View 162 where I've also added (orange) Associations between the departmental abstractions and their managing roles (this pattern will be derived in Section 25.6 "The Process Landscape in ArchiMate" on page 171 when we look into linking process models in BPMN with Enterprise Architecture models in ArchiMate). Now, of course, we would probably almost never model an organization to the employee level. But this exercise is to get to the bottom of the structure, later we might look at which patterns to use for what. Looking ahead: if you want to model rights management, for instance, the HR structure does not allow you to Associate rights with a Department. You might for instance want to give all the employees of the department, including the manager, the right to access a certain part of the building. But on the right hand side of View 162 does not have an easy element to Associate these rights with. You do not want, for instance, for the employees to inherit all the rights of the manager (right hand side) as you would like all employees (including the manager) to inherit the rights of the department (left hand side). This illustrates a limitation of the HR structure.

Now, a Business Role is 'responsibility for certain behavior'. How should we model this behavior? It must be either a Business Process or a Business Function. Here, it is clear that for the 'Job' roles, the Business Function is most appropriate for the behavior. But the actors themselves are executing internal processes. We are going to ignore the Business Function aspect now and look at the relations between actors, roles and processes and their IT support. We will get more into process details in Sections 24 "A Very Short BPMN Primer" on page 151 and 25 "Linking BPMN and ArchiMate" on page 156.

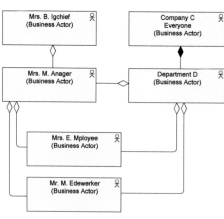

View 161. *Very Basic Organizational Structure*

Our simple example can be expanded with a few systems P, Q and R that are used by the business. To start with: there is no formal process description that use System P. Think of the application people use to report their worked hours, for instance. It is something everybody of Department D has to do, but there is no formal process description. System Q is being used by the Real Estate Trader Job in Process 'Trade Real Estate', where the Real Estate Trader performs some tasks. Finally, System R is used in Process 'Trade Grain', in which Job 'Commodities Trader' performs some task, but the process description is more detailed than that. For example, the job is 'Commodity Trader' but the role as mentioned in the process descriptions is more specific, like 'Grain Trader'. The elements are shown in View 163.

Process 'Trade Real Estate' is behavior performed by Job 'Real Estate Trader' and thus *may be* performed by Actor Mr.

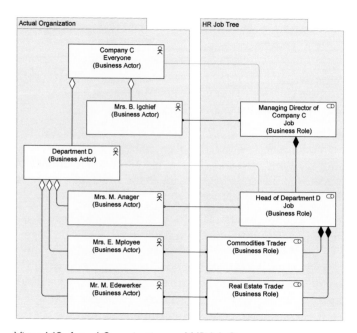

View 162. *Actual Organization and HR Job Structure*

M. Edewerker. Process 'Trade Grain' is performed by the 'Grain Trader' Business Role which is one of the roles that is contained in Job 'Commodities Trader' and thus Process 'Trade Grain' *may be* performed by Actor Mrs. E. Mployee. Here, by the way, is a confusing issue in ArchiMate: though I can draw *derived* Used-By relations from the Application Services to the Actors, since ArchiMate 2.0 this means quite something different than the use of those applications by the Actors in the context of performing that process.

Question 6. Can you tell what a *derived* Used-By between Application Service 'Real Estate Trading' and Actor Mr. M. Edewerker (allowed in ArchiMate 2.0) would stand for in ArchiMate?

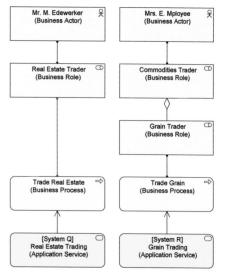

View 163. *Process Landscape for Organization Example*

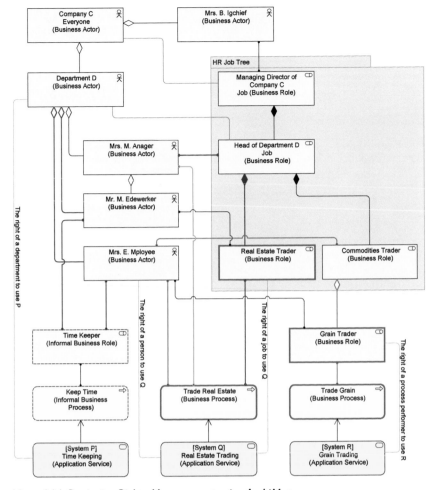

View 164. *Designing Rights Management using ArchiMate*

uses the process result instead of performing it.
Actor Mr. M. Edewerker. In other words: Mr. M. Edewerker
Business Service (not shown) which is (directly) Used-By
a Business Process 'Trade Real Estate', which Realizes a
By Application Service 'Real Estate Trading' is Used-
Answer 6. *Application Service 'Real Estate Trading' is Used-*

I can make a valid direct Used-By ArchiMate 2.0 relation between Application Service 'Time Keeping' and both actors directly, but I cannot derive it from the situation with a process and a role as I could in ArchiMate 1.0. This illustrates once more the limits of derived relations.

15.2 Using an ArchiMate landscape to design an object model

Now that we have a basic pattern for a detailed view on our organization, coupled to real jobs and real actors, we can use that to design a setup for rights management. I include this to show as an example how you can use an ArchiMate-based analysis to design a informational structure. I will be using View 164.

First, note that I have completed the process landscape by adding an (Informal) Business Process 'Keep Time' and (Informal) Business Roles 'Time Keeper' elements. These are useful for our analysis. Now, we are going to answer the question: which Actors may use which Application Services and how should rights be granted?

Let's start with Mr. M. Edewerker. He is assigned to Job 'Real Estate Trader'. Job 'Real Estate Trader' performs Business Process 'Trade Real Estate' which uses Application Service 'Real Estate Trading' from System Q. Mr. M. Edewerker therefore needs access to the Q System as a result of fulfilling Job 'Real Estate Trader'. *It must therefore be possible to Associate a right to use an application (or part thereof) to a Job from our HR Job Tree.* This is shown by an Association from the 'Real Estate Trader' Job to the 'Real Estate Trading' Application Service.

Next is Mrs. E. Mployee. She fulfills Job 'Commodities Trader'. She is also Assigned-To the process-specific Business Role of Grain Trader. By checking both routes (direct from Mrs. E. Mployee to 'Grain Trader' and the pink relations via her Job description) we can see that she may perform that role. Everyone who fulfills the role of 'Grain Trader' must have access to System R and its 'Grain Trading' Application Service. *It must therefore be possible to Associate a right to use an application (of part thereof) to a Business Role that is a performer of a Business Process.* This is shown by an Association from the 'Grain Trader' Business Role to the 'Grain Trading' Application service.

There is however a problem in View 164. Mrs. E. Mployee is Assigned-To (in red) the 'Trade Real Estate' Business Process, but she is a 'Commodities Trader' and not a 'Real Estate Trader'. So either this is an error or maybe we have an exception on our hands. Maybe our Real Estate Trader has left and we need a temporary solution. That does not mean we let Mrs. E. Mployee fulfill two jobs formally. But she will still need access to the 'Real Estate Trading' Application Service of System Q. She will get a personal exception. *It must therefore be possible to Associate a right to use an application (of part thereof) to an Actor (a specific person).* This is shown by an Association between Mrs. E. Mployee and the 'Real Estate Trading' Application Service.

Next, everybody who is part of Department D has to keep time using System Q's 'Time Keeping' Application Service. A Business Process and a Role are not really defined for that, so we cannot attach it to the role. But if we put the role and process in temporarily, we can see that the routes in blue provide a way to link Department D with the 'Time Keeping' Application Service. *It must therefore be possible to Associate a right to use an application (of part thereof) to a Business Actor that represents a Department.* This is shown by the Association from 'Department D' to the 'Time Keeping' Application Service.

Then, one Friday afternoon, we find Mrs. M. Anager using the 'Real Estate Trading' Application Service. This is OK, because every manager is allowed to order their subordinates around in our example organization. As a result we say that every Actor that fulfills a Job that is up the tree from a Job that is allowed to use a System may use that same system.

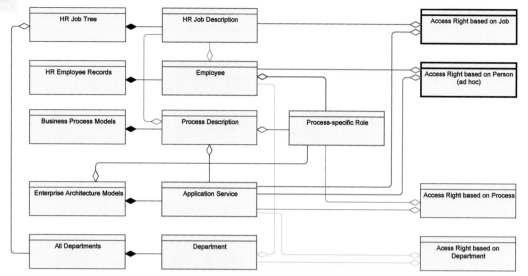

View 165. *Information Model derived from View 164 on page 109*

Of course, the rules in a real organization may be different (and probably are), but in our example, the orange Assignment from Mrs. M. Anager to the 'Trade Real Estate' Business Process means she also is allowed to use that system because of the purple relations.

The elements that have green borders in View 164 are elements you will normally find in business layer of your enterprise architecture models. In reality, the granularity of your process descriptions are far higher than is shown here in this pattern example. We will return to this in a later section, when we will go into process details in BPMN and how they can be linked to ArchiMate. There we will see that we can link Business Roles and Application Services from ArchiMate to detailed Activities in BPMN and thus link actual relations between roles and application services. If you have a detailed BPMN model and a detailed ArchiMate model linked to each other, you will have a serious foundation for providing some basic business information to your rights management environment.

What is left now is the final step. Now that we have identified the relations between the various elements we can turn it into an information model for rights management. After all, the rights management system does not manipulate real actors (let alone abstract notions like roles) but representations of them as information. This is like a client of a company: that client is an *Actor* in your EA model, but it is also a *Business Object* in your EA model, realized by 'client records' Data Objects in your applications and the database Artifacts realizing these Data Objects.

The information model is shown in View 165. On the left are the sources of information we can import automatically.

The purple outlined elements are the source information we need to maintain in our rights management system and which are the basic building blocks of the rights. All these can be automatically derived from the sources on the left. On the right, we see the four different types of rights we have found. Each right is a Business Object that is an Aggregate of an Application Service and something else:

- The right for any employee of a department requires that we know what department an employee is in. This can be generated automatically using the orange relations;

- The right for an employee that performs a process (using blue relations) can be derived automatically if the role that performs the process is a HR Job Description. If the role is a process-specific role, we need to manually link the employee with the process-specific role, this is illustrated by using a thick relation (all thick relations require manual interventions);

- The right for an employee based on his job description requires a manual link of that job description and the Application Service (green relations);

- The right for an employee directly (ad hoc) requires a manual link of that employee and the Application Service (green relations).

We can like wise identify the processes that are needed for Rights Management, some of which can be automated.

Now this is a simplification of the real thing of course, where we will have also requirements like separation of functions, (limitation of) access to Business Objects and Artifacts, and much more next to just access to Application Services. Furthermore, the rights management processes and affected systems are pretty complex. Because your rights management system may keep the right of Employee X to access an Artifact like Directory Y on your file server (based on whatever right from View 165), in the end it needs to be configured like that on the file server itself and the right in one system must translate to actual settings in another.

16. Virtual Machines (Parallelization)

There used to be a time that computer hardware was simple. It started even with only hardware: hard-wired analog components, together performing a mathematical function, like calculating shell trajectories for naval guns (war, indeed, being the great innovator that it is).

When computers were built for breaking enemy encryption — war again — they had to be digital, because their subject matter was digital. Soon thereafter, digital computers became 'general purpose' computers. Their architecture was generic. *What* they did, was left to software. What you did was that you loaded the program in the computer memory somehow and then started it by telling the hardware to start executing the instructions you just loaded. Any application ran directly on the hardware. Soon, this loading became a program itself: the system software, or the operating system. This was the program that was running, that was capable of loading and starting other programs and if they finished, the control was handed back to the op-

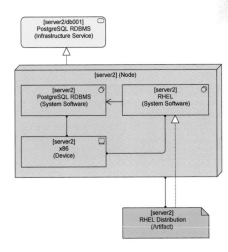

erating system. This program was the *supervisor*, nowadays called the operating system (literally: the application that operates the hardware so that humans don't have to).

But still, the situation was simple: there was a *single* device, on which ran a *single* operating system. On large mainframes, the operating system soon became (pre-emptive) multi-tasking: they enabled running various programs in parallel. Now, this parallelization is a an illusion: what happens in modern pre-emptive multi-tasking is that there runs a clock. And every 10 milliseconds or so, the operating system gives a little bit of operating time to another program, thus creating the *illusion* of parallelism to the end user.

Recently, in operations of computer infrastructure for organizations, parallelization of operating systems (sometimes called 'server consolidation') has become popular, as it enables the efficient use of expensive to acquire and run hardware by multiple independent operating system instances. Surprisingly, this type of parallelization/virtualization (the possibility to run various *operating systems* side by side on the same hardware) is also pretty old. It is also more complex than running multiple applications in an operating system which is designed for such parallelism. Because the operating system is supposed to be low level, some of the tightly coupled interaction of the hardware and operating system must not be interrupted or overwritten. The operating system is the *supervisor* of what happens on the computer.

View 166. *Two real servers which we will turn into virtual servers*

Being able to run multiple hardware supervisors in parallel, each with its own 'supervisor state' was invented by IBM in the 1960's. To manage these supervisors, a special piece of logic is needed (in hardware or in software) which is called the *hypervisor*.

These days central processing units of computers often have hardwired support for hypervisors. In other words: hardware devices have become capable of supporting operating system parallelism. The hardware can keep multiple independent 'states'.

So, the question is: how do we model that in ArchiMate? We will start with two simple servers that we are going to consolidate on single hypervisor-ready hardware using one of two approaches:

- *Bare-metal*. This means that the hypervisor sits directly on top of the hardware and the operating systems sit on top of that. Examples are VMWare ESX or Microsoft Hyper-V (which runs directly on top of the hardware even if it is managed from one of the OS-es on top of it);

- *Hosted*. This means that there is an operating system on top of the hardware and in it runs an application that also contains a hypervisor. This is the case for instance when you use Parallels Desktop or VMWare Workstation.

The distinction is not always clear, but that is not important for our goal. Now, when we start to model virtualization, we are going to look into detail first, before thinking about what the practical approach might be (e.g. when modeling a Current State Architecture). We start with a standard pattern (see section 1.9 "Using a Node to encapsulate infrastructure" on page 22) in View 166 for two independent servers that we will transform into virtual servers using the *hosted* virtualization approach. First, we remove the Node that we use to isolate the server's contents from its surroundings. This gives

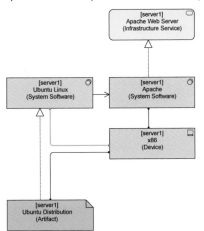

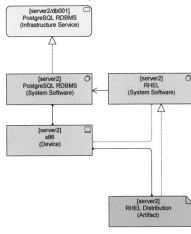

View 167. *Two real servers which we will turn into virtual servers, but without the encapsulating Nodes*

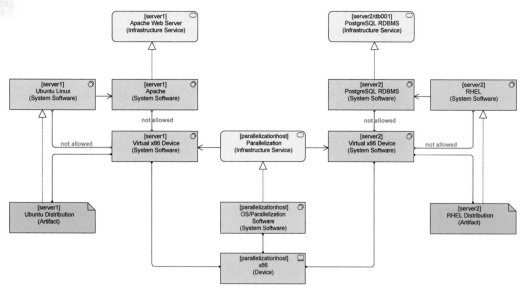

hardware into *software*, to be precise: software that mimics hardware. Software at the infrastructure level means using the System Software element. So, we are going to introduce new hardware (the virtualization host) and on it is deployed an operating system and hypervisor on which our virtual devices will run. This is shown in View 168 on page 112. Let me first draw your attention to the red Assignments. These are (currently) not allowed in ArchiMate. My modeling tool allows them but that is officially wrong. Personally, I think the fact that these are not allowed

View 168. *Our two real server Devices transformed into virtual server System Softwares, hosted on a new Device*

us View 167. Note here the two Assignments from each Device. One goes to the software distribution Artifact which Realizes the System Software element. The other directly goes to the System Software element. We will discuss the orange one in some more detail in a Chapter "Discussing ArchiMate" on page 179, when we discuss ArchiMate's (often historical) peculiarities.

Now, when we want to turn our real servers into virtual servers, we turn

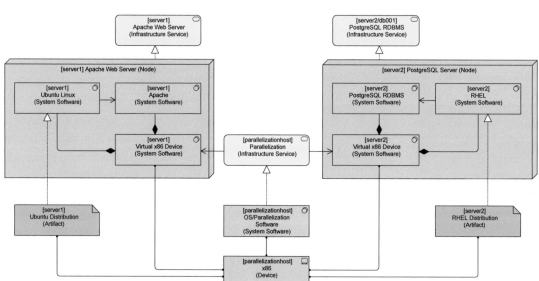

View 169. *Our two virtualized servers encapsulated in Nodes following the standard pattern*

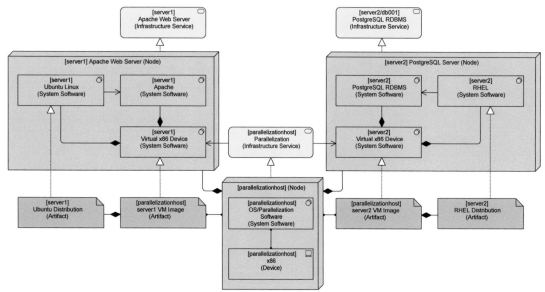

is because of ArchiMate's history and an oversight and I will get back to this in that later chapter.

If we want to remain within ArchiMate's current formal prescriptions, we need to use another relation. I opt for Composition for the rest of this section. The virtual device System Software elements are of course Assigned to the real device (the Parallelization Host). To show that the OS with hypervisor capability is required to actually run the virtual servers, I have added a Used-By relation

View 170. *Our two virtualized servers with a Node-encapsulating pattern for the parallelization host and partial Artifact modeling* between a Realized 'Parallelization' Infrastructure Service and the virtual devices.

We now add the encapsulating Nodes again, so that our virtualized servers are modeled in a pattern comparable to the real servers. This can be seen in View 169. And if we add Node-encapsulation to the parallelization host as well we get View 170. In this view, I have added the virtual machine images to the mix. This illustrates that it is not a bad choice to use Composition as the relation between the System Softwares of a virtual machine, as it mimics the structure of the Artifacts that Realize the System Software elements. We can argue that the Linux System Software is a part of the Virtual Device System Software, as the Virtual Device System Software is Realized by an Image that also Realizes Linux. I have left out the sub-Artifact for Apache in this example. I have also added Composition relations between parallelization host and the (virtual) guest computers. A Nested version of View 170 is shown in View 171. As I do not model internal Infrastructure Services, I have left these out. Personally, I prefer View 170, because it keeps the overall model simpler in terms of the number of different patterns employed. The pattern for the parallelization host is in fact a standard server pattern. Also, for architectural discussions outside the IT infrastructure provider, the fact if a server is virtualized or not is — apart from the cost issue — in most cases not very relevant (as long as the applications run, everybody is happy regardless if a server is real of virtualized).

Finally, to finish the hosted virtualization discussion, in View 172 you see a new example with a real server on the left and virtual servers on the right. This view shows a number of possible solutions to relate the parallelization host to the (virtual) guest devices. The blue Composition relations and the route via the VM Image Artifact are equal to what has been used in View 170. The other shown alternatives are:

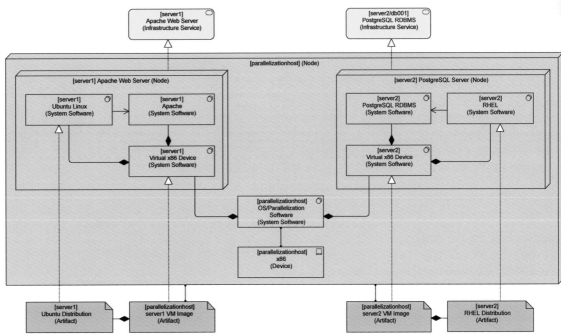

View 171. *A Nested version of View 170.*

- The orange Assignment is illegal in ArchiMate but shows the relation between the active parallelization host element and the virtual device.

- The green Used-By shows that the virtual device requires the parallelization host to function.

- The red Realization is derived from the route via the VM Image Artifact.

There are of course many, many more ways to model hosted virtual servers. There is a myriad of choices in what you show, leave out, etc. Here again, it becomes clear that you

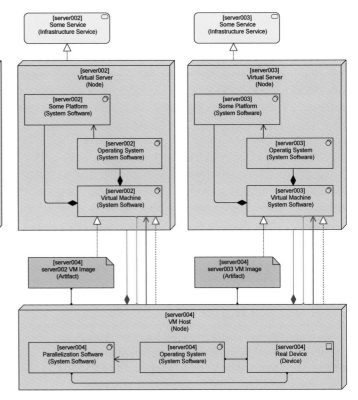

View 172. *Another real server versus virtual server, side by side*

need to find your own pattern based on what you like and need.

Now, with all these details for just a few simple servers, you do get a rather complex picture. It could be worse (e.g. recall the development of the basic server pattern in section 7.2 "A Basic TI Pattern: A Database" on page 47), but still, there is a lot of detail.

There is of course the question you need to answer: do you need all this detail? Via an approach to model the *bare metal* virtualization (instead of *hosted*), we can come to a pretty simple solution. The first step can be seen in View 173 on page 114. Instead of modeling the virtual devices as System Software, we model them as Composite children of the Device of the native (or bare metal) host. (A bit confusing this virtualization nomenclature: you have *native/ bare-metal* versus *hosted*, but the parallelization machine is always called a 'host'). The first effect of this is that the

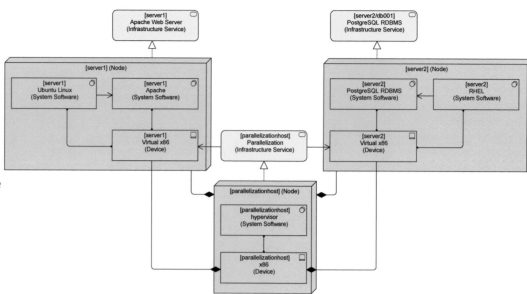

View 173. *Virtual servers in a 'bare metal' variation, where the virtual servers are modeled as sub-Devices of the host device (a suggestion from colleague Jos Knoops)*

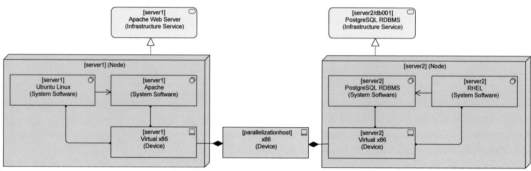

View 174. *Virtualized servers in a simplified pattern where from the parallelization host only the Device is modeled.*

Assignment which we tend to use between a Device and System Software is allowed again. What we say here is that the virtualization is in effect a splitting of the parallelization host in (time separated, as in: they never exist concurrently but 'existence' switches very rapidly between them) sub-hosts.

Which leads me finally to my preferred pattern for hardware virtualization: View 174. The whole issue has been simplified by making the Devices Composite children of the parallelization host's Device, without encapsulating the parallelization host in a Node. I would then only use the pattern of View 170 on page 112 for *emulation*: a software

program that emulates hardware of a different type (actually another IBM invention from the 1960's). Since hardware virtualization has become widespread and common (it might even be found on the desktop of a normal user, whose Mac runs Parallels Desktop so he or she can also run MS-Windows-only programs in a virtual machine, or in other words: me using my ArchiMate modeling tool) this is seldom seen anymore, except in attempts to keep software for obsolete hardware platforms (e.g. older game consoles) running.

Question 7. Can you spot the ArchiMate error in most of the views in the section?

Answer 7. There are many elements with multiple Composite parents as the Node Nestings represent Composites

17. Using Abstractions

17.1 The price one pays

We architects *love* abstraction. Abstraction makes the nitty-gritty and complex details disappear. Abstraction makes the unmanageable manageable. Our business colleagues also love it when we produce abstractions. It makes our end products easier to digest. In

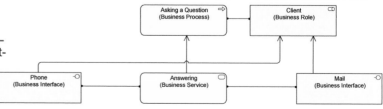

View 175. *Two interfaces for one Business Service*

ArchiMate, you can do both, which means that — apart from the precision-like modeling that you for instance do when building 'current-state' descriptive models — you can use the ArchiMate language in a more 'loose' setup, e.g. when designing a landscape top-down.

For instance, when designing, if you have a Business Process that requires the services of an application, you generally start with defining that application service in terms of 'what the business needs' and then you design how this service will be realized by one or more applications. Or, to stay completely at the business layer, you define the Business Service you provide to your clients in terms of what your client's process need and then move down to define what processes are needed to provide that service. A simple example can be seen in View 175. Here, we have recognized that our clients may want to ask us questions. So, we have defined the 'Answering' Business Service that provides these answers. We have decided answers may be asked by phone and by mail and ArchiMate supports that a service is exposed through multiple interfaces, which is useful in a situation like this. In our example, both are Business Interfaces that the client may use if it wants to use the (generic) 'Answering' Business Service.

View 177. *A Business Service exposed via two Business Interfaces*

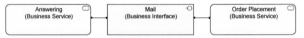

View 178. *A Business Interface exposes two Business Services*

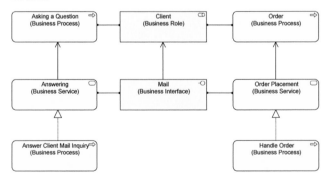

View 179. *Two independent Business Processes, Realizing their Services and exposing them through a single Business Interface*

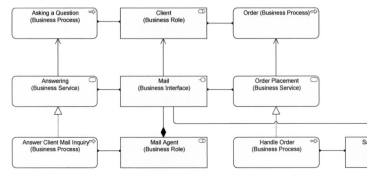

View 180. *Business Roles added to View 179*

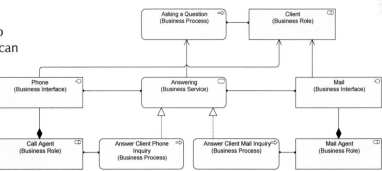

View 176. *The Answering Business Service is Realized by two independent Business Processes, one for answers by mail and one for answers by phone*

Having concluded we need an 'answering' Business Service, we turn to the question how this Business Service is to be Realized and we define two Business Processes that are performed by different roles with different skills. The Call Agent performs the 'Answer Client Phone Inquiry' process through the 'Phone' Business Interface. Something like it happens on the mail side. This can be seen in View 176.

So, we have *a single* service that is defined top-down from how it is needed. It could be considered a collection of two services realized by two processes, one for answering by mail and one for answering by phone. (If they were not separable as processes, we would have to use an Interaction instead and a Collaboration to perform it instead). If you look bottom-up, the 'Answer Client Mail Inquiry' Business Process for instance must Realize its own Business Service (Answering by Mail). A process, after all, is a causally related set of behaviors that is intended to produces something. That is true of the processes in this view too. But we can choose not to model those details, we *abstracted*.

So, ArchiMate's definition of a service allows it to be exposed via multiple interfaces as is shown in View 177.

But its definition of an interface also allows it to expose multiple services. Adding to our example, suppose we have not only an 'Answering' service but also an 'Order Placement' service, which also is available to our customers via mail (we are a mail order company with a phone help desk). This is shown in View 178.

From a management perspective, it is quite a nice simplification, these two Business Services that we provide through that single 'Mail' Business Interface. But a problem lurks here. If we add the processes for both services, we get View 179, and if we add the roles we get View 180.

As both roles are exposed via the Mail interface, ArchiMate expects the Composition relation between role and the interface. But that leads to something that my tool (and any other as far as I know) accepts, but that is illegal in ArchiMate itself: two Composite relations to the same child. (To be honest, I think there could be reasons to relax this restriction, as I describe in section 28.5 "Allow multiple parents in a Composition" on page 192) in the section where I describe my proposed improvements of ArchiMate.

Now, I do not show this as a critique on ArchiMate. It is to illustrate that as abstraction always leaves something out, it can lead to problems. There are many such potential problems. It depends on your intended use of a model if you run into one of them. For a relatively small Future-State like 'broad strokes' model, it is probably not a problem. For a detailed, used for analyses, Current-State or Project model it is definitely risky. Sooner than later you run into the problem caused by missing information.

ArchiMate has enough freedom to be used to make models with a lot of abstraction, and as such it also supports an approach to Enterprise Architecture design that sees services as abstractions defined top-down (from the needs of those that use the service). In fact, such thinking was an important aspect of the design process of ArchiMate in the first place. But ArchiMate also supports a more specific and precise use that is useful for creating precise 'current-state' models. ArchiMate's power of expression is good for both.

17.2 Too much detail?

If you run the 'ps' command in Unix/Linux or if you look at the processes in Window's TaskManager, you see all these processes that run. How should these be modeled?

Just to show that you can actually do this in ArchiMate: have a look at View 181. Here I made an attempt at modeling the processes that run in an operating system. It shows that the 'Operating System (System Software)' Realizes (indirectly) an Infrastructure Service that allows other System Software, such as an FTP-server to run.

I would model the process either as the 'FTP Server (System Software)' element or the 'FTP Server (System Software)'element together with its (possibly Nested) Assigned 'FTP Server Functionality (Infrastructure Function)' element.

I am still leaving out a lot of detail that I could also model (see for instance section 7.2 "A Basic TI Pattern: A Database" on page 47

for a lot of irrelevant detail from an enterprise architecture perspective). So, I would say that it is illustrated that you can go to insane level of details in your ArchiMate modeling. Or in other words: apart for illustration purposes in a book like this, I guess you would never do this in real life. There is an end to the meaningfulness of 'ever more detail', you can kill your modeling endeavor that way. Choosing the right level of detail/abstraction for the job is one of the main reasons why this is more an art than a science.

This is especially true when you're at the start phase of a project. It is not doable to design all the details in advance. So, you need to model simpler and/or more abstract diagrams on what will be delivered as was shown in View 159 and View 160 on page 107 when we discussed the ESB.

17.3 Software distribution

View 181 also shows another aspect you can model which is both detailed and abstracted. Suppose you have a server image that you can roll out for every FTP Server you need. Some sort of fixed setup. You could model this as the Artifacts in this view. There will be some source image somewhere, the 'FTP Server Software Image Source Instance (Artifact)' that resides somewhere. When a new server is created, this image is used to create a copy on that device. In View 181 this copy is called 'Deployed Software Image Instance (Artifact)'. Now you can also model an element that stands for all the 'standard FTP server instances. As these are real copies, using Specialization is not proper. But you can put them into a collection which is a sort of abstract Artifact. This is also shown. 'Software Image Distribution (Infrastructure Function)' is of course part of your secondary architecture (see 12.5 "Secondary Architecture: System Exploitation" on page 90).

17.4 Infrastructure Instances versus Infrastructure Configurations

On the server side, I tend to model the real world, that is, only the elements that we need. That has an underlying reason: servers tend to be pretty specific beasts (unless you are of course in the business of Google, Amazon or any of the infrastructure-in-the-cloud providers). But in *your* business, chances are that your servers all need their own specific setup. I discussed this with ArchiMate modelers from another company once who started out with modeling Server Configurations instead of Server Instances. They ended up with so many different configurations that in the end they

View 181. *An attempt at modeling the processes inside the operating system* would have been better off had they started with instances in the first place.

But for desktops, the situation is different. Generally, organizations use standardized basic desktops, with maybe a limited amount of specific configuration.

In that case, I think it is senseless to keep to the dictum that you want to model as close as possible in the real world, not even in a detailed 'Current State Architecture' model. Here I would suggest only modeling the specific 'configurations', like a 'standard desktop' or 'Trader PC', C# Developer PC, etc.

18. Complex Applications

The examples so far have been mostly minimal, to address certain aspects of basic patterns. But in reality, especially applications maybe be far more complex than those simple basic patterns. That same large system your organization deploys may offer many, many Application Services to the business.

Incidentally, this is one of the reasons why 'application rationalization' initiatives are useful, but do not deliver the expected ultimate simplification of the application landscape of an organization. Replacing those twenty different applications with one big system in part only shuffles complexity around instead of removing it. This is especially true when you are using platforms that are in themselves just rich development environments: install one and it doesn't do anything useful for your business yet. You need to create all kinds of configurations that are just again forms of applications, just running in your new platform instead of directly on top of the operating system. One instance of business complexity has been transformed into another instance of that same complexity. The new platform is richer and supporting this typical need will probably be simpler. But the cost is often that the platform itself as an architecture that also limits you in certain ways, as its core application architecture does not necessarily fit your organization very well, and complexity-increasing workarounds are often needed. You win some, you lose some.

Going back to our core subject, modeling in ArchiMate, this section addresses some of the aspects and consequences of complex application landscapes and platforms.

18.1 Reducing ownership clutter

Suppose you have modeled an application as in View 182. We see here some basic pattern approaches, namely the logical setup of an Artifact (the distribution of the application), which Realizes the Application Component, which is Assigned-To the Application's Function, which — in this case — Realizes five different Application Services. Following the approach laid out in 12.9 "Making it Practical: shortcuts" on page 93, we have Associations between a number of Roles like the application's Owner, the Application Manager, etc. I have colored the Associations orange in View 182 and the other views in this section.

As we can see, the fact that we want to link the Owner to the Application Service means we get five links, one for each Application Service. This clutters the view, and we would like to get rid of that, even more so if we have an application where this substructure approach is necessary on many levels, as can be seen in View 183 on page 118. There is another problem: those Owners, Application Managers, Change Managers and such do not think of themselves as owners of 'five services' or 'five functions'. They look at the system as a single whole. The Owner sees him- or herself as owner of 'System X' and not of 'the five

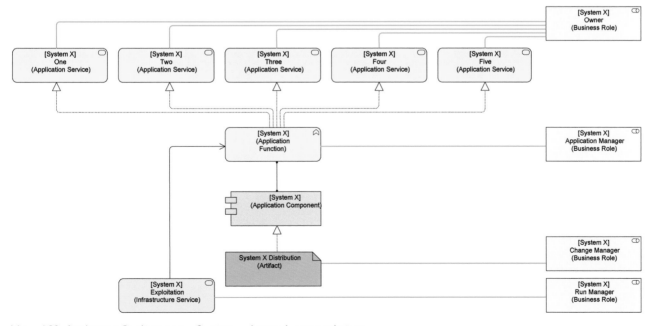

View 182. *Application Realizes many Services - cluttered owner relations*

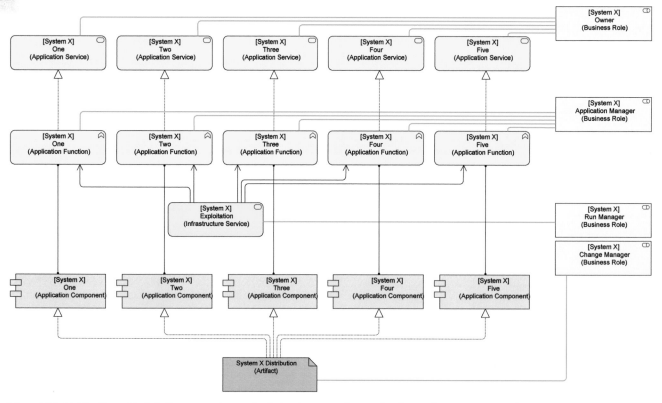

View 183. *Application with Sub-Structure: cluttered relation between the application and management roles.*

Application Services of System X'. Reporting from the model in a way that produces this substructure is therefore not acceptable.

This can be solved by putting the substructure in an Aggregation or Composition and relating management to those. The result is in View 184 on page 118.

That solution immediately poses its own questions, namely: "do you want the red relations in View 184?", or even: "do you want red relations instead of some of the other ones?".

The answer for me is no, because your model will end in chaos if you do. The problem is that not all applications have this complexity. Some are really simple. They just are

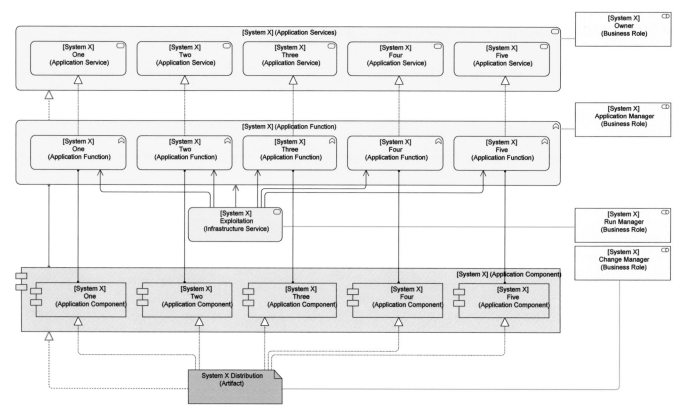

View 184. *Using Aggregation to simplify the mamagement relationships to systems*

a basic one-on-one from Artifact to Application Service. Some other might be complex in any of the other areas of Application Architecture. Some may just have multiple Application Services as in View 182 on page 117. Other may have just a single Application Component, but multiple Application Functions and Application Services. Some may have all aspects of the application landscape in a multiple way as in View 184. To illustrate what happens when some applications have and some do not have the Aggregation structure, I have created View 185 on page 119. On the left you see the simple application. Now suppose, you want to use your model to answer the question: which distributions relate to which owners? The left column is simple: there is only one route. In the middle column you see what happens if you add the Aggregation at the Application Component 'level'. Suddenly, we have three different routes from distribution to owner: the original blue one and two red ones (one follows the Aggregation that is depicted by Nesting). And add one Aggregation extra and the number of routes becomes five if you only count routes that are valid as ArchiMate derived relations (and more if you don't). The example is not perfect (creating a real example would mean that you get a very large picture with many patterns and relations), but I think you will get the picture from this. If you have all these routes, trying to answer questions from analyzing your model becomes rather difficult, because you need many, many variations of 'route traversal' in your analysis to make sure you do not miss anything relevant. And if there are multiple routes, pruning becomes a problem because you will find many conclusions multiple times.

This is why I think you should stick to as few patterns as possible. Hence, in View 184 on page 118 we do *not* add the red relations and we model everything between Artifact and Application Service with the same pattern: the left column in View 185. We do not try to get a combination of both.

We accept that *if* there is a need to model substructure, we model it all the way. We do not model it half. So, deciding to model substructure or not also means answering the question: do we need it?

Sometimes we do need those additional structures though. With only the model as in View 183 on page 118, we cannot provide the owner of the system with a simple 'you own System X'. To be able to say that to the owners and managers of the system, we do need the Aggregations of View 184 on page 118. That is why we keep to the dictum: we may add additional structures to the core modeling patterns, but we make sure that they cannot confuse each other in analysis. Thus, the Aggregations to link owners and managers only exists for that goal.

This problem exists because ArchiMate offers freedom in how you model something that a very formal approach (especially one without derived relations) doesn't as much. ArchiMate is less formal, there are (like with natural language) more 'correct' ways to say something.

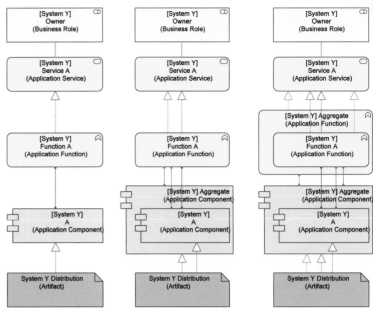

View 185. *Side-by-side illustration of the existence of multiple possible routes from distribution to owner, depending on pattern*

18.2 Complex Software Stacks

A platform is a software program that can load and execute software that is specifically written for it. We encountered the platform-approach from this book for example in sections 7.3 "Modeling Spreadsheet Applications" on page 48, 7.4 "Modeling an Internet Browser" on page 50, 7.5 "More 'application platforms'" on page 51, 9 "An Example from the Real World" on page 69, and 14.2 "ESB" on page 101.

The pattern used in this book follows what ArchiMate says what System Software is: "System software [...] is used to model the software environment in which artifacts run. This can be, for example, an operating system, a JEE application server, a database system, or a workflow engine. Also, system software can be used to represent, for example, communication middleware". We take the idea of software being deployed in a platform one step further: if an application can be `configured', the configuration can be seen as an Artifact that Realizes an Application Component which runs in the platform. This use of System Software enables us to make clear that there is little difference between configuring on the one hand and building on the other. The difference between the two has become blurred anyway by graphical programming environments.

The possibilities that a system offers in configuration can be seen as a programming environment on its own. For some systems with scripting languages and such, it is clear that the system is not only an application, it is also a platform to run those scripts in. For systems that contain just configurable options on the far other end of the spectrum, we might feel uncomfortable calling those configurations 'programs' and the possibilities a 'programming environment'. So, we don't do that, we stay pragmatic and practical. But specifically defined workflows, checks, etc., those are clearly business logic that is 'programmed' and 'executed' within the system and that makes the system a platform. Complex Application

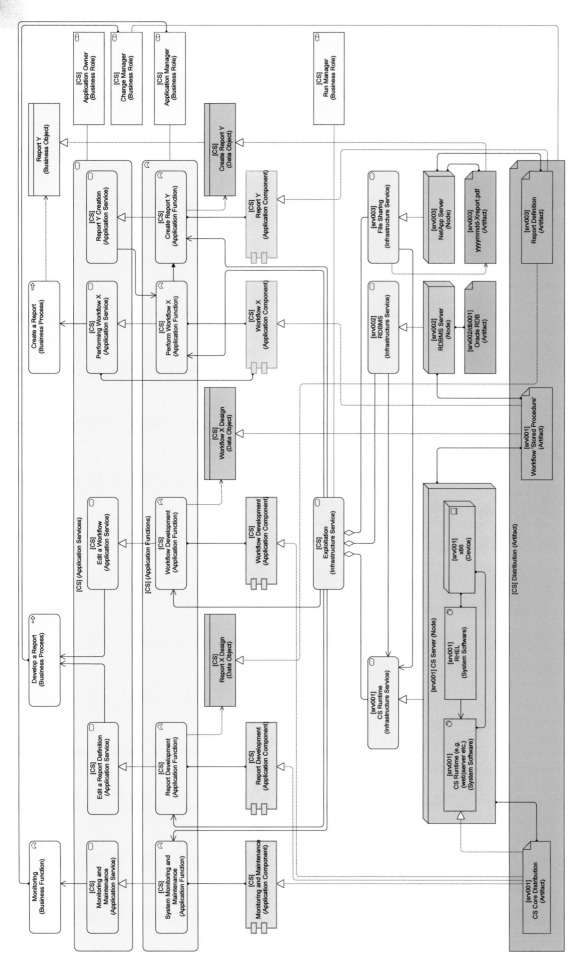

View 186. *A simplified example of a complex application platform,*

Platforms, as we have seen are often a collection of both. A very common pattern is that the complex system has a couple of applications to monitor, maintain/develop, etc., and that specific modules are implemented in that system which are programmed according to the requirements of the users. Some systems which are called applications are often not more than glorified toolboxes, e.g. master data management, warehousing, reconciliation systems are often 'empty'. You need to build your own business logic (work flows, data manipulations) in them.

Now, suppose you buy a scalable analytics platform. This platform consists of a couple of separate architectural domains:

- A Client, consisting of a couple of native Windows programs that talk directly to the back-end, like:

    * A workflow builder;

    * A report definition builder;

    * A monitoring application that enables you to keep track of what your workflows are doing;

- A runtime environment capable of running those workflows which use the report definitions to create actual reports;

- A database that is used by the back-end.

And it also requires (though it is not strictly part of its architecture) a file share to write the reports to. To produce a report we need a definition of that report and a workflow that uses the data and the report definition to produce that report. Report creation does not require human intervention, the workflow (once started) does it automatically.

An example is modeled in View 186 on page 120. In this slightly silly architecture we see:

- The report definition lives on the file share and so does the produced report;

- The workflow definition lives partly on the back-end and partly on the database server. Think of a description that partly consists of stored procedures written to a database (I know systems that work like that). The model shows that the workflow is created by a combination of data on the CS Server and the Database Server. Modeling this explicitly helps you when the time comes to access the possible migration of one database system to another: knowing that there are 'programming Artifacts' in that database makes you extra careful: do they still work the same? Passive data is far less vulnerable. This pattern might look like a type of pattern that we saw earlier when we modeled a message as a single Artifact to be Assigned to all the Nodes that have access to it (See section 14.2 "ESB" on page 101) but this is more like the 'informal collaboration' (See section 2.1 "Collaboration and Interaction" on page 23) as the Artifact is not something identical on each Node but consists of something that is separated across both Nodes;

- The red bordered Application Components and the red bordered System Software together form the platform

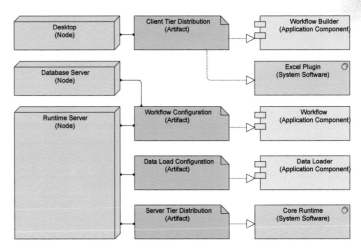

View 187. *Example of software 'tiers' with an irreducible part*

that you bought. Here you find the reason why (compared to Edition I) the Change Manager is Associated with the distribution Artifact and not an Application Component. The problem is that there is no good way in ArchiMate to aggregate System Software and Application Components in a single element. You may group them in a Grouping, but that has not structural relation, you cannot use that for analysis very well. But if you look at the example in View 187, you see that the 'Client Tier', consisting of a real application and a plugin for Excel consists of *both* System Software and an Application Component. So, how can I model this 'tier', so that I am in line with what the business knows from its vendor? The only structural option I have in ArchiMate at this time is falling back on the distribution Artifacts. This is acceptable maybe from the perspective of Associating the Change Manager with everything of and in this platform (both the core distribution and the stuff we have added ourselves), but to create structures that enable linking our model with the outside world is problematic;

- The orange bordered Application Components are the applications you have built in the platform. These contain your business-specific logic and the stuff what your organization bought the platform for in the first place;

- The business process Monitoring is done by the Application Manager, who is also associated with the application functions of the system;

- Developing a report means writing both a workflow and a report definition. In this simple example, the workflow is entirely internal. But in many setups you will find some sort of scheduling system kicking things off from the outside, e.g. at a certain time of day or when a certain piece of data has arrived;

- The business process of creating the report is fully automated. The workflow we have written performs that process. This is shown by assigning the Workflow X Application Component to the Create Report Business Process.

A good example of pretty generic complex application/platforms are SAS and Tibco. The MS Office Suite is also a collection of true applications (like MS Outlook) and application/platforms (such as MS Excel, MS Access).

18.3 A completely alternative platform approach

A quite different approach was suggested by Thomas Barnekow during a discussion on the LinkedIn ArchiMate Group. Before we describe it, we will first revisit the basic complex application pattern, where a system is both an application and a platform. A diagram is shown in View 188 on page 122. The orange bordered elements make up the complex application/platform including what you have built/configured in it. There are three components:

- The System Software element. This represents what is needed in the core to run any applications in the suite and any specific modules you have created;

- An Application Component representing the full applications that are part of the suite. Here they are modeled as one application that has two functions you can use out of the box: monitoring and developing/configuring/maintaining. This is part of secondary architecture (see section 12.3 "Secondary Architecture: Development" on page 89);

- An Application Component that represents a module/configuration you have created yourself.

In the example the first two are Realized by the distribution Artifact. The third is Realized by an Artifact you have created using the developing/configuring/maintaining Application Component. The Artifact Realizes both an Application Component (primary architecture) and the Data Object (secondary architecture). This is a simplified example of course: for instance the infrastructure support is very simple, whereas in reality it will be more complex.

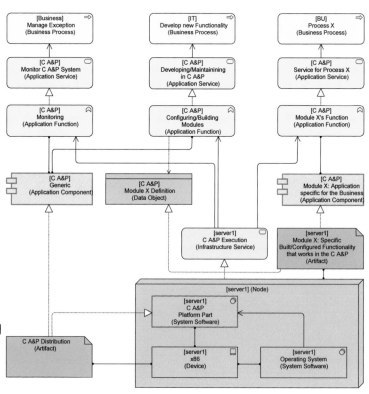

View 188. *Basic Complex Application/Platform system*

Now, Thomas Barnekow suggested a different pattern. His solution has the platform part modeled not as System Software (as what the ArchiMate standard more or less suggests with its definition of 'platform') but as an Application Component as well. Running your own built/configured modules then makes use of the internal 'run' capability of your application. Or in other words: running your module requires not the use of something from the *infrastructure* layer but something from the *application* layer. This creative use of applications using applications (see section 1.2 "The double use of Used-By" on page 17) makes it possible to Aggregate the entire suite into one Application Component, solving the problem depicted in View 187 on page 121.

I am adding this example because it is a beautiful example of the fact that ArchiMate enables you to model something in many different, sometimes even fundamentally different, *correct* ways. In any language (I know no real exceptions, though strictly logical ones — ArchiMate is not, as it requires interpretation — will have multiple ways that are *exactly* equivalent), you can say the same thing in many different ways. And ArchiMate is not even a real language, it is technically only a grammar.

I have personally decided to keep my approach to model the platform aspect of complex application suites as System Software. I think Thomas' solution is perfectly correct, and has some advantages, but also some disadvantages. Automat-

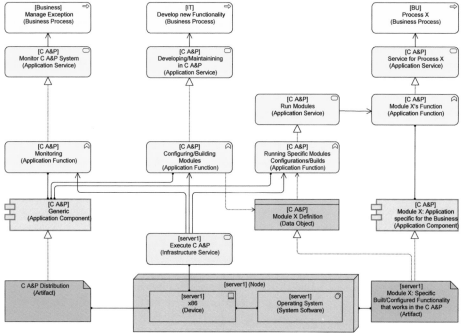

View 189. *Complex Application/Platform system with platform aspect modeled in application layer. From a suggestion by Thomas Barnekow*

ed analysis becomes slightly more complex, I think as you will be using the 'application uses application' pattern for two different meanings. Adding to that: our existing pattern choice (View 188 on page 122) serves us well. So, I keep to my existing setup.

There is one thing I cannot stress enough: Whatever you choose, make certain that you do it always the exact same way in all your models.

18.4 Complex Application Components

Not every organization can buy its software from vendors. Even if they do, we have seen the 'applications' are often (partly) platforms that require quite a bit of configuration and/or building before the application does exactly what your business needs.

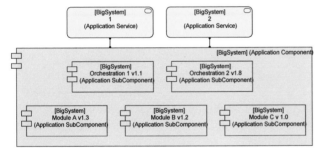

View 190. *Big Monolithic Complex Application*

But for those organizations that cannot purchase a platform that meets their requirements, there is no other route than building the software in-house. Generally this is only the case for very large organizations, whose needs (e.g. regulatory or technically) are so specific that a commercial tool vendor will be confronted with a market size of (close to) 1. So, we will find still complex 'monolithic' applications built in-house. Maybe less so that a few decennia ago, and more of them are interconnected, but it still happens. Besides, those application/platforms you

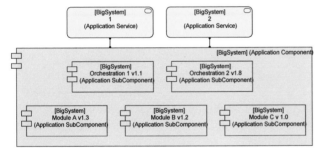

View 191. *Typical substructure modeling of monolithic complex application*

buy are in themselves often (partly) 'monolithic' applications. There is no free lunch: a true web of small interconnected programs (as envisioned by the people who gave us Unix) has never really materialized.

So, these are applications that contain a lot of internal complexity. A lot of sub-applications and parts that weave everything together (the 'orchestration' inside the monolithic application). How do we model that? Let's start with a simple example in View 190.

Our BigSystem monolithic application provides two Application Services for the business: '1' and "2. Of course, in reality there may be tens or hundreds of specific services, but for the exposé, this will do.

Typically, when we want to model that the Application Component is made up of many sub-components, we model those sub-components as Composite children and Nest them, as in View 191.

However, there is more to the structure than just the division

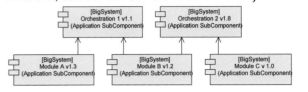

View 192. *The original substructure of BigSystem*

into sub-components. These sub-components have relations which — in the case of a large monolithic system — become as interesting for an enterprise architect as the landscape of applications is for less monolithic solutions. After all, the inside of the monolithic application is a landscape in itself which might have to be managed as parts may interact with the rest of the world. So, View 192 shows us some (derived) relations between the sub-components. Not shown is that 'Orchestration 1' Realizes Application Service '1', etc..

If you wonder why this may be interesting from an Enterprise Architecture point of view. Let's assume our big monolithic

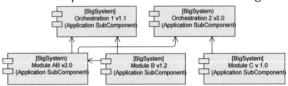

View 193. *BigSystem Update Phase 1*

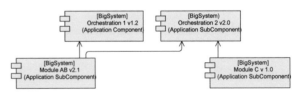

View 194. *BigSystem Update Phase 2*

application needs serious rebuilding. In fact, the work that needs to be done would be comparable to changing application *landscapes* in cases without monolithic systems. Such efforts are substantial enough to put them under Enterprise Architecture governance. Take for instance the following two phases that we foresee (View 193 and View 194): the two-step phasing out of 'Module B'. First we will update 'Orchestration 2' and 'Module A' such that 'Orchestration 2' becomes independent from 'Module B'. The new 'Mod-

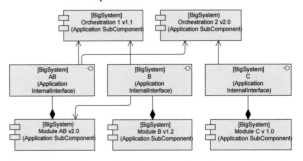

View 195. *BigSystem Update Phase 1 with internal interfaces added*

ule AB' is going to use 'Module B' itself, provide 'AB' to 'Orchestration 2', so we have two sub-component updates. Then, we will change 'Orchestration 1' so it uses 'Module

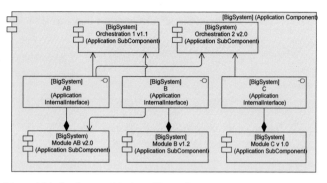

View 196. *BigSystem Update Phase 1 with internal interfaces in Nested fashion*

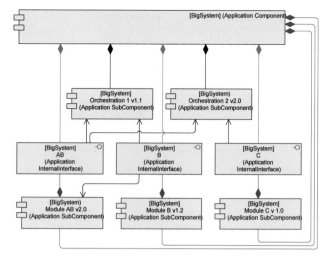

View 197. *BigSystem Update Phase 1, expanded version with all relations.*

AB' and we will have 'Module AB" create 'AB' without the help of independent 'Module B', which subsequently can be removed.

So, the stage is set for a series of changes to our Complex Application Component 'BigSystem'.

We will now return to the situation of 'Update Phase 1' as seen in View 193 on page 123 to illustrate a very small problem in ArchiMate. The diagrams that so far did show the dependencies used derived Used-By relations between the various sub-components. The first thing we want to do is to add the internal Application Interfaces so we know what we are actually saying with those derived relations. This is shown in View 195 on page 123.

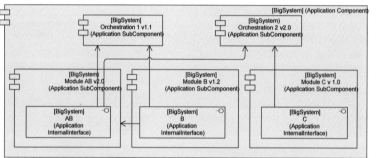

View 198. *BigSystem Update Phase 1, in double-Nested fashion*

What happens if we Nest this again in the BigSystem overall Application Component? This is shown in View 196.

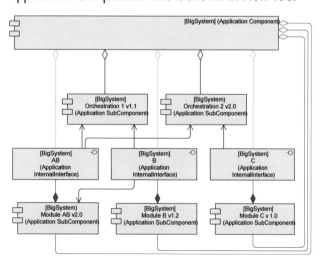

View 199. *BigSystem Update Phase 1, overall application modeled as Aggregation instead of Composite*

But what is the relation between the overall BigSystem Application Component and its constituents? Well, we know that the sub-components are Composite children of the overall component. They do not have an independent existence after all. The relation between the overall Application Component and the Nested (internal) Application Interfaces is likewise a Composite. There are two ways in which this is true, but they end up in the same way as shown in View 197.

• There is a direct Composite relation (red) between the overall Application Component and the Nested (internal) Application Interfaces. What this means is that these interfaces are interfaces of the overall Application Component, directly. This, of course is problematic.

• Even if you say that the interfaces are not of the overall Application Component but of the sub-components, there still is a derived Composite relation (red) between the overall Application Component and the internal Application Interfaces (blue route).

And the (very) small grammatical problem is this: the Application Interfaces now have *two* Composite parents, but ArchiMate forbids that any element is part of more than one Composite, and it does not limit that constraint to direct (versus derived) Compositions.

Even if we only use a direct relation we have a small problem: Nesting is allowed to represent a relation (Composition, Aggregation and Assignment for the core metamodel), so if you nest the internal Application Interface in the overall Application Component, there must be a relation. A direct Composition relation would mean that you let the internal interfaces be owned by the overall component, leading to the same multiple-ownership problem. So the only relation allowed between the overall Application Component and the internal interfaces in View 197 is an Aggregation.

In fact the only solution entirely without grammatical problems is if you not only Nest, but you Nest all the way down (this is shown in View 198) *and ignore derived relations*.

If you do *not* ignore the derived relations, the situation presents a true contradiction in ArchiMate: rules for derivation

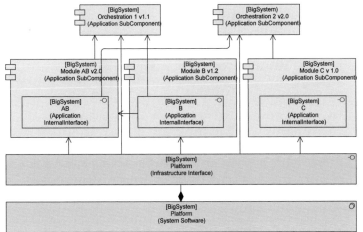

View 200. *BigSystem Update Phase I, overall application modeled as System Software (platform)*

say the Composition from the overall Application Component to the internal interface is allowed. But the rules for composition itself say it is forbidden.

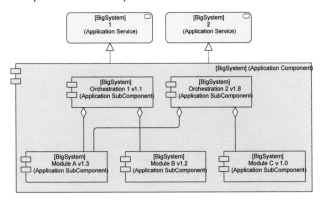

View 201. *The substructure of the Current State of BigSystem (View 191/View 192 on page 123) modeled with Aggregation instead of Used-By*

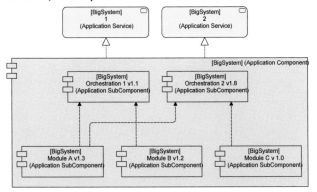

View 202. *The substructure of the Current State of BigSystem (View 191/View 192 on page 123) modeled with Flow instead of Used-By*

So, you need to prevent the derived Composition relations. This can be done by using Aggregation instead of Composition between the overall Application Component and its constituents. This is shown in View 199 on page 124. The orange Aggregation are derived from the blue Aggregations and Compositions. But, frankly, that is not what you mean when you have that big system and you want to show the substructure. After all, it *is* a single bit monolithic system and you only want to show substructure that is not independent from it.

There is another way to prevent the technical problem in ArchiMate 2. We could say the overall BigSystem application is a platform modeled as System Software. This is shown in View 200. Though technically correct ArchiMate, this is pretty artificial. After all, this allows us to let the overall application exist without its constituent parts. Besides, we have to make up an Infrastructure Interface that in reality does not exist.

There are more ways to model this substructure. View 201

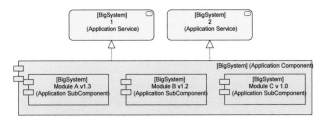

View 203. *The BigSystem system modeled without explicit orchestration subcomponents*

has the relations between subcomponents modeled as Aggregations. This view says that the subcomponents refer to each other. View 202 models their relation with (derived) Flows, here the dynamic character of the relation between subcomponents is stressed. And, finally, View 203 leaves out the orchestration elements altogether. This functionality is modeled as being part of the overall Application Component. As you can see that there are many ways of modeling application *landscapes* or application *structures* (or hybrids of these) in ArchiMate.

Personally, I would just use the pattern in View 196 on page 124, and ignore that small grammatical problem and thus just do something that might formally be illegal in ArchiMate. We might even see ArchiMate solve this issue in one way or another in a next release. Or we might use a Nested version of View 193 on page 123, but personally I would prefer having the interfaces in this case as they are important in the development and maintenance.

So, why did I make such a big production of this non-issue about the Composition relation? It is to show you another example that there are many ways in ArchiMate to model the same state of affairs. And secondly, that you should not be fanatical about following the standard in its literal detail. You use patterns that suits you best (and hope an upcoming release of your tool does not forbid the pattern in the future).

18.5 Business logic at infrastructure level

So far, the modeling approach has been to make a split between application layer and infrastructure layer largely on the basis of the question if there was business-specific logic or not. If not: the software would be modeled as System Software in the infrastructure layer, otherwise, as it was business-specific, the software was modeled as Application Component in the application layer.

This choice has the advantage that business-specific logic is always in the application layer and can thus be coupled (used by) the business layer in an appropriate manner.

There is a disadvantage to that approach as well: application logic cannot manipulate Artifacts and sometimes the business logic is just about manipulating Artifacts. This becomes especially clear when your business uses Business Process Modeling, which — other than Enterprise Architecture — generally does not make a split in layers. More on BPM in Chapter "BPMN and ArchiMate" on page 151, but coupling Business Process Models — where Activities (from an EA perspective in the business layer) may directly manipulate Artifacts (e.g. files) — to Enterprise Architecture models in ArchiMate — which does not allow that — is obviously problematic.

We can model business logic in the infrastructure layer, but we run into problems if we do. An example is shown in View 204. This example is adapted from the Managed File Transfer (MFT) - Scheduler example of section 9 "An Example from the Real World" on page 69. In it, we see the MFT solution that is responsible for (somehow, not modeled) receiving the file 'filexxx.yyy' and then acting on that. What is has to do with the file is defined in a business-specific

'Workflow X'. This workflow copies the file to a file share (not very realistic as we have an MFT so we get rid of all those file shares, but it will do for now).

The MFT system comes with a development/maintenance tool that we can use to define (develop) workflows. For the development/maintenance application, the workflow is data. But the Artifact that Realizes the Data Object also Realizes the System Software that stands for the application logic which is now modeled in the infrastructure layer. Before, we modeled such logic in the application layer, e.g. the Primary/Secondary architecture pattern seen in section 12.3 "Secondary Architecture: Development" on page 89. As the 'MFT Workflow X Definition' Artifact Realizes System Software, its behavior is an Infrastructure Function. Basically, this is all just like the modeling we did in the application layer, only now with infrastructure components which are able to handle/manipulate Artifacts directly. Earlier, we were unable to model how the 'workflow' handled Artifacts as we cannot relate application layer elements with infrastructure elements that way (an Application Service cannot manipulate an Artifact).

But this comes at a cost, in fact it comes with three prices to pay:

- If the whole Business Process is automated, we cannot Assign the System Software to it in ArchiMate. I've modeled a purple Association to show where we would like to have an Assignment instead;

- We cannot Trigger (nor Flow to) an Application Function from an Infrastructure Function in ArchiMate. Such connections exist in the real world, where applications listen to infrastructure events (e.g. on a TCP port) and get triggered by such an event, but ArchiMate does not allow it. I've modeled an orange Association to show where we would like to be able to Trigger or Flow;

- We *can* technically let the Infrastructure Service Used-By the Business Process. But, though allowed, this relation means quite something different than a direct usage. It is a derived relation that assumes that some application sits in between. And that application does not exist.

So, though we can do it and solve our 'Artifact manipulation by a Business Process' by it, current ArchiMate is too limited to allow everything we need.

View 204. *Business Logic in the Infrastructure Layer*

19. Modeling Information Aspects

So far, we have mostly ignored the informational aspects of our landscape. From an Enterprise Architecture perspective, this is mostly not a problem. The active structure and its behavior are generally the key to your landscape. Besides, modeling the Artifacts in your landscape often feels like modeling brick and mortar while all you wanted to show was a house. But there are cases when informational elements (Business Object, Data Object, Artifact) are essential.

19.1 Messages and File Copies

In the real world of organizations connected to the outside world, there is a lot of data going in and out. An Asset

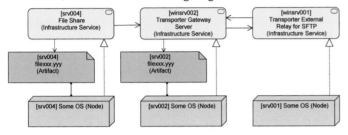

View 205. *Data transport: copying a file*

Manager, for instance, gets price and other master data from data vendors, cash positions from banks, holdings positions from custodians, the list is endless. And most of that data these days is still transported by shuffling files around, often via a very antique mechanism called FTP (albeit in a secure version). Take for instance price data. To get that from a data

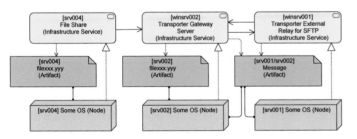

View 206. *Data transport: File copying and messaging side by side*

vendor, you may have to create a file in a certain format that contains information about your holdings. Then you upload that to an FTP site of the data vendor. The data vendor creates a reply, which again is a file with all the missing data (price and other aspects) filled in. This file you either have to collect yourself or they drop it on your own FTP server. This is a rather essential process for the business, and it is almost all low level data manipulation where the systems involved (like file transport, scheduling) are not interested in or aware of the content of the file.

Data transport has already been modeled before. In section 9 "An Example from the Real World", in View 111 on page 72, we see an essential piece of data transport modeled. Brought back to the file copying essentials, this becomes View 205.

On the right of this view, no Artifact is modeled. But if we want to add one that represents the data that is transferred

from [srv001] to [srv002], we get View 206. This was seen earlier in the lower-left corner of View 157 on page 105 in section 14.2 "ESB".

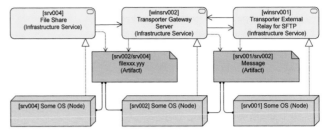

View 207. *Data transport with single Artifact for copied file*

I am taking a bit of liberty with ArchiMate when I model a message as something that is Assigned to multiple Nodes. Of course, if one digs deeper, even the messages become little stored Artifacts and moving something is implemented as copying and deleting the original. In fact, that is fundamentally true of digital technology. The internet is a good example: All those data streams are in fact built on top of IP

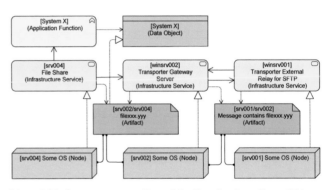

View 208. *Data transport: Shared Artifact Realizes Data Object*

(the 'Internet Protocol') which is just copying data over and destroying the original when the acknowledge of successful reception has been received. Do that copying and deleting quickly enough and you have an abstraction that looks like moving data around.

Now, the question obviously is: when do you choose one and when the other? Why not, for instance, use a single Artifact for the copying pattern? An example is shown in View

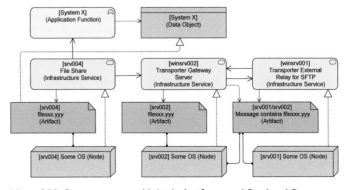

View 209. *Data transport: Multiple Artifacts and Realized Data Object*

207. But suppose this Artifact is used by some application and represents a real Data Object? If we add a Data Object it looks like View 208. Now, this suggests that System X depends on srv002. Now, in a certain way, this is true: If srv002 dies, no more new files can be copied to srv004. But if you start to reason that way, soon everything depends on everything. So, to prevent drawing weak conclusions too easily, the Multiple Artifact pattern is better in this situation. This is shown in View 209. Other problems appear when there are multiple systems employed to transport the Artifact around in a couple of steps, if the Artifact changes name, etc..

Now, suppose our message contains price data which is created by one system and imported by another. An example is shown in View 210 on page 128. Note, this example leaves out a lot of my standard patterns for modeling, like Infrastructure Building blocks, etc.. What this view shows is that there is a 'Provide Prices' Business Process that uses both systems to get the price from one system into another. Both systems use the MQ Messaging Service for this, one as sender, the other as receiver. The message is modeled as a shared Artifact. But in the application layer, both systems have their own Data Object, these need not necessarily be the same, both may have different extra properties, for instance. But both Data Objects do represent that same abstract Business Object: a Price. Note also, that System B also keeps price data in a database (the infrastructure of which is not modeled). In fact it may read the price message but it writes its price data Object to permanent storage. I have modeled that as two Access relations (because my tool is unable to create a true read-write).

It is fair that System A is in some way dependent on serv001 via the message Artifact, because without srv001, the message, and thus the Data Object cannot exist, whereas in the file copy example, it cannot be created anew, but it can exist.

If our 'Price' Business Object is highly sensitive information, we can from this model deduce that we need to pay extended attention to the security of srv001 and srv002 (and srv003).

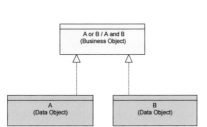

View 211. *Two Data Objects Realize a single Business Object*

19.2 Informational Structure

Now, from the explanation it is clear that our 'Price' Business Object is represented independently by both '[System A] Price Data (Data Object)' and '[System B] Price Data (Data Object)'. But what if we have a Business Object that is some sort of abstraction that is not kept in a single application, but that is distributed across multiple? Such things happen. The 'Customer' Business Object may be Realized by Data in the CRM system in combination with data in the Accounting system.

Or what if we have two systems, each holding half of the representations of a certain Business Object? Such things happen too. We may have a single 'Price' Business Object, but the vegetable prices are kept in a different system than the bread prices.

Here we hit on a weak spot of ArchiMate: it does not have much to help us to model this clearly. Those two Realization relations from two different Data Objects to that single Business Object (as in View 211) can have many different meanings that are not immediately clear from the model.

You might be tempted to use Composition and Aggregation at the business layer to solve this. View 212 has the AND-structure modeled as Composition. Technically, you lose the relation between the Data Objects and the overall Business Object, as a derived relation is not possible. But as we have seen more often, keeping to strict 'derived relations' when you think of meaning is generally too limited. The same is true for the relations in View 213 where an attempt was made to model the OR-structure.

The problem with both is that the meaning is still not clear. First, the Aggregation in View 213 generally means that its constituents have independent existence, which is not the case in our situation. And the Composition might be interpreted as the fact that the constituents cannot exist without the parent, that does not say they *must* exist in all cases. And we haven't even tried to model the difference between OR and XOR.

All in all, ArchiMate does not allow you to model informational structures precisely and unambiguously.

Note that the same ambiguities exist when modeling Services as Realized by

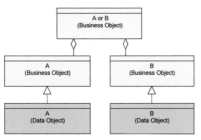

View 213. *Using Aggregation to model an informational OR-structure*

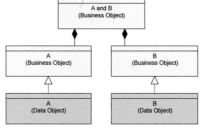

View 212. *Using Composition to model an informational AND-structure*

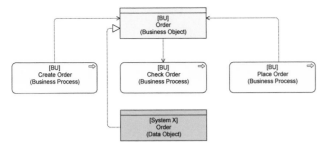

View 214. *Status Change of Business Object: Ignored*

multiple Functions (or Processes) in the same way as in View 211.

19.3 Status Change of Informational Objects

Suppose you have a process where an order needs to be checked by a supervisor before it can go ahead: an example of the four-eyes principle. The order's content itself does not change at all, it is only checked visually, e.g. in the system or via a printout.

If you have a situation like this you have a few options. The first is to ignore this in the informational part of your architecture. You model access of the check behavior to the Business Object and leave it at that. This is shown in View 214.

But being able to prove that the four-eyes principle was actually followed may be important in our enterprise design. For instance, we can show that only checked orders are placed. This is shown in View 215.

But since both Business Objects are Realized by the same Data Object, and assuming that we do not notify this check in the Order Business Object itself, we still cannot prove that we only place checked orders. We need some way to prove that. One way is to use the audit trail of the supporting system for that, which is a separate Data Object. Together with the order, the audit trail can Realize a checked order. This is shown in View 216.

Having separate Business Objects for order and checked order does provide clutter in our informational landscape though. We could do with just a single 'order' abstract entity and depending on the availability of the audit trail, the order is either checked or not. Because we can show that checking the order leads to a proof in the audit trail, and because the processes are modeled such that the order in which they are executed mean that no unchecked order can get placed,

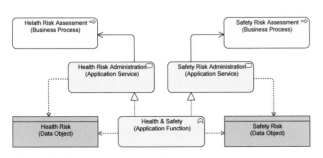

View 220. *Two ways to Access Information*

we might simplify our business architecture. This is shown in View 217.

Finally, View 218 and View 219 show the version where the proof is on a signed printout, modeled with a Representation

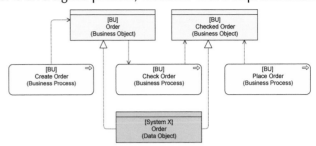

View 215. *Status Change of Business Object: in business layer*

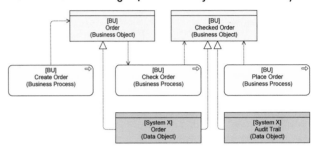

View 216. *Status Change of Business Object: in business and application layer*

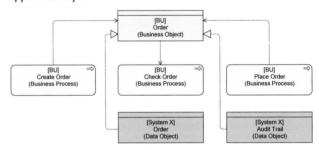

View 217. *Status Change of Business Object: in application layer*

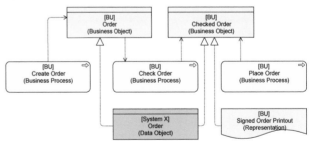

View 218. *Status Change of Business Object: in business layer and as Representation*

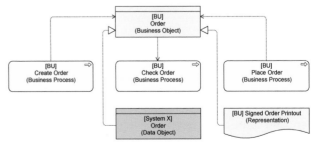

View 219. *Status Change of Business Object: Representation only*

element. Of course, there might be both an audit trail in the system and a paper trail, in which case these are combined. All in all, I would in most cases not model status changes by creating additional Business Objects, though if you want to be very precise, you can.

19.4 Access passive element from internal or external behavior?

The ArchiMate metamodel allows you to Access informational objects from both the internal and the external behavioral element. The two are shown in View 220: the blue Access relations from the external behavior (service) and the red ones from the internal behavior (function). The same pattern applies in the business layer and the infrastructure layer. Incidentally, the red Access relation is also the derived relation from the route via the Realization relation and the blue Access relation.

Now, in this book, I have most of the time modeled Access from internal behavior, but the other one is quite valid as well. The question of course is: when to use one and when the other. Here, I think there are a few aspects to take into account. First, using both means that your analyses in the model get yet another route to manage. And as you know it is important to keep your routes to a minimum if you want to use seriously large models. If you want to pay that price, then it depends on what the information stands for. If you

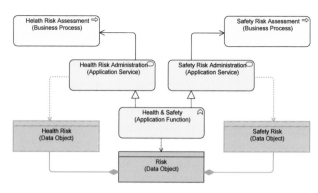

View 221. *Basic Access Pattern with optional service-specific objects*

follow the line that you do not create service abstractions (i.e. services Realized by multiple functions/processes), in other words you keep the relations between internal and external behavior as 1:n, then relating external behavior to information is more specific.

Personally I prefer:

*   Access information normally from internal behavior. It is after all that behavior that generally accesses that information for more than just the service;

*   Only Access information from the service if that information is the content of that service (and nothing else).

This is shown in View 221, with the optional service-related information and its relation in orange.

20. The Implementation and Migration Extension

ArchiMate comes with another extension (besides the one we described in Section 13.3 "The Motivation Extension" on page 97): The Implementation and Migration Extension. This extension was also added after ArchiMate was adopted by The Open Group and it (and its sibling the Motivation Extension) were designed so it would be possible to model certain aspects of The Open Groups Architecture Framework (TOGAF) in ArchiMate.

I am personally not a big fan of the view on enterprise architecture that is underlying these approaches. I do believe on the importance of (extensive) modeling in Enterprise Architecture, but for me, that modeling is by and large restricted to the *object* (the enterprise and what it does) and not the *subject* (the architect, or the project manager, and what he/she does). More on this in section 26 "The Role of ArchiMate in Enterprise Architecture" on page 179, part of the "Discussing ArchiMate" Chapter).

Now, for the Motivation Extension, as you might have read (see Section 13 "Modeling Risk & Security" on page 96), I found a useful application within *subject* modeling. For the Implementation and Migration Extension, I have not encountered such an application yet. So, I am only offering a basic explanation of the Implementation and Migration Extension here and some remarks on developing your patterns in case you want to use it. For this I am using View 222 on page 131.

In this view, the four elements of the Implementation and Migration Extensions are used.

This is the Work Package. The ArchiMate standard defines it as "a series of actions designed to accomplish a unique goal within a specified time". A Business Role may be Assigned to it. If that sounds as a Business Process to you, I'm with you. The ArchiMate standard says it is a 'behavioral element' just like that Business Process. It is however completely separate, it is not a Specialization of Business Process, so you cannot use it in your models as you would the Business Process element from the Core ArchiMate metamodel. It does accept the Trigger (———▶) and Flow (- - - -▶) relations between Work Packages, just as they can exist between behavioral elements of the same layer in the Core metamodel.

This is the Deliverable. The ArchiMate standard defines it as "a precisely-defined outcome of a work package". Deliverables are Realized (- - - -▷) by Work Packages. Now the 'outcome' of a Business Process is a Service or a Business Object (or a Aggregation of these in a Product). Again, this sounds like a passive element in the Core ArchiMate metamodel, but it isn't. Of course, deliverables could be very abstract, like 'a stable environment' but that kind of overlaps with Goals from the Motivation Extension.

This is the Plateau. The ArchiMate standard defines it as "a relatively stable state of the architecture that exists during a limited period of time". Plateaus are Realized (⸺▷) by Deliverables and may Aggregate (◇⸺) any Core metamodel element. Given that change is eternal in human endeavor, I would say that there is no 'plateau' that can exist for an indefinite period of time. I find the concept of a plateau (for me: any state of affairs of the landscape that will be in production, so for me the 'target architecture' of a project is a plateau as well) extremely useful. But here the idea is taken from TOGAF, where there is a clear current state (or baseline) and a clear future state (or target architecture) and the plateaus are intended to only model temporary intermediate states of affairs.

This is the Gap. The ArchiMate standard defines it as "an outcome of a gap analysis between two plateaus". Gaps are Associated (⸺) with Plateaus. Gaps may also be Associated with any Core metamodel element. Now, 'creating a gap analysis' sounds as a Business Process to me and the resulting Gap thus as a Business Object, both part of what I would call 'tertiary architecture' (see Section 12.8 "Tertiary Architecture: other roles" on page 92). Both firmly part of what the enterprise is and does. In the official standard, a Gap is not a Specialization of a Business Object.

You may Associate Locations with both Work Package and Deliverable. Strangely enough, this does not follow the normal relation from a Location to a structural element: Assignment. View 222 contains all Implementation and Migration elements and the Core elements that may be related to it in a simple example: a server must be updated from version 1 of the operating system to version 2. I would like to draw your attention to the following aspects:

- You must decide which Realization relations you want to draw from either Work Package or Deliverable (shown in orange). I would suggest using only a 1:n relation between Work Packages and Deliverables and not modeling any Realization from the Work

View 222. *Basic Structure of the Implementation and Migration Extension*

Package to Core elements, but only from Deliverables, which are more specific if you keep to 1:n;

- In the example, the device is not changed, only the operating system installed on it. This happens often when your landscape changes, not everything changes. So, I would not model Realizations from Work Package or Deliverable to elements that do not change. The ArchiMate standard does not allow any other relation, but in the spirit of ArchiMate, I would suggest using Associations (shown in blue) for affected but not changed elements. I would also not model this from Work Packages but from Deliverables only.

- You need to choose which elements to Aggregate in a Plateau (shown in green). In the example you need to choose if you want to Aggregate affected but unchanged elements (e.g. the Device) and you need to choose if you want to model direct Aggregations to elements that can be 'derived' (e.g. do you really need to Aggregate

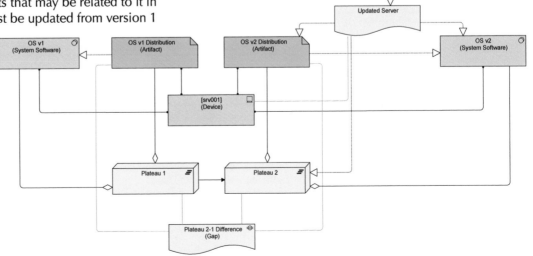

View 223. *Proposed pattern for using the Implementation and Migration Extension*

the System Software if you have Aggregated the 'distribution' Artifact?).

- If you want to model Locations (and this is a big 'if' as far as I'm concerned), do you Associate them with both Work Packages and Deliverables? It is possible that something is created at Location A and used at Location B, so you might have to. Personally, I would not use Locations at all.

- Gaps are Associated with the Plateau's they represent the difference of. It is allowed to Associate them as well with the Core elements that the Gap analysis is about (shown in violet). Do you include Associations to elements that remain the same but that are relevant?

- You need to choose if you use a single element or a multiple for each element that changes. In the example, two are modeled, but with many Plateaus this becomes messy. Use single objects, though, and the result may be difficult to read. Tooling may help here, e.g.. by offering viewing options and element versions depending on plateaus, but this is not part of the ArchiMate standard itself.

The proposed pattern is shown in View 223 on page 131.

I personally think that though it may seem nice to be able to connect architectural landscapes to this sort of change modeling, it becomes — except for the most simple of cases — rather unwieldy pretty quickly. Nice for simple examples but it does not scale well and as such does not offer much advantages over simpler ways.

But as a separate modeling structure for change it works rather well.

This page intentionally not left blank

Model Use & Maintenance

Model Use & Maintenance

21. Construction & Use Views

When you get *really* serious with ArchiMate, and you model your entire Current State in ArchiMate, your models will get pretty large. My own estimate of our model when we are

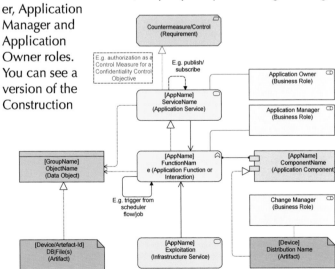

View 224. *Large Model Construction - Business Architecture View*

complete, with risks, secondary and tertiary architectures and more lies around 20,000 elements and 25,000 relations (and much more in satellite models, see below). This sounds unmanageable, but it isn't if you do it right (this comes from experience, we build & manage this with roughly one FTE after doing an initial stint with two FTE). And besides, if you have such a model, it will save a lot of work elsewhere in your organization. Now, apart from the right patterns to which you should stick religiously, you will need a way to model this. One big view of 20,000 elements and 25,000 relations doesn't cut it.

Before I describe the details, there is one important point and you might to choose differently. We decided *not* to model Interfaces so we could keep our models simpler (they are complex enough as is). My philosophy is that behavior is the core of what happens in the organization and we model around that. This is also the reason we chose the original

color setup (with a twist). Basically, it was all about keeping things manageable in the light of the huge scale we were planning to do our modeling in.

We decided to use a couple of 'view types' to maintain our current state model (and models for large projects). I think our end result is not yet finished, as we have found that maintaining construction views is not enough to publish the model, so we need other views, specialized for a specific audience. Using the viewpoints mechanism from the ArchiMate standard also doesn't cut it for us. So, we created a couple of 'view templates' to divide our landscape in and that we use to model our large environments, especially the current state. Note, these views are not truly ArchiMate 'viewpoints'. ArchiMate viewpoints restrict a view to certain element and relation types. Our views are not quite like that. For instance, the Application Architecture View does not allow all Business Roles, only explicitly the Change Manager, Application Manager and Application Owner roles. You can see a version of the Construction

View 225. *Large Model Construction - Application Architecture View*

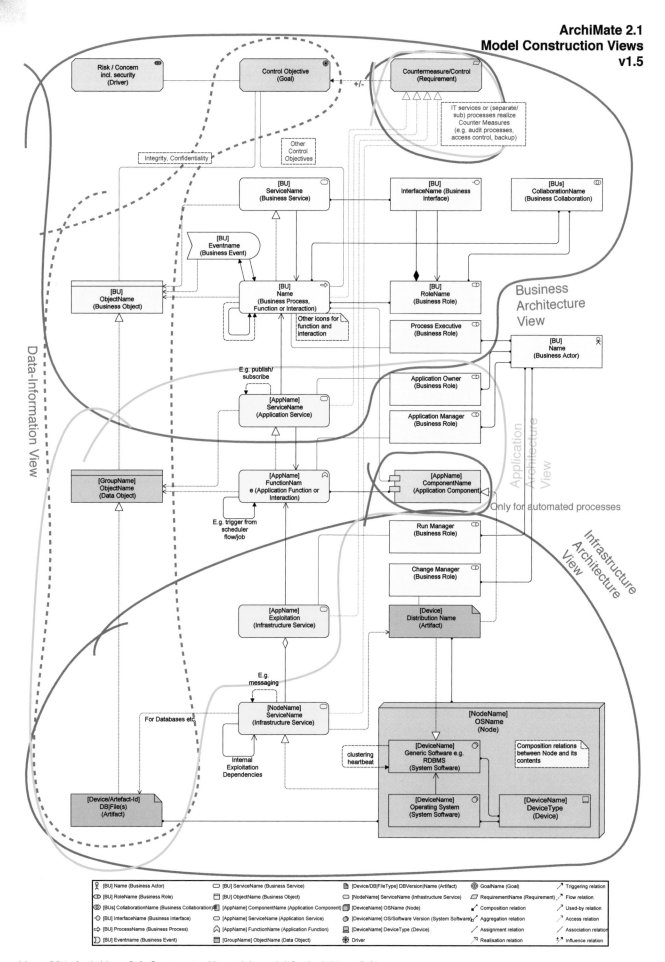

View 226. *ArchiMate 2.1 Construction Views (also valid for ArchiMate 2.0)*

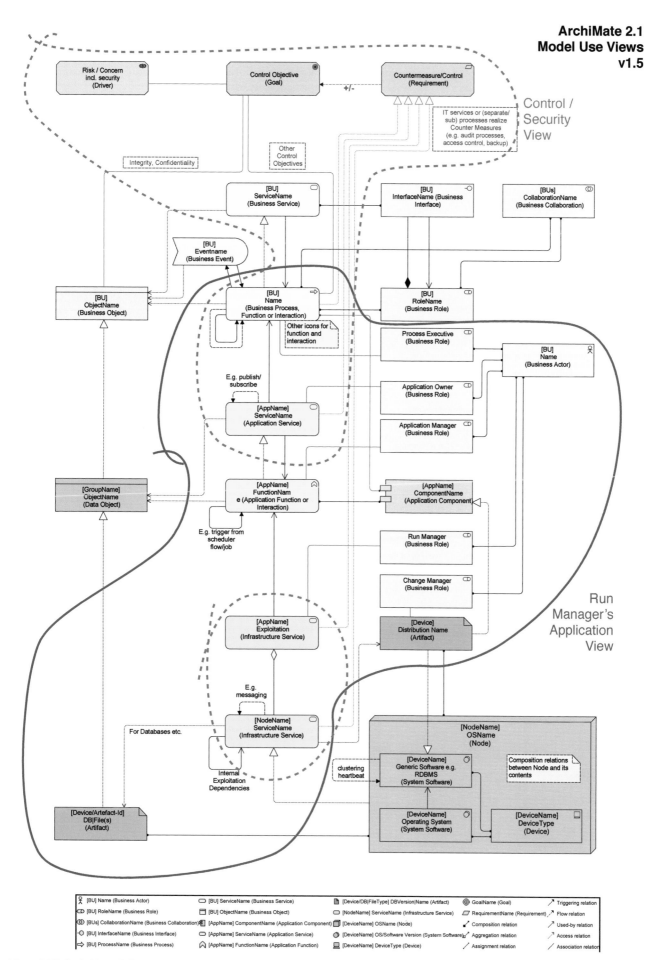

View 227. *ArchiMate 2.1 Use Views: Application Exploitation and Risk& Security (also valid for ArchiMate 2.0)*

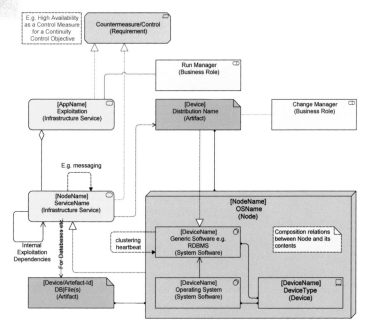

View 228. *Large Model Construction – Infrastructure Architecture View*

Views in View 226 on page 136. Here you see three view types:

- The Business Architecture View outlined in red. This view is for modeling the business architecture, but it also includes Risk, Control Objectives, Counter Measures (Section 13.4 "Modeling Risks and Controls" on page 98) and Secondary Roles (Section 12.9 "Making it Practical: shortcuts" on page 93). Note that for this and the other view types, if an element is not available in the view e.g. Infrastructure Service in the Business Architecture View, any relation to it is also not visible in the view. A special case is the Application Component: only the Application Components that perform (automated) business behavior are shown. The elements of the view together can be seen separately in View 224 on page 135;

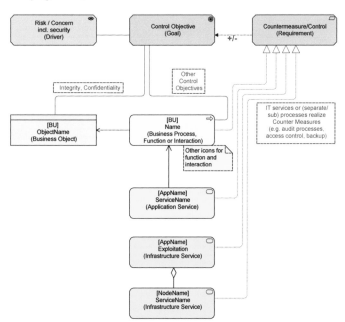

View 230. *Large Model Use – Risk & Security View*

- The Application Architecture View outlined in yellow. This view is for modeling the application architecture, but it also includes the 'Exploitation' Infrastructure Service (see Section 7.6 "Infrastructure 'Building Blocks'" on page 53), the 'Application Owner', 'Application Manager' and 'Change Manager' from Section 12.9 "Making it Practical: shortcuts" on page 93) and the Counter Measures (Section 13.4 "Modeling Risks and Controls" on page 98) that the Application Services have to Realize. We have been in discussion about adding the Business Processes that use the Application Services to this view, but you need to keep the number of elements down to keep it manageable. Besides, we had that there because it would make use by the Run Department easier and we decided on a special view for that (see below). Important: we do not use Application Collaboration and Application Interaction. The elements of the view together can be seen separately in View 225 on page 135;

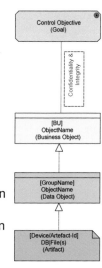

View 229. *Large Model Construction – Data-Information View*

- The Infrastructure Architecture View outlined in brown. This view contains the infrastructure, the 'Run Manager' from Section 12.9 "Making it Practical: shortcuts" on page 93) and the Counter Measures (Section 13.4 "Modeling Risks and Controls" on page 98) that the Infrastructure Services have to Realize (e.g. Intrusion Detection as a Counter Measure for Control Objective Confidentiality). It can be seen separately in View 228;

- The last view template on View 226 on page 136 is the Data-Information View in green dashed outline. This also contains the Confidentiality and Integrity Control Objective for the Business Objects (Section 13.4 "Modeling Risks and Controls" on page 98). It can be seen separately in View 229.

Now, with these views, you can model the entire setup. But that does not mean you have the best views for using the model. As my colleague Jos Knoops experienced, a bit of a specific view about an application helps the IT Service Management department a lot to understand what it is they are actually managing. So he created an application context view for the Run Department which can be seen in View 227 on page 137 as the blue outline. I call this the 'Run Manager's Application View'. it can be seen separately in View 231.

Since the Run Manager already knows who he is and what his or her responsibilities are, he or she is not in the view. What is in the view is the basic application setup, which processes it supports and who the most important stakeholders are (Process Executive, Application Owner, Application Manager and Change Manager) from Section 12.9 "Making it Practical: shortcuts" on page 93). Here, we do show the actual actors in our model. And we do not show the Counter Measures, because this is in informative contextual view about the application the Run Manager is responsible for to keep running.

Another view type you could add is a view for the Security Officer or the Operational Risk Officer. It is the light purple dashed outline in View 227 on page 137 and it can be seen separately in View 230. A view like this could show the Security or Operational Risk officer the most important elements related to Risk & Security management from the explanation in View 151 on page 99.

21.1 Exceptional Construction Views

In many cases, the approach with these Construction Views works fine. But in some cases, it is not the best or most pragmatic way. The nice thing about View of course is that you can have multiple views without changing the model (and thus the analyses you can do on the model) at all. I specifically say 'selections', because creating special views with derived relations added to that view adds those relations to the model as well, and as such may damage the usability of the model. But keeping the relations of the patterns exactly the same, different 'cuts' can be made than the Construction Views so far.

One situation where that is very useful is for very large and complex platforms. Such a platform has so many Application Services it provides to the business (and to other systems) that modeling these in single view becomes unwieldy. So, in that case you could cut that single Application Architecture View up into multiple Application Architecture Views.

But you can also go outside the standard Construction View setup. Take for instance our ESB. This will often be a very large platform with many, many Application Services. What the ESB does — providing the glue between many systems — leads itself to an alternative approach, an exception.

In the example of View 232 on page 140 (do not worry if it is unreadable because its elements are too small, you're not supposed to be able to read that view), the following has been modeled:

- Starting from a Business Process that is executed by a couple of systems and the ESB (top) we have created a type of Application Architecture View that contains all the systems that play a role in that process. In this case, on the left a major system, on the right some other systems and external services. This differs from the Application Architecture View, which normally only shows the architecture of a single system;

- Having multiple systems enables us to show how the Data Objects (this example *with* Data Objects differs from the one finally proposed in Section 14.2 "ESB" on page 101) and Artifacts play a role in the publications and subscriptions shown.

Such a view might be called an Application Orchestration View. And instead of modeling a pure, but unwieldy, Application Architecture View for the ESB platform, we create an

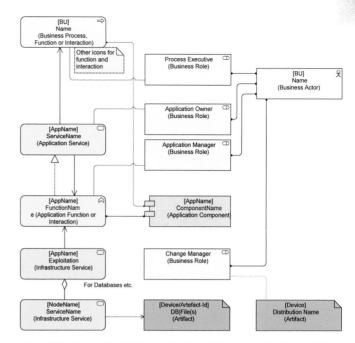

View 231. *Large Model Use – The Run Manager's Application View*

orchestration view for each orchestration, showing multiple applications, but only with the role they play in that orchestration.

One such an orchestration is shown in View 232 on page 140. Maybe 25% may not appear in a normal Application Architecture View. You can imagine that your organization has maybe thirty of these specific orchestrations, or maybe even more and you can immediately recognize that putting the application architecture of the ESB means putting the amount of elements of 25 of these views in a single view. That is way beyond what is reasonable and the standard construction view pattern breaks down.

Our 'ESB Application Construction View', might then be nothing more than links (if your tool supports it) to a series of Application Orchestration Views.

The key thing to remember is that you can design as many types of construction views as you like, but you need to keep an eye on:

- Do the views become unwieldy (too complex for easy maintenance)?

- Can you minimize repetition of model fragments (also an effect on maintenance, change something in one and you have to change all the occurrences of that model fragment wherever it appears)?

- Do not create new model patterns, only view-specific model-fragment selections.

For certain large and/or complex parts of your environment, blindly using the basic construction views may make life unnecessary difficult. One should of course never follow any guideline blindly, certainly not mine anyway...

Be pragmatic.

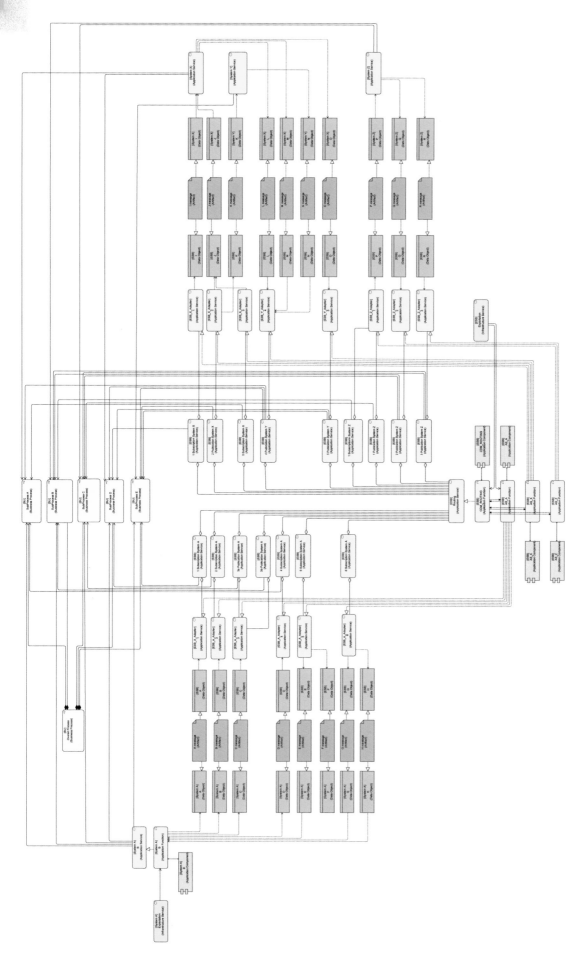

View 232. *Automated Process involving ESB, showing only a small portion of Application Services of the ESB (adapted from a view created by colleague Joost Melsen)*

22. Model Maintenance

A model, especially a large 'current state' model requires proper maintenance. For instance, you need to be kept up to date with changes. In our case, this for instance means that any change that the infrastructure people make in their tool is automatically mailed to the Enterprise Architecture department for maintenance. This must be so, because in our case, the CMDB is again fed from our ArchiMate model, so our model *has* to be correct. This feedback loop keeps the basic infrastructure information up to date. Here again, we meet Uncle Ludwig: through the link to the help desk, our Current State model is *used* and therefore acquires *meaning*.

For projects the situation is a bit different. Here the project first should have a project start architecture (PSA) that contains (the most relevant parts of) what the project is going to deliver. When the project finishes (generally, you can start with this when you are at the user acceptance testing phase, you make the model of the PSA complete and when the results of the project go 'live', you include the model of the PSA in your overall current state model.

When things change, you need a basic procedure for change. Here is mine:

- Views have a state:
  * *Work in Progress;*
  * *Draft;*
  * *Final;*
  * *Erroneous;*
  * *Research.*

Normally, views progress in a cycle: they are created by an architect and during that phase they have the *Work in Progress* state. When the modeling is done, the view moves to the *Draft* state and will be checked. Generally, this must be done in two accounts:

- Is the view content-wise correct? You check that with people who can vouch for the correctness. E.g. business people for the business architecture, infrastructure managers for the infrastructure architecture, etc.

- Is the view properly modeled according to the chosen patterns and guidelines (e.g. style)? It is generally the lead architect who has to vouch for this.

When the view is checked on both accounts, it moves to the *Final* state. When something has to change again (e.g. an error has been found, a change must be made), the first thing to do is move the view again from *Final* to *Work in Progress*.

We also keep some views in an *Erroneous* state. These are known to be wrong but are currently not worked on. And we may have some *Research* views, which are generally temporary.

There is one caveat with all these views, and especially with the Construction & Use Views of the previous section. You can't have too many or maintenance becomes increasingly more difficult. Tooling (see Chapter "Tooling" on page 201)

generally supports that if you change the label of an element in one view, it gets changed automatically in another (though label layout may suffer). If you remove a relation between element in one view, you might get warned it appears in other views. But if you add an element or relation that should appear in multiple views, you are on your own. Which means that the more views there are where a certain elements must appear, the more work changing a view becomes. Also, keeping a view easy on the eye (HVS, see Section 6 "Aesthetics (Style)" on page 41) sometimes means a lot of work. Add one little element and you sometimes have to layout 20 others and all their relations. Providing good readable views requires hand work (and hard work) and a good eye for layout, so prepare yourself. And don't expect a tool to be able to do this for you. Even the best tools in this area cannot produce the required cleanliness and organization of layout as View 51 on page 42 illustrates (to be fair, the changes in element sizes in that view were added by hand).

Finally: one important suggestion: Clean Up! On a regular basis, check your model for elements that are unused (do not appear in any view and are also not children of elements that are used in a view. We use a script in our tool to do this. And of course, when IT gets decommissioned, make sure you remove it from your model. In our setup that means simply removing the views and then running the unused elements script.

22.1 The Satellite Model Approach

Sometimes, you need certain details for analyses in certain cases, but most of the time those details just get in the way. Take for instance the following situation:

- Your company employs a Scheduler platform in which many activities have been automated. For instance, IT-maintenance jobs, or more to the point: some daily actions on your data like updating from external feeds or creating reports;

- Such schedules generally consist of a main (parent) action (in this example called the 'Flow') which is started at some time of day, and all kind of steps (in this example called the 'Jobs') that are executed in some complicated order when the parent runs;

- A Job is executed on a system (e.g. a server) where it may start an application that actually does something (like creating that report or importing into a system that data another Job has just fetched).

Data-intensive organizations may sometimes have hundreds or thousands of Flows, each consisting of tens of Jobs. Many of these Jobs in turn use several applications that exists in your landscape, the fact of which is sometimes hidden deep in the whole scheduling setup.

Personally, I want my main 'Current State Architecture' (CSA) model to be navigable graphically. That means that my CSA model will have construction views for all applications that are used. If I then publish my model, the organization has access to a usable overview of the whole jungle of dependencies that make up a modern Business-IT landscape. And what is more: I can run analyses when I need to. If I want to replace that large system, an analysis of the CSA will show me where this application or its data is used.

But in the example above, the Jobs are more like application architecture, the inside of the Flow, which is the application, which in turn requires the runtime environment of the scheduling platform. An example can be seen in View 233

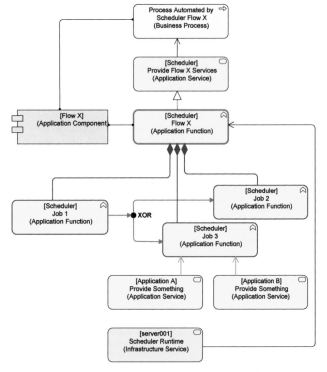

View 233. *Actual structure of Application Services being used by the Jobs of a Scheduler Flow.*

(ignore the colors for now). A very simple Flow is depicted. It contains two Jobs that each use a different application from which only the Application Service is shown here. Note that we have modeled the Scheduler as we did in Section 9 "An Example from the Real World" on page 69. The Scheduler is a *platform*, the Flow is the Application Component that is deployed on that platform. The Jobs are the components that make up the internal structure of the Flow.

If you have hundreds of Flows and you have tens of Jobs on average in each Flow, you are talking about thousands of Application Functions. That could be modeled, of course, if the Flows are not very volatile, but a main issue here is that you are duplicating the maintenance of information. How the Jobs make up the Flows has already been documented in the Scheduler platform. Keeping those two in sync is problematic.

But if you can export the information from your Scheduler system and import it into your EA modeling tool, you may be able to use the information directly. Adding these thousands of Jobs, however, into your CSA means you have to make them navigable, which is a lot of EA layout work (and

re-work if the structure is volatile). Besides, at the EA level, nobody is interested in those details.

Here, the trick of using a Satellite Model comes in. Creating a Satellite Model works like this:

• you clone your main CSA model;

• you import the details of the structure you need. In this case, that would be the whole Flows/Jobs structure. Example: the blue and red items in View 233;

• you add relations (by hand) between the elements that were already in your CSA model and the imported details. Example: the orange Used-By relations in View 233;

• you make sure your Flow's and Job's Application Function have an ID that is *unique across models* (e.g. add that to its properties). A possible candidate is the ID it has in the Scheduler system, but watch out for what editing on that side (e.g. modification by delete/add) can break.

There is no need to import the dynamic structure that is available in the Scheduler system (the pink relations) into your Satellite Model.

What you then do is set up a couple of synchronizations:

• From Scheduler system to Satellite Model: import Flows and their Jobs. Name changes can be carried over automatically if there is an independent ID;

• From Satellite Model to CSA Model: roll-up all the relations to the Jobs and turn them into relations to the parent Flow. This can be seen in View 234 where the Used-By relations between Application Service and Jobs have been turned into Used-By relations between the Application Services and the parent Flow;

• From CSA Model to Satellite Model: add/change all non-Scheduler elements.

You also need to set up a reconciliation. Once in a while you produce a report from the Satellite Model that contains the relations between Jobs and applications and this

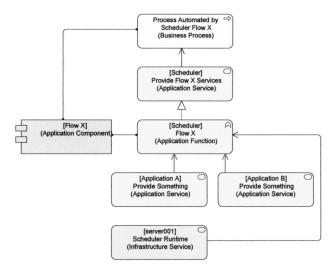

View 234. *Rolled-up view of Application Services Used-By the parent Scheduler Flow. of View 233*

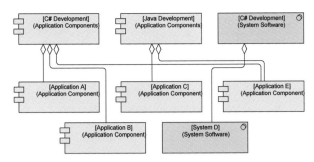

View 235. *Model analysis elements: Aggregation example*

needs to be checked by the Scheduler people for correctness

and completeness. Any 'breaks' need to be repaired in the Satellite Model.

Two final remarks. First, the relations used in the roll-up of View 234 on page 142 cannot be derived in the official ArchiMate sense of 'derivation' from the relations in View 233 on page 142. This illustrates a point made in 5.5 "On the limitations of derived relations" on page 36. Second, the relation between the 'model' in the Scheduler system and what you want in your CSA is an example of the fact that you will always have multiple models of the same reality in your organization. More on this issue will be said in section 29 "Multiple Models of One Reality" on page 201.

23. Requirements that influence your patterns

23.1 Additional elements for model use

A model — and Uncle Ludwig would agree — is only meaningful if it can be used. ArchiMate is not a language for yet another way of creating pretty pictures. It is a grammar that can be used to create *models*, and the nice thing about models is that you can analyze them.

To ease these analyses, or to provide better ways of integrating your model with other models in your organization, it is often useful to add extra elements. Some of these we have already encountered, such as the roles from secondary and tertiary architectures in a way that enables practical use (see section 12.9 on page 93 and their use in section 21 on page 135).

An example would be to model which development environment is needed for certain applications. Development platform and Run platform are not necessarily the same, e.g. program written in C# may run on Windows or on Linux. But sometimes it is: application developed inside the SAS-stack will also be developed using SAS-tools and SAS-language. As there is no 1-to-1 mapping from the runtime environment (via the Infrastructure Services which is used by the Application Function) and the development aspects, it may be useful to model these.

There are – as always – multiple ways to do this, but in this specific situation there are generally two:

- Add properties to elements. E.g. have a 'Development Platform' property in each Application Component and System Software component and fill these with appropriate information;

- Create additional model elements, e.g. a 'C# (Application Components)' element in which you Aggregate all Application Components that are developed/maintained in C#.

And — as always — both have advantages and disadvantages. A disadvantage of the former is that it is often hard to make this visible

in your views and analyses require some sort of scripting that accesses those properties. So it depends on the tool if this is doable or not. Besides, what if you have a hybrid such as 'Application E' in these views? How many property fields are you going to use? It gets pretty complex quickly, modeling is more powerful.

The disadvantage of the latter is that you will sometimes run into restrictions set by ArchiMate, e.g. you cannot Aggregate both System Software and Application Component in

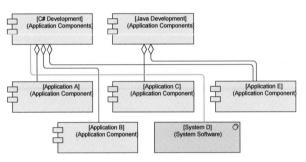

View 236. *Model analysis elements: using Association to overcome type differences*

a single element that says 'C#'. So, in View 235 a second Aggregation is required so we can Aggregate both Application Components and System Software.

You can get around this by using Associations, as partly shown in View 236, but that trick you can only use once in your model, or the same pattern (e.g. Application Component Associated with Application Component if you do it for the entire collection) might get two different meanings and become ambiguous.

You can also creatively use elements from for instance the Motivation Extension, e.g. you could let each Application Component for which you require to know the development platform Realize the (in your model) single Constraint 'Must be maintained in C#' as is shown in View 237. I prefer this one, as it also has a meaning I can

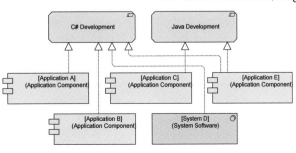

View 237. *Model analysis elements: using Constraints (or Requirements)*

understand: without C# maintenance skills to actually do the maintenance, you are helpless.

23.2 Keeping in sync with other administrations

In Sections 16 "Virtual Machines (Parallelization)" on page 110, 7.19 "Infrastructure Pattern: High-Available Database Cluster" on page 62, and 7.20 "Infrastructure Pattern: High-Available Server" on page 62 we already saw some slightly complex infrastructure diagrams.

Most of the infrastructure I model is generally simple: a repeat of the same basic pattern: a Node encapsulates the Device and System Softwares inside it and all the Infrastructure Services are Realized directly by the Node. We can have several Nodes, such as in 7.16 "Deployment Pattern: Providing a local ASP" on page 59, but the basic pattern remains fairly simple. Even the final pattern for hardware virtualization (View 174 on page 114) was simple.

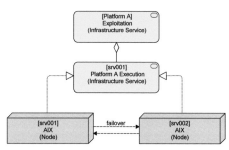

View 238. *Very simple failover setup with a single Realized Infrastructure Service*

But there are exceptions. Server Clusters in several variations present a challenge. Not so much designing a pattern, as we saw in View 89 on page 63. But what is difficult is to create patterns that not only give a good representation of what is going on, we also do not want to many pattern variations, as they make automated analysis more difficult, and in case of large scale Current State Architecture models we also want to be able to synchronize our models with other models that exist in our organization, e.g. CMDB models of the IT department.

Take that high-available server from View 174 on page 114. That outside 'cluster' Node might be something that cannot be found in the IT department's administration. Instead, we might find just two Nodes, one for each device. The fact that they are set up to form a cluster is part of unstructured information, say some sort of design or maintenance document. Whatever the way it is documented (and hopefully it is), when we want to remain in sync with their administration, we need to adapt. We need a pattern for this high-available server setup that can be matched to their administration of separate Nodes, while we want our landscape preferably to show that those Nodes form an inte-

grated and interconnected whole that as a whole Realizes the Infrastructure Services we need.

The simplest form of 'clustering' is a simple 'failover' setup. Here, one Node Realizes an Infrastructure Service and when it dies, we can fail over to the other one, maybe even requiring a manual intervention. Basically, that setup looks

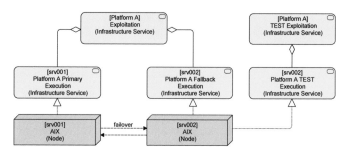

View 239. *Very simple failover setup showing separate Infrastructure Services for primary and failover and showing the use of the failover device for testing*

like the pattern of View 238, where I have left out the internal structure of the Nodes, but still show the approach of Section 7.6 "Infrastructure 'Building Blocks'" on page 53. The approach, though simple, contains an abstraction that can limit the use of our model: starting from the Infrastructure Service, we cannot see which one of the Nodes is the primary and which one is the failover Node. This may be important information, as we might try to save money by using the failover Node as test environments long the failover is not needed. As soon as failover is needed, the test device is switched to a production configuration and restarted. A very error-prone, low-tech, labor-intensive example of failover, but it does exist.

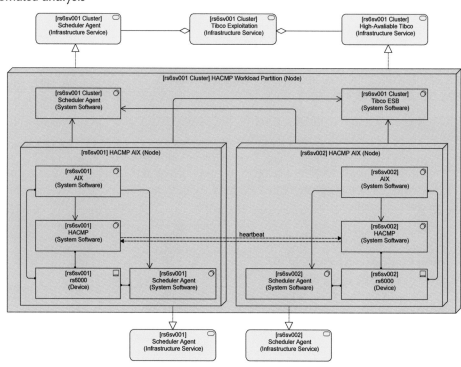

View 240. *The High-Available Server of View 89 on page 63 modeled to fit the IT department's administration*

View 239 shows the basic pattern where we have an independent Infrastructure Service for primary and failover, of course both again Aggregated in a single 'exploitation' Infrastructure Service that acts as a simplifier towards the application layer.

This all still fits nicely with both our basic infrastructure pattern and with the IT department's administration. But our high-availability server pattern of View 89 on page 63 does not. It consists of a 'cluster' Node that is unknown to the IT department and that also has a setup (with two devices and three operating systems) that is alien to the infrastructure people. So we need a solution that fits both our idea of the fact that this high-available cluster acts as a single Node and the IT department's idea that we are talking about just two Nodes (and the rest is just configuration). A solution is shown in View 240 on page 144. Both 'internal' Nodes now perfectly fit the administration of the IT department. We also let these Nodes Realize their specific maintenance-services. But for us, the important Node is the outer one. For us, that Node is a single element that Realizes the Infrastructure Services our application landscape needs.

To show that the software that is installed on the 'virtual' operating system depends on both Nodes, we just let both these Nodes be Used-By that System Software. And we let the flow relations connect to the inside of the Nodes to signify the tight coupling that is going on.

Now, nothing stops the really paranoid from creating a failover situation between two high-availability clusters. Some things should *never* fail, after all. Such a setup is modeled in full in View 241. If anything, diagrams like that prove that ArchiMate is not just a language for abstract high-level boardroom diagrams. Of course, we can create a simplified diagram. This is shown in View 242 on page 146. I have removed the details from the sub-Nodes and the Infrastructure Services for the secondary 'Exploitation' architecture (see Section 12.5 "Secondary Architecture: System Exploitation" on page 90) and for good measure added the data center locations. At this point it may be good to stress a point I have not stressed much in this book: both View 241 and View 242 are part of the *same* model, they are just different views of the same underlying reality. That means that if you change the label on an element in one view, it will automatically change in the other. It means that relations are there, even if they are not shown.

23.3 Server Farm

Now that I have my structure for complex clusters of Nodes, we can easily adapt this to 'farms'. A farm is a collection of Nodes that are all (generally) identical and that may all provide an identical service. Often, such a farm is combined with some sort of 'load balancer', which makes sure that labor is divided over all the Nodes. A typical use these days is Citrix or other terminal services to provide applications to thin clients. Another typical use are heavy-duty web servers or streaming services.

The basic pattern for a farm is rather simple, just a Node that contains a number of other Nodes and the outer Node

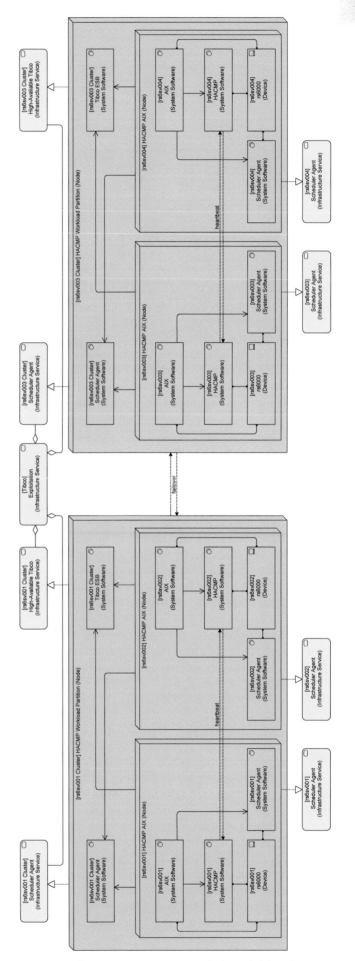

View 241. *A failover setup between two high-availability clusters*

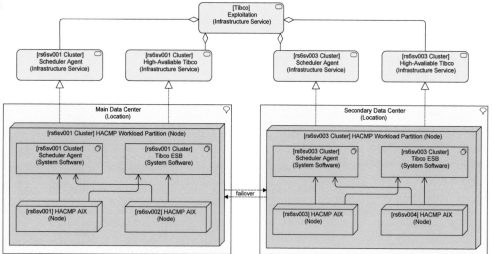

View 242. *Simplified version of View 241 on page 145.*

providing a service (or more services). It is shown in View 243. This pattern replicates some of the chosen aspects of the high-available server, namely Node-Within-Node, where the Nodes do have some sort of independent existence. Another standard pattern (for me) is that the Infrastructure Service is Realized by the outer Node, not by the actual System Software that is somewhere on the inside.

Different from the high available cluster is that the outer Node has no real 'existence', we cannot, for instance, deploy System Software on it. View 243 shows another aspect already as well: since all the Nodes of the Farm must be completely identical, any software installed on it must be identical on all the Nodes. This is shown by Assigning the Artifacts of the software distribution to all Nodes of the Farm. By the way, as an alternative, we could have also used the solution of View 244, taking parallel Realization of the Infrastructure Service to signify 'either'. I don't use this, because in our practice the farms do have a recognizable entry in the IT department's documentation and also because this parallel Realization is ambiguous and because both parallel relations have opposite meaning: the Realizations mean 'either', while the Assignments mean 'both'.

23.4 Citrix

Finally, now that much is in place, I end the collection of pattern and solution examples by showing a pattern for Citrix XenApp. For those who do not know what Citrix (or another Terminal Services solution) does, it allows organizations to run certain desktop applications in a controlled server environment instead of on the desktop: while the application runs on the server, e.g. in a data center, the user's in- and output (keyboard, mouse, screen) are connected to the application. Any movement of the mouse, any click on the keyboard on the user's desktop is sent to the server and handed to the application, any graphical output of the program is sent to the user's desktop and presented to him. For this, a special proprietary protocol is used requires very little bandwidth so it can be used to offer applications to users in

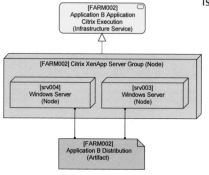

View 243. *Basic pattern for a Server Farm*

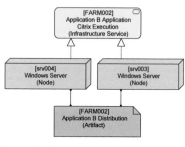

View 244. *Farm pattern with parallel Realization*

situations where there is little band-width. Terminal Services like Citrix are vulnerable for high 'network latency', but if you are relatively close to the data center, most applications work OK. Terminal Services are also bad at handling graphics-intensive programs like video, because it is hard to compress that kind of graphics for fast transport over a network.

Citrix is a suite of different kinds of solutions, from virtual desktops to streamed applications and may be used locally on a company network directly or provided via a web server intermediary. In that last form it is often used for working with your

organization's applications from home via the internet.

View 245 on page 147 contains a detailed display of the architecture. Note, there are many items and relations there for explanation purposes, not all of these are by definition useful as addition to your model.

Wen a user starts an application under Citrix, the following happens (I have left some bits out):

1. The Citrix Receiver on the mac desktop sends a request to the XML Broker to start Application A. In View 245 this is shown as the red Used-By between the Citrix Services and the Citrix Client Infrastructure Services;

2. The Citrix XML Broker requests information on the load of the servers in the FARM001 from ZDC (the Zone Data Collector), shown as internal Used-By in srv005 in View 245;

3. ZDC constantly collects information from all servers in the farms on how busy they are (load). Shown as the red Used-Bys from the farms to the ZDC System Software View 245;

4. Based in part on the information from ZDC, the XML Broker creates an ICA file. This contains the address of the server that is going to serve the Citrix Receiver on the mac desktop. The mac desktop gets this file. This is shown as the Assignments to both srv005 as well as mac desktop. It is also part of the Used-By between Citrix Services and Citrix Client Infrastructure Services;

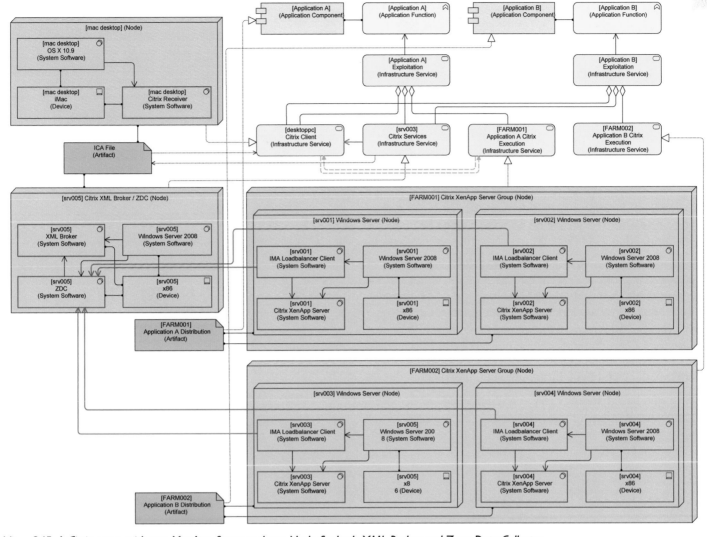

View 245. A Citrix setup with two XenApp farms and one Node for both XML Broker and Zone Data Collector.

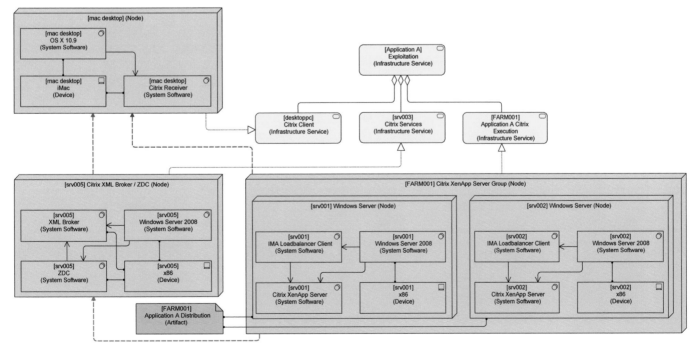

View 246. Current State infrastructure pattern for Citrix based applications

5. Based on the ICA file received, the Citrix Receiver sets up a connection with one of the servers in FARM001. The application is launched on either src001 or srv002 and XenApp Server connects its interface to the mac desktop's Citrix Receiver, where the user can interact with it. This two way interaction is modeled in View 245 on page 147 as the orange Flow relations between the Citrix Client and Application A Citrix Execution Infrastructure Services.

The purple bordered Software System elements are Realized by the (not shown) Citrix distribution Artifact. Now, as stated, you do not need all of this in your model, I am only showing for illustration purposes. From an Enterprise Architecture perspective, we can do with less details. After all, why model that ICA file?

Shown in View 246 on page 147 shows the infrastructure pattern that could be used in the Construction Views approach at the start of this chapter. In this view, I would only keep the red flow to model which XML Broker is managing which farm and remove the blue and green flows. These are also Citrix flows, but they can be omitted as they do not add anything substantial to what we can deduce from the structural relations and the infrastructure building block setup.

For a web-based intermediary, the situation becomes more complex, but not extremely so.

This page intentionally not left blank

BPMN and ArchiMate

BPMN and ArchiMate

Why is there a chapter on BPMN and ArchiMate in this book on ArchiMate? Well, there is a very good reason: powerful and flexible though ArchiMate is, it can't do everything. It is a language for Enterprise Architecture modeling and not for, say, software design (for which we may use UML) or process design (for which we may use BPMN). Business Process modelers need more than ArchiMate can provide, e.g. in detailed sequence flow modeling, decision point modeling, etc., and they often require tooling that not only let them model, but maybe also simulate or even directly execute a modeled process. Given that you cannot really support the needs of process modelers with ArchiMate, they will generally use their own language. But their processes are part of the Enterprise Architecture and thus also of your EA models of Current State or Project in ArchiMate. And as there is only one reality, the two models should not tell incompatible stories about your enterprise. There is, therefore, a need to use both, but to keep them in sync. In fact this is true for many, many more models that exist about your enterprise, be it the content of the Help Desk system where incidents are linked to systems and people, the Operational Risk models that link risks, controls and processes, etc. They might not be immediately recognized as 'models', but they are. That Excel spreadsheet with a list of applications and their security or business continuity classifications is also a model (a poor one, though).

ArchiMate, being the language that covers all layers of the enterprise and having a decent and flexible meta-model is a natural hub for all these models. For Business Processes, that superficially means that you may have Business Process elements in your ArchiMate model but that they represent processes modeled in more detail by the process modelers. There are many proprietary process modeling environments for sale and only one Open Standard: BPMN. Therefore, we will take BPMN as our process modeling language and show how an Enterprise Architecture modeled in ArchiMate can be in sync with a process landscape modeled in BPMN.

There is one other important aspect to consider. Business process models are generally used by, discussed with and therefore must be understandable by 'the business'. Enterprise Architecture models, especially those detailed models for Current State and Project Architectures far less so. Yes, the high-level abstracted models in ArchiMate can be used for discussions with the business (in a way not very different from presentation slides with a few graphical elements), and yes, ArchiMate is not rocket science, but it remains so that complex ArchiMate models will not be very usable in communication with your average business person. Process models on the other hand, must be understood by the people who actually perform them and that means there are important aspects to guard, especially with respect to too much abstraction. A nice example is that while in ArchiMate, a Business Process cannot directly Access an Artifact (it needs to be abstracted up to Business Object or a Representation may be used instead), the business will demand to see a description where a 'process' directly handles an 'Excel spreadsheet document' which is then for instance loaded into a system. Business process model views used for the documentation and design of human-based processes must be grasped more intuitively than Enterprise Architecture views.

24. A Very Short BPMN Primer

BPMN stands for *Business Process Model and Notation* (or *Business Process Modeling Notation* depending on which BPMN documents you read) and it is an open standard for Business Process Modeling which is managed by the Object Management Group (OMG). This book is about ArchiMate, so in this chapter I am going to assume you are familiar with BPMN. However, for those that want to read on regardless (I would) here is a very short primer. Note: if you want to

learn BPMN Modeling, I would strongly suggest using Bruce Silver's book *BPMN Method & Style 2nd Edition*.

We start with a simple high level process. A Portfolio Manager of an Asset Management firm daily checks his portfolio of investments against his or her targets with respect to performance, risk, etc.. And if he or she decides that the portfolio needs adjustments (buy or sell assets) he or she will have to come up with an investment idea (which may

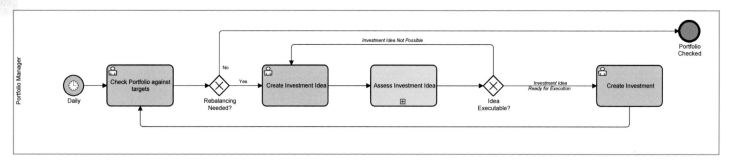

View 247. *BPMN Example – The Basic Portfolio Management Process*

be selling as well: a de-investment). After the creation of an idea, this idea has to be checked. This generally consists of many possible checks, like running simulations, checking against compliance rules, checking against the mandate from the client, etc.. If the idea is executable, an investment will be created and then it is back to the check if the portfolio is now balanced with respect to the targets. If the portfolio is still 'out of balance', this 're-balancing' process continues with the next investment idea. This goes on until the portfolio is back into a state that lets the portfolio manager sleep well at night. A basic overview in BPMN can be seen in View 247.

The large overall outer rectangle is called a Lane. A Lane in BPMN is nothing more than a visual organization of the process model. Lanes are generally used to group activities that are performed by a single role, but BPMN does not prescribe this. You may use a Lane as you want, it is more or less meaningless in BPMN. You might use it to divide activities into those that are done in different locations, have different risk profiles, etc..

In the Lane, we see a couple of elements and relations:

This is the Start Event of this process. The process starts here and a sequence of events follows. What follows depends on the arrow that leaves the Start Event. In this example, the Start Event is a timer event, it occurs at a certain point in time, in this example: daily.

This is a Sequence Flow. A Sequence Flow is used to model the order in which activities occur. In our example, after the process starts, the next thing that happens is the first activity, which is connected to the arrow head of that first Sequence Flow.

This is a Task. A Task is one of the possible types of Activity. In our example we see two of these and this is the most simple one. A Task is a not further detailed set of behaviors. As you can see, there is a little person-icon in the top-left corner of this Task. That icon says this is a User Task.

Here we run into a peculiarity of BPMN. BPMN has three types of simple Tasks: a User Task, a System Task (little gears as icon) and a Manual Task (no icon). In our example, the Task is a User Task and it is performed by a person. The definition of the three types of Tasks in BPMN leaves an interesting white spot. According to BPMN a Manual Task is performed with the help of *any* kind of automation and examples given are like digging a hole or something other purely physical. The User Task is defined as a Task that is

orchestrated by a process engine but performed by a person. The System Task is performed by a computer. As you can see, there is formally no room for a Task that is performed by a user but that still uses automation, e.g. writing a letter using a document processing application.

There are more curious parts of BPMN (one of which we will encounter below). One of the reasons there are peculiar parts of the BPMN specification is probably that its development has been driven largely by the desire to model automated processes that are orchestrated by workflow engines. The fact that a few large companies that sell workflow engines have financed the development of BPMN is probably to blame.

This is a Gateway. Gateways require some attention. From the view it is clear what effect this Gateway has: the sequence is split and the process proceeds with *either* of the outgoing sequence flows. It follows either of these, because this type of Gateway is an XOR Gateway. The large X signifies that. As the XOR Gateway is also the default Gateway you may leave out the X icon inside. But I like to be explicit in my modeling, so I always explicitly show it. It is important to realize that a Gateway is not an activity that is performed. The Gateway only *represents* something, namely the possible outcomes of the Activity that went before it.

There are many types of Gateways. Some have multiple inputs and multiple outputs and are very complex. They are seldom used. The ones generally used are the XOR Gateway above and the Parallel Gateway. The Parallel Gateway has a large + as icon. The Parallel Gateway signifies that all outgoing Sequence Flows will be followed.

What is useful to remember when handling Sequence Flows, Gateways, etc. is the concept of the *token game*. Think of tokens as a marble that travels along the Sequence Flows. Every Start Event produces a single marble thus creating a single *instance* of this process. Our marble rolls into the first Task and when that Task is done it comes out at the other end. Then the marble rolls into the XOR Gateway. Here the marble goes either way. Had it been a Parallel Gateway with two exits, *one* marble would have gone in and *two* marbles would have come out. The idea behind the marbles is that when the process is finished, all marbles must have been consumed. The most common and obvious consumer of a marble is an End Event. But a Parallel Gateway can also consume all marbles of all incoming Sequence Flows and then spit out only one.

This is the End Event in our example. It consumes the marble and the process ends. A process may have multiple end states and all should be represented as an End Event. We will get back to this below.

It might be good at this point also to explain that a process description contains a generic description of a single instance of a process. That is, it is possible that the same process happens simultaneously multiple times in your organization. Bruce Silver gives a good explanation in his book, including situations that you have one process that has to work together with multiple instances of another process. Think of a sale to a customer that happens many times and billing to that customer that happens only once a month. Or more to the point: the single process of filling a specific position in your company related to the multiple instances of a process to handle a single applicant for that function. Again: if you haven't been studying BPMN a lot, I can recommend Bruce's book.

There is only one element left in our example in View 247 on page 152.

This is a SubProcess. A SubProcess is a kind of activity that has details that are available and are modeled as a separate process. You can expand this Activity in place, but here it is shown in a collapsed state. We see the details of this SubProcess activity in View 248 on page 153.

This SubProcess models what happens when we 'assess an investment idea'. The first thing we do is check if this idea is actually allowed by the mandate that we have from our client. If this checks out OK, we check if for this type of investment a portfolio is available. Assets are generally organized in portfolios and we need to decide in which portfolio this asset must reside. If a proper portfolio is available we prepare the idea for execution and move to the end state 'Investment Idea Ready For Execution'. All these Tasks are performed by the Portfolio Manager, hence they have been modeled in a Lane that is labeled with 'Portfolio Manager'.

But there are two situations where we are forced to leave this 'happy flow'. The first one is if the client's mandate actually does not allow the portfolio manager to make this investment. If he or she thinks the idea is good enough, he or she might try to get the client's mandate updated. But that is not something that the portfolio manager does by himself in our example or-

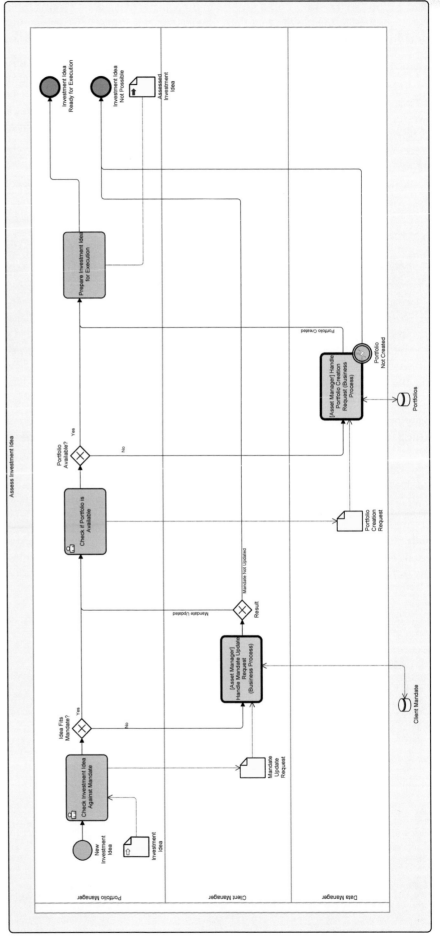

View 248. *BPMN Example – Expanded SubProcess from View 247 on page 152*

ganization. So, he shoots off a request to the Client Manager for an update to the client's mandate. The outcome of that activity might be that the client's mandate is either updated or not. If not, we move to the end state 'Investment Idea Not Possible' and the SubProcess finishes. If the client mandate is updated and the idea becomes allowed, we move back to our 'happy flow'. The same kind of thing happens when we do not have a portfolio ready to accept the investment: a new portfolio has to be created. In our example organization this is the domain of a Data Manager. The outcome of this is a new portfolio and we return to the 'happy flow'. Unless, that is, some error occurs and the portfolio cannot be created. In that case we move to the 'Investment Idea Not Possible' end state. The green activities are of a new type:

[Asset Manager] Handle Mandate Update Request (Business Process) — This is a Call Activity. What it represents is that we are going to *call* another process. This looks like the SubProcess of before, but while the SubProcess is an integral part of our process, the Call Activity is a temporary handover to another process, generally some sort of 'reusable process' that can be re-used from within many other processes. Technically, in BPMN, Call Activity and SubProcess look very much alike. You are allowed, for instance, to expand the called process in place in the Call Activity, just like a SubProcess.

Having come so far I must make an important remark on using color. BPMN, like ArchiMate, is color-neutral. Color has no official meaning in BPMN. The other aspects of form, like thin/thick borders, rounded corners or not, etc., are part of the BPMN specification.

Note: I do not follow Bruce Silver fully here. Bruce advises to put the Call Activity in the Lane of the role that 'makes the call'. I agree that this is more correct, but it has a slight practical disadvantage when communicating with the business. By putting the Call Activity in a Lane of the role that per-

forms the called process, the view itself immediately shows who is involved and that improves understanding of what happens by people who do not model for a business.

Our Call Activity 'Handle Mandate Update Request' is followed by an XOR Gateway with two outgoing Sequence Flows: 'Mandate Updated' and 'Mandate Not Updated'. In fact, this only makes sense (as we shall see) as the process called has two End States, one for each outgoing flow.

More to the right in View 248 there is another Call Activity. This one has a single Sequence Flow coming out, but something else too:

Portfolio Not Created — This is an Error Boundary Event. BPMN has a rich set of event type elements which make up for pretty sophisticated modeling. I'm not going to describe them at all, just this one because it is used in the example. What happens here is that the process called by the Call Activity throws an error. Here it means that some error in the called process interrupted the process in mid-flow, thereby also killing it. It is often a matter of taste if you consider something a normal situation or an error. Personally, from long ago working with Abstract Data Types, I find the difference not that important: you need to be complete (all non-error end state and all errors need to be accounted for to be robust).

Both Call Activities in the example have two possible outcomes, one is modeled with two proper end states (not seen yet) and a Gateway, the other is modeled with a single outgoing Sequence Flow and one coming from an error that was produced.

The only remaining elements of View 248 on page 153 not yet described are the informational elements. While tasks, activities, subprocesses etc. are not that uncommon from the ArchiMate perspective (they are all business behavior, most likely to be modeled as a Business Process), the infor-

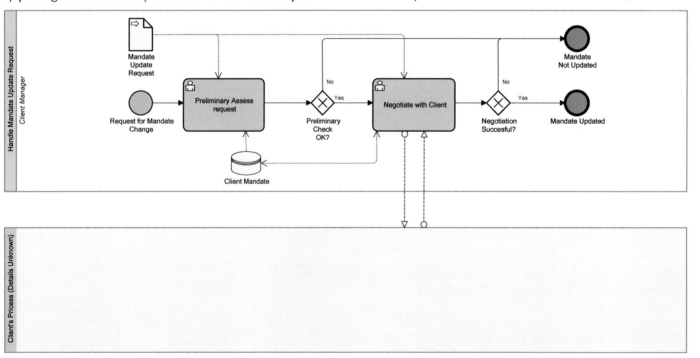

View 249. *BPMN Example – Collaboration between the Asset Manager's (our) process and the Client's (their) process*

mational perspective from BPMN is quite different. BPMN knows about data and has generally two types:

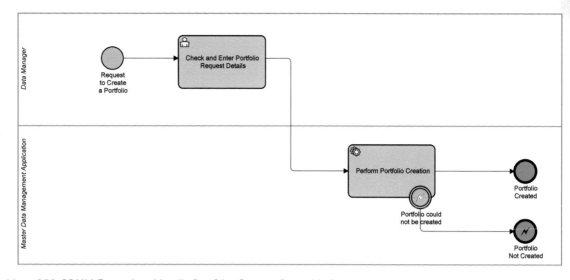

View 250. *BPMN Example – Handle Portfolio Creation Re-usable Process*

This is a Data Store. A Data Store stands for data that exists independently from a process. This is *permanent* data. BPMN thinks about data in quite a technical perspective, coming from its 'process engine' background. So, in terms of ArchiMate, these are best seen as permanent Artifacts in ArchiMate. From an ArchiMate perspective BPMN (and other process modeling notation styles) often seem to link the business layer (process) and the infrastructure layer (artifact) indiscriminately. However, they make sense without automation too: that "locked filing cabinet stuck in a disused lavatory with a sign on the door saying Beware of the Leopard'" is a Data Store in BPMN terms too. Still, it is a rather physical approach and is easiest associated with infrastructure.

This is a Data Object. This is *temporary* data that only exists as long as this process instance still runs. Again, this makes perfect sense from a technical perspective with 'process engines'. This is data that is kept 'in memory' of the process engine for that particular process. In that sense, it is easiest associated with ArchiMate's Data Object at the application layer. Some modelers say that data like this should not be modeled as internal data is implicitly available to all Activities in the Process, but sometimes it can be useful, for instance if you need to document certain aspects of that data. And of course, in executable processes running in workflow engines you will need to model it explicitly.

The Call Activities in our example call other processes. The first Call Activity in View 248 on page 153 calls a process named 'Handle Mandate Update Request'. As this process communicates with another independent process (that of the client) we draw visible proxies for both processes. One for our process and one for their process. We do not know the details of their process, so we leave them out. But we do know we communicate with them, asking their permission to update the mandate and getting a decision in return. This is shown in View 249. There is a new element here, that is shown in its two possible appearances.

This is a Pool. To be precise: this is a Black Pool as it does not have any process details in it. A Pool is a somewhat troublesome element in BPMN (as far as I'm concerned) as I'll explain below. Technically, 'Pool' is not even the right name for this element. The correct name from BPMN's meta-model is

Participant and a Pool is the 'visual representation of a Participant'.

If a Pool has process details in it, like Lanes and Activities it is a normal Pool. A Participant/ Pool just may or may not contain a Process. If it does not contain a Process it is a Black Pool, but still a Participant.

This is a Message Flow. An important thing to know about Participant/Pools is that between Participant/Pools only messages may flow. A sequence of activities is only allowed *within* a Process (using Sequence Flows) and communication (using Message Flows) is only allowed *between* Processes. Message Flows can be connected to either Activities or to the Pool/Participant itself (the latter generally in the case of Black Pools).

Now the trouble with Pool/Participant in BPMN is this: the text of the BPMN 2.0 Specification clearly suggests that a Participant is a kind of either role or actor in the collaboration. A 'Client' or a 'Seller' or 'Company X'. But the meta-model of the BPMN 2.0 Specification suggests something quite different. A Participant is a kind of ephemeral proxy. It sits between Party or PartyRole (e.g. 'Company X' or 'Seller') and the Process. A Participant may — according to BPMN's meta-model — only 'have' one Process or none (in case of a Black Pool). Now that does not sound right for a Party; after all a Client may have multiple Processes, e.g. 'Buy Something' and 'Complain'. Also interestingly enough, the Process can be 'of' multiple Participant/Pool elements. That does not make sense at all, unless all these different Pools/ Participants are proxies for the Process itself or for the Party behind it. I have written elsewhere in more detail about this and I do not blame you if it is confusing. But it becomes important later on when we are talking about integrating BPMN and ArchiMate.

Something else that becomes important later on is that the BPMN language does not have a visual representation for Process. Yes, you read that right: *The most important Business Process Modeling language (BPMN) does NOT have a visual representation of its 'Process' element*. This, again, becomes an interesting fact when trying to link BPMN and ArchiMate.

Back to our example, we see that the called process as shown in View 249 ends with two possible End States: 'Mandate Updated' and 'Mandate Not Updated'. When you go back to View 248 on page 153, you see that those two End States match with the Sequence Flows that leave the Gateway immediately following the Call Activity. There is nothing in BPMN that says that this must be so and that forces this kind of a correctness upon you. It is a matter of 'Method & Style', to speak with Bruce Silver. In this case, I normally slightly digress from Bruce's advice as he differs between '2' and '3 or more' End States. In the first case, he suggests using the name of one of the End States as label for the Gateway that follows and 'Yes' and 'No' for the Sequence Flows leaving that Gateway. I know from private communication he does not disagree with using his rule for '3 or more' for '2 or more'. The advantage of that is that you may get tool support for that, while changing an End State label into a 'yes/no answerable question' is something quite beyond digital computers and thus cannot be supported by automation. The hard link between End State labels and Sequence Flow label can be supported, though and good modeling tooling will help you here to keep your models internally consistent and maintainable (not something easy to do with word processing files and images).

Returning to our BPMN example, we have one called process from View 248 on page 153 left. That process is shown in View 250 on page 155. There is one new element here.

 This is a System Task. A System Task is a Task that is fully performed by a computer, a fully automated task. Now, as you can see, since the task is performed by a computer, I have labeled the Lane in which it is modeled with the name of the application that performs this. In fact, you can probably already guess what this means in ArchiMate terms where an automated Business Process can be performed by an Application Component by assigning one to the other.

The process in View 250 is pretty simple: the Data Manager enters the details and then the application goes on to create everything that is necessary. That should always succeed, so if it does not it is considered an error. This error leads to an Error End State of the process 'Portfolio Not Created'. Here again, if you go back to View 248 on page 153, you see that the label of this Error End State corresponds with the label of the Error Boundary Event in View 248. Not something BPMN prescribes, but it is good practice anyway.

25. Linking BPMN and ArchiMate

Now that we have introduced the basics of BPMN (or for some readers, rehashed what they already knew) we can discuss how ArchiMate and BPMN can be linked. Note: the contents of this section have not yet seen sufficient use to count as a 'real world' solution for me yet. The basic mechanism has been tested and works, though.

Thinking about this linkage starts simple: use ArchiMate for the Enterprise Architecture and BPMN for the details of the business layer, more precisely the business processes, that are shown in ArchiMate. There are various overlapping questions that arise:

- How should we link the processes themselves? For one, though BPMN does have a Process element in its meta-model, it does not have it visually where you do your modeling and what you show to others;

- What to do with the Pool/Participant in BPMN? It is tempting to use it for ArchiMate Actor (for the high level BPMN 'Parties'), for ArchiMate Business Function or GOFBF, for some high level Business Role;

- As far as Process is concerned, one visual option is to create an outer Lane level for any process that holds the link to the ArchiMate Business Process but that means that for simple single-Lane processes you still will have two levels of Lanes;

- You can choose to take Pool/Participant as a proxy for a Process instead of a proxy for a Partner. A Process then more or less always requires a Pool visually, unless you can find some way to link a Process view without a Pool to the ArchiMate Process;

- The BPMN Data Objects seem a bit more difficult to pin down. BPMN separates them according to their 'permanence' while ArchiMate separates them according to the layer (infrastructure, application, business) they belong to. The easy answer is that you can link whatever you want here, it is a matter of style/taste what pattern you prefer (only, as always, choose a pattern and stick to it);

- Then there is the question where to maintain specific linkages: at the ArchiMate side, the BPMN side or both?

Less problematic is the use of an Application by a Process. You may link any Activity or Process to an ArchiMate Application Service in some way. Also, linking an ArchiMate Application Component to a BPMN Service Task or entire Process will be a good way to link fully automated behavior between BPMN and ArchiMate.

Working together with Dick Quartel from BiZZdesign, who did test implementations in the BPMN module of BiZZdesign Architect and discussed options with me, choosing solutions and abandoning them again because of problems and disadvantages, this is what resulted:

25.1 An ArchiMate–BPMN Linkage Pattern

First: I wanted to have a linkage that was independent of tooling. Though it is necessary to add things (especially to the BPMN side because that is the side where the actual links have to be maintained as the details are there) it is necessary to design something that could be implemented for

ArchiMate and BPMN models to be part of different modeling environments.

The basic technical/syntactical structure of linkage is like this:

- Added to the BPMN model are objects in 'Other Domain' libraries. These objects become available in the BPMN modeling tool in a way described below. Example 'Other Domains' are 'EA Application Services', 'EA Application Components', 'EA Business Roles', 'EA Locations' and 'EA Business Processes'. In these domains, we can load the elements from another environment, in our case we load the elements that we have exported from the EA tool. We can also create new 'Other Domain' elements ourselves in those libraries, as these are just simple elements with a name and a type, e.g. name: *Data Manager* of type *EA Business Role*. Three 'Other Domains' are available in the setup we use (the icons are provided by the tool I use):

  ⊠ The Enterprise Architecture domain;

  ♡ The Locations domain;

  ⚠ The Risk Domain.

  While the BPMN tool supports these three separate domains, we fill them all from the same ArchiMate model. A separate risk environment could be the true source of the elements in the Risk Domain, but we provide them via the central ArchiMate model;

- We add links to the BPMN elements to these 'Other Domain' elements. These links are stored as properties of the BPMN elements. This is an extension of BPMN. Examples are:

  * If we link an *EA Application Service* to a *BPMN Task*, it means that the Application Service (from ArchiMate) is used in that Task;

  * If we link an *EA Application Interface* to a *BPMN Task*, it means that the Application Interface (from ArchiMate) is used by the performer of that BPMN Task. As the performer is not an official part of visual BPMN, we must later infer the real connection to a real performer (role);

  * If we link an *EA Business Process* to a *BPMN Pool*, it means that the Process embedded in the BPMN Pool is the equivalent of the ArchiMate Process linked to it. Note that we have chosen to use the BPMN Pool as proxy for the *process*, not for the *party*. We also do not use (ugly) constructs like having always an outer Lane Set that can carry the name of the Process. Not using the 'extra Lane Set' construct means that when we have a BPMN Process visualization without a Pool, we do not have a direct way to link the two, because as said before, the amazing situation is that BPMN does not have a visual representation for its foundational element: Process. But tooling can offer a way around this (as we will see);

* If we link an *EA Business Role* to a *BPMN Lane*, it means that this role performs the BPMN Activities in that Lane;

* If we link an *EA Application Component* to a *BPMN Lane*, it means that this application performs the (automated or 'System') Tasks in that Lane. This is the equivalent of the way in ArchiMate an Application Component can be assigned to a Business Process, signifying an automated Business Process. All Tasks in such a Lane should be Service Tasks of course. It also means that we will have to be strict in using BPMN Lanes for Roles/Application Components;

* *BPMN Data Objects* and *BPMN Data Stores* may be linked at will to *ArchiMate Artifacts*, *ArchiMate Data Objects* or *ArchiMate Business Objects*. The relation between ArchiMate's passive structural (informational) elements and BPMN cannot be made very hard. Business Process Models are generally not described in a very abstract way and do not link well to more abstract notions like ArchiMate's Business Object. Also linking with internal application architectural structure like the ArchiMate Data Object does not work very well. If the modelers are also very much aware of the EA structure as modeled in ArchiMate, some more links are possible;

* *BPMN Activities* and *BPMN Data Stores* may be linked to *ArchiMate Location* elements to signify where the activities are performed or where data is stored;

* *BPMN Activities* may be linked to *ArchiMate Requirement* elements, for instance when these elements are used to model Risk Controls. But also from other environments (e.g. a specific Risk Management environment) can we use the data to fill this 'Other Domain' in the BPMN model;

- In some situations, the link is a type of 'equivalence' link. For instance, when linking a *BPMN Process* to an *ArchiMate Business Process*, we want it to mean that they represent the same in both models. The same may be when we use *BPMN Lanes* for performers and link it to either an *ArchiMate Business Role* or an *ArchiMate Application Component*). If we want 'equivalence' we must make sure that the labels of the elements in both models are the same. Given that we have added the ArchiMate elements as 'Other Domain' to the BPMN environment, we must have the means to link the label of the BPMN element to the linked ArchiMate element. E.g. if you link multiple ArchiMate elements to a single BPMN Process, e.g. a Risk Control, a Location, a few Application Services and a Business Process, the last one is an equivalence link and we want the BPMN Process in the BPMN model to have the same name as the ArchiMate Business Process in the ArchiMate model. This we call the 'label link';

- At the BPMN side we ignore ArchiMate's Business Functions or any other functional concept like GOFBF (see

10.3 "Good Old Fashioned Business Function" on page 79) or abstract roles. The 'business functional landscape(s)' are ignored at the BPMN side. I tried looking at ways to make a linkage with a business functional approach, but none of these worked out properly and it is therefore left to the EA side to have this structure.

Now that we have introduced the basic setup, we can expand our example BPMN with a linkage to ArchiMate and show how such a linkage can be represented in the ArchiMate model. We start with the BPMN Process in View 250 on page 155. What we want to do here first is:

- Have the ArchiMate Business Process linked to the BPMN Process and make it a 'label link';

- Have the Service Task in the lower Lane linked to the Application Service that defines what the application actually does.

In my environment, when I add a link to a BPMN element, it shows up as a little icon in the element as can be seen in View 253 where we see one of the Tasks from View 250 on page 155.

If I click that little icon a graphical object becomes visible displaying the names of the linked ArchiMate elements.

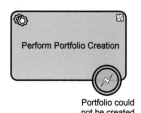

Portfolio could not be created

View 253. *Icon in top-right corner shows there are links to the EA Domain*

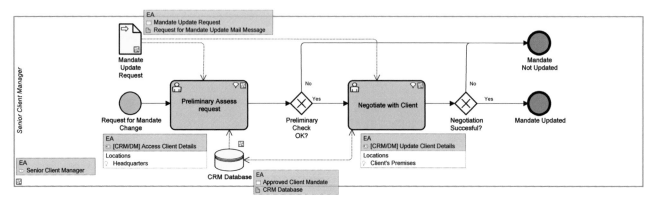

View 251. *View 250 on page 155 with added EA Domain links (visible)*

In View 251 this is shown. As you can see, I have linked ArchiMate elements to both Tasks and to both Lanes. The Task elements have been linked to ArchiMate Application Services, signifying that these are the Application Services that are used by those tasks. It is a good idea to let the Business Process modelers define these services if possible, unless you already have a set that is usable by them. In any way, they must have a strong say in their definition when you are designing a new solution.

- Have the upper Lane linked to the right ArchiMate Business Role and make it a 'label link';

- Have the lower Lane linked to the correct ArchiMate Application Component and make it a 'label link'. The little icon showing there is a 'robot' to signify automated performance by the application, it could of course simply be the icon of the Application Component;

- Have the Human Task in the upper Lane linked to the Application Service that is used by the human's behavior. The little icon is an ArchiMate Application Component icon inside an ArchiMate Service icon in my Application-Behavior color;

If you look at the Lanes in View 251, you see that not only are there ArchiMate elements linked to the Lanes, but the Lanes have changed names too with regard to the situation in View 250 on page 155. That is because I have also set these linked ArchiMate elements to be the 'label links'. The Lanes now have labels that are copies of these ArchiMate elements. To show that a label is linked, my tool shows that label in *italics*. If you go back to View 247 on page 152, you will see some other labels in italics, namely the Sequence Flows following the Gateway that follows the SubProcess. That is because I have linked these labels to the End States of

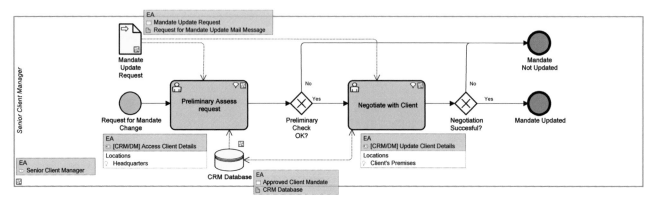

View 252. *The Process from View 249 on page 154 expanded with some Other Domain links.*

that SubProcess before the Gateway. As that is not about the relation between ArchiMate and BPMN, but about elements within the BPMN model I will ignore that here.

Our setup has more 'Other Domains' in BPMN. As mentioned above, we have a 'Risk' domain and a 'Location' domain. These are also filled from the ArchiMate model, but we have chosen to model them as separate domains in BPMN. That makes it for instance easy to use an Operational Risk Management system as source for Risks, etc. As an example, I have added a Location to the Human Task in View 251 and I have added Risk Controls to both Tasks. The result can be seen in View 254.

Question 8. Can you see what is wrong with View 254 (best seen in the lower expanded version) from a BPM perspective?

Answer 8. The RC1 Risk Control suggests that the human can decide not to enter the portfolio but there is no Gateway or End State for that.

Now the question becomes what the effect of all these links should be on the EA side in the ArchiMate model where the process details are aggregated but all the business-IT links should be visible. We do not want to replicate all these SubProcess and Activity details of BPMN in the ArchiMate model. After all, the whole idea was to have only a rough identification of Business Processes and such in the EA ArchiMate model while keeping a synchronized detailed description of the processes in a BPMN model.

Before we see what the result might be, we complete the rest of the BPMN model with some 'Other Domain' links in View 255 on page 160. Note: the expanded Assess Investment subprocess of View 248 on page 153 has been extended with a Lane representing the Fund Manager who has to OK the request to update a Client Mandate to illustrate something on the ArchiMate side which we will address below. In this example,

we have defined a few Application Services that are used in certain Tasks,e.g.:

- *[PM/OM] Enter Order*, the 'Enter Order' Application Service from the 'Portfolio Management/Order Management' Application, used in the 'Create Investment' Task;

- *[PM/OM] Access Portfolio Details* and *[DSS] Calculate Portfolio Characteristics*, DSS being the Decision Support System used in the 'Check Portfolio against targets' Task.

The first question is: Which processes should be visible as Business Process on the ArchiMate side when we do a roll-up of process details on that side? I choose to show two types of processes on the ArchiMate side: The *End-to-End* process and the *Re-usable* process, so, for instance, subprocesses are not shown separately in the ArchiMate model. The End-to-End process is a process that starts with an important business event and that runs to its full completion producing something of value to the business. This includes every part that has to contribute,even if we are talking about wildly different Business Functions and the widely different Business Roles assigned to them. In our example, we have a single End-to-End process: Daily Rebalance Portfolio. Though this

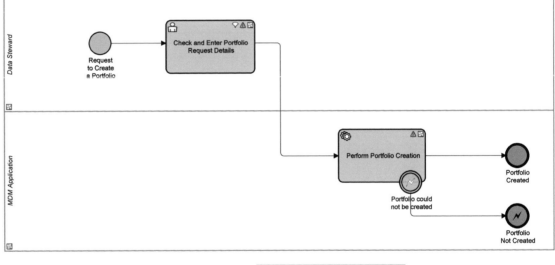

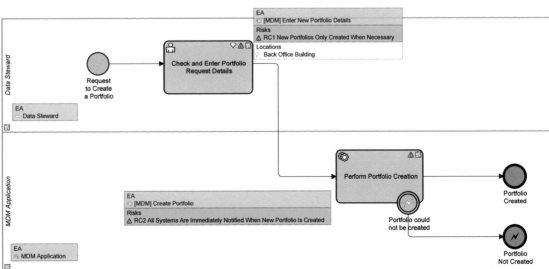

View 254. *View 251 on page 158 with added Location and Risk Domains. Above with only the icons that there are such links and below with the contents of the links of the Tasks visible.*

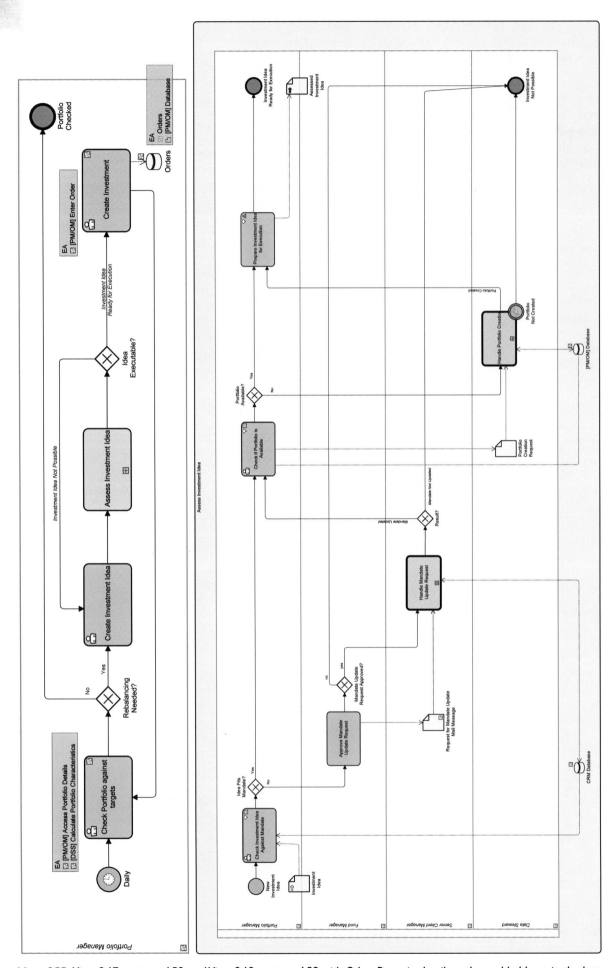

View 255. *View 247 on page 152 and View 248 on page 153 with Other Domain details and an added Lane in the latter*

Mastering ArchiMate Edition II

process is generally seen as part of the Fund/Portfolio Management Business Function, we have already seen that in it other functions, like Master Data Management and Client Management may play a role.

The Re-Usable processes are those that I model as started from another process via a Call Activity. We have two of these in our example model.

In View 258 on page 162, you see such a *possible* Roll-Up of the links that have been created in the BPMN Model. All the red-rimmed elements have been used in the BPMN Model, linked to a BPMN element. All the orange (structural) and purple (dynamic) relations can be constructed from the links in and contents of the BPMN Model. Of course in a real Current State model, you would not model everything in a single view, it would become too unwieldy to read (this one could probably be organized better too and I've left a few things out even). And you can choose what you want to model depending on how you want to use the model.

Here are some things to note:

- It is possible for a Business Process to have assignments from more than one performer (Business Role and/or Application Component) as a result of this roll-up. ArchiMate suggests that you should assign only one Business Role or Application Component to a Business Process and use Collaborations and Interactions if multiple performers work together to perform a process. I have ignored that (see also section 2.1 "Collaboration and Interaction" on page 23 and 8.1 "Application Collaboration is an Anthropomorphism" on page 66 and 10.2 "Business Function or Business Process?" on page 76 about the use of Collaborations and Interactions) and instead have modeled de facto 'informal' collaborations and interactions (see View 23 on page 24). In our example, Business Process, 'Handle Portfolio Creation' has two performers, one of which is an application that performs an automated part of the process. And our main end-to-end process 'Daily Rebalance Portfolio' has two human roles assigned to it: the 'Fund Manager' and the 'Portfolio Manager';

- The Roll-Up of View 258 on page 162 ignores the Call Activities when deciding which Business Roles are assigned to a Business Process on the ArchiMate side. That means that Business Roles 'Data Steward' and 'Senior Client Manager' are not assigned to our main 'Daily Rebalance Portfolio' end-to-end Business Process, even though they do play a role in some situations. Instead: the Call Activities in a BPMN Process result in that in ArchiMate the main-process and the re-usable-process-that-is-called are linked via Trigger and Flow relations. I prefer — and this is illustrated in View 259 on page 163 — showing the dependency on the called processes by modeling (structural) Aggregation relations;

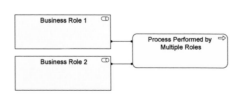

View 257. *ArchiMate Roll-up of BPMN Process performed by two Roles*

- The ArchiMate Artifacts that have been used in the BPMN model to link to BPMN Data Stores are

not the real Artifacts as I should have in an ArchiMate model, certainly not a Current State or Project model. That is because an Artifact like "[server1/db01] Oracle DB" is meaningless for the business modeler. So, I have extended my normal modeling patterns with 'abstract' aggregates that hold the Artifact names that can be understood by the business (modeler). You will need very good cooperation between architecture modelers and business modelers anyway to make linked models like these work;

- If a project starts out with designing the rough processes and imagining what Application Services (or automated tasks) are needed, you get a very nice start for the IT side of the project in terms of what is to be realized by the applications. Also, if you already during the rough design phase identify which processes or activities need to be performed automatically (hence, by applications), you already start both detailed BPMN business process modeling as well as detailed EA modeling on the right track.

Now, let's address a few basic patterns, some of which have already been hinted at in the previous example. The first is a simple one.

25.2 BPMN/ArchiMate: Multiple Roles performing a Single Process

On the BPMN side, this is a very simple pattern shown in View 256.

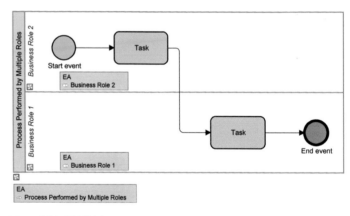

View 256. *BPMN Process with two Roles performing a Single Process*

As my tool can show it, you see the EA 'Other Domain' elements displayed. The process itself is linked to the ArchiMate Business Process and the Lanes are linked to the ArchiMate Business Roles. Rolled-up in ArchiMate this becomes View 257.

This is not quite how ArchiMate purist modelers would like to see it, as I should have either used a Aggregation of those two Business Roles in a parent Business Role or in a Collaboration. In the latter case, the process would have to change into an Interaction.

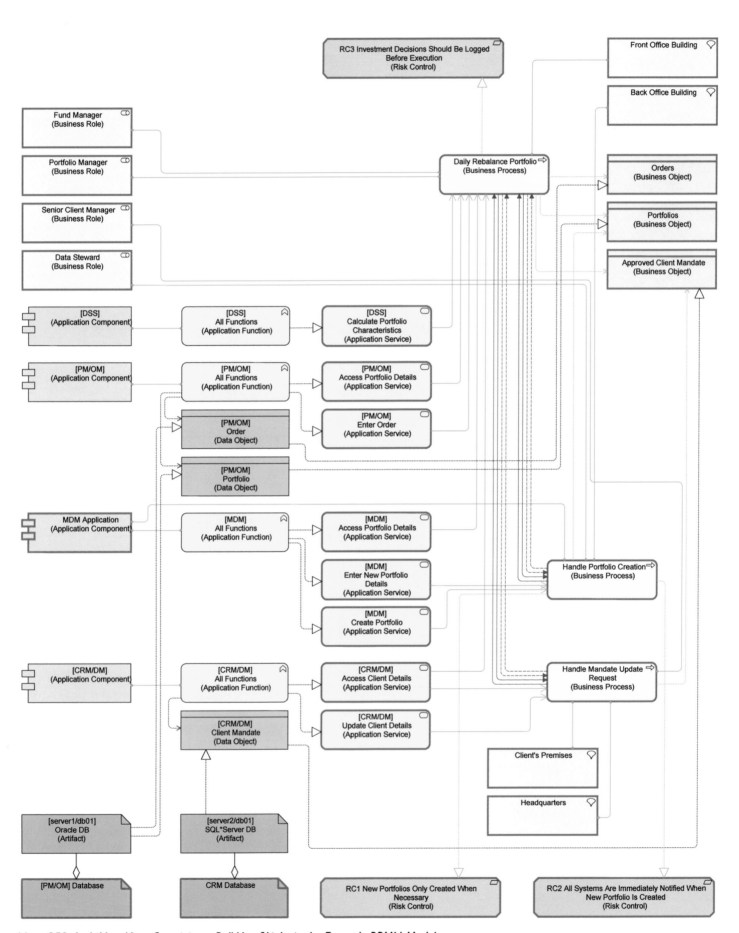

View 258. *ArchiMate View Containing a Roll-Up of Links in the Example BPMN Model*

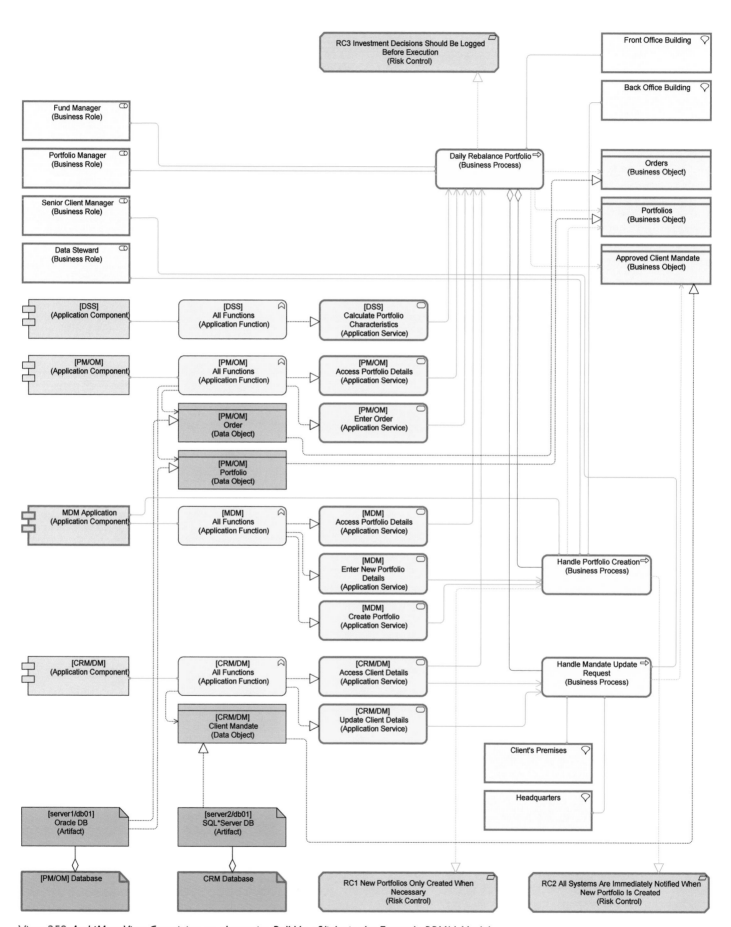

View 259. *ArchiMate View Containing an alternative Roll-Up of links in the Example BPMN Model*

The first option (just Aggregate the roles in ArchiMate) results in View 260.

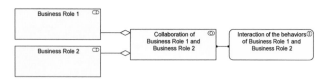

View 260. *ArchiMate Roll-ip of BPMN Process performed by two Roles – Aggregate Business Role performs the Business Process*

There are a few disadvantages:

- Formal ArchiMate now does not allow you to draw a derived relation between each of the roles and the process. This is not really a problem in the real world. It just illustrates that ArchiMate's idea about derived doesn't always really work out in practice;

- The aggregated Business Role needs to be modeled explicitly in ArchiMate (it is implicit in BPMN) and it needs a name. You cannot create that name in an automated way, that would require artificial intelligence, unless you do something like "A collaboration of Role 1, Role V, Role X, etc.". So, you end up having to maintain these aggregates in the ArchiMate model by hand and the logic on updates of both models becomes very complicated. Furthermore, for every combination of roles that perform a process another explicit aggregated Business Role is needed. Apart from the ArchiMate model, nobody in your organization looks at it this way; nobody has a lot of 'named' sets of roles in their head when they think of roles performing processes in collaboration.

You can even do it in a pure ArchiMate way, which means using a Collaboration of Business Roles for every collaborative behavior. That results in View 261.

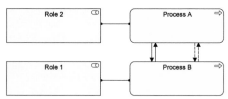

View 261. *ArchiMate Roll-ip of BPMN Process performed by two Roles – Business Collaboration performs a Business Interaction*

Though ultimately most correct in terms of ArchiMate 2.0, this has the same disadvantages as the previous solution and an additional one: all your Business Processes will be Business Interaction elements, another bottleneck in your communication with the business.

Most importantly, these aggregates, both Business Collaboration or Business Role, do not add any information to your model, they only make matters more complex than needed and you cannot draw extra inferences.

As an aside: in very complex BPMN cases, where for instance meetings are modeled, it may be a pragmatic necessity to keep the meeting as a single Task in a single Lane. In that case one could decide *not* to link a role (or a Collabo-

ration in ArchiMate terms) to the Lane, but instead link all roles to the Task and label the Lane independently.

25.3 BPMN/ArchiMate: A Process calling another Process

The next one is also pretty simple: Some process is calling another independent process through a Call Activity. In a very simple form this looks in BPMN like View 262.

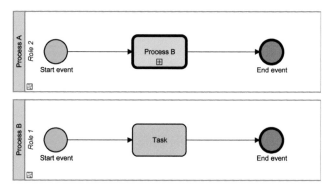

View 262. *BPMN Process calls another Process*

I've shown both processes in separate pools for clarity and to be able to show the process name (as the Pool name). In ArchiMate, the Roll-up becomes View 263.

Modeling the triggers and flows between these processes assumes the BPMN processes exchange information (which is optional) and trigger each other

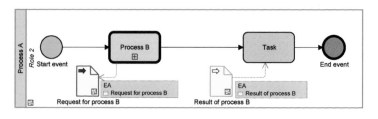

View 263. *ArchiMate Roll-Up of BPMN Process calling another Process*

(which is a necessary result of the call and return). In BPMN, modeling the information exchange explicitly would require Data Outputs and Data Inputs (neither using a Data Store or Message Flows would be proper, I think). Now, with Data Inputs and Data Outputs it could look like View 264.

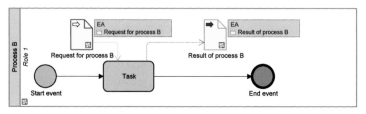

View 264. *BPMN Process calls another Process – with Data Inputs and Data Outputs*

What I did in this view was use two Business Objects at the ArchiMate side: 'Request for process B' and 'Result of process B' and linked these (label link) to the Data Inputs and Data Outputs. Hence, via the ArchiMate model, the Data Output of Process A and the Data Input of Process B have been linked together. BPMN itself does not offer this, though of course tooling might. But in BPMN these objects are fully independent.

The ArchiMate Roll-up now can show Business Objects for the data that was passed from Process A to Process B and back. This is shown in View 265.

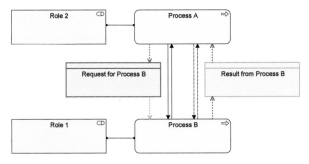

View 265. *ArchiMate Roll-Up of BPMN Process calling another Process – with Data*

To ease the comparison, I have color coded the elements in both views. The red BPMN Association relation corresponds with the red ArchiMate Access relation. The purple bordered BPMN Data Input and Data Output correspond with the purple bordered ArchiMate Business Object.

In the ArchiMate Roll-up, the information flow is in fact modeled twice now. Both the Access actions to the Business Objects and the Flow relations represent the same.

Given that, when information flow is not explicitly modeled in BPMN with BPMN Associations to Data Objects/Inputs/Outputs, there might be no ArchiMate Flow at all, it is I think best to forget about Archi-Mate's Flow relation. Just model the Triggers and model Access via Business Objects if the Data Objects/Inputs/Flows are explicitly modeled in BPMN and linked to ArchiMate Business Objects. That looks like View 266 (with data) and View 267 (without data).

25.4 BPMN/ArchiMate: BPMN has no Architecture 'Layers'

So far, the previous pattern was pretty easy and linking BPMN and ArchiMate worked well. The more details BPMN has, the more can be represented in a Roll-Up in ArchiMate. But there is a snag.

When ArchiMate models information, it is available in three versions:

- Artifacts for the low physical level at the technical infrastructure, generally used for files, data bases, etc.;
- Data Objects for objects inside applications, generally if permanent Realized by those infrastructure Artifacts;

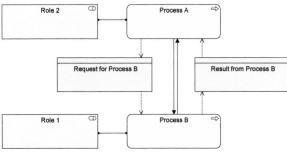

- Business Objects which are Realized by those Data Objects and are more abstract concepts, like for instance 'Bank Account' or 'Invoice'.

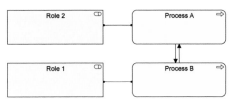

View 266. *ArchiMate Roll Up of BPMN Process calling another Process – with data*

View 267. *ArchiMate Roll-Up of BPMN Process calling another Process – without data*

BPMN does not have abstraction at all. It is intended to model executable processes and the way BPMN separates data into different concepts is not by abstraction but on the split temporary/permanent: Data Objects/Inputs/Outputs exists as long as the process is running, Data Stores exists independently from processes. In ArchiMate, the closest equivalent is a Data Object in memory versus a Data Object Realized by a file or a data base Artifact.

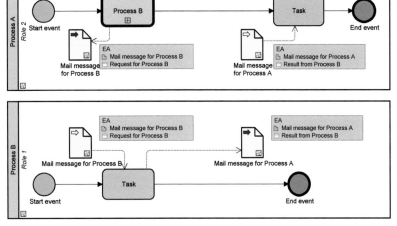

View 268. *Artifact links in BPMN model expanded to Artifact + Business Object links.*

When business modelers model non-executable processes, these are often described in what from an ArchiMate perspective is a mix of layers. Tasks (clearly business behavior performed by a human role) 'access' files (clearly Artifacts from the infrastructure layer). This cannot be modeled in ArchiMate; Business behavior cannot access Infrastructure Passive Elements. An ArchiMate Business Process cannot Access an ArchiMate Artifact. But that is exactly how the business sees its actions and one of the reasons why the layered Enterprise Architecture approach generally feels alien to them. They do not think in abstractions, they think in concrete activities and objects.

Suppose we change our processes of View 264 on page 164 so the data represents ArchiMate Artifacts instead of Business Objects? This is shown in View 269 on page 166. Here, the process designer had to model a process where the business tells him "we have to handle this or that incoming mail message' and he models Data Objects that are those mail messages (or 'Excel file' or 'Word file with allowed counter-parties').

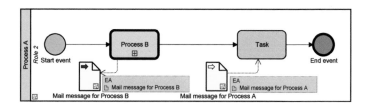

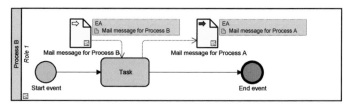

View 269. *BPMN Process calls another Process - Data Objects are infrastructural (e.g. mail messages)*

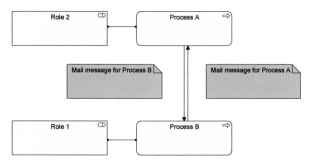

View 270. *ArchiMate Roll-up of BPMN Processes in View 269*

Now, when we Roll-up this into ArchiMate, the basic structure can be seen in View 270.

The problem is that we are not allowed to draw Access relations from an ArchiMate Business Process to an ArchiMate Artifact. So, how are we going to represent what is in the BPMN model? We cannot 'invent' a Business Object separate from the Artifact. There might not be a clear intermediate ArchiMate Data Object (e.g. the Business Object 'Customer Complaint' is directly Realized by the 'Mail Message' Artifact). And even if we ignore the ArchiMate Data Object issue, a single Artifact may in the end Realize many Business Objects. How do you choose which one? You can't. We have some options:

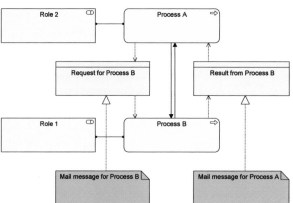

View 271. *ArchiMate modeler expands Artifact link from BPMN to Business Object*

- We can silently promote the Artifact on the BPMN side to a Business Object on the ArchiMate side. In the example above we would get a 'Mail message for Process B' Business Object, etc.. This will work, but as soon as there is also a real Business Object at the ArchiMate side, say 'Customer Complaint', it becomes tricky. You can't overwrite the name of the BPMN Data Object 'Mail message' with 'Customer Complaint' just like that, the business after all thinks in (and requires the visibility in their process descriptions of) mail messages and not in abstract business objects;

- We can use Associations between the Artifacts and the Business Processes. This is pretty ugly as it adds a new incompatible pattern to our ArchiMate landscape.

A possible solution is this: if the BPMN model contains only links to Artifacts from a Data Object/Input/Output/Store, they are represented as Artifacts in ArchiMate with Associations to the Business Process. But if the ArchiMate modeler finds out which Business Object is meant by the Artifact, he or she models that Business Object and creates an Access relation from the Business Process to the Business Object and a Realization Relation from the Artifact to the Business Object. He produces View 271.

And when synchronized back to the BPMN model, this turns into View 268 on page 165.

On the synchronization back to BPMN, the Business Object is to be represented as 'Other Domain' object and it has been linked to the same BPMN Data Object/Input/Output/Store elements as the Artifact is.

The whole setup above is not a perfect real world example. For instance, an ArchiMate setup may have the Mail Agent (e.g. MS Outlook or Apple Mail.app) at the application layer and the mail message then becomes a Data Object Realized by a (probably never modeled) Artifact. A better example might have been to model an application maintenance Process that gets an Excel spreadsheet with names to add to the application's user table. But I'm too lazy to change all the images and text at this point. Maybe later.

The whole link-up requires quite a bit of technical sophistication and there are no tools yet that support this in full.

25.5 The Process Landscape in BPMN

Most companies I have seen wrestle with linking their processes up to some other structure. Not long before writing this, a senior consultant of a major world-wide operating consulting firm presented to an acquaintance a process framework he had just designed for a company. What is noteworthy about this is that he had to do this at all. What is strange is that after all these years of modeling businesses there isn't a standard way to do it. The consultant had invented a new setup. To this day, many hours are spent in many companies on yet another way of modeling a process landscape.

At a high level, there are many variations of a single theme: processes as a chain of functions. Such a pattern was expanded in 10.2 "Business Function or Business Process?" on page 76. Incidentally, the framework presented by that consultant was fundamentally flawed even: the end-to-end processes that consisted of behavior of various departments, (various business functions) was presented as an *internal* process of one of these departments. No surprise then, that as soon as people tried to use it in earnest, it died a quick death.

Starting from BPMN Processes, I am going to build yet another... process landscape setup. I am starting with a sketchy end-to-end process for investing in stocks. It is a Process Chain of three processes of three parts of the company: Portfolio Management creates an Order, Trading receives the Order and makes the deal, Administration receives the details of the deal and administers it. I am at this point purposely vague about what 'Portfolio Management' stands for — a Business Function?, a Business Role?, a Business Actor? — as we get to that later.

The three processes (caricatures of the real thing, I can assure you) are shown in View 272, View 273, and View 274.

- Process 'Create Order' begins when the analyst starts to create an order for some reason we do not know. This analyst does two things: first create the investment proposal (e.g. invest in X for amount Y). This may mean running all kinds of calculations and reading a lot of company documents, newspapers and web sites. When he has decided what to invest in, the second task is creating an order for the trading desk. This task is done by the portfolio manager, presumably using some order entry system.

- Process 'Create Trade' starts when the order has been received. A trade analyst checks the order if it can go though, e.g. adding missing information, checking correctness, etc. Then the order is handed to the trader who goes to the outside world to make the trade.

- When a deal is struck, the trading process ends. Now the trade must be settled. Settlement means "you get your

money and I get my goods" (or the other way around of course). It means that we have to instruct our bank to wire the money to our counter-party and they have to instruct their custodian to wire the stock to our account. The administrator waits for the settlement details as received from the outside world, checks them against what was expected and administers.

Note, all messy exceptions that can occur are left out of these caricatures of processes.

Question 9. Can you see what is wrong with View 274 from a BPM perspective?

Answer 9. The description assumes that the External Settlement Details arrive *after* the instructions. But what if there is a problem and it happens the other way around? There is no process waiting for those instructions..

Either of these processes has no use without any of the others. The processes are related, in fact they form a, what is generally called, 'Process Chain'. Note: a 'Process Chain' is not necessarily a single thread of processes, there may be branching, merging, etc.. In fact, there is no modeling difference between a 'Process Chain' and a 'Process', but we need a different name, because organizations generally see a difference between a process that exists inside a certain responsibility and one that crosses multiple responsibilities.

Everybody agrees about the existence of these chains, but the question is, how does these chains fit in the company? The chain crosses departments, responsibilities, etc. and thus becomes a subject of intense discussion. The consultant I mentioned earlier sidestepped the issue by making a setup where you did not see those responsibility conflicts. As there is no standard model to use, I'm going to use one of my own. This one works from the practice of most organizations. Top-down, it is created from the responsibilities within the organization, which starts from the top. I am not using ArchiMate here (but we'll return to ArchiMate later). In my model, the highest level is a *Mandate*, something that a board member of a company or business unit has. Such a mandate is a combination of people, roles, resources, etc., everything the high level manager is accountable for and makes the final decisions about.

Now, this Mandate is often a collection of recognizable different 'units of business' of the company. Say, the Chief Financial and Risk Officer may be responsible for

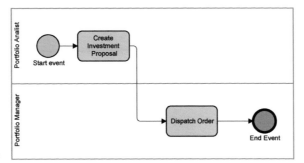

View 272. *The Sketchy Create Order Process*

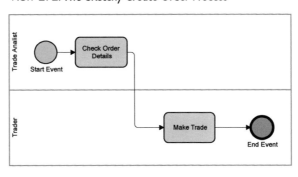

View 273. *The Sketchy Create Trade Process*

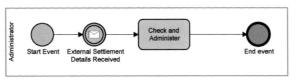

View 274. *The Sketchy Settle Process*

(surprise) finance and risk. And the Chief Operations Officer may be responsible for Administration and IT Support. Such responsibilities may in practice be swapped about. A Mandate of a C-level officer may be any set of these (with some constraints, like separating risk or auditing from the primal process). So we might see a Chief Finance and Operations officer, etc.. These 'swappable' units of business could — in my view — be the *Capabilities* of an organization. Generally, a Capability has a manager too, one level below the C-level. Of course, a Capability can be subdivided in sub-Capabilities etc.. What then is the definition of Capability? There are many around, but here is one: resources giving the ability to undertake a particular kind of action.

These Capabilities all can contribute to processes and (end-to-end) process chains. In fact, technically I would find the term 'Cross-Capability Process' a far better name than 'Process Chain' as the term 'chain' gives a misleading one-dimensional suggestion.

In View 276 there is an example. We see the Capabilities 'Risk', 'Operations', and 'Investment Management' and the Cross-Capability Process (or Process Chain) 'Invest in Developed Equity', which is made up of the three processes we described above: 'Create Order', 'Create Trade' and 'Settle'.

Below it, we see another Cross-Capability Process 'Create Compliance Report', which we will use down below to illustrate a variation on our theme.

Now, interestingly enough, BPMN has three ways to model this 'Process Chain':

- The processes can be in a separate Pool each and communicate via messages. This is shown in View 275. Note the message start and end events;

- The processes can be SubProcesses of an overall process. This is shown in View 277 on page 169 (with Data Inputs and Outputs to take the place of the messages) and in a collapsed state in View 278 on page 169.

- The processes can be called from an overall process via Call Activities. Those called

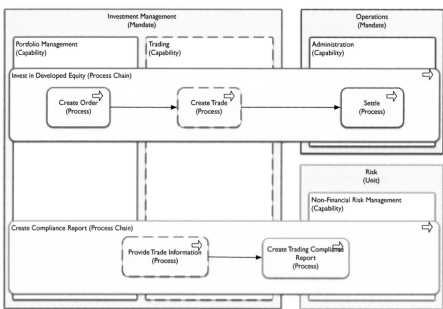

View 276. *Example from a potential process framework*

processes look exactly like the ones depicted as SubProcesses.

The question of course is: which one do you take? To begin with, in our example, the Process Chain is not really a process that is performed where such a thing makes sense. Our Process Chain is a managerial abstraction that is performed by a loose collaboration of the roles that perform the individual processes the Process Chain is made up of, as depicted in View 118 "A Business Process using Business Functions is performed by a (loose) Business Collaboration" on page 78. That would suggest using a 'chain of Pools' (technically a Collaboration in BPMN) as in View 275. BPMN does not have a graphical representation for the total, i.e. you cannot embed the pools in some outer object, so you are restricted to having some sort of view represent the 'process chain'. The sequence of the 'Order', 'Trade', and 'Settle' processes cannot be modeled using Sequence Flows, but that seems at first hand not to be a big problem. In fact, sending a message from a Message End Event to a Message Start Event as in View 275 effectively creates a sequence, even if our 'sequence token' is consumed by the end event and produced new by the connected start event. Even if the 'chain' is more complicated than a straight chain, but has branches we can do without the gateways.

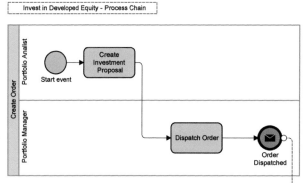

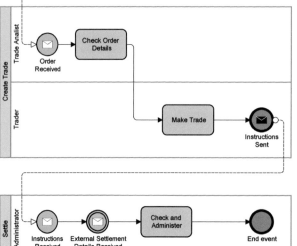

View 275. *Process Chain depicted as a Collaboration in BPMN*

After all, each end state of a process can send a message to a different 'next' process. Sadly, though, we seem to be stuck when we have processes that do not clearly send messages to other processes. What if the Create Order process just writes the Order in a Data Store and the Create Trade process has a continuous loop of looking at the available Orders in that Data Store? This is in fact a pretty common pattern. However, following the principle that we should stay as close as possible to reality we can in fact show what happens. After all, each process in the 'chain' can read from or write to a store (of Orders, of Trades) and it will still work and it can be modeled. In fact, it is what really happens, the sequence of processes in the chain is 'loose' and implied, not 'hard'.

The second and third way are identical in most ways except for one. Modeling the 'process chain' as a process in itself makes it possible to use Sequence Flows and Gateways to produce more realistic complex chains directly. An example using SubProcesses can be seen in View 277. Though it can of course be left out, I have modeled the data too, so you can couple the BPMN data elements to 'other domain' ArchiMate informational elements. SubProcesses can be collapsed and a nice simple overview of a process chain can be created as can be seen in View 278. Creating a 'simplified view' or 'collapsed view' of the process chain of Pools as in View 275 might be possible as well, depending on your tooling. It might look like View 279 (my tool cannot really do it well, so you cannot see the difference here between the collapsed state and a black pool).

Using SubProcesses for the processes in the process chain has a serious disadvantage, though. Say that you have a process chain for 'Investing in Developed Equity' (as shown in these examples) but also a process chain for 'Investing in State-backed Credits'. The processes for creating an order or a trade are quite different and require different capabilities, but the settlement is handled by the exact same generic 'Settle' process. When you use SubProcesses, you need to define that same 'Settle' process twice and keeping them in sync will be a problem. Luckily, BPMN has a way of re-using processes using Call Activities and the example is shown using Call Activities in View 280 on page 170. You can of course use a mixture of SubProcesses — for processes that are unique to the chain — and Call Activities calling Re-Usable Processes — for processes that are not unique to the chain.

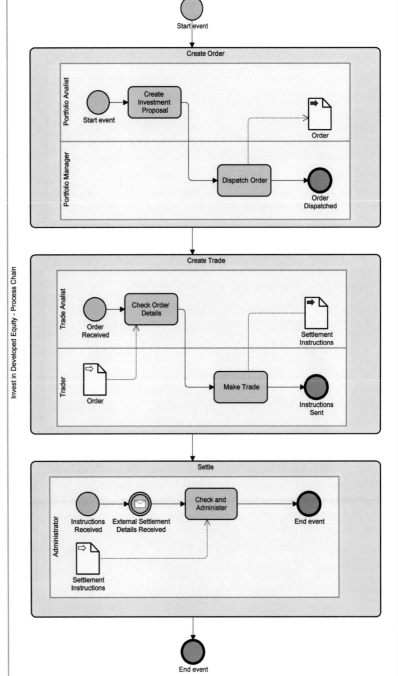

View 277. *Process Chain depicted as a Process with SubProcesses in BPMN*

Which brings us back to the question on what to use. Using different Pools has the disadvantage that you cannot really model process chains that —as a chain — are under workflow engine support: Sequence Flows cannot be used. It has the advantage of having natural visible elements (the Pools) for the processes. Whether you like to use Pools for

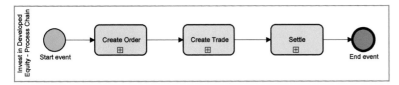

View 278. *Process Chain depicted as a Process with SubProcesses in BPMN — Collapsed*

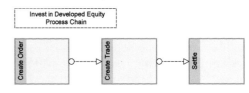

View 279. *Process Chain as a Collaboration in BPMN – Collapsed*

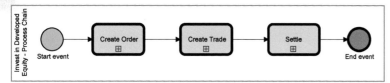

View 280. *Process Chain depicted as a Process that calls other Processes in BPMN*

processes that are wholly internal to your organization is a matter of taste, but in principle there is nothing against it. In fact, as Bruce Silver shows in his 'hiring' example: sometimes multiple Pools are the only way possible to model certain processes, especially when there are 1:n relations between them (one 'fulfilling vacancy' process and many 'screen applicant' processes for instance). Looking at it now, my personal preference is using Pools for the processes in the process chain. One aspect that plays a role here is that these processes are still very high level and require detailing in actual subprocesses and call activities anyway.

Now that we have decided what to use, we can look at a slight variation. Our example processes above were processes that clearly belonged to a single 'Capability'. But this is not always the case. Take the bottom process chain in View 276 on page 168. This is a process chain 'Create Compliance Report' consisting of two processes 'Provide Trade Information', which comes from the Trading Capability and 'Create Trade Compliance Report' which comes from the 'Non-Financial Risk Management' Capability. These processes are depicted as crossing Capability boundaries, however. That is, because in both processes a Task needs to be done by another Capability. In 'Provide Trade Information', there is a small task for the Portfolio Manager, he has to sign off on the data generated by Trading. And the same thing happens when the report is created, the final report needs to be signed off by Trading. For these small and simple steps it is overkill to create entire processes (or SubProcesses if you chose to model chains that way). So, we accept that it is possible that not only a process chain can cover multiple capabilities, the roles that are part of the capabilities may perform a task somewhere else. In fact, this is one of the reasons why we might use the 'Capability' concept, to differentiate between a role performing activities that are part of a capability and performing activities that are part of another capability. The processes in this second example chain are shown in View 281. I have color coded the edges of the Pools and Lanes so it relates to View 276 on page 168. The upper Pool contains a process from the Trading Capability which contains an action of a role that 'belongs to' the Portfolio management Capability. The lower Pool contains a process from the Non-financial Risk Management Capability which contains an action of a role that 'belongs to' the Trading Capability. How it is shown in View 276 on page 168 cannot always be realized: suppose it is the Portfolio Manager who has to perform a Task in the 'Create Trading Compliance Report' process? The element would overlap Trading which has no part in the process at all. So, though View 276 looks nice, it's method of displaying a role belonging to one Capability performing a Task in a process from another Capability does not scale. In reality, I think

such processes should be shown just as the ones from the upper process chain: inside the Capability where it belongs to. The detail that a role from yet another Capability does something is then ignored.

Before finishing this slightly off-topic exposé and return to modeling in ArchiMate, I'd like to say something about ownership of processes and process chains. For me, a process should be owned by the one who is responsible for its results. Which means that in View 276 on page 168, the 'Settle' process is owned by the Administration Capability under the Operations Mandate. But the 'Settle' process is also part of the 'Invest in Developed Equity' process chain (or cross-capability process, or end-to-end process). And the Capability that drives this process, for which the results are, is Portfolio Management. We do not do Portfolio Management because of Trading and we do not do Administration because of Trading. We do all of this because we want to do Portfolio Management. But we do the 'Provide Trade Information' because of 'Create Trading Compliance Report', so here Non-Financial Risk Management owns the chain. Often, owners of processes are afraid that they lose effective ownership of their process if a 'process chain owner' is appointed. But that should not be so. If there is disagreement between Trading and Administration about what happens in the 'Invest in Developed Equity' process chain, the Portfolio Manager should make sure that 'Create Trade' and 'Settle' are aligned. That means talking with the Trading and Administration Capabilities (who still own their own processes) to solve the issues.

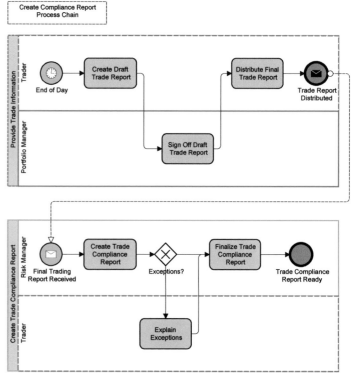

View 281. *Create Compliance Report Process Chain*

25.6 The Process Landscape in ArchiMate

How would the landscape of View 276 on page 168 look in ArchiMate? Given that ArchiMate does not have a 'Capability' element (it probably should, see Section 28.9 "Capability and Product, Skills" on page 194) and that we need to make a choice what to use for 'Mandate', we start in the details and we try to abstract away until we get something resembling View 286. Here we have adapted View 276 so that 'nested' elements are not nested by 'performer' but by 'owner'. The former, after all, is not really possible

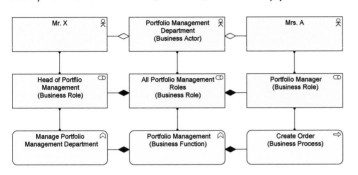

View 282. *The Portfolio Management Capability in simple ArchiMate 2.0*

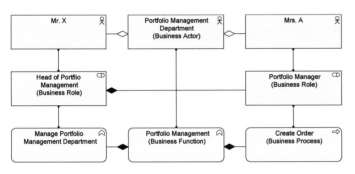

View 283. *The Portfolio Management Capability in simple ArchiMate 2.0 using HR's Job Tree from View 162.*

in real situations (we would need a rather large number of dimensions to do this 'nesting' coherently and we only have two...).

Suppose we think of a Capability as some sort of department with its behavior. For instance for a Portfolio Management Capability we could start with View 282.

I have created a Business (sub)Function for 'managing the department' because that is not really a single process with a single recognizable result.

Now, if we want our 'Jobs' to be compliant with what is in HR's systems (we want this because otherwise we have to (a) make things up and (b) maintain them ourselves) as in View 162 on page 108, there is no Composite element containing 'all Portfolio Management roles'. Leaving it out (and using the HR Job Tree as pattern) produces something like View 283. As we wrote before, there is something to say for this HR Hierarchical Job Tree as the manager is generally able to overrule (and thus perform) the role of the managed employee. That is what hierarchy is about.

Now, modeling this hierarchy presents us with something ugly: to keep the Portfolio Management department as the performer of the Portfolio Management function we can draw a direct Assignment between them. But that Assignment is in fact a derived relation of some role that sits (hidden) in between. We might have removed that 'All Portfolio Management Roles' element from the view, but it is still assumed to exist in the background as otherwise the derived relation would not be possible.

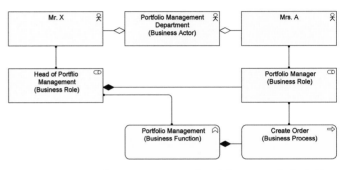

View 284. *The Portfolio Management Capability in simple ArchiMate 2.0 using HR's Job Tree and using only direct relations.*

To solve it we can instead Assign the 'Head of Portfolio Management' role to the Business Function of the behavior of the department. In that case, the specific 'manage department' (sub)Function can be removed as well as can be seen in View 284.

This result was used in 15.1 "Basic Organizational Structure" on page 107. Hiding relational details and using Nesting may produce View 285.

If we model the details of our Process Landscape of View 276 on

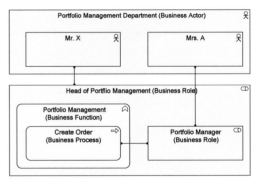

View 285. *Nested version of View 284*

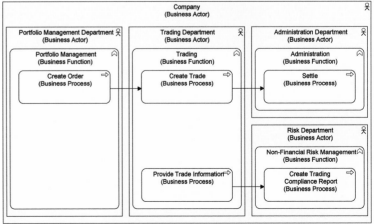

View 286. *Process Landscape attempt in ArchiMate (from View 276 on page 168)*

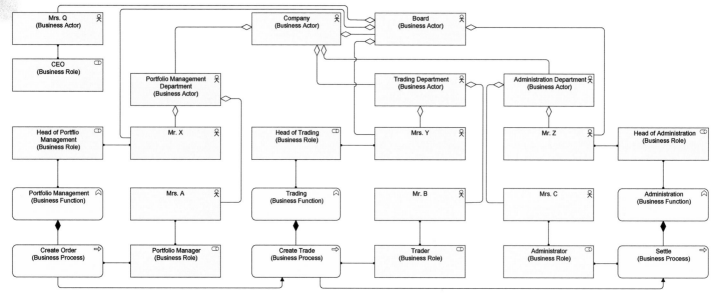

View 287. *The Process Landscape of View 163 on page 108 in ArchiMate with far too much detail*

page 168 in ArchiMate, using the pattern of View 284, we get something like View 287 on page 172. Let me reiterate: examples like these are not meant as example patterns for Enterprise Architecture models, I am just using ArchiMate as an analysis tool.

Now, if I remove all the elements from View 287 that are not in View 286 on page 171, and I add missing relations, I get View 288. This can be shown nested and if you do that, View 286 on page 171 (which was derived from the non-ArchiMate View 276 on page 168) results and that was what we set out to do.

What does this show us? Well, for one, that thinking in terms of Board Mandates leads to defining a 'mandate' as the responsibility for a unit-of-business (department) which somewhat represents a 'capability'.

In summary, with respect to process landscapes:

- Processes need to be grouped by 'owner' (and not 'performer') to create a coherent landscape that can be correctly shown in a simplified 'nested' form;

- A process chain (end-to-end process) requires its own separate owner;

- Ownership is based on who requires the result of a process or process chain.

25.7 Processes handling Artifacts

In ArchiMate, processes do not handle Artifacts, they handle Business Objects. But if you look at actual business process documentation, it often happens that there are actual steps in the process (Activity, Task, SubProcess) that manipulate for instance files.

Take the following example. We have a situation where we have to report to a regulator. These reports are created and sent. But there is also an 'ad hoc' question handling process, which is shown with a lot of detail in View 289 on page 173. The regulator asks us a specific ad hoc question, maybe a clarification question after we have sent our generic report. For this, the people responsible for answering those questions need to collect a number of files, then use these files as input for

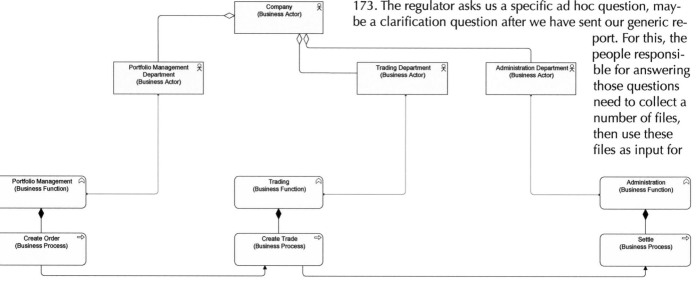

View 288. *View 287 with all elements removed that are not visible in View 286 on page 171. To make the connections required, the red Assignments have been added.*

a new report and send that as answer to the regulator. In this process, there is a step where we 'collect files' and a next step where these files are loaded into a system which makes sense of them, e.g. extract exactly the right information from them.

Now, suppose from the process modeler's perspective the step of collecting the files is crucial and needs to be explicitly described, e.g. because its effect is that the performer of that step needs access to specific information. The effect oft hat requirement is that in the process documentation we have to describe a process activity — which in ArchiMate terms is part of the business layer — that accesses a file — which in ArchiMate terms is part of the infrastructure layer.

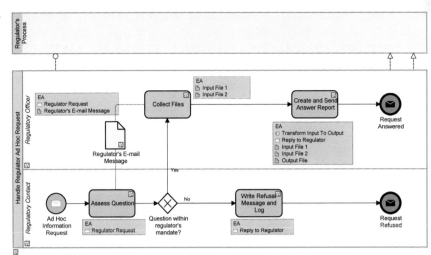

View 289. *A process that handles artifacts with much detail shown*

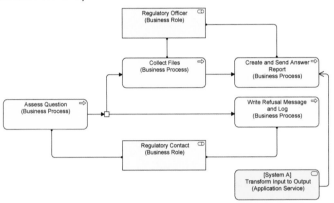

View 290. *Detailed ArchiMate version of process of View 289, without data*

Now, earlier we decided not to model the details of the process on the ArchiMate side. For this section, we are going to step away from that a little to make our options clearer. So, we are going to start with the process, but modeled in detail in ArchiMate, which is shown in View 290. Here we have modeled the activities on the BPMN side as Business Process on the ArchiMate side. On the BPMN side, the ArchiMate Business Roles have been linked to the Lanes, as was proposed before.

Now, the question is: how do we model the passive side (data) in the ArchiMate model?

A first attempt could be to follow ArchiMate strictly and use Business Objects for the passive elements. The simplest way is to make a Business Object that represents the file to be handled. This is shown in View 291. From an ArchiMate perspective, this is definitely weird. We have passive elements that are obviously Artifacts, but they end up in the model as Business Objects.

A second attempt would be to represent the artifacts in the BPMN model as Artifacts in the ArchiMate model. This is shown in full in View 292 on page 174, where I have left out the Application Function as it is not relevant to this analysis. Now, we have Business Objects that represent the Artifacts, and these have gotten a more logical

name, e.g. instead of 'system1extract.csv' the Business Object has been named 'System 1 Extract'. Though much better from an Enterprise Architecture perspective, we now have two (and adding the application layer even three) elements all representing what in the eyes of normal people (such as the business) is just a single easy to understand thing: a file. It is not surprising that you run into trouble sometimes when the tools and mechanisms of Enterprise Architecture have to be read or used by the business. It is a 'light' version of confronting a couch potato with the schematics of his or her TV.

There is a special problem in View 292 on page 174 as well, and it is illustrated in red. What happens in this view is that we have a full layer route from Artifacts to Business Objects because one of the processes also uses an application to manipulate them, hence, there is also an intermediate Data Object. But leave out that application, and what we need to do to model both Artifacts and Business Objects are Realizations such as the one shown in red. Now, these Realizations are valid ArchiMate relations. But there is a hidden problem: they are not *direct* relations, they are *derived* relations. This means that even if the intermediate

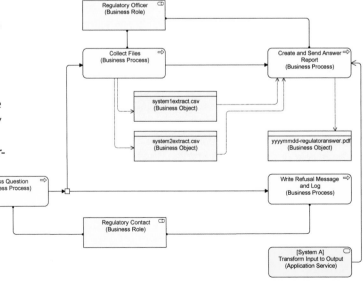

View 291. *The Process of View 289 in ArchiMate with files represented as Business Objects*

Data Objects are not shown, they are implicitly assumed to be there. Of course, being intelligent humans, we can step over that problem and just use them as if they were direct Realizations.

A third option is also ArchiMate-compliant. We can directly link the Business Process elements to the Artifacts. We use the generic Association relation to model the 'access' between the two. This is shown in View 293 on page 174. Effectively, we are working around a limitation of ArchiMate.

Question 10. What other relation is allowed between Artifact and Business Object and why is it not appropriate?

Answer 10. A Used-By is allowed. But what this means is that the Artifact Realizes an Application Component that has a derived Used-By with the Business Process.

This solution does come with a disadvantage, though. Because, what is not shown is what happens in the 'Create and Send Answer Report' Business Process with regard to the application that is being used. The application layer needs that Data Object and that Data Object can Realize a more appropriate Business Object as in View 292.

Having seen three different options, what is best? Personally, I would prefer to use the solution of View 292 and give the business process modelers freedom to link either Artifacts or Business Objects or both. The ArchiMate model could contain a 'direct' Realization relation between Artifact and Business Object if there are activities in the BPMN model that do not use an application to access the data.

25.8 Processes communicating via an ESB

Combining some subjects from earlier in the book, I am going to present my true ESB pattern. Earlier, I presented modeling the ESB in Section 14.2 "ESB" on page 101. The story there wasn't finished yet. First, the patterns there used dynamic (flow) relations to show the flow of data between systems, processes and infrastructure. The disadvantage of using flows, however, is that you cannot link the flow to the passive structure of your architecture. Not having Business Objects or Artifacts to represent the content of the flow becomes a real problem when you want to link BPMN and ArchiMate as above.

Hence, we need a solution for the ESB that does not depend on (dynamic) flow relations, but that uses the (structural) Access relation and passive structural objects. To illustrate the patterns, I am going to start with the processes. Suppose we have two processes: one is a process that produces price information (e.g. by using data vendors, which we will not show here). This price information is sent (via the ESB) from the Master Data Management system to the Accounting System. To make matters a bit more realistic, both the pricing process and the valuation process are not fully automatic, but they have human exception handling. The setup is seen in View 294 on page 175. At some time of day, the application *[MDM System]* generates the prices. A check follows if there have been exceptions during that automated

process. If there haven't been, the prices are distributed and the process ends with a Message End Event. If there have been exceptions, the role [MDM] Data Steward manages the exceptions, after which we end up in the same Message End Event. From this End Event, a BPMN Flow connects the

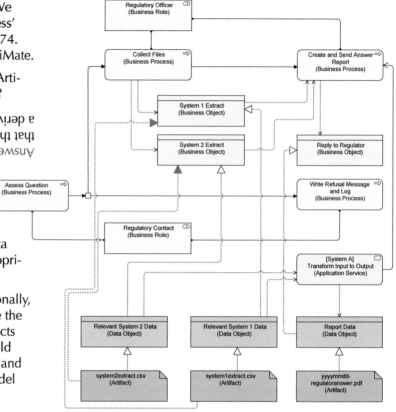

View 292. *Business process of View 289 with files represented as Artifacts as well as Business Objects.*

[MDM] Create and Distribute Prices process to the *[Accounting] Valuation* process. This, therefore, starts with a Message Start Event and the first Activity is that the [Accounting System] performs the Valuation automatically. Here too, there is

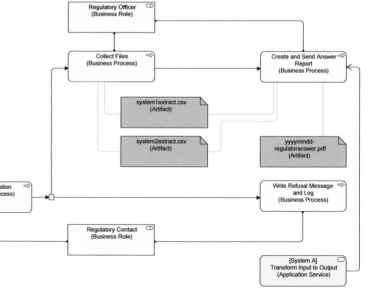

View 293. *Business process of View 289 on page 173 with Associations used to link Business Processes and Artifacts*

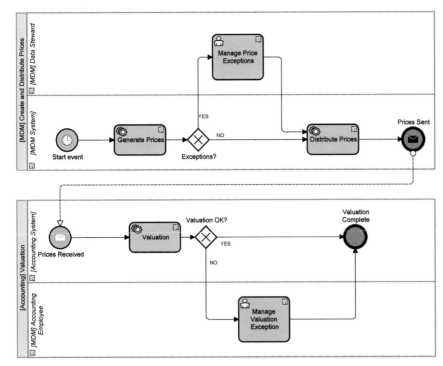

View 294. *Pricing Process delivering Prices to the Valuation Process*

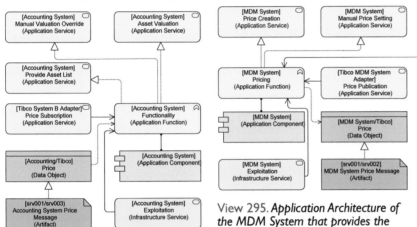

View 295. *Application Architecture of the MDM System that provides the prices.*

View 296. *Application Architecture of the Accounting System that provides the assets and receives the prices*

subscribed to them gets them. One of these, we already know, is the Accounting System itself and it is shown in View 296. In both views, we see the Artifact that represents the message that is going from MDM to Accounting. And finally, the Tibco Application Architecture is shown in View 297. Tibco is shown, as it was in Section 14.2 on page 101 as a platform in which we have created and deployed three applications: the adapter specific for the MDM System, the Adapter for the Accounting System and the application that represents the internal routing logic. We follow the 'Construction View' approach from Section 21 on page 135 here.

Now, all these applications are used in the Business Process. They either are used by Tasks (actually providing the Task with some sort of Application Service that supports it) or they even perform the Task, if it is fully automated. As we saw before, we may link the ArchiMate elements to a BPMN description. This is shown in View 298 on page 176. The Lanes have been coupled with Business Roles and Application Components imported from the ArchiMate side and they have become 'label links'. To the Tasks the various Application Services are linked (and shown) in popups. And we have added a BPMN Data Input and a BPMN Data Output element, both linked to the message Artifacts and the Price Business Object from Enterprise Architecture. We've selected the Artifacts to be the 'label link'. And, of course, the BPMN Pools themselves have been 'label linked' to the Business Process elements of the ArchiMate model. Following the same 'roll-up' mechanism we described before, the business architecture part of the ArchiMate model looks like View 299 on page 176. There are a couple of interesting

an exception-handling Activity and it all ends in the *Valuation Complete* End Event. Both processes have System Tasks that are performed by a system (shown as label on the lane that contains the System Tasks) and that run automatically. Both have human Tasks that obviously use IT too.

Let us first look at the architecture of the Master Data Management System. This is shown in View 295. The MDM System provides two Application Services and uses two. First it uses the *Provide Asset List* Application Service from the Accounting System directly to get a list of assets that need to be priced. Then it creates the prices for those assets, this is the *Price Creation* Application Service that can be used by the Business Process. It also offers a *Manual Price Setting* Application Service that can be used by the business when it manages the exceptions. And finally, it uses the *Price Publication* Application Service of the specific adapter that has been created for our MDM System in the Tibco environment. We publish the prices via Tibco so that every system that has

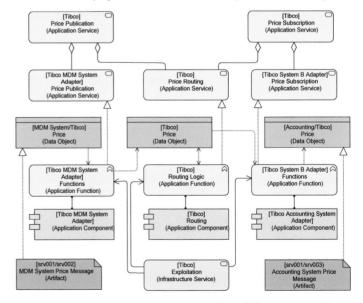

View 297. *Application Architecture of the Tibco ESB connecting Master Data Management and Accounting*

aspects of this roll-up. The first is that the processes are performed by a collaboration of Business Roles and Application Component, shown as an 'informal collaboration'. This is logical, because both processes are examples of 'exception-based architecture', or in other words: one automates as much as one can. The second is that the

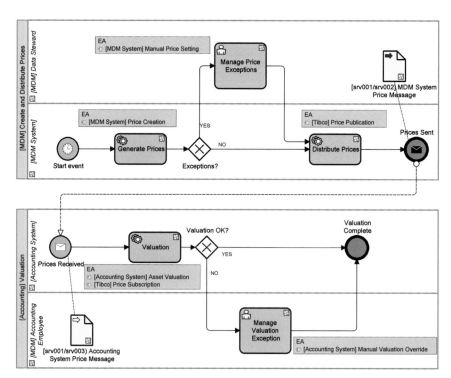

View 300. *Infrastructure for the MDM System*

part played by the *Price* Business Object can be derived from the BPMN Message Flow in View 298, as it connects two BPMN Data Objects (Output and Input) that are both linked (not shown) to the Price Business Object, next to being linked to their own specific message Artifact. I would like to be able to connect the BPMN Message Flow to the Business Object, but my tool does that allow that (yet), it is, however, the ideal linkage for this scenario.

Of course, we also have infrastructure views on our model. Following the 'construction view' approach, we get View 300 for the MDM System, View 301 for the Tibco environ-

View 298. *View 294 on page 175 extended with ArchiMate links.*

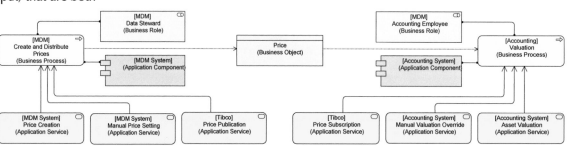

View 299. *Business architecture in ArchiMate, derived from a roll-up of the linkage in the BPMN model.*

ment and View 302 for the Accounting System. A full overview of all layers and relations can be found in View 303 on page 177. Here, you can also see a choice I have made that is an exception to a rule. As a rule, I keep Data Objects specific to applications. But in this case, I make an exception because the Data Objects are so very clearly exactly the same for both. As a result, the flow of information can be easily seen by following the Access to the Business Object in the business layer and the Data Objects in the application layer. We do not have to go to the infrastructure layer to see the shared messages or use Flow relations. Note that Tibco's Price Data Object has no Artifact that Realizes it. It is quite ephemeral and its Realizing Artifact is internal detail that we need not show. It is only there to show the flow as Access relations instead of Flow relations.

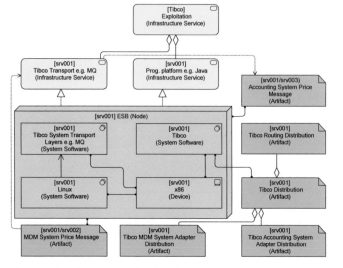

View 301. *Infrastructure for the Tibco environment*

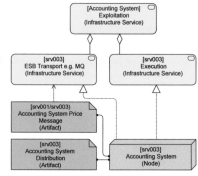

View 302. *Infrastructure for the Accounting System*

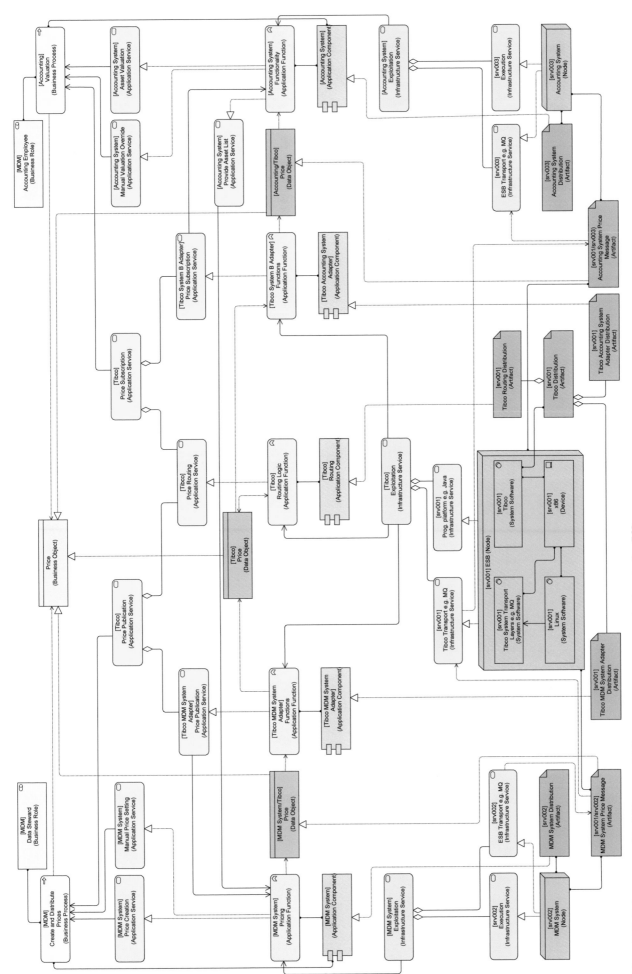

View 303. Full overview of ArchiMate model for two processes communicating via the ESB

Discussing
ArchiMate

Discussing ArchiMate

26. The Role of ArchiMate in Enterprise Architecture

ArchiMate started out as a university/business collaboration with the idea to create a modeling language for the elements that make up an enterprise. This has, in my view, resulted in a very usable and practical Core ArchiMate language which in my experience has been tested to the extreme for that goal and passed with flying colors, resulting in a 75,000 elements and relations model/satellite Current State: a true 'model of the enterprise', maintainable with relatively little effort and in sync with other 'models of the enterprise'.

One of the key insights during that development came when we had to address the question "How do we model the owner of an Application?", the answer of which led to the 'Primary/Secondary/Tertiary Architecture' approach in section 12 "Secondary and Tertiary Architecture" on page 89. The main insight behind that approach is that *everything* that happens in your organization is part of the 'enterprise' in Enterprise Architecture. Not just your primary processes, but also HR, finance, IT development, etc.. When you model a business, you may leave some out (it is all a matter of there being a business case to spend the energy on modeling), but even if you do not model them, they remain part of that enterprise. Even your activities in EA are part of the enterprise. There needs to be a business case for them, some advantage they give you or some pressing need. EA then seems special, because when EA is seen as part of the enterprise, you get the situation that EA is the activity that models itself. But take a step back and you will see that this is not such a special situation: the finance department will also 'model' their own finances, the HR department will also do their HR-work for their own HR people, the IT department has its own IT to develop and maintain.

Looking at it that way, it would, in fact, be very strange if a purported EA modeling language like ArchiMate would *not* already be able to capture the secondary, tertiary, etc. activities in an enterprise. Which then begs the question: why were the extensions (Motivation Extension and Implementation Extension) added to ArchiMate 1?

Both extensions seem to stem from a specific — I would say 'classic' — approach to 'doing EA': working with principles and guidelines and working with 'As-Is' and 'Future-State' architectures with 'gaps' that direct your projects and programs intended to change 'As-Is' into 'Future-State'.

There are many definitions of the term 'Enterprise Architecture'. The one I like is: "Enterprise Architecture is about understanding all of the different elements that go to make up the enterprise and how those elements interrelate" from the Institute For Enterprise Architecture Developments. Not that it means I concur with everything of that institute, it is just a definition I encountered and agree with. Many other definitions exist, from MIT, the US Government, etc. The one from the ArchiMate Foundation was: "A coherent whole of principles, methods, and models that are used in the design and realization of an enterprise's organizational structure, business processes, information systems, and infrastructure". Here you see a more detailed role for EA. EA consists of 'models, methods and principles' that are 'being used in the design and realization' of the enterprise. Here EA is not about the 'elements of the enterprise' and their relations (in other words about the 'design (of the enterprise) itself'), but it is something at a more abstract level: EA *steers* 'design (and realization)' (of the enterprise). The ANSI/IEEE Std 1471-2000 standard, which is most often used, combines both in its definition of Enterprise Architecture: "The fundamental organization of a system, embodied in its components, their relationships to each other and the environment, and the principles governing its design and evolution". It says more or less:

- Architecture is the design of 'the thing in itself' as in 'the architecture of a building' or 'the architecture of an enterprise'. This is sometimes called 'operational space';

- Architecture is also the *process* of *creating* the design of the 'thing in itself', as in 'the way a building is designed' or 'the way an enterprise is designed'. This is sometimes called 'architectural space'.

Now, 'architects of the physical' do not confuse the two. If they model, they model 'the thing in itself'. They model buildings, bridges, airports, etc. Their models do not also contain the 'principles' or 'method' of modeling, though they normally will in some way document requirements (what the future owner wants) and constraints (legal, physical) and the like. And of course, the major stakeholder's signature should be on the contract or the architect does not get paid. Enterprise Architects, however, are more often seen to model 'aspects of designing' (principles and such) than the design itself. There is of course a vision behind a design.

Enterprise Architecture has 'fuzzy edges' which are useful to include in your 'models of the enterprise (to be)' such as the risks and control objectives that were modeled in 13.4 "Modeling Risks and Controls" on page 98. These are indeed not 'elements of the enterprise' per se, they are often vague, abstract environmental aspects of the enterprise. But they still are not elements of 'architectural space', they still are elements of design: the 'model of the thing in itself'.

I think modeling 'architectural space', or in other words modeling 'the principles governing its design and evolution' *in combination with* 'the fundamental organization of a system, embodied in its components, their relationships to each other and the environment' ('the thing in itself') often has limited practical value. The relation between the two is far too complex, volatile and fuzzy to be modeled adequately and usefully. It works only in 'toy models', little examples often used to explain a method, but it does not scale well. The reasons and intentions for anything as complex as the setup of an enterprise just cannot be modeled with a couple

of simple concepts. The assumption that this is useful in practice has a lot in common with the (failed) assumptions behind AI on digital computers. It may be one of the reasons too why EA generally is not seen as very valuable by the business and too detached from reality. Methods that do not scale well are —sadly enough — a common aspect for methods that result from academic institutions. ArchiMate is an exception (most of it scales rather well), but maybe that is because not just academia designed it, but businesses were closely involved and the result was quite something different than the founders envisioned originally: they were thinking of a language that was also a dynamic system, where you could animate the architecture instead of just draw pictures, hence the name ArchiMate (for Architecture-Animate).

Having said that, one should not be too principled against guidelines. After all, the Enterprise Architect's position differs substantially from that of the architect of physical structures. For one, the physical architecture process is part of an old and well-established and relatively slowly changing human activity with often very clear and concrete goals. The enterprise on the other hand, is confronted with huge amounts of freedom (certainly at the start of change initiatives) and a lot of volatility. This leads to a deeply felt need for stability, in which guidelines may play an essential role. But turning guidelines into principles comes with substantial risks, a subject that is outside of the scope of this book.

27. Problem Areas in the ArchiMate 2.1 Standard

I might rightly be called a fanboy of ArchiMate, but that doesn't mean I am without criticism. There are a few generic problems with the ArchiMate 2.1 Standard as far as I'm concerned. Here are a few:

27.1 Hidden Structure and Specialization Confusion

ArchiMate has a hidden structure (or leftovers from the past, whichever way you want to interpret it) at the business layer. Pre-TOG ArchiMate used to have a Business Behavior concept from which Business Process, Business Function, Business Interaction and Business Event are Specializations. As a result, Composition and Aggregation relations are possible between each of these. ArchiMate 2 has lost this generic Business Behavior concept and somewhat vaguely talks about "Business Process/Function/Interaction" without using Specializations to link them together, but the resulting Compositions and Aggregations are still allowed (and thus have 'ad hoc' status. In 'Section 9.2 Specialization of Concepts' of the ArchiMate 2.1 Standard, we encounter a pre-ArchiMate 1.0 example of a *generalized* (not *specialized*, note) 'Business Process/Business Function" concept of which Business Process, Business Function and Business Activity are Specializations. Pre-TOG ArchiMate has the "Business Behavior" concepts, but Business Interaction and Business Event do not Specialize from it. The ArchiMate 2.1 Standard contains the leftovers of the removed 'parent concept' in the 'allowed relations' tables at the end.

There are several other 'Specialization' relations possible according to those tables, which also define hidden structure or are even based on a confusion about the Specialization relation. Some of these are weird. Collaboration, for instance, is a Specialization of Role, but according to the standard a Role may also be a Specialization of Collaboration. Here the designers seemed to have used the idea that a if A is a Specialization of B and B is a Specialization of C then A is a Specialization of C. But if that is true, a Role that is a Specialization of a Collaboration is a Collaboration itself and may be Assigned to an Interaction. In technical terms: given the fact that Collaborations has Constraints that do not hold for Role (in other words: you cannot always use the parent Role instead of the child Collaboration), the Liskov Substitution Principle does not hold and ArchiMate's Specialization is therefore not pure enough to use this daisy-chaining. Besides, and what is worse, what they in fact did was set up a circular dependency in a type/class tree: Role is a Specialization of Collaboration, which is a Specialization again of Role. Or in layman's terms: a Ball is a kind of Toy and a Toy is a Kind of Ball. Hmm, I think not.... The same problem exists between Business Object and Contract.

Personally I would have left Specialization out of the 'allowed relation table' as Specialization in modeling is about creating new concepts from existing ones (and thus actually about changing the number of columns and rows in the table), not about modeling relations between existing ones (the contents of the cells).

Luckily, though the use of the specialization/class/type concept in the standard is messy, the usability of ArchiMate is not really impacted. But sensitive architectural souls may sometimes balk at the invasion of their aesthetic senses and rightly complain about the mess.

Another mistake concerning Specialization is in the definition of Viewpoints. Viewpoints are an idea in Architecture that sound neat, but their big advantage would be if you could have a model and Views could be automatically derived from your model using Viewpoints. Automatic layout requires Artificial Intelligence (which is quite beyond digital computers for reasons that can be found elsewhere) and even if you do not get a good layout, automatic generation of Views using Viewpoints requires a perfectly completely modeled architecture, which hardly ever is the case.

Having said that, ArchiMate comes with Viewpoints. View View 304 contains one of these in Mastering ArchiMate style.

Now, a Viewpoint is meant to be a way to look at your model: combine a Viewpoint with a model and what

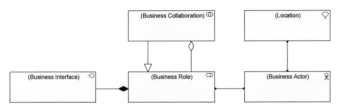

View 304. *ArchiMate's Organization Viewpoint as shown in the Archi-Mate 2.0 Standard Section 8.4.2 but in Mastering ArchiMate Style*

results is a View. This Viewpoint, however, also contains the meta-model Specialization relation between Business Collaboration and Business Role. Now, this relation exists in the meta-model but you will never model it like this in your real architecture model. That the relation shows up in those Viewpoints only illustrates that the authors never looked at it from the perspective of real models but just copied parts of the metamodel to the Viewpoints.

While it was probably just an oversight by experienced ArchiMate modelers, what happens here is the same as the beginner pitfall that was mentioned in Section 4.3 "Mis-

understanding the standard meta-model diagram" on page 33.

Another question mark is the fact that the 'allowed relations' table allows a Flow or Trigger relation from — say — Business Actor to Business Collaboration. As ad hoc addition to the meta-model this is nowhere explained. And if it is meant as a derived relation, then it is a confusion about a real model versus the meta-model. In a real model, this derivation is not possible, because there, the Specialization relation between a specific Collaboration and a 'superclass' does not exist. The fact that 'a' Business Collaboration is 'a' type of Business Role in the metamodel, does not make 'the' specific 'Sales & Legal Collaboration' in a real model a Specialization of any specific Business Role.

27.2 Sloppy Examples

The ArchiMate 2 Standard has some sloppy examples. Take for instance "Example 4 Business Interface"on page 19 of the ArchiMate 2.0 Standard. This problem was fixed in the ArchiMate 2.1 Standard (as were some others).

Recall, a Business Collaboration is a 'temporary role' that can be assigned to its (temporary) behavior: the Business Interaction. That means that the activities of that Business Interaction must be performed by both roles. But if you look at View 305, the Call Center Business Interface is As-signed-To the Medical Insurance Seller. The model says that it is the Medical Insurance Seller which has the interface to the customer (Call Center) and who thus makes the sell. But implicitly, the model says that there is a Business Interaction that Realizes the "Combined Insurance Selling" Business Service.

A problem that remains with Example 4 in ArchiMate 2.1 (and 2.0) is that the Luggage Insurance Seller has a Web Form as Business Interface. A Web Form is an Application Interface, so we are probably talking about an automated process here that is performed by some *application*. If it really is a human role, we have modeled a Web Form where the poor humans fulfilling the 'Luggage Insurance Seller' role are typing very fast to make it look to the customer that he or she is interacting with a computer...

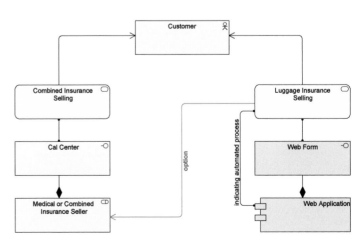

View 305. *Example 4 Business Interface from the ArchiMate 2.0 Standard in Mastering ArchiMate Style*

View 306. *Repaired version of View 305*

Actually, this example would have been better if a Business Collaboration had been left out as in View 306 on page 181.

In this view, the red Used-By shows a possible way the 'Medical or Combined Insurance Seller' could offer the Luggage Insurance: by entering the customer's data into the Web Form him- or herself. In fact: quite an efficient solution from an IT-perspective.

The example is not really 'wrong'. You can actually think of an explanation to make it right, but you need to take quite a bit of liberty with the model if you do so. The same 'Web' interface of a human role returns in Example 6 of the standard.

Example 6 on page 21 also contains the first appearance of a small but meaningful mistake that is often repeated: the service offered by the insurance company to a customer is called "take out insurance". But "taking out insurance" is informal language for the process of *buying* insurance, not selling or providing it.

This kind of error is not always a matter of a wrong label, it is sometimes also made in a structural way. Example

View 307. *Example 15: Product from the ArchiMate 2.0 Standard laid out in Mastering ArchiMate style.*

View 308. *View 307 with Nesting removed*

View 309. *View 308 with missing Business Process added.*

15: Product is also questionable. Analyzing this is useful, not just to show that the example might be questionable, but it is also educational about what ArchiMate views actually mean. In Mastering ArchiMate style the example looks like View 307. The accompanying explanation says:

A bank offers the product 'Telebanking account' to its customers. Opening an account as well as application support (i.e., helpdesk and the like), are modeled as business services realized by the 'Customer relations department'. As part of the product, the customer can make use of a banking service which offers application services realized by the Telebanking application, such as electronic 'Money transfer' and requesting 'Account status'.

If we un-nest the diagram it looks like View 308.

The Used-By relations between the Application Services and the *Banking* Business Service is a derived relation. To find out what actually happens, we can add the missing part, a Business Process or Business Function. If we add a *Provide Banking* Business Process that Realizes the *Banking* Business Service we get View 309.

This Business Process, note, is a process of the *Bank*, not of the *Customer*. But we wanted to model that it is the Customer who uses the Telebanking application to look at the account status and to transfer money.

So, expanding the derived relation makes it clear that the example, as modeled, actually says that the Application Services are used by a Business Process of the Bank's Employees, not of the Customer Business Actor.

Now, might this still be OK if we would say that the Banking Business Service is a Business Service performed by an automated Business Process. In that case we don't model Bank Employees using the Telebanking application instead of the Customer. For that we would have to add an Assignment from the Telebanking Application Component to the Provide Banking Business Process, which is shown in View 310.

I renamed the Business Process and Business Service to *Automated Banking* so it is clear what is being offered. This would in fact be the pattern that I have put in section 2.7 "Automated Processes" on page 27 as the pattern

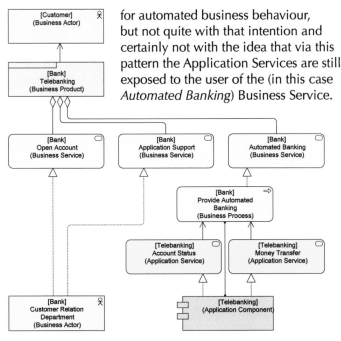

for automated business behaviour, but not quite with that intention and certainly not with the idea that via this pattern the Application Services are still exposed to the user of the (in this case *Automated Banking*) Business Service.

View 310. *Alternative 1 for View 309: make clear that the Banking Service is an automated Business Service.*

So, I have removed the Application Service from the Product Aggregate and our Product is now fully modeled at the business layer.

If I Nest that, I get View 311.

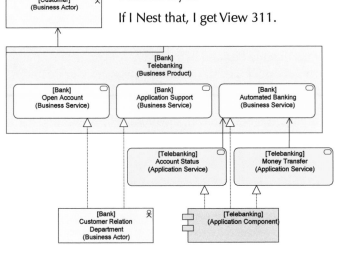

View 311. *Nested version of View 310. The Product offered to the Customer is now entirely at the business layer.*

Actually, we can leave the Application Services out of this picture, as they are not longer relevant for our model of what we offer the customer: it has become 'internal detail'. So we get View 312.

This is a clean solution, but it hides the core of what the Customer gets: the use of the Telebanking environment. If we want that in and we want to stay close to the original diagram, we could instead create View 313.

The Automated Banking Application Services is now Composed of the Account Status and Money Transfer Application Services. We now have that overall element that was in View 307 on page 182. Un-Nest it and you get View 314.

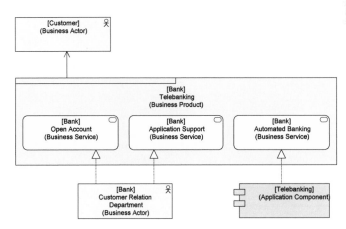

View 312. *Simplified version of View 311. Application layer details are now hidden.*

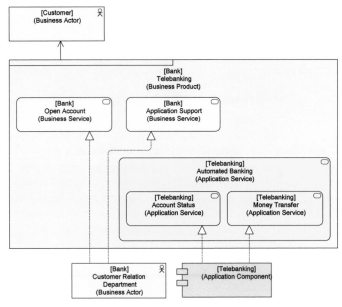

View 313. *Telebanking Example: Automated Banking as Application Service instead of Business Service.*

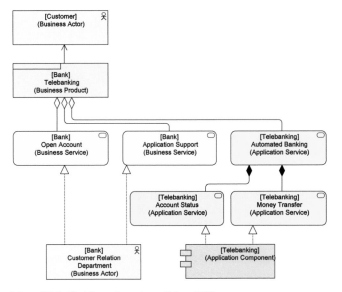

View 314. *Un-Nested version of View 313*

That 'overall element' does not add anything useful, so we can remove it and get View 315.

And if we Nest that result we get View 316, which — if I wanted to model the original diagram, and with the Contract added — would probably be my preferred solution.

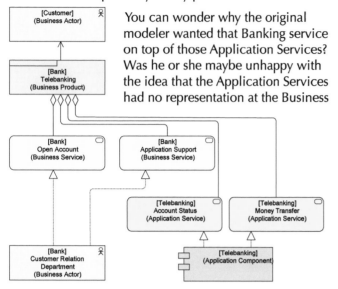

You can wonder why the original modeler wanted that Banking service on top of those Application Services? Was he or she maybe unhappy with the idea that the Application Services had no representation at the Business

View 315. *View 314 with the aggregated Application Service removed*

Layer? Maybe he or she should shave realized that these Application Services are used by the Business Layer of the *Customer's* Architecture. Whatever the reason, the original Example mixes two different approaches where it is better to use either one.

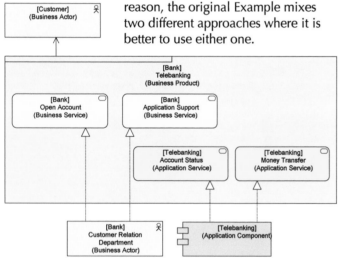

View 316. *Nested version of View 315*

27.3 Fuzzy Concepts

ArchiMate 2.1 has too much fuzziness in some of its concepts. Examples are the infrastructural concepts Network, Communication Path and Infrastructure Service. For instance, ArchiMate 2.0 suggests that "message queuing" would be a good use for the Communication Path concept. But this overlaps with using a Flow relation for the 'logical communication' between Nodes (as derived from the communication between the Infrastructure Function. Also, "message queuing" would probably be a good candidate for an Infrastructure Service that is to be Realized by infrastructure so it can be Used-By the application layer. Network, accord-

ing to the standard, 'represents the physical communication infrastructure'. But while for a business oriented 'enterprise architect', a thing like a "100 Mbit/s LAN" (example used in the standard) might sound physical, infrastructure architects know this is all in the digital domain: packets and such with bits and bytes. So, the real physical domain might be the "CAT5E cabling", and the Communication Path may be "1 Gbps Ethernet". ArchiMate's Network and Communication Path are not overly helpful, and I have never seen it really used outside The Open Group's (or Novay/Telin before them) own materials.

A major area of fuzziness is the use of the Assignment relation in the Infrastructure layer. In ArchiMate 1, System Software was a *behavioral* element and the Device was the active element that 'performed' that behavior. Assignment is used for such a relation between an active and a behavioral object in ArchiMate. With ArchiMate 2, the Infrastructure Function was introduced behavioral element in the infrastructure layer, and System Software became an active element, that — just as Device — could be Assigned to that behavioral Infrastructure Function element. The Assignment from Device to System Software was kept (probably for backward compatibility).

ArchiMate states both in version 1 and 2 about Devices and their Assignments:

> *Artifacts can be assigned to (i.e., deployed on) devices. System software can be assigned to a device.*

The Assignment between an Artifact and a Device is clear: it means that the bits and bytes of that Artifact reside on that Device. In ArchiMate 1, the relation between Device and System Software was also clear, because it was Assignment between active element and its behavior. But now that System Software is not behavior anymore, it becomes unclear what this Assignment means.

About Node, ArchiMate says:

> *Nodes come in two flavors: device and system software, both taken from UML 2.0. A device models a physical computational resource, upon which artifacts may be deployed for execution. System software is an infrastructural software component running on a device.*

(which is clear) and

> *A node is often a combination of a hardware device and system software, thus providing a complete execution environment.*

(which is clear) and says about Assignments:

> *Artifacts can be assigned to (i.e., deployed on) nodes.*

This is a pattern we have adopted. In this book, we also have kept the ArchiMate 1 Assignment between Device and System Software. We encountered a problem when we modeled virtual hardware as System Software in Section 16 "Virtual Machines (Parallelization)" on page 110 and found out that ArchiMate does not allow us to Assign from our virtual machine System Software to other System Software and I opted to use Composition instead.

Have a look at View 317 where the structure of Infrastructure is shown, on the left with an Artifact Realizing an Application Component and on the right with the same Artifact Realizing System Software. Note:

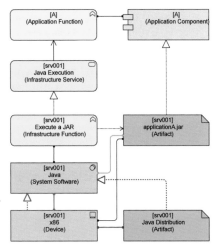

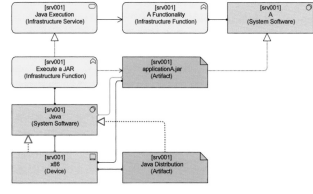

- The red Assignment is the leftover from ArchiMate 1 with undefined meaning in ArchiMate 2, though generally read as 'runs on';

View 317. *Basic Pattern of deployed Artifact as Application Component (left) or System Software (right)*

- The blue route leads to the green Realization relation. Later I will make an improvement suggestion that amongst other things cleans this up.

Now, what does the orange Assignment signify? Only the description of System Software says something about it:

> *Artifacts can be assigned to (i.e., deployed on) system software.*

So, the meaning of Assignment here is 'deployed on'. Deployment in ArchiMate means 'it resides on/in'. An Artifact that is Assigned-To System Software must somehow become embedded on it, like an Artifact that is deployed on a Device becomes embedded in (part of) (the storage of) the Device. Deployment does not mean execution. Execution of the Realized active element is modeled using the Used-By. But if our System Software is a Java engine and the deployed Artifact is a '.jar' file, in the real world the .jar' file must be deployed on the *Device*, hence the orange Assignments in View 317 are nonsense.

So, is there a way in which that orange Assignment is meaningful? View 318 contains two ways that fail to be meaningful. On the left the stored procedure Artifact is part of the passive element of the setup, on the right it is an extension of the distribution Artifact of the System Software. In both cases, the Artifact is, either directly or indirectly) deployed on the Device.

I can think of a scenario where I would say that I am really deploying on System Software, and that is in a situation like the one depicted in View 319. Whereas I could manipulate the files on the Device in View 318 to add the EJB to the JEE environment,

I probably cannot do that realistically if I want to install the Amiga Game on the Amiga emulator. Technically, however, the Game distribution is still destroyed when I destroy the Amiga emulator distribution, so I would not be lying if I would draw a Composition between the two as with the JEE example.

The concepts from the Motivation Extension have their overlap and fuzziness as well, see Section 28.16 "The ArchiMate Extensions" on page 198.

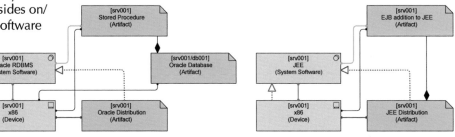

View 318. *More ways for the Assignment between Artifact and System Software to be meaningless*

And a final example of fuzziness is Grouping, which according to the standard is a relation, but which is shown as a sort of Nesting. See 28.8 "A Group concept, a 'Fourth Column', Nesting" on page 193.

27.4 The 'Required' Interface concept

ArchiMate's description (still) contains the *Required* versus *Provided* Interface concept. A 'provided' Interface fits nicely with the fact that it is Used-By another active element and the service-oriented approach of ArchiMate, so no problem here. E.g.: the Application Interface is used by the Business Role or by another Application Component. Originally, ArchiMate, without the Motivation Extension, did not have the possibility to model requirements very well. This was 'solved' — but only for the interface concept, not for the service concept, strangely enough — by the introduction of the concept of 'required' interface, which is explained as "which functionality is required from the environment". Now, functionality is behavior, so this is not only half, but also a mix-up between active structure and behavior.

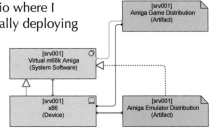

View 319. *Amiga Game deployed on Amiga emulator System Software*

27.5 Derived Relations

Finally, the whole concept of 'derived relations' needs a review. While the idea was originally theoretically neat, in practice it is often too limited and sometimes over-permissive (see also Section 5.5 "On the limitations of derived relations" on page 36). One more example: One cannot derive use of the Aggregate parts of a Product (i.e. the Business Services) from using the Product itself.

There are even some ad hoc workarounds for its problems in the metamodel and it has not been fully employed (e.g. not in the extensions).

28. Proposed Improvements

Overseeing the construction of a current state model of over 75,000 elements and relations (with links to other models of the enterprise, e.g. like process models and CMDBs) has proven to me the usability of ArchiMate and has exposed a wealth about the reality of seriously using the language. In this section I'll make some proposals to improve the language. Now, while I of course prefer to see these changes implemented, I find the language without them still very powerful and usable for modeling Enterprise Architecture. It is just that our experience has been a very good test for the language and out of that test come these suggestions.

The first three suggestions are interrelated.

28.1 Service as Composite Part of Function/Process

There are two views of what a service is.

One is that the service is *visible* behavior that is *strongly coupled* to the *invisible* behavior. E.g. if you describe a selling process that creates a service which is used by a buyer, all the behavior that is visible to the buyer is an inseparable part of the process (and its description). It is not only part of the service, it is *at the same time* part of the process and the service is seen as the (visible) Composite part of the process. This, we could call the 'constructionist view' of a service.

The other is that a service provides some value to the environment and that it is an *abstraction* from the nitty-gritty details of the *internal* behavior (e.g. a function). In other words, some people want to see a service as an abstraction that is *weakly coupled* to the (independent) internal behavior. For them, the service is disjunct from and realized by *independent* internal behavior. This we could call the 'abstractionist' view of a service.

In ArchiMate 2 metamodel, the view on service is abstractionist and the view on interface (the other side of the

coin) is constructionist, as can also be seen in the basic pattern of View 320.

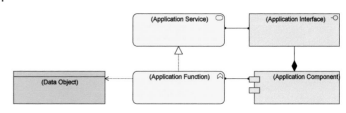

View 320. *The Basic Application Pattern*

I am going to take a little detour to come to a precise as possible interpretation of the 'abstractionist' view. For that, I start with View 321, with the service outlined in red. What is shown here is two different processes of a supermarket that both Realize the *same* service. As far as the abstractionist is concerned, that service is what the customer uses. The internal behavior of the supermarket — the process — is not seen. Now, in this example we show two different ways the supermarket can handle the transaction: using cash registers and using hand scanners. These are quite different processes, but according to the abstractionist view they can be exchanged as they Realize the same service to that customer.

If a constructionist would model this, the result would look like View 322. The services (outlined in red) that are provided by those processes are inextricable parts of the process (shown as Composites) and also specific for each interface. An explicit abstraction can be modeled (the elements outlined in blue).

The problem with the first view is that the service might be modeled as the same, but it it isn't. I cannot just replace one process by the other without affecting the customer's experience. After all, at the cash register, payment with cash is an option. But the hand scanner checkout only accepts electronic payment, e.g. via a credit card. So, the service is modeled as 'the same' but it isn't. The abstraction hides relevant detail.

Now, I am being unfair as this is not quite what the abstractionist has in mind. According to the abstractionist, we can change the 'independent' internal behavior with something else, provided it results in *exactly* the same experience of the service user. The abstractionist thinks therefore not only of internal details that are *invisible* to the customer but which are also *irrelevant* for the customer (or more precisely for the service definition).

So, what the abstractionist means (View 323) is that there might be an alternative and *different* 'internal' process that

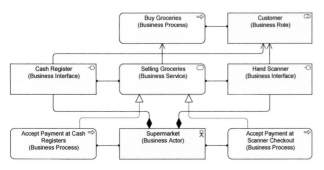

View 321. *Note quite the Abstractionist View of the Service Concept*

realizes *exactly* the *same* service: it only differs in — for the service — *irrelevant* details and the 'external' behavior that is exposed to the user of the service is *exactly* the same.

Now, note that same/different/exactly are all words that are influenced by your level of detail. In detailed models, it will be hard to find examples of a different process providing exactly the same 'externally visible' behavior. Or, not so surprisingly, the abstractionist view is usable mainly when we define our services in an abstract manner. If you do that, the service definition quickly begins to resemble a set of requirements. And that is in part, I think, what the abstractionist view entails.

The constructionist view fits reality better. Suppose, for instance, you have a Business Process that Realizes a Service — say a Sell a Luggage Insurance Business Process that Realizes a Luggage Selling Business Service which can be Used-By a Luggage Insurance Customer — the behavior that the Luggage Insurance Customer actually uses must be part of the Sell a Luggage Insurance Business Process. It cannot be otherwise. *There exists no behavior* used by *the customer that is not* performed by *the seller.* Suppose at some point in the Sell a Luggage Insurance Business Process the contract is presented to the customer. This is definitely part of what the customer experiences, it is external behavior, but it is definitely *also* part of the 'internal' behavior, because it is part of the process.

In other words: the insurance seller's 'offer the contract for signing' activity is both part of its process but also a part that is externally visible/usable. It is the *same* activity.

Important to note for this is that I am not talking about modeling nitty gritty details, even if my argument to make the split different stem from the analysis that the 'external' (detailed) behavior must be part of the 'internal' (detailed) behavior. Both the internal behavior (e.g. process) and the external behavior (service) may be abstract in your model. After all, the fact that, e.g., Business Process and Business Function are hidden from the outside world does not mean they must be detailed. We think in 'hiding the details' but in Enterprise Architecture models you will not want to see something like the process details anyway. For that, we have languages like BPMN (see 24 "A Very Short BPMN Primer" on page 151). The Business Service is always an abstraction of actual behavior, but so is Business Process in ArchiMate.

Hence, from a constructionist view, the external behavior must be a part of the internal behavior, just as the external interface already is a Composite part of the Node, Busi-

View 322. *The Constructionist view of the Service concept*

ness Role or Application Component that offers that interface to the outside world. In other words: from a constructionist view we have 'behavior' and 'external behavior' which is part of 'behavior' and the obvious relation is a Composition.

Service originated in ArchiMate as something of a two-face: It was both seen as a 'requirement' kind of concept as well as a 'construction' kind of concept (and even more as the latter). So, when thinking along the lines of 'business requirements drive service definition', hence outside-in, service also got a role as the 'requirement/value' side. At the interface side this thinking was mirrored in required/provided interfaces.

But now that ArchiMate has the Motivation Extension to cover the requirement side, I think that we have the means to make a clean cut: the Requirement concept from the Motivation Extension covers the 'requirement/value' side and we can see the service itself — cleanly — as the 'externally usable *part*' of the provider's behavior (which has a meaning for the environment). In fact, it has been originally defined that way by the ArchiMate designers. The standard says about the generic 'service' concept:

View 323. *What the abstractionist really means*

A service is defined as a unit of functionality that a system exposes to its environment, while hiding internal operations, which provides a certain value (monetary or otherwise).

The standard explains:

Thus, the service is the externally visible behavior of the providing system, from the perspective of systems that use that service [...] The value provides the motivation for the service's existence. For the external users, only this exposed functionality and value, together with non-functional aspects such as the quality of service, costs, etc., are relevant. These can be specified in a contract or Service Level Agreement (SLA).

The point I am making can be summed up as:

- the service is behavior and *all* behavior, is behavior of the performer;

- the fact that you can (and probably should) *design* a service independently does not mean it should *exist* independently.

Given that we can follow Uncle Ludwig in saying that meaning is hidden in correct use, we could give the following coherent definitions instead for the services in Archi-Mate:

- A business service is a usable part of business behavior. It may be used by business processes or functions (and by roles and actors);

- An application service is a usable part of an application function. It may be used by either business processes or functions or by other application functions (and by application components);

- An infrastructure service is a usable part of an infrastructure function. It may be used by either application functions or by other infrastructure functions (and by Nodes).

The structure surrounding the service concept then becomes like View 326 (example at business layer level), where the service is a Composite part of the function. Using the Motivation Extension, the service Realizes a Requirement which is Associated with a Value. This more or less states that the Value is only there when the Requirement has been Realized, which is kind of nice. Together these two orange relations allow the derivation of the red Association linking Business Service to Value. Business Service A can be used by Business Function B. Together the red Association and the green Used-By can be used to derive the blue Association. In other words: Business Function B has an association with the Value (because that Value is only there when Business Function B uses Business Service A.

There are many pointers in ArchiMate (both versions 1 & 2) that a service is a 'unit of functionality' where the partition external/internal (and its meaning) is based on actual outside use. I suspect that in the behavioral column, it has been easy to talk about a service as being 'created' (realized) because the behavioral column is all about 'doing' and 'creating' is a verb. In the active structure column, it could only be sensibly seen as an interface being 'part of' an Application Component or Node or Business Role. But it works as well (even better) if we just see the service as a (usable) part of the function, just like the interface is a (usable) part of the role/component/node. Not external/internal but visible/all.

Changing the Realization relation (between function/process and the service it provides) to a Composition relation also removes the unnecessary difference between the behavioral column and the active structure column. The result looks like View 324.

View 326. *Constructionist Interpretation of Service, Combined with Motivation Extension Requirement*

This also has the effect that the relation between an active element and its service is always Assigned-To, it does not depend anymore on the route taken, which is also kind of nice.

28.2 Automated Processes

There are several problems with automated processes in ArchiMate, and they stem from the view the ArchiMate designers had on the Business Layer Architecture. They saw the Business Layer as all-human. This, by the way, is also a classical business process modeling approach, which then has the effect that automated processes end up being invisible in a business process model view of an organization. The growth of process automation in the world is turning that into a serious problem in business process management circles.

In ArchiMate, the human-oriented elements in the Business Layer use the Application Layer elements. Or, in the case of passive elements, the human-layer elements are realized by the Application Layer elements, as shown in View 325.

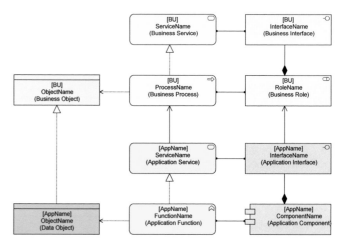

View 325. *Human processes: Business Objects are Realized, applications are Used*

So, when the designers wanted to add automated Business Processes, they came up with the solution to have an Assigned-To relation between elements in the Application-Lay-

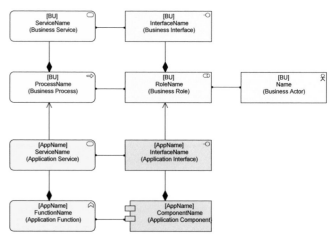

View 324. *Proposal: A service is the Composite usable part of a Function*

er and the Business Layer as shown in View 327. This way, the Application Component takes the position of the Business Role in non-automated processes. And the Application Interface takes the position of the Business Interface.

ArchiMate is not perfectly clear about how this should be used. Because there are two ways:

- Use *both* the Used-By (in green in the image) from Application Service to Business Process and the Assigned-To (in red) from Application Component to Business Process. Here you choose to keep the normal pattern (Application is Used-By the Business Process) and the Assigned-To is *extra*, to signal automation.

- Use *only* the Assigned-To from Application Component to Business Process. Here the Assigned-To comes *in place of* the Used-By.

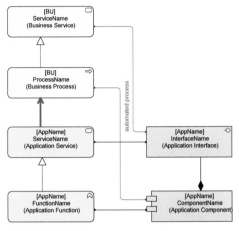

View 327. *Automated Process: the Application Component is Assigned-To (performs) the Business Process and the Application Interface is Assigned-To (is the 'protocol' for) the Business Service*

The second method has the following problem: though the Application Component Realizes a service for the business, you cannot model its use by a Business Process anymore, breaking the 'IT is used by the Business' pattern. If you leave out the Used-By that starts from the Application Service, there is not even a route from Application Service to Business Process that gives a valid derived relation. This makes the Application Service a dead end, so why still model it?. But if you leave it out, the Application Function becomes a dead end instead, so why model it? And if you remove that, where is the behavior of the Application at the Application Layer? Because that might not be exactly the same as the Business Process. And besides, do you want an Application Layer behavior description in your Business Process? Something you discuss with the Application Architects?

The Assigned-To relations from Application Layer to Business Layer are therefore efficient, but rather messy shortcuts. A bit like the missing Infrastructure Function and the resulting behavioral status of the System Software element in ArchiMate 1.0 that were repaired in ArchiMate 2.0.

There is another related problem. Suppose you have an automated work flow in a Business Rule Engine. Most of your Business Process runs automated. But once in a while, an exception happens and a human needs to do something. This is quite a common pattern and ArchiMate does have problems with it. View 328 shows how it basically looks.

Now suppose I do not want to show the internal details of 'Process Total'. The cleanest way to do this is to leave out the subprocesses, make the roles Aggregate parts of a Collaboration and Assign the Collaboration to the process. In a fully human world, it looks like View 329.

Question 11. Can you spot the ArchiMate error in View 329?

Answer 11. You're only allowed to Assign an Interaction to a Collaboration.

But with our *automated* process as one of the parts of the overall process, we cannot do that. An Application Component is not allowed as a child of a Business Collaboration in ArchiMate. In fact, when we have automated processes,

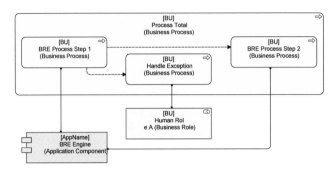

View 328. *An automated process with human exception handling*

ArchiMate does not allow us to use Business Layer elements to model an active business side of the architecture properly at all. So modeling processes that are *partly* automated becomes problematic.

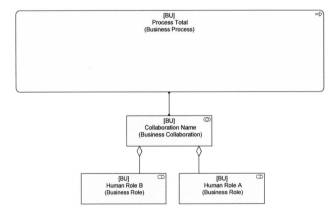

View 329. *When two roles separately do the (sub) Business Processes, the overall Business Process is performed by a Collaboration*

There is a straightforward way to solve this. We can look at the automated process as being performed by a robot element of sorts at the business level. There are various ways to implement this, but my preferred solution is to have an Application Component *Realize* a Business Role (Realizing a Business Actor leads to unnecessary complexity, I will not go into that here). To make the whole setup simpler, I also make the relation between a process/function and its service to be the same as between the actor and the interface, namely Composition, as proposed in 28.1 "Service as Composite

Part of Function/Process" on page 186. That is not strictly necessary for my argument, but I think that also could be an improvement for ArchiMate.

It looks like View 330 for an automated process.

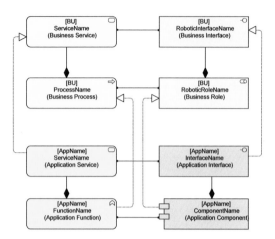

View 330. *Proposed meta-model Realization relations for automated processes*

And it looks like View 331 for a non-automated process.

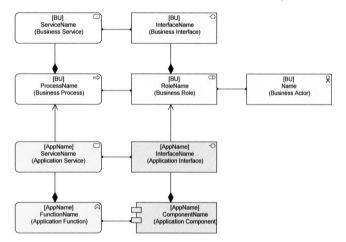

View 331. *Proposed solution for non-automated processes*

In my opinion, this cleans up and improves ArchiMate in a few ways. First, the types of relations between layers have been reduced to Realization and Used-By. A lower layer active/behavioral element is Used-By a higher layer, or a lower layer passive element Realizes a higher layer element. A direct Assigned-To has become limited to layer-internal relations.

When we add the possibility for an Application Component to Realize a Business Role (and for the Application Interface to Realize a Business Interface) like we have done here, the older cross-layer Assignment relations have gone. The derived relation between Application Component and the automated Business Process is Realization, and this is true too for the derived relation between Application Interface and Business Service. This breaks the clean use of Assignment between active and behavioral components and it is so because Assignment is a stronger structural relation than Realization. Hence:

28.3 Switching Strength of Assignment and Realization

The strength order of structural relations was decided upon, but I have no documentation of why that particular order was chosen and privately I have been told it was more intuitively decided than reasoned. Part of it may have been the 'abstractionist' (weakly coupled) view on the service concept.

What happens if we were to switch Assignment and Realization in the strength table for deriving structural relations? If we start in the middle of the ArchiMate 2.1 meta model, the basic Application Pattern (see View 320 on page 186), the *derived* relation of the route from Application Component via Application Function to Application Service changes from Realization to Assignment. Incidentally, that is the same result that we get if we follow the route from Application Component via Application Interface to Application Service.

This is kind of nice in two ways: first, because it does not matter which route you take what the derived result is. But secondly, because it is kind of nice to have Assignment as the resulting relation between an active component and a behavioral component. It means that you never break the pattern that an active element is Assigned-To a behavioral element. Incidentally it also allows View 89 on page 63.

In the real ArchiMate 2.1 meta-model, the derived relation from Node, via Assigned-To to Artifact, via Realization to Data Object and via Realization to Business Object is Realization. If we switch strengths of Assignment and Realization, the resulting relation would become Assigned-To in its meaning of 'resides on'. In other words, follow the earlier suggestion and not this one, and the Node is Assigned-To the Business Object, or, the Business Object resides on the Node, which is I think a slightly cleaner way of looking at it.

When we change these strengths, the derived relation of "Device Assigned-To Artifact Realizes System Software", becomes Assignment, which is also the direct relation that still exists in the metamodel.

Another effect is that System Software that is Assigned-To Artifact that Realizes an Application Component becomes a derived Assignment. We get an active structure element Assigned-To an active structure element. There is a prece-

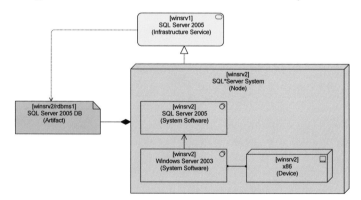

View 332. *(Structural) Artifact as Composite child of (structural) Node*

dent for this (from Business Actor to Business Role), but it is not very nice. However, if we would change the Assignment relation for 'resides on' to Composition (we allow an Artifact to be a Composite child of a Node, as a Node may contain both passive and active structural elements, even if itself is an active structural element), this problem is solved. This is illustrated in View 332 on page 190. The effect of this, though, is that the derived relation of "Device Assigned-To Artifact Realizes System Software" (which we so nicely had designed to be the direct Assignment relation, above) becomes Realization, as in Device Realizes System Software. But that Assignment is a leftover from ArchiMate 1 where System Software was behavior, so we should get rid of that anyway...

28.4 Summary of the previous three change proposals

The three proposals on the previous pages were:

- Change the strength order of Assignment and Realization;

- Let a service be the Composite part of the function/process that is responsible for it;

- Make sure automated processes become properly represented in the Business Layer Architecture, by making an Application Component able to *Realize* a Business Role.

If we would implement all three proposals, the effect would be:

- We can correctly make collaborations of automated and non-automated business processes (e.g. automated business processes with human exception handling);

- We are ready for a future in which more and more IT agents will be recognizable as actors at the business level (e.g. automated phone services or interactive web sites of today, but then on steroids);

- Only Realization and Used-By are possible between architecture layers. This is both intuitive and more simple than in ArchiMate 1.0 & 2.0. Also, Realization is only possible *between* layers, making it a pure layer-abstraction relation;

- The (derived) relation between an actor and the behavior it is responsible for becomes Assigned-To *in all cases*. This is a more proper derived relationship between a structural component and a behavioral component than Realization;

- Note: The old layer-crossing Assignment relation is saved as a derived relation, which makes the set of changes backwards compatible on that point. For this we need either composite services or the switch in strength between Assignment and Realization;

- Conversion can probably be automatic: Existing Realizations to service elements can be automatically converted to Composition when they come from an internal behavioral element and to Assignment when they come from another type of element (this still needs more extensive checking for all scenarios). In an n:1 scenario, this breaks the 1:n rule for Compositions (see next section).

We can top this off with an example in View 333. There you'll see how a Business Process that is automated using a Business Rule Engine has a manual part that handles exceptions. Here, the human uses a spreadsheet on his desktop to calculate something and then enters it manually into the

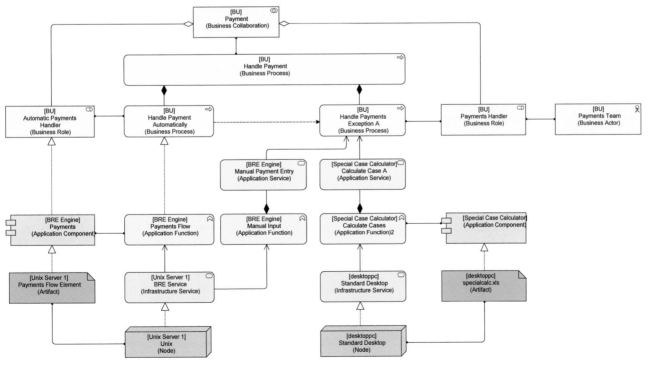

View 333. *An example that uses the proposed changes to ArchiMate from sections 28.3, 28.1 and 28.2 A Business Process is performed by a Collaboration of humans and applications. The process is automated using a BRE, humans handling the exceptions, using a user interface of the BRE and some hand work.*

BRE-based system. Note, the actual 'rule set' artifacts and such of the BRE have been left out here. They can be seen in the basic BRE Pattern in View 72 on page 52.

28.5 Allow multiple parents in a Composition

In ArchiMate, it is stated that an element can only be part of a *single* composition. It has taken that from UML, the modeling language for software engineering.

Now, in software engineering, composition and aggregation are (also) about memory management. Who owns what piece of memory? Who should free the allocated memory? When an element is a composite child of another element, if the parent is deleted, the child should be deleted also. However, when an element is an aggregate child of another element, and the parent is deleted, the child should be left alone. An aggregation only *points* to another element, it does not *own* it. In software engineering, accessing freed objects used (e.g. as a result of 'memory sharing') to be a major source for crashing applications and not freeing objects used to be a major source for 'memory leaks'. Hence, 'memory sharing' and 'memory leaks' became a sign of bad programming in the early days and a paradigm has stuck, has become a foundational part of OO and UML:

- Composition means that you own the child. That means that if you are removed, you should also remove (free up) your composite parts (the 'children');

- Aggregation means that you do not own the child, you only point to it. That means that if you are removed, you leave the reference ('child') alone.

This software engineering paradigm has been transported into ArchiMate (see Section 1.7 "Composition and Aggregation" on page 20). But ArchiMate has not transported it in full, it has also added a restrictive paradigm: with a few exceptions in the metamodel: Composition and Aggregation are only allowed between elements of the same (sub)type. This differs from software engineering where elements can both composite and aggregate elements from wildly different types. This is necessary in ArchiMate, because allowing any aggregation and/or composition would play havoc with the ArchiMate metamodel.

But relaxing the multiple-composite-parent restriction for Enterprise Architecture might be very useful as we *do* have real and unavoidable sharing in the real world outside of software engineering (and with Garbage Collection, Automatic Reference Counting and such, the issue has become less of an issue in software engineering as well, where people now start talking about 'strong' and 'weak' composition). Take the following example. Suppose we model our Infrastructure Services for the exploitation of applications

as being composed of several parts, which we name 'infrastructure building blocks' (see 7.6 "Infrastructure 'Building Blocks'" on page 53). For instance, suppose an application requires a file share, a relational database and a system where the application is executed. In a previous chapter, we modeled this by creating a specific abstract Aggregation of Infrastructure Services, that together form the Aggregated 'Exploitation' Infrastructure Service that provides TI-support for the application. An example can be seen in View 334.

This aggregation breaks the possibility to have derived Used-By relations between the individual building blocks and the applications that depend on them. Using derived relations, we cannot say, "[rs6sv001/db001] Oracle RDBMS (Infrastructure Service" is Used-By "[App Y] Reporting (Applica-

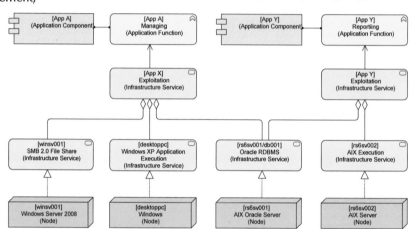

View 334. *Exploitation Infrastructure Services based on Aggregation of (shared) Infrastructure Service Building Blocks*

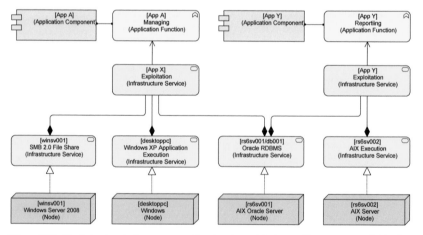

View 335. *Exploitation Infrastructure Service based being a Composition child of Multiple parents*

tion Function)".

But what if we were to release that restriction on multiple parents in a Composition? Suppose we would allow true sharing as in the nasty 'memory sharing' of the early programming years? We could model it like in View 335 on page 192.

In the Enterprise, true sharing is not only real, it is often even a desirable state of affairs, cost-wise. Now, if we would allow multiple parents in a Composition in ArchiMate, we could create real sharing in our models. Remember, if one of the now 'parent' Infrastructure Services breaks, the 'child' Exploitation Infrastructure Service, which in the case of App A in View 335 has three 'parents', breaks too. Which is as it should be. Now we *can* say: "[rs6sv001/db001] Oracle RDBMS (Infrastructure Service" is Used-By "[App Y] Reporting (Application Function)". So the advantage for this pattern (apart from enabling modeling true sharing as it is real in the enterprise) is that the official derived relations still can be used. Other advantages are that abstraction less quickly lead to problems (e.g. see View 180 on page 115), enables constructions like several of those in Section 16 "Virtual Machines (Parallelization)" on page 110 (which are technically illegal) and removes the problem that when you have a Composite of a Composite the derived relation between grandfather and grandchild is technically illegal.

There is however also a disadvantage when used as in View 335. The aggregation version is easier to read for people and the use of the symbol becomes different from UML and that means another addition to the learning curve (this time especially for software architects). Multiple parents confuse. So, personally I can live with the aggregation version (the ArchiMate derived relations are too limited for most analyses anyway) and the fact that it does not clearly shows the real 'make or break' dependency of the abstract 'Exploitation' Infrastructure Service on all its building block components.

We could also let a collaboration element be jointly owned by its parents. This is more realistic also from a derived relations point of view: If two Business Roles together perform an Interaction (or Process, see below) which Realizes a Service, there is currently no derived relation between any of the roles and the service, which we know both roles must be there for the service to exist. But the 'directional' limitation of derivation forbids the derivation.

And if the Contract and the Business Services co-own the Product through Composite relations, we can rightly derive service-use from product-use.

All in all, relaxing the single-parent limitation makes sense because true 'sharing/co-owning' is both reality and often a desirable state of affairs for the Enterprise (and thus ArchiMate models of that enterprise). It is not necessary to limit our view of the real world by software engineering sensibilities. After all, do we not all state from time to time that it is in the end about the business and not about IT? We are Enterprise Architects, not software engineers after all...

28.6 Get rid of Interaction

When we discussed Business Functions and Business Processes (Section 10.2 "Business Function or Business Process?" on page 76) and Business Process Modeling (Section 10.4 "The 'End-to-end' Business Process" on page 79) we used Business Collaborations, but we (illegally) assigned them to Business Functions or Business Processes instead of Business Interactions.

But these Business Interactions were in fact processes or functions that were performed by a collaboration of roles.

And then you have to ask yourself: what is an Interaction? Is it a type of process (defined 'outside-in' on the basis of what it produces) or a type of function (defined 'inside-out' on the basis of what it needs? An Interaction can be needed in either situation.

If you think about it, the way a Collaboration is Assigned-To a Business Process (as in View 118 on page 78) makes a lot of sense. And that end-to-end process is in fact performed by a collaboration. Technically, I can Assign the Collaboration to that process, but ArchiMate says in its definition I'm not allowed to: a collaboration should only be assigned to an Interaction.

There is no need for this special status of interactions. If you keep collaborations and remove interactions, ArchiMate becomes simpler and sense-making models like that one from View 118 on page 78 become legal.

In the end we even removed the Business Collaborations altogether in our modeling and used the 'informal collaboration' technique of 2.1 "Collaboration and Interaction" on page 23. I would keep Collaboration in the meta-model as there are times that you explicitly want to model it, but I would keep that for moments that the collaboration actually has a very specific meaning. I would still normally use 'informal collaborations' because of their simplicity and because often (see for instance the results of BPMN-ArchiMate coupling in Section 25 "Linking BPMN and ArchiMate" on page 156) they are the best way forward.

28.7 Infrastructure Collaboration to model Clustering

There might be a structural way to support the modeling of various ways of clustering (instead of using dynamic relations like flows for this, as in the patterns of for instance 7.19 "Infrastructure Pattern: High-Available Database Cluster" on page 62) in the infrastructure layer if the infrastructure layer would support its own Collaboration element.

28.8 A Group concept, a 'Fourth Column', Nesting

Nesting, in ArchiMate is a way to graphically represent three relation types:

- Composition;
- Aggregation;
- Assignment.

Grouping, though it looks graphically as an element is not an element, it is officially a relation between all the 'nested/elements.

I think a better solution for the latter would be if we would not have the Grouping *relation*, but the Group *element type*. Basically, a Group would be an element that is generic and that can Aggregate every other element type. Nesting a group (or more precisely: The effect is visually exactly the same as the current Grouping relation, but the grouping has become truly part of the network of elements and relations.

A Group would be part of a fourth column in ArchiMate (next to Active and Passive Structure and Behavior, category: Miscellaneous, proposed default color: white). Such a fourth column could hold concepts that are neither structure nor behavior. A possible name for the category is 'Collections'.

ArchiMate already has some concepts that do not really fit the 3-column structure very well. Location and Product would be obvious candidates for the Collections category. A Product already is an Aggregation of both (passive) structural and behavioral concepts. The relation from Location to structural elements would then have to become Aggregation, or Location would be a Specialization of Group that can be Assigned-To structural elements, or we might change the Assignment relation to Aggregation for Location. Another possible member of the 'Collections' category would be Capability (see below).

I suggest to define Nesting as a way to visually hide relations between elements and force elements to have at least one relation if they are to be nested. Making it a purely visual construct would also allow views where an element is part of two different Nestings (e.g. as in View 127 on page 80).

28.9 Capability and Product, Skills

One of the most often heard complaints about ArchiMate is that the concept Capability is missing. People often use ArchiMate's Business Function for Capability as it comes closest. Are they right? And: What is 'Capability' and how should we model it in ArchiMate?

Capability is widely used as a concept in many different definitions, both in Enterprise Architecture and in natural language. For instance, TOGAF 9.1 gives the following definition of Capability:

> *Capability*: An ability that an organization, person, or system possesses. Capabilities are typically expressed in general and high-level terms and typically require a combination of organization, people, processes, and technology to achieve. For example, marketing, customer contact, or outbound telemarketing.

From an ArchiMate perspective, that sounds like (potential) behavior. But TOGAF also says this when it describes the Core Metamodel:

> *Function*: Delivers business capabilities.

Here, from an ArchiMate perspective, TOGAF's Function sounds like an active object. But TOGAF also says:

> *Function describes units of business capability at all levels of granularity The term "function" is used to describe a unit of business capability at all levels of granularity, encapsulating terms such as value chain, process area, capability, business function, etc. Any bounded unit of business function should be described as a function.*

Here, the description of Function casts a very wide net which not so much delivers but is Capability at a more fine-grained level. Then, when discussing 'implementing' an Architecture (the domain of ArchiMate's Migration Extension) TOGAF gives a second, different definition of Capability:

> *Capability*: A business-focused outcome that is delivered by the completion of one or more work packages. Using a capability-based planning approach, change activities can be sequenced and grouped in order to provide continuous and incremental business value.

> *Work Package*: A set of actions identified to achieve one or more objectives for the business. A work package can be a part of a project, a complete project, or a program.

Are you confused yet? Anyway, TOGAF 9 uses (and as we know from Uncle Ludwig: meaning lies hidden in use) 'capability' as a concept mostly when discussing realizing an architecture (e.g. in 'capability based planning') and secondly as something that is encapsulated by a Function. TOGAF's idea of what a Function is differs fundamentally from what ArchiMate says it is. While ArchiMate's functions are purely behavioral siblings of separate active elements ('the other side of the same coin'), in TOGAF Function seems more like an form of 'GOFBF' (see also Section 10.3 "Good Old Fashioned Business Function" on page 79), a mixture of active and behavioral objects. It also makes the ease with which many use the Business Function concept from ArchiMate for Capability slightly suspect. Do they have ArchiMate's function concept or GOFBF in their mind when they use the word 'function'? Are they "bewitched by language" as Uncle Ludwig would say? Or are they just illustrating the power of human analogy/'family resemblance' thinking over strict logic?

Such differences, by the way, make plans to integrate TOGAF and ArchiMate fraught with peril: though names of concepts may be the same (think 'Function') their meaning is quite different in both standards and trying to link them will be difficult in the extreme as you have either to fundamentally adapt one of the current meanings or you have to live with the utter confusion of two related but different meanings ('uses') for the same word. Before you know it, you will be, as suggested above, "bewitched by language". It seems that for any chance of success with respect to integration, TOGAF could adopt ArchiMate's metamodel of the enterprise and re-phrase its method. Adoption the other way around (apart from some additions like Capability that can be made in the proper ArchiMate way, see below) would probably destroy a unique contribution of ArchiMate: looking at active versus behavioral concepts to describe multiple aspects of what is essentially one 'thing'.

Now, TOGAF's metamodel is not metamodel about 'operational space', it is more like a metamodel about the artifacts of enterprise *architecture* (TOGAF artifacts instead of enterprise artifacts) and its use (again, I am not a TOGAF expert), i.e. 'architectural space' (see Section 26 "The Role of ArchiMate in Enterprise Architecture" on page 179). ArchiMate on the other hand, has a Core metamodel that consists of artifacts that are about the *enterprise* (the artifacts in the extensions are meant for modeling change and architecture). So, when TOGAF talks about 'capability' it is often in the context of capabilities that are realized by 'implementing an architecture' via 'work packages' which sounds like a metamodel for enterprise *change* instead of a metamodel for enterprise.

Still, these concepts are close enough and the first definition given above seems pretty usable to me from an ArchiMate perspective. So, I will start from the TOGAF definition of Capability (the first one, not the second one) and see where that takes me when looking at it from the ArchiMate side. In fact, I am looking here at how ArchiMate could get inspiration from TOGAF.

From ArchiMate's perspective, what a business produces are (above all) Services and these are — in ArchiMate — purely behavioral objects (though in principle always linked to an Interface — an active object). ArchiMate is a bit skimpy on allowing passive objects to be produced. ArchiMate's Product concept aggregates Services and a Contract, and that's it. No Interface or other active objects at all. No passive objects other than Contract. So, if your business for instance builds web sites to customers, you can model the offering of a 'web site building' Service, but you cannot model the 'web site' code itself as part of the ArchiMate Product. That seems to be an omission in ArchiMate. I think it would be a good idea to have the possibility to aggregate a Business Object as well in a Product, then the Business Object could be 'web site' and this one is realized by — for instance — a zip file (Artifact) with a Joomla setup, both can be used to model a Product.

So, given that Capability, as defined initially above, is missing from ArchiMate, how would we add it? My initial thought would be to create a concept related to Product as shown in View 336. At the abstract level, we say that a Product is Realized by a Capability. Below that level, we say that a Product may consist of:

- A Contract, obviously;

- Any produced Service (like that 'building a web site' service I mentioned above);

- A produced passive element, either modeled as a Business Object ('a web site') or modeled as an Artifact ('a ZIP file containing the code of the web site').

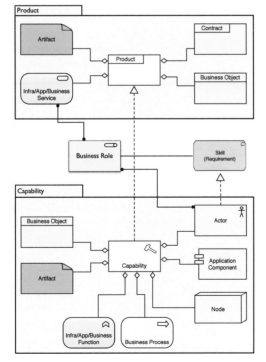

View 336. *Proposal for Capability Concept, illustrated with a possible link from Actors as part of Capability to (Business) Service as part of Product.*

Now, to Realize a Product, we need to have a Capability. What makes up a Capability? What can we possibly need to Realize that Product? My proposal is:

- A Business Process;

- Any Service;

- Humans (Actors), Systems (Applications Components and Nodes), in other words all the 'actors' of every layer. Each 'actor' can be essential for the production of services or passive elements that are part of the Capability;

- Passive elements: modeled as Artifacts or Business Objects. Data Objects are application-internal and are irrelevant detail from the Capability perspective.

For the icon, I think a hammer would be appropriate, as one of the proverbial tools. A wrench maybe better, but was too much work to draw.

Now, the two elements in the middle of View 336 are to illustrate a specific question regarding Product: Should we be able to add active objects to the Product aggregate? Suppose we offer support on-site, could the Actor or Role also not be part of the Product?

I think not, as what we offer is the service. I have doubted about adding Role to the Capacity aggregate, but in the end decided against it. A Role is a 'responsibility' and as such seems not tangible enough to add to a capability, and again, it is the service that the user of the Product wants. Then again, it is not enough to have just any Actor to add to a certain Capability. After all, the Actor must be able to perform the right activities. In other words, what we need is Actors with certain Skills. Would Skills be another potential new ArchiMate concept? Maybe, but for now I see those Skills as a form of Requirement for the Actor. Which brings me temporarily to the different subject of Requirements in ArchiMate, currently available in the Motivation Extension, something that can be Realized by any other type of object. Skills, then, could be modeled by a Requirement object that is Realized by an Actor.

So, what we can do is add the Actor to the Capability, let this Actor Realize a 'skill' Requirement which is Assigned to the Role, which is Assigned to the Process which Realizes the Service that is part of the Product.

Summarizing:

- We could add Capability as a new concept to ArchiMate 3, a bit like the current Product concept: an aggregate of other objects from the Core metamodel;

- Product too, could be extended to aggregate passive and active concepts;

- A Capability could Realize a Product;

- Product and Capability would be neither active structural, passive structural or behavioral, but in the fourth

Miscellaneous category of concepts (see 28.8 "A Group concept, a 'Fourth Column', Nesting" on page 193).

28.10 Allow Junctions for all relations

Let's start with the classic ArchiMate way of modeling two Actors performing some business behavior together, using the concepts of Collaboration and Interaction. An example is seen in View 337. In this example, our organization has a yearly process which is 'Organize the yearly office party', which by tradition is a collaboration of the Customer Support Department that handles logistics, like organize music, food and beverages. The whole publicity is done by the Sales Department. And this is a real collaboration, Support comes with the idea for the party, Sales advertises it and depending on the success rate of Sales, Support needs to buy different amounts of food, drink and beverages.

But what if we have the situation that each year either Sales or Support organizes the party? The

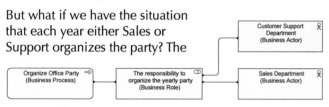

View 338. *Possible solution for two Actors that may both fulfill the same Role independently*

easiest way to model that is shown in View 338. Technically, this is stretching ArchiMate's intention, as the standard suggests that a Business Process should be Assigned-To a single Business Role. We can try to solve that, but such a solution is really ugly, modeling-wise. Examples are given in View 341 and both make my skin crawl. The upper one (also doable with Specializations) creates some sort of non-existent abstract department (outlined in red), the lower one creates multiple instances (outlined in red) of what in fact is exactly the same role.

But there is a change we could apply to ArchiMate that makes this problem go away (and opens many nice possibilities). We could allow Junction relations for more than just Triggers and Flows. In View 339 I am using an OR-Junction to model that either Sales or Support organizes th eoffice

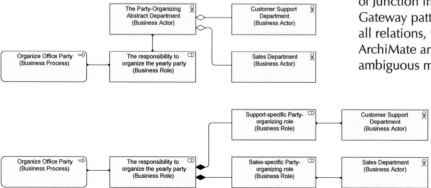

View 341. *Two ugly solutions to model correctly that either department organizes the yearly office party*

party. And in View 340 I model, using an AND-Junction, that Sales together with Support organizes the office party. And yes, this is in fact a simple way to model a collaboration.

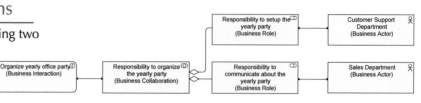

View 337. *Classic Collaboration in ArchiMate: two Roles (fulfilled by two Actors) perform a single process.*

As we saw in Section 25 "Linking BPMN and ArchiMate" on page 156, using a typical EA-construct 'named Collaboration' is really impractical in many situations and hard to explain to the business, who do not think in such structures when they describe business processes. But

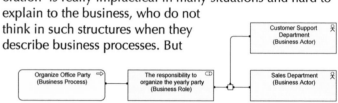

View 339. *Alternative way to model that either of two Actors may fulfill a Role*

the use of a Junction to show that multiple roles together perform a process is perfectly acceptable.

There are many more ways in which using Junctions for the other relations are practical. One such an example is shown in View 343 on page 197. Here, it is mod-

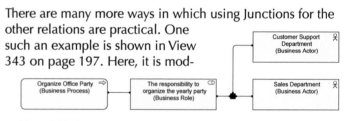

View 340. *Alternative way to model a Collaboration, using the Junctions on Assignments*

eled that our (conceptual) Business Object 'Bank Account' is Realized by either a Data Object of application A *or* a Data Object of application B. And that Data Object of application B is either stored in the '[db001] Oracle Database' *or* in the '[db002] PostgreSQL Database'.

By reusing (and expanding, e.g. include Specializations of Junction into AND, OR, XOR, maybe by adopting the Gateway patterns from BPMN) the Junction concept for all relations, we could significantly increase the power of ArchiMate and give the modelers the means to produce less ambiguous models.

28.11 Make the Access relation bidirectional

ArchiMate 2.0 removed the bidirectionality of the Assignment relation that existed in ArchiMate 1, and that was a good move. The bidirectionality in ArchiMate 1 led to all kinds of senseless derived relations. ArchiMate 2.0 re-

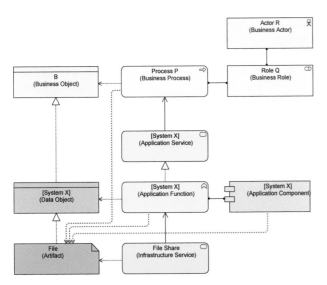

View 342. *Three useful (derived) Access relations*

moved all of those and added the ones that made sense 'by hand' to the core meta-model.

So, why propose now to make another relation bidirectional? Well, what drives this is a couple of realities, like:

- Some processes are just about Accessing an Artifact. You can imagine Data and Business Objects, but the labels you give these are just representations of the Artifact. They add to the complexity of the model, they do not add to the informational content of the model;

- Behavior may depend on passive elements, not only the other way around. A good example is application maintenance from 12.6 "Secondary Architecture: Application Maintenance" on page 91. Here, the application maintenance process edits a file, say an ini file, that influences an application's functionality. The application's functionality is dependent on the settings in the file (on the 'Settings' Data Object the Artifact realizes). Though the Artifact is shared, the Data Object isn't, which shows up when you make errors in that ini and the application crashes.

To illustrate what derived relations we can have when Access becomes bidirectional, have a look at the green and blue Access relations in View 342.

The green one follows from: Artifact is Accessed-By the Infrastructure Service, which is Used-By the Application

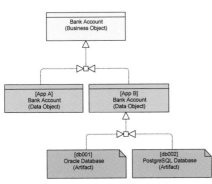

View 343. *Using OR-Junctions to show more detail on the dependencies between informational elements*

Function. The result is Artifact is Accessed-By the Application Function. And frankly, that is not a weird derivation. But ArchiMate as is does not allow it. The blue one follows the derivation up to the Business Process.

As Assignment is (rightly) unidirectional, Access relations

from higher layer *active* components must be added 'by hand' to the core model, like the red one.

It could be (but I am uncertain) even better to make the direction of the Access relation depend on its 'read/write' status:

- Read Access: direction from passive structure to behavior;

- Write Access (including Create and Delete): direction from behavior to passive structure;

- Both read and write Access: bidirectional.

28.12 Allow some direct relations between business layer and infrastructure layer

The layering of Enterprise Architecture in three layers (business & information, application & data, infrastructure) is widely accepted by Enterprise Architects. What we Architects tend to forget is that most of our coworkers do not have that layering in mind. A good example was the way BPMN handles 'passive elements'. It does not divide these into infrastructural, application and business, instead it divides them into 'temporary' and 'permanent' (see Section 24 "A Very Short BPMN Primer" on page 151). The same sort of confusion happens when we talk to other coworkers, e.g. when a software engineer thinks a 'business service' is a service that is realized by the application that has business value (which he or she opposes to a technical service that exists because of the IT-integration).

Especially the abstraction of the business layer could use some reality by allowing the business layer to directly Access Artifacts or use Infrastructure Services and Interfaces. Allowing it enables you to model how things really are without the 'invention' of non-existent intermediate elements. It would also make the problems described in 25.7 "Processes handling Artifacts" on page 172 go away.

This is especially true if we want to model non-informational elements as Artifacts. That steel mill might want to have a Business Process that Accesses a steel beam. That is a physical Artifact directly Accessed by a Business Process. No data in between.

Another example is that it would be useful (and realistic) to let the infrastructure layer also perform a Business Process. This can either be done by allowing Assignments from infrastructure layer active elements to business layer behavior elements, or along the Realization of a Role pattern of 28.2 "Automated Processes" on page 188 (Node Realizes Role).

28.13 Improve the description of Business Function

The specification's description of Business Function stresses the classical picture of the use of Business Functions by end-to-end processes too much and ignores how a Business Function in reality Realizes a service (e.g. by an *internal* Business Process as described in 10.2 "Business Function or Business Process?" on page 76. The description of the complex relation between Business Functions and Business Processes could be improved, I think.

28.14 Drop the 'required' interface concept

See Section 27.4 "The 'Required' Interface concept" on page 185 for a description of this aspect of ArchiMate. I would drop this half-baked aspect from ArchiMate suggest using Requirement from the Motivation Extension instead of a 'provided interface' (if at all there is someone who still uses it, which I doubt).

28.15 Allow cross-layer triggers and flows; Events in all layers

There are many examples where triggering and flow between layers makes perfect sense. A system engineer resetting infrastructure in case of calamities, for instance. Or IT triggering the start of a Business Process. Or an Application Function not only using an Infrastructure Service, but also dynamically influencing that layer. One use (but there are many) was shown in View 204 on page 126.

Additionally, events may also exist in other layers than just the business layer.

28.16 The ArchiMate Extensions

Besides the problem with complexity of real enterprises that makes the use of modeling 'architecture space' problematic, the concepts of the Motivation Extension themselves are fuzzy, which also shows in the examples the standard provides, e.g. sometimes 'making profit' is modeled as a Driver, another time as a Goal. A specialized concept for a 'constraint' is also fuzzy. Why is 'Applications should be written in Java' a Constraint and not a Requirement? If

you think about it, this constraint most likely comes from a requirement elsewhere, like the IT department not being able to support all computer languages on the planet. And it clearly is not just about the realization, because to run, the application will need the Java runtime platform (System Software): there is a real requirement for the enterprise architecture too.

Also problematic is the difference between a Requirement and a Principle. It looks simple at first: according to the standard "A principle defines a general property that applies to any system in a certain context. A requirement defines a property that applies to a specific system". But what is a 'system'? When describing Requirement the standard says: "The term "system" is used in its general meaning; i.e., as a group of (functionally) related elements, where each element may be considered as a system again." So, Requirement can apply to something as broad as Principle. When the standard explains the relation between a Principle and a Requirement, it says:

> A principle needs to be made specific for a given system by means of one or more requirements, in order to enforce that the system conforms to the principle. For example, the principle "Information management processes comply with all relevant laws, policies, and regulations" is realized by the requirements that are imposed by the actual laws, policies, and regulations that apply to the specific system under design.

This not only shows the classic top-down approach to EA (start with principles and then 'realize' these in specific solutions), but it also introduces Realization as a relation between what for the secondary and tertiary processes in your enterprise are just Business Objects. Either Specialization or Aggregation of a Requirements landscape would have covered this as well.

The links between the Extensions and the Core metamodel are also questionable. Most of ArchiMate's Motivational Elements (Assessment, Goal, Principle, Requirement, Constraint) can be easily seen *also* as types of Business Objects. The easiest is Assessment. An Assessment has to be made by a process and it can be Accessed-By by a process. But you can say the same about the other Motivational El-

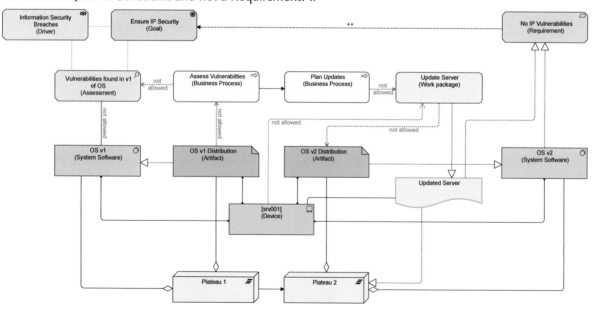

View 344. *Various examples of real relations we cannot do in ArchiMate 2*
This is because of a lack of integration between the Core metamodel and the Extensions. Also shown forbidden
Access relations from business layer to infrastructure layer

ements, except maybe Driver (though 'recognizing external Drivers' might be something your business needs to do and as such it becomes part of the operations of your business).

Doing this makes it easier to link the secondary and tertiary processes (See 12 "Secondary and Tertiary Architecture" on page 89) like Operational Risk Management and Continuity Management in your enterprise to your primary process. A Work Package from the Implementation and Migration Extension is clearly a behavioral object that should be (or be a Specialization of) Business Process.

View 344 on page 198 contains some examples of forbidden relations that would both make sense and would be possible if the Extensions were integrated properly in ArchiMate instead of taken from TOGAF and more or less haphazardly grafted onto ArchiMate as they are now:

- I cannot Associate Assessments with a Core element. Such an Association obviously makes sense and is useful;

- Work Package is not (a Specialization of) Business Process. As a result, modeled Business Processes (like Change Management processes, from secondary architecture, see Section 12 "Secondary and Tertiary Architecture" on page 89) cannot Trigger or Flow-To Work Packages, Work Packages cannot Access their descriptions (e.g. project plans) etc.. The Work Package is also unable to use IT itself, it is therefore a seriously handicapped Business Process.

28.17 Why change ArchiMate?

I think ArchiMate is great. It is the best thing since sliced bread for Enterprise Architecture modeling. The language is not strictly formal, but its concepts and relations have been selected for usability, and as Uncle Ludwig explained to us, that it one of the best tests of meaningfulness.

The world of Enterprise Architecture stretches from the strictly logical world of bits and bytes to the not-always-so-logical world of human behavior. It is unavoidable that such a stretching exercise leaves its marks. So, it is easy to find (logical) fault with the language, as I have shown. But from a business perspective (a human perspective) it is very good at enabling you to model to the extremes of Enterprise Architecture. And the fact that — even without all these improvements — we still were able to use the grammar to the extent we did shows how powerful the language already is. And we are daily innovating with it still.

With the right use of patterns and the right discipline and a good knowledge of the powerful underlying ideas, you can take this language far. Even without the improvements proposed by me in this chapter.

But I do think cleaning a few things up and improving the language here and there would make it greater still. It is up to the — by nature (and rightly so) conservative— standards body to take that step. Standards bodies *should* be conservative and slow, or the standard would be too volatile to be a real standard. On the other hand: when 'backwards compatibility' becomes your main worry, and you cannot innovate, the standard will probably die.

It is up to The Open Group.

Tooling

Tooling

29. Multiple Models of One Reality

You can create your views in a decent drawing tool, like OmniGraffle Professional for the Mac or Visio for Windows. For both applications, so-called 'stencils' are available, and you can use these to create views. In fact, you can use any drawing tool, the stencils and the smart behavior of the graphics only make life a bit easier. But the main problem of tools like these is that they generally are just that: a *drawing* tool, they create views but they do not create a *model*. What you really need is a good *modeling* tool.

Now, it is important to realize a very important aspect. *There will* by definition *be multiple models of the same reality in your organization*. There is no single model-based tool that supports all uses of any model of your enterprise. The help desk needs a model of all the infrastructure and applications that run on it and if they are professionals, they want to know what business processes are supported. They might want to add aspects like application owners, process owners and such. All this you can do in ArchiMate. But their model needs more: they need to log incidents against applications, they need incident management work flow support and case management, etc.. The operational risk managers need a model with risks, control objectives, control measures and also the business processes, functions,roles and actors involved. ArchiMate can do that. But they also need to store assessments, have work flow support for incident management, require strict access to maintained data, etc. The Business Continuity Managers need Continuity Plans with business processes and the Business Control people need detailed process descriptions with more detail than what is in your Current State model. In section 22.1 "The Satellite Model Approach" on page 141 we required information about the detailed structure of scheduler jobs, something we do not need nor want in our main EA models. The list is long and all these different uses require often subtly or not-so-subtly different IT support. And there will not be a single tool that is going to support them all. Your Enterprise Architecture modeling tool is not the tool to log incidents, store improvement plans, etc.

The consequence of this is that it is very important to realize that you will always, *by definition*, have multiple models of your Enterprise reality in your organization. And these different models even need to be used in conjunction sometimes, for instance when auditors check how well prepared you are for calamities, and they want to look at your Security Architecture, your help desk setup and your Risk Management. If these three systems have an incompatible description of, for instance, your Business Processes, Business Functions, Roles, IT Services, etc., it will be impossible to get a good look. So what generally happens is that the people helping the auditors, create their own 'model' of the organization with everything that specific auditor need. What they create is often incompatible with what has elsewhere in the organization been documented and it will certainly be a duplicate or triplicate effort with another maintenance burden you do not want. You don't want that state of affairs.

Since you have to start from the assumption that it is unavoidable that there will be multiple models needed of your reality, the question does not become: "How do I create *the* best model?", but "How do I make sure the *different* models tell a *single* story?" and "How do I prevent a duplicate of effort?".

There are two ways to make that happen:

- Have one model be the slave of another (master) model. E.g. you export your Enterprise Architecture model from your EA modeling tool and you import it in another tool;

- Make sure all models are compatible enough so they can be translated into each other or reconciled against each other.

Which you use and — in case of the first approach — who is master and who is slave, how does synchronization work, is something that you need to design carefully.

For instance, where I work we use our EA Current State model effectively as our CMDB. Our EA tool has a decent scripting language and import/export facilities. We export our model (the master) in a way that it can be imported in our IT Service Management (ITSM) system (the slave). Projects that go live are added to our Current State model and thus exported to the ITSM system. But during day-to-day operations, small changes are documented in our ITSM system. The system automatically sends these to a mailbox of Enterprise Architecture and we add the changes to our model. New items get an id in the ITSM system and this id is fed back into our EA model as a property of certain elements. If we change something in the Current State model and export to the ITSM system, we can change names of elements, and the id makes sure the new names are adopted by the ITSM system. Once in a while, we run a reconciliation to find any item that has slipped through our net. It is difficult to get this right, but it is doable.

As you have seen in Section 25 "Linking BPMN and Archi-Mate", we also have linked our Process Models with our

Enterprise Architecture models. Again, linking these is done with two-way synchronizations, which is slightly more elaborate, but also offers freedom in tool changes.

For other systems (the software engineer's design system, the operational risk manager's risk management system, the process modeler's process modeling tool) we must make sure that their model is compatible with the Enterprise Architecture model, which plays the role of a central core repository.

30. Tool Requirements

Depending on your requirements, different tools may fit your bill. If all you want is directed drawing with not too complex views, many tools will do what you want.

From a perspective of very large models, the following aspects are important:

- Does the tool support everything in ArchiMate?

- Is the tool not overly restrictive?

- Can the tool handle large complex models and views without crashing, slowing down, etc.?

- Does the tool support a modeling style that is usable for large complex models and views?

- Is it possible to configure/use the tool such that it supports your preferred style?

- How good is the support for drawing tricks (e.g. layers, etc.)?

- Can you influence layout (colors, standard labels, attachment points for relations, ordering of relations, etc.)?

- Does the tool have a scripting language?

- Can elements and relations be augmented with properties?

- Does the tool have good import/export facilities?

- Can the tool produce or make available reports for people that do not use the tool themselves? Do these reports work when:

  * Views are large and complex (e.g. it is not scaled such that the contents become unreadable)?

  * Some views should be reported but others not (e.g. do not report work in progress views)?

- Can the tool produce vector-based output of diagrams (e.g. PostScript, SVG or — preferably — PDF), e.g. for large poster prints?

- Is the tool well supported?

- Is there an active and experienced user community for the tool?

- Is the tool's file format open for inspection (and emergency repairs)?

- Is it possible to anonymize models? This is useful if you want to send models to tool support or forums without having to disclose company sensitive information.

I will not provide Tool reviews in this book. If I ever write anything about tools, it will be on the Mastering ArchiMate blog.

The diagrams in this book have been made with BiZZdesign Architect. I am not affiliated with BiZZdesign.

This page intentionally not left blank

Index

Enterprise Architecture 10

   Architectural space vs operational space 179

   Critique

      Specialization Confusion 180

   Fragmentation 10

   Layers 11

   Role of Enterprise Architecture 179

Event 22

Excel

   as an Application Component 49

   as System Software 50

F

Flow relation 22

Future State Architecture 11

G

GOFBF 79

Grouping

   not using the Grouping relation 45

   using the Grouping relation 27

H

Hacker, P.M.S. 10

I

Modeling Information 109

Infrastructure Function 18–19

Infrastructure Interface 19

Infrastructure Layer 11

Infrastructure Service 19

ITIL 94

J

Junction relation 29

M

Meaning 26

Model Use & Maintenance

   Multiple Models of a Single Business Reality 201

N

Nesting 21–22

Network 26–27

Node 18–19

   using for infrastructure encapsulation 22

P

Pattern

   Anti-Pattern 66

      Application Collaboration 66

      Association 68

   Application Platform 51

   Business

      Business Functions 81

      End-to-end Business Process 79–81

   Business Pattern

      Enterprise as loose collaboration of Business Functions 76

   Concurrent Realization 64

   Database Server 47

   Deployment Pattern

      Classic Two-Tier Application 54–55

      Providing a local ASP 59–60

      Remote ASP 56

      SaaS 58–59

      Standalone PC 53

      Standalone PC with Shared Data 54

      Three-Tier Application 56

   Infrastructure Building Blocks 53

   Infrastructure Pattern

      Database Cluster 62

      Database Replication 61

      Server Cluster 62

   Internet Browser 50

   Real World Example 69–73

   Secondary and Tertiary Architecture

      Pragmatic set of Roles to add to your model 93

   Spreadsheet 48

   Using collections in a model 63

Patterns 46

   Application Deployment 53–58

Print License 12

Product 26

Project Start Architecture. *See* Change Architecture

R

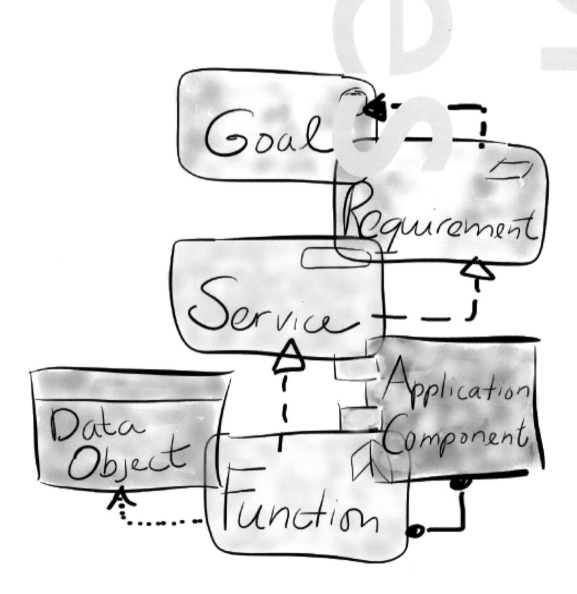

List of Figures

Finger

Finger

This Chapter contains material for easy reference while reading the book You keep one finger between this page and the next as the next page has the ArchiMate meta-model.

Additionally: here is an overview of the Style Guide Items:

Style Guidelines

1. Make your relations in general go in vertical and horizontal directions only.

2. Don't let relations overlap

3. Minimize the number of line crossings

4. As much as possible: Group relations according to either source or destination

5. Align relations, even unrelated ones

6. Align elements, even unrelated ones.

7. Use as few as possible different element sizes (this is like not using too many font sizes in a text document).

8. Align elements and attach relations such that relations are as simple as possible and with the least number of line crossings, preferably straight lines from one element to another.

9. If you have a nested element or groupings, align the elements that are on the inside as well.

10. Distribute elements evenly within their `group'.

11. *Make a view as easy on the eye, as 'quiet' as possible without losing essential information.*

One important remark on sizing and arranging: the above guidelines lead to views that are rather 'boring'. For technical views for your fellow architects, that should not be a problem. But when you communicate to non-architects, you will need to take far more freedom to get the message across (technical views do not have a 'message' per se).

Therefore, when I want to commnicate with non-architects (e.g. management or users), I will relax the approach above, or, I will use something else than ArchiMate for that specific message. A message is often only valid at a certain moment in time anyway, so doing a one-off is not really a problem.

This page intentionally not left blank

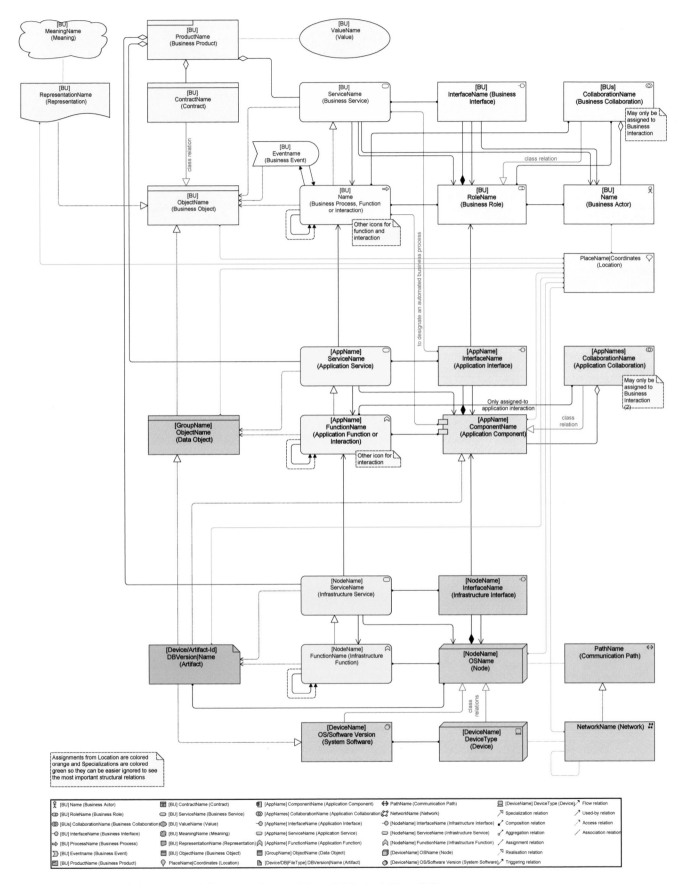

View 345. *ArchiMate 2.1 Metamodel. for easy reference (also valid for ArchiMate 2.0)*

Green-colored relations are Class-relations. The Associations from the Location object are orange-colored so they can be more easily ignored when looking at the other relations

Lightning Source UK Ltd.
Milton Keynes UK
UKIC01n2359120515
251392UK00006B/10